Three More Screenplays
by
Preston Sturges

Three More Screenplays
by
Preston Sturges

Edited with Introductions by
Andrew Horton

Foreword by Tom Sturges

UNIVERSITY OF CALIFORNIA PRESS

Berkeley   Los Angeles   London

University of California Press
Berkeley and Los Angeles, California

University of California Press, Ltd.
London, England

Library of Congress Cataloging-in-Publication Data

Sturges, Preston.
    Three more screenplays by Preston Sturges ; edited with introductions by Andrew
Horton ; foreword by Tom Sturges.
        p.   cm.
    Includes bibliographical references.
    Contents: The power and the glory — Easy living — Remember the night.
    ISBN 0-520-21003-4 (alk. paper). — ISBN 0-520-21004-2 (pbk. : alk. paper)
    1. Motion picture plays.   I. Horton, Andrew.   II. Title.
PN 1997.A1S853   1998   ·
791.43'75—dc21   97-53062
                                                                      CIP

Manufactured in the United States of America
9 8 7 6 5 4 3 2 1

I claimed that talking film was one of the great gifts to mankind and the greatest boon the theatre had ever received, making it universal.

PRESTON STURGES

Contents

Foreword

For the last fifteen years I have been working toward a goal. Simply stated, it was to ensure the complete preservation of my father's films and screenplays. I am most happy that the task is nearly completed. With the publication of this third volume of screenplays, there are now twelve of the very best Preston Sturges screenplays in print, preserved and protected forever.

My thanks to the University of California Press for dedicating itself to and allowing itself to become the center of Preston Sturges screenplay studies. MCA Universal has promised (at the time of this writing) that most, if not all, of their Preston Sturges films are to be re-released in a new compendium of laser discs and home videos to be called The Preston Sturges Collection. This collection will make its appearance in stores around the fall of 1998. My thanks to MCA Universal for so graciously accepting the responsibility as guardian of his works.

August 1998 will mark 100 years since Preston Sturges's birth in August 1898, and this centenary will be celebrated by the publication of this book and the re-release of the movies. In addition, there will be film festivals and celebrations, and maybe somewhere a decent print of *The Power and the Glory* will be discovered. In the near future there will be a play about his remarkable life, but that is another journey.

Other special contributors to the Preston Sturges preservation story are: The UCLA Special Collections Library, Lilace Hatayama, Diane Jacobs, Bruce Goldstein, Paramount Pictures, the Samuel French Agency, Film Forum, *Buzz* Magazine, Marlene Swartz, Sandy Sturges, Tommy Malecky, Allan Mayer, Ed Dimendberg, Joe Roth, Chick Callenbach, American Movie Classics, David Packard, Jim Curtiss, Donald Spoto, Franz Schwartz, *People* Magazine, Louis Feola, Cindy Chang, the Director's Guild of America, the Writer's Guild of America, Debra Rosen, Charlie Katz, and The Disney Channel.

Tom Sturges
Los Angeles
19 November 1997

Acknowledgments

It has meant a lot to me to have gotten to know Sandy and Tom Sturges while working on this project. Not only did they generously give of their time and energy to make suggestions and discuss details of Preston Sturges's work, but they also read an early version of my introductions with the trained eyes of copy editors. Their assistance is much appreciated.

Ed Dimendberg, the film studies and humanities editor at the University of California Press, deserves special credit for inviting me to take on the pleasurable task of working on this volume devoted to my favorite American screenwriter of comedy.

Introduction

"Laughter Is All Some People Have"

Directing was easy for me because I was a writer director and did
all my directing when I wrote the screenplay.

PRESTON STURGES

Preston Sturges remains one of the most memorable American screenwriters for his particular ironic comic vision that wins us over and often catches us by surprise. No matter how many times one sees his films or reads his scripts, his work continues to delight and instruct.

At the end of a comedy seminar I taught several years ago I asked each participant to come up with his or her own "comic epitaph." We had a lot of fun going around the group hearing witty and sometimes touching "final words." When the group asked me what I wanted on my tombstone, there was no question. It had to be a line from Preston Sturges's *Hail the Conquering Hero,* with only the verb tense altered: "Everything was perfect except for a few details." On the last day of the seminar I asked the members of the group to name the one comedy they had most enjoyed seeing, from among films featuring Mae West and Whoopi Goldberg, Buster Keaton and Woody Allen, and from European examples such as the Oscar-winning *Mediterraneo* to Jean Renoir's splendid works. The overwhelming majority voted for *Sullivan's Travels,* Sturges's timeless send-up of Hollywood and celebration of the spirit of film comedy. They particularly remembered the final line of Sullivan (Joel McCrea) when he turns down the chance to make the serious social drama *O Brother Where Art Thou?*—"Laughter is all some people have in this cockeyed caravan."

It is encouraging that Sturges has recently begun to receive the recognition he deserves after several decades of almost complete neglect following his death in 1959. For instance, Diane Jacobs has written a fine critical biography, *Christmas in July: The Life and Art of Preston Sturges,* and we have Sturges's own unfinished autobiography, which was adapted and edited by his wife, Sandy Sturges, to mention but two works.[1] Clearly Sturges is now appreciated for his multiple accomplishments. As Geoffrey O'Brien notes, Sturges wrote "the most consistently lively dialogue that any American has written for stage or screen."[2]

Vincent Canby comments further that, "aside from Lubitsch, Sturges had no equal in Hollywood at the time he was in residence there. He was our premiere *satirist*."[3] And David Thomson remarks that Sturges emerges as "the organizer of a convincingly cheerful comedy of the ridiculous that is rare in American comedy."[4] Furthermore, thanks to the active support of Sturges's youngest son, Tom, the careful editing and detailed film scholarship of Brian Henderson, and the production skills of the University of California Press, two volumes of scripts written and directed by Sturges have already been published to high praise.[5]

This volume marks the third and final collection in this University of California Press series of Sturges's works, and one that takes a different direction from the first two. Assembled here for the first time are three scripts Sturges wrote *but did not direct: The Power and the Glory* (1933), an epic drama of the American dream-cum-nightmare, which had a profound impact on other films, including *Citizen Kane,* both in content and in narrative approach; *Easy Living* (1937), an exemplar of the screwball romantic comedy at its brightest and nuttiest; and *Remember the Night* (1939), an unusual Sturges original that blends romantic comedy and courtroom drama.

This volume thus allows the reader the pleasure of savoring and observing Sturges's talent in formation before he began directing his own screenplays in 1940 with *The Great McGinty.* In fact, the focus of this introduction will be on Sturges the screenwriter. I will discuss both his craft and the major themes and patterns he explored during the 1930s as he moved from his success as a Broadway playwright to his new role as a sought-after screenwriter, in a decade when the "screenplay" was still a fluid element as "talkies" gained a foothold in Hollywood.

There is an additional pleasure for me in exploring these examples of Sturges's early screen work, for I am a practicing feature screenwriter and teacher of screenwriting with a particular leaning toward comedy in all its flavors. My hope is that the following discussion will be of interest not only to Sturges's fans, students of comedy and American cinema and culture, but to screenwriters generally, who can learn much from reading and re-reading, viewing and reviewing these continually fresh works.

Sturges did not "officially" direct any of these three projects. But as his words in the chapter epigraph make clear, even before he gained the title of "director" he had learned a valuable Hollywood lesson: directing is best done through the writing of the script. He was a self-taught playwright and screenwriter who never took a screenwriting class or seminar, for no such courses existed in this infant industry. He mentions one book, however, that did have an influence on him: Professor Brander Matthews's *A Study of the Drama.*[6] Matthews's book is still a good survey of the elements of drama, treating not only examples from world drama including Aristotle, Sophocles, and Aristophanes down to Ibsen, but also topics such as the actor, the audience, the theater, dramatic characterization, dramatic definitions, dramatic analysis, and the three unities of time, place, and action.

We should note at the outset a point that Sandy Sturges rightly emphasizes about the way he "wrote" his scripts: he dictated them. "He almost literally became the characters he was creating as he paced around the office, speaking as they would speak, moving as they would move." He would laugh at particularly good lines and cry at the more emotional moments.[7] I would suggest, therefore, that in reading these scripts we should also imagine the "performance art" dimension of Sturges's creativity. Sturges obviously possessed a powerful ability to "see" his films before him even as he spoke—and well before they were recorded and edited into the movie we would see on the screen.

Thus, part of our interest in these early works lies in seeing what skills of the dramatic and movie trade he absorbed, experimented with, revised, and refined. We will pay close attention to how Sturges managed to profit from and at times avoid the pitfalls of being a hired writer in the complicated business of filmmaking, where the screenwriter is always being told what to do, how to do it, and when. John Gregory Dunne does a good job of articulating the tough role screenwriters play in Hollywood:

Beating up on screenwriters is a Hollywood blood sport; everyone in the business thinks he or she can write, if only time could be found. That writers find the time is evidence of their inferior position on the food chain. In the Industry, they are regarded as chronic malcontents, overpaid and undertalented, the Hollywood version of Hessians, measuring their worth in dollars, since ownership of their words belongs to those who hire and fire them.[8]

Given that filmmaking is a team effort and always an uneasy bonding of craft and commerce, with an emphasis on the latter, how does a writer not only survive but also develop and thrive? These three scripts help us answer this question as we chart Sturges's remarkable development through the 1930s.

Most of the attention paid to Sturges to date has naturally focused on the films he directed. But let us remember that all together he worked on at least twenty-eight films, including credited and uncredited writing, complete screenplays as well as dialogue only. He embraced a full spectrum of genres and approaches, ranging from an adaptation of Tolstoy's *Resurrection* (*Never Say Die*, 1939) to songs written for *The Gay Deception* (1935) and *One Rainy Afternoon* (1936), and from biting satire of the movie industry (years before *Sullivan's Travels*) with the unproduced script *Song of Joy* (1935) to both serious (*The Power and the Glory*) and comic (*Diamond Jim*, 1935) studies of the rise and fall of tycoons. Once again, the three scripts in this volume allow us to better understand the many "voices" that add up to the carnival we call Preston Sturges.

Sturges the Man

Sturges's life has been thoroughly documented elsewhere. We should nevertheless keep in mind the great diversity of lifestyles and cultures he was exposed

3

Preston Sturges. Courtesy The Museum of Modern Art.

to during his life. Critical to his perceptions was his exhilarating and painful boyhood, living throughout Europe with his free-spirited avant-garde mother, Mary Desti, friend of Isadora Duncan and wife or lover to an array of men from countries as different as Turkey and Mexico. On the other hand, we cannot fail to note Sturges's admiration for the man who adopted him, Solomon Sturges, the conservative Chicago businessman who clearly gave Preston more love and attention than his mother ever did. As Diane Jacobs puts it, "The country where Preston *belonged,* where he would write his plays and films and conceive his comic vision, was no single place."[9] Sturges himself said, "At best my efforts have been a French sense of humor filtered through an American vocabulary."[10]

I have stated in my book *Writing the Character-Centered Screenplay* that we are all a feast of contradictions and that we can never completely fulfill Socrates' directive to "know thyself."[11] Thus we never completely know anyone else either. This is certainly true of Sturges. Even so, without delving deeply into psychoanalytic theory, we can see from the biographies and his own autobiography that he in fact occupied a middle ground between all the elements in his life: between European culture and American capitalistic society with its often puritanical small-town values; between the pain of being ignored by his mother and his ability to gain attention through his storytelling; between moments of depression and periods of joyful exuberance; between the pull of creativity and that of puttering with inventions, heading up an engineering company, racing boats, running a restaurant, and more. The tension between these disparate impulses fueled his life and his art. Although much of Sturges's laughter is genuine, flat-out fun, the distinctive ironic flavor of his work may well come from sources deep below the surface of his whirlwind activity, perhaps unacknowledged by Sturges himself.

Before turning to Sturges the storyteller and screenwriter, we should consider the volcano of interests and projects that he indulged in beyond those related to writing and the silver screen. We are not speaking of a single-minded, focused writer who gave all to his craft. For there is Sturges the businessman who helped run his mother's perfume industry, who made investments in other businesses, and who later started up and ran the famous Hollywood restaurant The Players. There is also Sturges the inventor who delighted in devising new gizmos of all kinds. Listed in his archives at UCLA are patents registered for new planes, cars, a helicopter, a laugh meter (1934), and exercise machines, among more than thirty inventions. He even claimed to have introduced the club sandwich to Germany.[12] As a screenwriter myself, I marvel at how Sturges both thrived and managed to survive as a writer in the midst of so many interests and demands on his time and energy.

Sturges as American Storyteller

> By the very nature of his art, which depends on invention and
> innovation, *a story teller* must depart from the beaten track and,
> having done so, occasionally startle and disagree with some of his
> associates. Healthy disagreement we must have.
>
> PRESTON STURGES

Before discussing Sturges the screenwriter, let us view him in the larger role of an original American storyteller. For Sturges told stories in endless conversations, in plays written for the stage, in scripts written for the screen, and he absorbed stories wherever he went, from whomever he met. In fact, he often described himself as an American humorist working in film, thus foregrounding story over medium. Donald Spoto, in his biography of Sturges, says much the same thing: "He never developed a self-consciousness or snobbery about his work. . . . He was simply a genial entertainer who was the first to enjoy his own stories."[13]

Storytellers, after all, must by definition be good listeners—and just imagine the stories Sturges heard in his life, in Europe, in New York, in Hollywood. His ear for dialogue could only develop from *listening* to what he heard around him on several continents. His mother's multinational husbands and lovers were fuel for satirical tales and sources of lines. He tells us, for instance, that the Mexican millionaire Gabriel Elizaga once told the young Sturges, "Your mother is really a superior person, and I am not such a much."[14] So it comes as no surprise that Sturges delighted in creating minor "ethnic" characters. Here is Louis Louis, the owner of the failing Hotel Louis, talking to our comic heroine, Mary Smith, early in *Easy Living:*

LOUIS LOUIS

(interrupting)

Miss Smit, I'm a man like dis! I don't beat around de bush to
come in de back door. I tell you dis is vere you belong and dis is
vere you got to be.

Invention, innovation, and "healthy disagreement" are the key ingredients Sturges recognizes in a master storyteller's art. The first two are obvious: no storyteller worth his or her salt will simply repeat a story. You need to make the story pass through your imagination and come out stamped with your own embellishments, concerns, characteristics. Most of Homer's tales in *The Odyssey* and *The Iliad,* for instance, can be traced back to earlier sources; what made them "epic" was the particular spin and shape Homer gave them.

But Sturges asks us to consider the storyteller on that third level as well, the level of healthy disagreement. This notion of entering into dialogue with a tradition or a culture suggests a dimension of comedy that has been with us at least since Aristophanes, whose comedies, in condemning war-oriented cultures, offered his fellow Greeks a healthy and cathartic counter-view of the major politics of the day.

Any storytelling can be simultaneously a celebration and a critique of a particular culture. Aristophanes took this dual task seriously: in the *parabasis* of many of his comedies, he would drop the comic mask and identify himself as a *komodidaskelos,* a comic teacher and critic. Although Sturges, working within a comic tradition that did not allow for so direct a dialogue with the audience, never called himself a "comic moralist" or a "teacher through humor," we can still view each of his scripts as a storytelling crossroads in which innovation, invention, and healthy disagreement both celebrated and critiqued the codes, formulas, conventions, and even the morality of American culture.

Sturges was a storyteller, not a moral philosopher or preacher. But he certainly created an edge to his material. As Geoffrey O'Brien notes, "What lingers finally from his movies is not their wildness, but their unsentimental rigor."[15] This "unsentimental rigor" is immediately apparent when we compare Sturges to Frank Capra, who in film after film, from *It Happened One Night* (1934) and *Mr. Smith Goes to Washington* (1939) to *Meet John Doe* (1941) and *Mr. Deeds Goes to Town* (1936), glorified a simplistic populist doctrine of American virtues in which little guys win out against evil capitalists and democratic small-town heroes take on and beat the crooked politicos. Sturges's stories are the opposite of Capra's sentimental tales. In fact, David Thomson could easily be quoting Sturges when he writes: "Deeds and Smith admonish indolent or cynical government assemblies with a soulful list of clichés that Capra persuades himself is libertarian poetry rather than a call for unadventurous conformity."[16]

Sturges would have none of that, and this volume is testimony to the bard's healthy disagreement with American culture—beginning with our recognition that his very serious script *The Power and the Glory* was written before his famous film comedies. The story of the rise and fall of a tycoon, viewed unsentimentally through the eyes of his best friend and assistant, suggests Sturges's lifelong concern with a system that could create at once so much wealth and happiness and such poverty and suffering. "Sucker sapien" is the term used to describe the average guy or gal in *The Lady Eve* (1941), a film that, like so many of Sturges's stories, builds a romance between a trickster female character and a "sucker sapien" male (though sometimes the reverse occurs). This ironic take on romance—and culture—is seen time and again in Sturges's early scripts, most especially in this exchange in *Remember the Night* as Lee, a clever female thief whose trial has been postponed, winds up with Jack Sargent, an innocent assistant district attorney, for Christmas. Attraction builds as exact opposites attempt to understand each other:

SARGENT
(Hopefully)

I mean maybe you're a kleptomaniac.

LEE
(Placidly)

No, they tried that. You see, to be a kleptomaniac you can't sell any of the stuff afterwards . . . or you lose your amateur standing.

SARGENT

I don't understand it. First you think it's environment and then . . . Whitney goes to jail. Then you think it's heredity . . . and you get some bird with seven generations of clergymen behind him.

LEE

I don't think you ever could understand because your mind is different. Right or wrong is the same for everybody, you see, but the rights and the wrongs aren't the same. Like in China they eat dogs.

SARGENT

That's a lot of piffle.

LEE

They do eat dogs.

SARGENT

I mean your theory.

LEE

Try it like this: suppose you were starving to death . . .

SARGENT

Yes.

LEE

. . . and you didn't have any food and you didn't have any money and you didn't have any place to get anything.

SARGENT

Yes.

LEE

And there were some loaves of bread out in front of a market, and you were starving to death and the man's back was turned . . . would you swipe one?

SARGENT

(Vehemently)

You bet I would!

LEE

(Smiling with pleasure)

That's because you're honest. You see, I'd have a six-course dinner at the table d'hote across the street and then say I'd forgotten my purse.

As Sargent looks at her goggle-eyed she concludes sweetly:

LEE

You get the difference?

Unsentimental rigor, and great fun—not to mention the beginning of a healthy romance built on disagreement. "Cynical, Sturges explosively, joyously, is neither nihilist nor dogmatic," remarks Raymond Durgnat. "He appeals to no ideology, no perfectionism, no despair, but rather to intuitive decencies and horse sense."[17]

Sturges the Screenwriter

> At the risk of sounding pontifical, I believe the success or failure
> of any writing depends upon the *residual.* By this I mean what the
> reader has left in his mind after closing the book; what the
> spectator takes home with him after leaving the theater or movie
> palace.
>
> PRESTON STURGES

The residuals from reading these three scripts are long lasting and numerous. Volumes One and Two of Sturges's screenplays reveal Sturges the director-writer. Once more we emphasize that this collection shows us the screenwriter, pure and simple, yet at the same time it reveals how that screenwriter was preparing to take on the role of director so as to protect, nurture, and realize his original screen visions as far as is possible in the collision of business and art called "Hollywood."

We will discuss Sturges's craft from a variety of viewpoints in the individual introductions. For now, let us examine six particularly notable aspects of Sturges's screenwriting, ones that contribute to the strong residual impressions left by these scripts.

This Cockeyed Caravan: Sturges's Carnivalesque Humor and Vision

Sturges's writing embraces a very wide view of comedy. We can easily find influences from silent film as well as from smart Broadway comedy, from vaudeville and also from French and Italian farce, from Molière (whom he deeply loved and admired and often saw staged in France), Aristophanes, and Shakespeare as well as from the characters Sturges met in his own life.

All of this "cockeyed caravan," as Sullivan calls life at the end of *Sullivan's Travels,* adds up to truly a carnivalesque vision of humor and comedy. As Mikhail Bakhtin explains, "Carnival is not a spectacle seen by the people: they live in it, and everyone participates because its very idea embraces all the people. While carnival lasts, there is no other life outside it. During carnival time life is subject only to its laws, that is, the laws of its own freedom. It has a universal spirit."[18]

Easy Living turns New York and the high ranks of American capitalism into a romantic comic romp, a fairy tale "subject only to" the laws "of its own freedom." Meanwhile, *Remember the Night* hovers between comedy and drama, in an uneasy balance that continually threatens to break down. Finally, *The Power and the Glory,* Sturges's earliest work here, is an example of the carnival gone wrong, for in the rise and fall of Thomas Garner we see a realistic world in which the freedom and celebration of true festivity can be neither established nor maintained.

Consider, too, that the carnivalesque embraces all forms of comedy, from pure slapstick farce to parody and satire, from joking to romantic and sexual coupling, and you begin to appreciate more fully the broad range Sturges worked within. In fact, the comments of Brander Matthews, Sturges's admired author-

Preston Sturges in the director's chair, a screenplay in hand. Courtesy The Museum of Modern Art.

ity on drama, could apply to Sturges and his comic worldview as easily as to his actual subject: "The comedy of Aristophanes was a medley of boisterous comic-opera and of lofty lyric poetry, of vulgar ballet and of patriotic oratory, of indecent farce and of pungent political satire, of acrobatic pantomime and of brilliant literary criticism, of cheap burlesque and of daringly imaginative fantasy."[19] Like the ancient Greek comic poet, Sturges is not afraid to include an always surprising variety of elements between FADE IN and THE END in each script.

We can be even more specific in suggesting that Sturges managed to fuse the two most important comic traditions in American film, "anarchistic" comedy and the romantic or "screwball" tradition.[20] According to Henry Jenkins, for a while in the early 1930s, when sound was being introduced in Hollywood, it was far from certain what the dominant comic genre would be. Romantic comedy came to Hollywood with sound as a Broadway import; indeed, Sturges, with such stage successes as *Strictly Dishonorable* (1929) on his résumé, was a prime practitioner in the genre. Classic romantic comedy, as in Frank Capra's *It Happened One Night,* is by definition pro-social; it aims in its "happy ending" at reconciliation of opposites in a socially viable manner that will help the "community" survive and thrive. In the very early days of sound, however, an "anarchistic" comedy that had grown out of vaudeville was also a going concern. Anarchistic-comedy films, Jenkins explains, are "characterized by a subordination of visual and aural style, narrative structure and character development to foregrounded comic performance; they are marked by a general questioning of social norms."[21] Sturges's comic vision embraced both traditions simultaneously. Thus *Sullivan's Travels* has a romantic thread, with Sullivan falling for "the girl," yet the whole film is episodic, as each segment subverts the others. Similarly, while romance blooms in *Easy Living,* the scene in the automat restaurant is pure vaudeville and Mack Sennett combined.

I would argue that the healthy anarchistic streak in Sturges helps to explain the "edge" his comedies have. When, at the beginning of *The Palm Beach Story,* we see a wedding and the words "And they lived happily ever after . . . or did they?" we know we are in the hands of a major ironist who will treat no tradition as sacred. This vision, this talent, finally, epitomizes the Mardi Gras spirit that Sturges acknowledged in the closing pages of his autobiography. He speaks of himself, a man in his sixties waiting for a plane, in the third person: "While waiting, he thinks back on his life and to him it seems to have been a Mardi Gras, a street parade of masked, drunken, hysterical, laughing, disguised, travestied, carnal, innocent, and perspiring humanity of all sexes, wandering aimlessly, but always in circles, in search of that of which it is a part: life."[22] Carnival, then, is not a genre for Sturges, but life itself.

Pushing the Envelope: Experimentation with Narrative and Genres

> It was actually the enormous risks I took with my pictures, skating
> right up to the edge of non-acceptance, that paid off so hand-
> somely.
>
> PRESTON STURGES

According to Sandy Sturges, Sturges usually began a project having the "ending in mind" but almost always being unsure of how to get there.[23] This tension between the known and the unknown, I suspect, helped Sturges experiment with characters and narrative in the same spirit of playful freedom with which he experimented in his noncinematic inventions and projects.

Beginning with his invention in *The Power and the Glory* of a new form of storytelling, which the publicity department coined "narratage," Sturges never seemed satisfied with imitating others or telling a story simply. He played with narrative structure, with genre boundaries; he pushed scenes as far as they could go and then some, and blended pathos and comedy in unusual combinations. *Remember the Night,* for instance, has some absolutely classic screwball romantic moments, but then Sturges throws all the rules—especially as written by the likes of Frank Capra—out the window when, in a harshly touching scene, the naive assistant D.A., Jack Sargent, takes the streetwise thief, Lee, back to her Indiana home to confront the mother she has not seen since she ran away. We are suddenly in a very different world of straight-on melodrama shaded by film noir. The family home has "junk in the yard," and a dog barks. With no word of welcome, the mother jumps into a list of condemnations about Lee. She concludes:

THE MOTHER

A fine lot of work you ever did!
    (She turns to Sargent)
The great lady! We weren't good enough for her here . . . A
Christian home, a hard working father and mother.

LEE

Nobody said you weren't, Mama.

THE MOTHER

    (To Sargent)

With a crook for a daughter . . . so the neighbors can read about it
in the paper . . . and pity me . . . and wait for her sister to turn out
the same.

LEE

How is she?

THE MOTHER

She's gone too.

It's a turning point in Sturges's script in a number of ways. Most important, the relationship between Lee and Jack now begins to take on much deeper meaning as, at the home of Jack's mother and aunt, Lee next comes to know the good side of small-town midwestern American values. But Sturges is definitely pushing the envelope and mixing his genres for his own purposes here—and getting away with it. This will become apparent in the ending, which is not a simple fade-out on an embrace following difficulties overcome, but a question mark: we really do not know what will happen next, though we are sure of the protagonists' affection for one another.

We will look for this experimental, risk-taking side of Sturges in each of the three screenplays printed here.

Dialogue with a Hook

The hook is a word or an idea spoken by one character which
gives the next character something to hook onto when he
responds, or like a trapeze artist, gives him something to swing
from on his way to another point of view.

PRESTON STURGES

Whenever I teach a screenwriting class I turn to clips from Sturges's scripts and films to illustrate what crackling fine dialogue can be. We have already seen several fine examples in this introduction, but allow me the pleasure of another to more clearly establish what Sturges does with a "hook." Early in *Easy Living,* a fur coat lands on the head of clueless Mary Smith as she rides an open-air bus down Park Avenue. The coat belongs to the wife of J. B. Ball, the "Bull of Broad Street," one of the richest men in America. When she tries to return the coat to him, he tells her to keep it and then drives her in his limo to get a hat to replace the one destroyed by the falling sable coat. The hook in this scene is the word *boys,* which is part of the title of the magazine for which Mary works, *The Boys' Constant Companion.* They are inside J.B.'s Lincoln:

J.B.

The Boys' what?

MARY

The Boys' Constant Companion. It's a magazine . . . for boys.

J.B.

I never heard of it.

MARY

(A little crossly)

It's got a million readers.

J.B.

(With satisfaction)

It hasn't got me.

He looks at her a moment, then lifts the speaking tube.

J.B.

Stop at a hat shop.

MARY

(Nervously)

It's terribly sweet of you but I really haven't the time and the coat
more than makes up for . . . for . . .

13

J.B.

(With inward amusement)

Listen: If I can keep waiting what's waiting for me, the Boys'
Constant Reminder can wait a few minutes also.

MARY

Companion . . . Boys' Constant Companion.

J.B.

Companion.

A less experienced or less talented writer of comedy would surely add much
more in terms of description or direction that would clog up the flow of the scene,
the speed of the exchanges, and the pure fun with which these lines (and thus
the characters) "hook" into each other.

Comic Density and a Bevy of Minor Characters

Every Sturges film, in addition to one-on-one scenes, has moments when the
frame simply bursts with multiple pursuits, actions at cross-purposes, and a bevy
of minor characters. In *Hail the Conquering Hero,* for instance, it seems that
half of small-town America is inside Mama's home when Woodrow returns a
"hero." And think of the feisty parade that breaks out on the Palm Beach express train as the Ale and Quail Club cuts loose in *The Palm Beach Story.* Turning to our scripts, by the time the food starts flying in the automat in *Easy Living,* a large sampling of New Yorkers are involved in throwing and grabbing,
stealing and eating the abundance of free food that rains down on them. At work
here is Sturges's love of silent screen comedy as well as his delight in writing
for a host of great character actors, including William Demarest, Franklin Pang-
born, Sig Arno, Robert Dudley, Roscoe Ates, Dewey Robinson, Chester Con-
klin, Robert Warwick, Robert Greig, and many more.

Never do these scenes suggest a dangerous world. Rather, they are testimony
to life as a ceaseless parade of fascinating and, yes, silly characters who are all
part of the same show. Sturges's world is not the darkly humorous (or should
we say, humorously dark) universe of Quentin Tarantino or the edgy assortment
of quirky characters in the Coen Brothers' *Fargo* or even *Raising Arizona.* The
small-town Christmas and New Year's Eve celebrants in *Remember the Night*
are all affable folk, halfway between cartoonlike caricatures and drawn-from-
life figures in the spirit of, say, Charles Dickens. Only in *The Power and the
Glory,* and in *Remember the Night* in the scene with Lee's mother, does Sturges
dare to venture outside the realm of comedy to look at a harsher, colder world
of human failure and failings.

We treasure the gallery of minor characters Sturges has conjured up. *Easy
Living* sparkles not just in the witty exchanges between Mary, J.B., and Johnny,
but also in the nutty cross-purposes of characters such as Louis Louis with his
broken English, whose hotel J.B. now "owns" unless the hapless Louis can come

up with some fast cash to pay off his long-overdue loans. Consider this exchange between Louis and J.B.:

                              LOUIS

Gimme six weeks.

                              J.B.

(Reluctantly)

I'll give you a week.

                              LOUIS

(With fire)

What good is a week?

J.B. – OVER LOUIS

                              J.B.

(Roaring)

All right I WON'T GIVE YOU a week!

LOUIS – OVER J.B.

                              LOUIS

(Desperately)

All right, I'll TAKE a week! . . . Goodbye, I got to hurry.

He puts on his derby.

                              J.B.

(Puzzled)

What're you going to do?

                              LOUIS

(Scatter-brained)

I don't know, but I only got a week to do it in.

Look, first of all, at the sheer fun of this exchange. J.B. is a tough business-man who has acceded to a one-week deadline, which Louis is forced to accept. The hotelier's sudden move to leave surprises J.B., who obviously enjoys the cat-and-mouse game-playing that finances involve. Thus his question, "What're you going to do?" Louis's answer is, as Sturges notes, scatter-brained, but his lack of command of the English language makes it all the more hilarious: "I don't know, but I only got a week to do it in." Although our main focus in *Easy Living* is on Mary Smith and J.B., the proceedings gain much from the offbeat characters such as Louis Louis, who only add to the comic confusion Sturges thrives upon.

Adaptation: The Art of Borrowing Well, Stealing, and Transforming

Of the three scripts reproduced here, *Easy Living* is an adaptation. I have written elsewhere about adaptation as a "lively and creative art,"[24] and Sturges proves this point in his own work. In fact, "adaptation" is perhaps too limiting a term for what Sturges accomplishes with original material written by others. It would be much more accurate to describe his rewrites as "based on ideas" he found in other stories and plays.

Easy Living, according to documents in the UCLA Special Film Collection, was originally a thirty-five-page "screen story" by Vera Caspary, dated May 1, 1935. The tale begins in a Manhattan blizzard as "a girl," Mary Winslow, makes her way to the Park Avenue home of a rich woman, "Madame," to give her her regular massage. As the story unfolds, Madame "loans" Mary a mink coat, with payment to follow when Mary can afford it. An argument ensues, however, and Mary is fired. As she leaves, she manages to steal the mink. Caspary tags the end of her tale with a clear punch line: "This is the story of a girl who stole a fur coat . . . Pure and simple"; and finally, "Easy living is often uneasily maintained."[25]

Sturges turned this tale around 180 degrees. Instead of the coat being stolen, it becomes an instrument of pure accident when Mr. Ball, the "Bull of Broad Street," heaves it off his Park Avenue balcony during an argument with his wife and it lands on the head—or, more precisely, the hat—of Mary Smith as she rides on the open-air upper level of a double-decker bus. Suddenly it's the story of chance (accident) as a naive young woman is thrown with full comic force into a world of wealth and capital. And it's also now a very funny story as opposed to a somber tale of a fallen girl in the city.

Adaptation? Only in the most remote sense. A highly original work inspired by a spark in another tale? Yes!

Polishing and Rewriting: The "Well-Directed" Script

Any screenwriter knows that the heart of writing is in rewriting. Linda Seger and Edward Jay Whetmore remark that it is with the first draft completed that "the collaborative nature of filmmaking begins to come into play."[26] Publishing a Sturges script with its handwritten notes and crossed-out segments—as we do here with *The Power and the Glory*—allows the reader to see the writer at work. Such versions give us a lot of insight into Sturges's constant revisions, for a script is never finished until it's on the screen.

On Reading Sturges's Scripts

Sturges's scripts bring us a multitude of pleasures, not the least of which is the frequent urge to call friends up and read whole segments out loud. He has that kind of effect on us. Such urges, of course, are wholly desirable and should be encouraged.

In this section I would like to suggest some of the themes that appear in these early scripts, themes that Sturges developed even more fully in the later works he directed as well as wrote. Four of the most striking are the development of strong female characters; a fascination with rags-to-riches or fish-out-of-water stories; a love of "good-fairy" tales, with all their comic and ironic implications; and a delight in food as well as its opposite, hunger.

A brief consideration of these themes will illuminate not only Sturges's personal interests but also some of the social realities and dreams within American culture of the 1930s. For certainly the Great Depression gave a new perspective to the "rags-to-riches" stories and myths within American society and the tension between the millions who went to bed hungry and those with great wealth. Given such times, who wouldn't dream of a "good fairy" who would swiftly turn a dull life of drudgery into the stuff of living fairy tales.

Strong Female Characters

Many film scholars and critics have commented on the inadequacy of roles for women in American cinema in recent years, especially compared to the feisty, independent women seen in screwball comedies of the 1930s and 1940s. This seems particularly true when we think of Sturges's comic heroines. Who can forget Barbara Stanwyck in *The Lady Eve* or Claudette Colbert in *The Palm Beach Story,* whose blend of street smarts, flirtatious cunning, and solid intelligence puts them miles ahead of their men. The early scripts we will be examining here show Sturges developing these "prototypes" with verve and obvious pleasure.

Barbara Stanwyck's high-class thief Lee in *Remember the Night,* for instance, was clearly a warmup for Eve in almost every sense. Then there is Jean Arthur's Mary in *Easy Living,* who exhibits that rare quality in American film comedy: a balance between complete innocence and a native intelligence that sees immediately to the heart of an issue, a moment, a person. Finally, although *The Power and the Glory* is a tragic drama, Colleen Moore's Sally is set up as the brains behind Spencer Tracy's Tom Garner, as well as a love interest who becomes a forceful wife. That her strength as a character spills over into greed and finally suicide suggests Sturges's interest in what can happen when ambition outstrips love and contentment. We do not have to dwell long on the probable influence of Sturges's strong-willed and independent mother in the formation of these memorable women.

Rags-to-Riches Narratives

All three of our scripts explore sudden transitions in socioeconomic status: the "fish-out-of-water" narrative model. *The Power and the Glory* captures the joy and then tragedy of Tom's swift rise to wealth; *Easy Living* catapults Mary out of her scraping-by workaday life into J. B. Ball's sphere of luxury and extravagance; and *Remember the Night* sends Lee from the "rags" of the street into the "riches" of a loving and supportive family that Jack has known and wishes to share with her—*after* she has served her time. In a sense, the rags-to-riches theme is the American dream. But when it crosses boundaries with the fish-out-of-water motif, Sturges's particular brand of irony and critique kicks in. Irony always involves a double vision—an awareness of multiple realities—and in comedy as practiced by Sturges this translates to double laughter. We can laugh both at and with Mary in *Easy Living* as she tries to make sense of the rich and famous who mistakenly think that she is "somebody" too. Such intertwined narrative strands offer endless comic possibilities.

Good-Fairy Narratives

The good-fairy motif is also important to Sturges's scripts. We see this in *Remember the Night,* where Jack rescues Lee from a life of meaningless crime, and in *Easy Living,* where J. B. Ball introduces Mary to a new, exciting world. Sally is Tom's good fairy at first in *The Power and the Glory,* and later he becomes a good fairy for both his mistress, Eve, by agreeing to marry her, and his son, by supporting him even though he has done nothing to deserve it. That these good deeds are misplaced and ultimately backfire tragically leads to the vastly different tone and impact of this work of drama.

Food and Famine Motifs

Sturges's use of food and hunger motifs provides the culinary equivalent to the rags-to-riches schema. Certainly this man, who ran two restaurants during his career, both thought about and enjoyed good food, and all that it suggests: a shared community of kindred souls, festive times, and a general sense of well-being and happiness. Who can forget the automat scene in *Easy Living,* when the homeless and the wealthy alike become a classless society feasting on free food. In *Remember the Night* many important dialogues occur over meals, including the beginning of romance between Jack and Lee as they eat in a fancy New York restaurant. And *The Power and the Glory* is narrated from Henry's kitchen toward the end of the evening meal. Likewise, the lack of food helps define characters and create comedy as when, in *Remember the Night,* Jack has cause to be grateful when he remembers that his butler has prepared sandwiches to go, after he and Lee find themselves stranded in the middle of a field. A far cry from the custard pies of silent comedy, food in Sturges's scripts is, as a symbol of love, friendship, and community, merely part and parcel of what the Mardi Gras of life is all about.

A Final Take

Sturges endures. The three scripts gathered here help us understand better how and why this is so. The reasons have to do with more than mere laughter or entertainment. Dana F. Sutton ends *The Catharsis of Comedy* with these

18

words: "Almost like prophets and shamans . . . comic writers and comic actors become privileged members of the community."[27] Preston Sturges might well have scoffed at such a remark, but his scripts, his films, and his career suggest otherwise. Certainly part of Sturges's status as a privileged member of the Hollywood community was that he could turn rewriting and alteration into a positive activity that led to an even better final artistic product. As he put it, "The crafts of the tailor and the storyteller are not dissimilar, . . . for out of a mass of unrelated material, each contrives to fashion a complete and well-balanced unit. Many stories are too heavy in the shoulders and too short in the pants, with the design of the material running upside-down."[28] *The Power and the Glory, Easy Living,* and *Remember the Night* stand as well-tailored works, complete and perfectly balanced, that will not go out of fashion or style.

NOTES

1. Diane Jacobs, *Christmas in July: The Life and Art of Preston Sturges* (Berkeley: University of California Press, 1992); and *Preston Sturges by Preston Sturges,* adapted and edited by Sandy Sturges (New York: Simon & Schuster, 1990).

2. Geoffrey O'Brien, "The Sturges Style," *New York Review of Books,* December 20, 1990, 6.

3. Vincent Canby, "The Pragmatic and Falling-Down-Funny Films of Preston Sturges," *New York Times,* January 14, 1983, 16.

4. David Thomson, *A Biographical Dictionary of Film,* 3d ed. (New York: Alfred A. Knopf, 1995), 725.

5. *Five Screenplays by Preston Sturges,* edited with an introduction by Brian Henderson (Berkeley: University of California Press, 1986); and *Four More Screenplays by Preston Sturges,* edited with an introduction by Brian Henderson (Berkeley: University of California Press, 1995).

6. Brander Matthews, *A Study of the Drama* (Boston: Houghton Mifflin, 1910).

7. Sandy Sturges, interview, July 5, 1997.

8. John Gregory Dunne, *Monster: Living Off the Big Screen* (New York: Random House, 1997), 7.

9. Jacobs, *Christmas in July,* 43.

10. Quoted ibid.

11. Andrew Horton, *Writing the Character-Centered Screenplay* (Berkeley: University of California Press, 1994), 5.

12. *Preston Sturges,* 64.

13. Donald Spoto, *Madcap: The Life of Preston Sturges* (Boston: Little, Brown, 1990), 147.

14. *Preston Sturges,* 82.

15. O'Brien, "Sturges Style," 9.

16. Thomson, *Biographical Dictionary,* 107.

17. Raymond Durgnat, *The Crazy Mirror* (New York: Horizon, 1969), 120.

18. Mikhail Bakhtin, *Rabelais and His World,* translated by Helene Iswolsky (Cambridge, Mass.: MIT Press, 1968), 7.

19. Brander Matthews, *The Development of the Drama* (New York: Charles Scribner's Sons, 1903), 90.

20. Andrew Horton, ed., *Comedy/Cinema/Theory* (Berkeley: University of California Press, 1991), 10–12.

21. Henry Jenkins, *What Made Pistachio Nuts? Early Sound Comedy and the Vaudeville Aesthetic* (New York: Columbia University Press, 1992), 22.

22. *Preston Sturges,* 339.

23. Sandy Sturges interview.

24. Andrew Horton, *Modern European Filmmakers and the Art of Adaptation* (New York: Frederick Ungar, 1981), 1.

25. Vera Caspary, "Easy Living: An Original Screen Story," May 1, 1935, UCLA Special Film Collection, 34–35.

26. Linda Seger and Edward Jay Whetmore, *From Script to Screen: The Collaborative Art of Filmmaking* (New York: Henry Holt, 1994), 38.

27. Dana F. Sutton, *The Catharsis of Comedy* (New York: Rowman & Littlefield, 1996), 118.

28. *Preston Sturges,* 268.

The Power and the Glory

"You Can't Judge Him by Ordinary Standards"

The Power and the Glory was Sturges's first script not based on a previous work. He wrote it because he wanted to write it, not because he was under contract. That this script made an immediate impact on producer Jesse Lasky, who ordered William K. Howard to shoot it without changing a word, means we should take it seriously: such an order is rarely heard in an industry that seems to pride itself on making endless revisions straight down to the last editing session before a film's release.[1]

The film opened on August 16, 1933, to strongly positive reviews. Among them was that of the *New York Times* critic Mordaunt Hall, who wrote:

Told in a manner which is a distinct departure from the ordinary talking picture, there came to the screen of the Gaiety last night Jesse L. Lasky's latest production, *The Power and the Glory,* the story of the success and tragedy of two lives, a husband and a wife. It is a compelling and forceful film, thoroughly human and always believable. The new treatment, which the producer calls "narratage," is eminently well suited to this particular dramatic vehicle.[2]

The film impressed Europe as well. Billy Wilder, the great director of such films as *Some Like It Hot, The Apartment,* and *The Lost Weekend,* later explained that when he first came to Hollywood, Sturges was one of his heroes: "I had seen *The Power and the Glory* in Paris six or eight times after I left Germany. Being a writer, I was fascinated by it and was later vividly reminded of it when I saw *Citizen Kane.*"[3] Indeed, of the many rise-and-fall-of-American-tycoon films made in the 1930s, *The Power and the Glory* had an especially apparent influence on the writing and shooting of Orson Welles's *Citizen Kane.* Herman Mankiewicz, who wrote the script, was a drinking friend of Sturges. It was Mankiewicz who decided to focus nonchronologically on the search for the meaning of Kane's last word: "Rosebud." And Welles and *Citizen Kane* cinematographer Gregg Toland both expressed admiration for the visual style of James Wong Howe's cinematography in *The Power and the Glory*.[4]

Synopsis

The script we have is the version begun December 6, 1932, and completed January 16, 1933, as dictated to Bianca Gilchrist. Because of the nonchronological order of events, a synopsis will be particularly useful to our discussion of the script. Note that I have added here a sense of actual narrative time in Tom's life and indicated the number of pages in a sequence. At each cut in the script a brief adjustment may be necessary as the reader determines what time period is being portrayed. In addition I have noted some of the differences between the script and the final screen version.

Sequence A (5 pages)

The present

The first page is missing. But we begin at "the end" with Tom Garner's funeral, where we hear the preacher praising the deceased. A gray-haired man in his mid-fifties, Henry, described as "the bookkeeper type, if there is such a type," leaves during the service. We then watch as he enters a building marked "The Chicago & Great Western Railroad." (In the film Henry begins narrating during this scene.) A sharp exchange takes place in the elevator as the elevator man says in lines added in Sturges's own hand, "I'm glad he croaked . . . The old b. . . ." Henry responds crisply, "Aw shut up!"

The sequence ends with Henry in his office looking at an imposing bust of Tom and then at a tintype photo as organ music from the cathedral builds to a crescendo.

Sequence B (16 pages)

The present

We see Henry and his wife in the kitchen doing dishes and discussing Tom's life. "He was good for nothing," the wife claims, but Henry comes to Tom's defense with, "You can't judge him by ordinary standards—they wouldn't fit him. He was too—too big." Established from the onset is a controversial double view of Tom's character and accomplishments.

Henry's voice-over now takes us back to:

The past: Tom's childhood

We have a swimming hole scene with the young Tom and Henry, establishing how they became friends. Also set up is Tom's daring personality as he dives from a high cliff. Henry, in contrast, is much more passive; in fact, he cannot

Tom Garner (Spencer Tracy), the railroad-owning tycoon in *The Power and the Glory,* talking to his best friend and assistant, Henry (Ralph Morgan). Courtesy The Academy of Motion Picture Arts and Sciences.

even swim. But they strike up a friendship when a local tough kid shows up looking for a fight and Tom, standing up for Henry, gives him one. Henry is able to repay his new friend when Tom injures his hand in a dive: Henry bandages Tom's hand after treating it with leaves he claims will take out the poison. Henry's voice in the present continues to speak to us about his friend who is now gone.

Sequence C (8 pages)

The recent past: Tom as president of "the finest railroad in America"

This rapid cut to Tom at the height of his power catches him negotiating to buy another railroad, the Santa Clara (haphazardly corrected by hand in the script from the Santa Fe). Now a hard-nosed businessman, Tom orders stocks to be purchased before he goes in to the board of directors to argue for his actions. Significantly, Sturges does not at first identify Tom as Tom; he is simply called "The Big Man" for some four pages, at which point Sturges playfully adds, "We might as well call him Tom from now on." In a tough dialogue with the directors he comes out with the winning votes needed to purchase the railroad, and then, as he moves to leave, he mentions: "One thing more, gentlemen . . . I want to congratulate you . . . you bought the Santa Clara ten minutes ago," referring to his stock purchases before the meeting.

Henry—who is identified in these voice-overs simply as "The Narrator"—then sets us up to go further back in Tom's life, saying of his friend and boss, "It's funny when you think he couldn't even read and write when he was twenty . . . had to sign his name with a cross . . . it's funny."

Sequence D (13 pages)

The past: Tom as a young, uneducated railroad "trackwalker"

Henry sits at a desk writing a letter; in voice-over he informs us that "in a way I was responsible for Tom and Sally getting married." In a series of short scenes we follow Tom, now in his early twenties, as he learns to read and write from Sally, who is a schoolteacher in a small mountain school. (These pages are shortened in the film.) Then comes the "proposal" scene, in which Henry relates events as told to him by Sally. The scene is played for comic effect as Tom, too shy to put his intentions into words, drags Sally up a mountain. Tom succeeds in his mission, however, and Henry tells us, "They stayed happy for quite a while too."

Sequence E (12 pages)

The recent past: Tom meets Eve

Before we see any scene of Tom and Sally's marriage, we cut to shortly after the purchase of the Santa Clara railroad and the meeting of Tom and the railway's former president together with his beautiful daughter, Eve, whom Henry describes as "kind of aristocratic." From the beginning it is clear that Tom is smitten with her. Henry plays the role of Greek chorus, not only reporting events but also commenting about Eve: "Right then and there I knew there was trouble coming."

We then meet Tom's twenty-year-old son, Tommy, who has just been bounced out of Yale for poor grades and boozing. Tom solves the problem of an unemployed son his own way: he gets him a job at the bottom of the corporate ladder. Sally and Tom quarrel over this handling of the situation, and Tom storms off. (In the film this scene is made even more compelling, for it is clear that Sally senses that Tom is having an affair. She confronts him about his attitude, remarking, "You wouldn't have amounted to so much without me, and you know it.") The sequence ends with mother and son drawing closer together in their hatred of Tom.

Sequence F (11 pages)

The past

We are now roughly halfway through the film. Henry, in voice-over, muses: "Tom might be a trackwalker yet, happy and satisfied, if it wasn't for her"—meaning Sally.

Tom Garner (Spencer Tracy) proposes marriage to Sally (Colleen Moore) on a mountaintop in *The Power and the Glory*. Courtesy The Academy of Motion Picture Arts and Sciences.

We have returned to the beginning of their marriage, finding them ensconced in "a little shack in the mountains." Sally urges Tom to make something of his life so "we could have good clothes and a better house and . . . and . . . maybe even a horse and carriage." She volunteers to take on Tom's trackwalking job if he will go to business school. And we learn, ironically, that she's already asked about the job before talking to Tom—a technique to be replayed in the purchase of the Santa Clara.

We cut to Tom a short time later as a business student. He is a very serious young man, but his classmates are able to talk him into joining them for a few beers at the local bar. A comic scene follows (abbreviated in the film) in which a very hungry Tom partakes of the bar's advertised "free lunch," all the while nursing a single beer.

As the sequence ends we see Sally walking tracks, and Henry tells us that she supported Tom through school, sending what money she could.

Sequence G (6 pages)

The recent past

We jump to the affair between Tom and Eve, about which Henry comments: "Maybe it was fun for her, but with him, it was madness." Eve has reached a point where she wants him to choose: her or Sally. When he proves unable to commit, she leaves their restaurant table, saying, "Well . . . call me up some day . . . when you've made up your mind."

Back at the office, Sally asks him to take her to Europe to help save the marriage. Tom confesses. Sally takes the blame for all: "I made you work and grind and push up—not because you wanted to . . . because *I* wanted you to. *I* wanted the power and the money . . . you wanted to go fishing."

Sally walks out in a daze and throws herself under a streetcar.

Sequence H (19 pages)

(The film adds a short scene at this point between Henry and his wife. Once more, Henry's wife attacks Tom, but Henry defends him, pointing out that the two of them had "thirty years of love and kindness and devotion." Thus Sturges continues the "dialogue" on a life, demonstrating that everything can be seen from more than one perspective.)

The past: Tom and Sally early in their marriage

Sally, in a joyful and comic scene, tells Tom she is pregnant. The script sets up the action elaborately as Sally is hoisted, among workmen and steel cables and girders, up to Tom, at work on "a great railroad bridge under construction."

The scene dissolves to the recent past. Tom tells Tommy that he'll be getting married soon and says he hopes Tommy will come live with them, that they "ought to be friends." The old man also offers to support his son while he has a good time, commenting, "I guess I can earn as much as you can spend, huh?"

The distant past

We are present at Tommy's birth. Tom, in his joy, simply yet emotionally says, "My son . . . my son. I've got a son. Oh Sally, they'll never stop me now. Thank you . . ." In the final version, it is this scene that gives us the title of the film, as Tom goes on to recite the Lord's Prayer, including the line ". . . the power and the glory for ever and ever. Amen."

The recent past: Tom and Eve's wedding

A swift wedding takes place soon after Sally's death, with Tommy as best man—something that Henry confesses was "strange to see." The honeymoon is canceled, however, when a railroad strike breaks out. Tom goes and tries to quash the strike, screaming that "nobody runs this railroad but me." In a montage of images we see that over four hundred workers die as Tom brings in troops, police, and strikebreakers. Meanwhile, Tommy becomes more than friends with Eve during what should have been her honeymoon.

The present: Henry and his wife after the funeral

The two continue to discuss why Tom killed himself. Henry's wife feels he did so out of shame. Henry explains that since Tom died on his wedding anniversary, his death must have been connected to love. In any case, he states, "He didn't kill himself."

Sequence I (15 pages)

The recent past: Tom's discovery of Eve's deception

At the office, Henry reminds Tom that it is his anniversary. Tom rushes to a jeweler's shop and buys a string of black pearls and, on the street from a peddler, a fuzzy toy monkey. When he arrives home early carrying the gifts he finds Eve on the phone, talking lovingly to someone. At her feet a baby is playing, about whom she says, "[He's] like a little blond angel . . . he looks just like you." The person on the other end is clearly Tommy. When Eve discovers that Tom is there, she tries to cover up, but Tom is unmoved. He leaves the gifts for her and the boy and departs.

There is a brief shot of Tom in his car, "trying to dispel the horrible thoughts he has entertained," and then we cut to Tom at a board meeting. He comprehends nothing, for he is "hearing" Eve's words come surreally out of the executive Elmer's mouth. Sturges tells us that Tom's eyes "wander around the room insanely."

He leaves the meeting propped up by Henry, headed for home. Henry tries to get him into bed to await the doctor, but Tom wants to see Eve. When she comes in, Tom takes her to the nursery, with Henry following at a distance. They look at the baby, and Tom asks, "Who does he look like?" The rest of the scene plays out quite differently than in the film. In the script, Tom looms menacingly over the child. Eve refuses to name the father. When he takes the baby by the neck as if to strangle him, however, she screams: "Don't! I'll tell you. Oh God, I couldn't help it. I'm young, I fell in love. Oh God." Finally she confesses: "Oh God . . . it was Tommy." By now Eve has sunk to the floor. Tom kicks her weakly and tries to spit on her; he then "turns back to the crib, looks down in it. His great hands begin to work." Does he mean to murder the child? Meanwhile Henry, watching all this from the door, looks on "horror-stricken."

Tommy arrives, and we learn the baby is still alive.

Tom staggers to his bedroom and tells Tommy to come in. Tom pulls out a revolver and points the gun at Tommy's heart. When Tommy pleads for his life, Tom gets another idea. Saying, "You've done everything else to me, now . . . ," he points the gun at his own chest, places Tommy's hand on the handle, and commands, "Pull."

Henry hears an explosion and rushes in only to see Tom, "with a supreme effort," take the gun from Tommy's hands and fall to a kneeling position. As he lies dying he whispers to Henry, "Suicide." His eyes close, and after a moment he utters the words he spoke when Tommy was born: "I've got a son."

Finally, we flash back to the earlier childbirth scene, with the young Tom kneeling by Sally's bed. The script ends with this moment from the past, now made tragically ironic as Tom recites the Lord's Prayer: "Our Father, Who art in heaven, hallowed be Thy Name, Thy kingdom come, Thy will be done, for Thine is the power and the glory. Amen." The script closes with the organ music at Tom's funeral—Schubert's "Ave Maria"—bringing us full circle.

The film itself ends quite differently, beginning with Tom's confrontation with Eve. When he asks her whom the child looks like, he repeats one of Sally's lines about freedom and happiness; then, as Henry goes to check on the doctor, we hear a shot ring out. When Henry rushes in, Tom is sinking to his knees. Henry helps him to his bed, and Tom says his last word: "Sally." Tommy does not appear at the end of the film.

The film closes on the present, after Tom's funeral, back in Henry's kitchen: Henry falls asleep and his wife gets up, pats him on the shoulder, and leaves, turning out the lights.

A Tale of Two Suicides:
Marriage, Friendship, and Business American Style

The idea for *The Power and the Glory,* Sturges explained, came from the many stories his wife Eleanor Hutton had told him about her grandfather C. W. Post, the founder of the Post cereal empire, who rose from poverty to become a very wealthy industrialist and then, at age fifty-five, committed suicide.[5] But there are also echoes of Solomon Sturges's father, Albert, who founded a railroad, and of railroad barons such as Jay Gould and Jim Fisk.[6] In the next section we will discuss the unusual, nonchronological way in which Sturges narrates his tale, but let us first consider the subject matter and tone of the story and its implications for Sturges's subsequent career writing comedy.

Irony is perhaps Sturges's strongest suit, and it is ironic that his first original screenplay was a darkly emotional drama about an American tycoon's lifelong friendship with another small-town boy, Henry, and about his joyous yet troubled marriage to Sally, an ambitious schoolteacher who helped him rise . . . and fall.

There is much to be learned about Sturges the writer and about Sturges's comic vision from a close read of *The Power and the Glory*. At dead center, of course, to have such a serious film located at the beginning of Sturges's Hollywood career suggests what wise observers of comedy have always known: that very critical concerns often lie at comedy's core. Put another way, *The Power and the Glory* demonstrates that Sturges had a real interest in the whole spectrum of issues and themes related to the American dream and its multiple realities. In particular, the film embraces the topics of success and failure, wealth and power, as well as love, family, personal fulfillment, and friendship. Viewed through a lighter, more playful lens, these become the same themes Sturges explores in his comedies. As Brian Henderson points out, for example, *The Great McGinty* can be considered the comic counterpart to *The Power and the Glory.*[7] And as we have discussed, the rags-to-riches theme winds through many of Sturges's films, including, from our present collection, *Easy Living*.

Irony plays out also in the endings of the film and the script. The film is quite powerful in its bleak dramatic revelation and suicide in the closing scenes. But the original script is even darker. There Sturges tracks a good man who falls so far and so hard that he is ready to strangle the illegitimate child of his second wife and son, and he lashes out bodily at his unfaithful wife; finally he resorts to self-destruction, turning a gun on himself but wrapping his son's fingers around the grip—though in his dying breath he does call the act "suicide." The relentless pain of these closing minutes is much more reminiscent of Dostoyevsky than of American cinema of that era. The irony of a fake suicide becomes Tom's revenge, for it is he who will receive a hero's funeral, while his son, Tommy, must live with his deed all his life.

The script ends with a final flashback to a happier time, when Tom was thrilled to be a father, when his dreams were beginning to come true, when he and Sally were still very much in love. We are thus left with a bittersweet taste of the joys of the past and the sorrows of the present.

The film puts this birth scene, together with the "power and the glory" prayer moment, earlier and closes with Henry falling asleep and his wife taking care of him—patting him, turning off the light, leaving him to his sleep. It's an even better ending than in the script, I suggest, for it leaves us with a sense of loving care, perhaps the most important thing that evaporated in Tom's life.

Three strong concerns run through the film: friendship American style, marriage, and capitalism. A fourth theme, the role of memory in preserving—or distorting—the past, will be addressed in some detail in the following section.

Friendship

The narrative strand of the rise and fall of an American industrialist is contained, in this film, within the tale of Tom and Sally, each of whom ends life in suicide. But even this narrative is wrapped inside a longer relationship: the friendship of Tom and Henry, thanks to which Tom and Sally meet in the first place. Friendship, therefore, anchors the script, which is why Henry is the perfect narrator for this sad tale. Part of the power of the script and the film is that we, the audience, come to realize that Henry is not only telling us Tom's story; he is also remaining loyal to his friend in his efforts to justify Tom's behavior to his own wife (who is never identified by name). What remains is a friend's memory, powerful enough to "evoke" the images and scenes we experience.

Marriage

Significantly, this retelling of Tom's life and his relationship to his wife Sally falls within the purview of another marriage. *The Power and the Glory* is framed as a heated dialogue between Tom's best friend, Henry, and Henry's wife as they attempt to "size up" Tom's whole life. Within that framework, the wife is ready to pass down strong judgments, while Henry, who does not exonerate Tom, nevertheless insists on a more tolerant assessment.

What Sturges gains in having a narrator who is involved with, but apart from, the film's main protagonist is not only a certain degree of concerned objectivity but also an alternative perspective on marriage. That is, whereas Tom and Sally wind up divorced and dead through their own actions, Henry and his wife remain married and their relationship stays healthy, as witnessed in their ability to express their differing opinions openly. The wife even gets the final moment on screen, having taken care of Henry so he can sleep. After all the violence and horror, we end with an example of love that endures. A happy ending? Not exactly. But it somehow acts as a counterweight to the tragedy of Tom's life.

American Business

We need not overemphasize Sturges's own fascination with the pros and cons of American capitalism and the insights into business gained from his personal relationships, for instance with his adoptive father Solomon and his wife Eleanor Hutton. In the rags-to-riches tale related in this film, the American dream—in this case, Sally's strong desire for a better life—plays no small role. However, ambition quickly turns into overambition on Sally's part, even as Tom, having trouble balancing the public sphere—business—with his private life, succumbs to self-destructiveness.

It would be a very different tale if Sturges settled on someone born into money or even someone from an urban background who acquired wealth. Instead, and influenced by the stories of C. W. Post, he built his script around a small-town boy who makes good and then falls. The early scene at the swimming hole is critical, for it establishes a rural America untouched by cities, capital, and industry. In fact, it is a pastoral nineteenth-century scene, conveying no suggestion of the twentieth century. Sturges has thus carefully constructed a script that resonates across a number of American myths, ideals, and realities.

These themes appear in his comedies as well. *Easy Living* crosses private romance and the public sphere of the stock market in a satirical critique of American fortunes gained and lost. And *Remember the Night* reverses the movement of *The Power and the Glory* by taking our district attorney and his criminal lady back to their roots in rural Indiana. There they regain some simple values that will help them survive the upcoming trial back in New York.

Sturges does not condemn American capitalism. It, like Tom, is too big to be judged by ordinary standards. But in both *The Power and the Glory* and his comedies, he is able to suggest the tensions, dangers, and contradictions that can occur in a system where chance rather than logic appears to rule and where vast inequities can and do exist.

Pleasures of the Text

Let us briefly mention three of the many pleasures of reading *The Power and the Glory*. First, there is the "author's note" at the beginning of shot C-2 concerning the Santa Clara railroad: "This stuff will have to be checked; I don't really know anything about it. P.S." Of course, the note makes sense when we consider that Sturges dictated his scripts. This message, then, is more like a work reminder for the future. Nevertheless, the fresh straightforwardness to this admission of lack of expertise is appealing.

Next is the highly original courtship sequence represented in D-10–D-15, narrated by Henry. Tom Sturges has commented that in screenings of the film he has attended, audience members often say they thought that Tom and Sally actually speak during the scene, though of course it is Henry in voice-over recapturing the past as he quotes the actual lines. The double effect of hearing Henry's voice in the present mouthing the words of the young lovers in the past is pleasurable in and of itself. But the scene gains a carefree sense of romance with the final joke, when, after an uncomfortable climb to a mountaintop, Tom finally screws up the courage to ask Sally to marry him, and she agrees, but then adds: "Tom, couldn't you have asked me at the foot of the mountain?"

As a last example of a well-written scene—one that did not make it to the screen—consider F-5. Tom, now a college student, is about to go into a bar. He pulls out three one-dollar bills and some change. We watch as he pockets specified amounts for room, tuition, and carfare. Finally "he looks at what he has left in his hand and weighs it speculatively, then turns and goes into the saloon." Without dialogue, Sturges has shown us both Tom's dire financial straits and his pragmatic sense of fiscal responsibility as he heads into the bar to enjoy what pleasure he can afford.

"Narratage" and Fragmented Storytelling

It was neither a silent film nor a talking film, but rather a combination of the two. It embodied the visual action of a silent picture,
the sound of the narrator's voice, and the storytelling economy
and the richness of characterization of a novel.

PRESTON STURGES

Mordaunt Hall in his *New York Times* review comments that *The Power and the Glory* is full of "surprise" scenes that please and move us. This effect is due in large part to the imaginative fractured narrative structure and the extensive use of a narrator to tell the tale, a dual technique that studio producers called "narratage." What Sturges accomplished by telling the story in a series of flash-backs related in the "present" by Henry, Tom's lifelong friend, was as revolu-tionary to Hollywood storytelling as D. W. Griffith's experiment in narrative structuring in *Intolerance,* where tales from different historical periods were linked by the title theme. Sturges stated that he owed this unusual approach to narrative to Eleanor, who often sharpened the effect of the stories she told of her family by reordering events for heightened emphasis.[8]

The Chinese-box-within-a-box layering of narrative in the film places Tom and Henry's friendship at the center. This is surrounded by Tom's relationship with Sally, whom he meets through Henry; Tom's business success, which he owes to Sally's urgings and help; and finally Tom's personal decline as his mar-riage to Eve, who is out for herself, becomes a disaster in every sense.

Sturges's decision to fracture the narrative by juxtaposing distant-past, pres-ent, and near-past events in sudden and unexpected ways was a daring move that paid off handsomely with the critics. But there is another level to his "nar-ratage" that we should keep in mind, and that is that *The Power and the Glory* is absolutely *cinematic.* We learn from this script that Sturges in the few months he had been in California had definitely made the transition from New York play-wright to West Coast screenwriter. Sturges clearly understood what film can do best. The jumping around in time, the use of montage to convey the passage of time, the mixing of light and dark, and of dramatic and carefree moments, are a use of cinema as cinema par excellence. That this approach to screen narra-tive also increased the emotional impact he wished to create makes his tech-nique all the more impressive. Sturges, in short, demonstrates with this script that he had the feeling for cinema and the freedom of imagination to do what-ever he had to do to create original work.

Add to the screenplay the strength of the direction, the radiant performance by a youthful Spencer Tracy, and the excellent cinematography of James Wong Howe and you have a memorable film indeed.

There was one serious problem, however: the public didn't buy it. But al-though box office receipts proved poor, it almost didn't matter to Sturges,[9] for he was suddenly respected in Hollywood as a classy, talented writer who should be taken seriously. In this sense, his "on spec" approach to writing paid off. He could now enter Hollywood on something close to his own terms, rather than becoming a hack writer from the East Coast writing to commands from producers. And there was more. Sturges first understood during the shooting of *The Power and the Glory* that he passionately wanted to be a film director. Unlike other writers in Hollywood at the time who moved swiftly from one project to the next, Sturges chose to be on the set or in the editing room from start to finish. He thus learned from the outset to appreciate the complexity and thrill of making movies: "It was during this period that I decided to change my profession once more and become a director instead of a team writer. . . . I was sure I could direct because I had just seen it done while I was directing the dialogue on *The Power and the Glory.*"[10]

Preston Sturges would never call himself merely a screenwriter again.

NOTES

1. James Curtis, *Between Flops: A Biography of Preston Sturges* (New York: Limelight Editions, 1984), 83.

2. Mordaunt Hall, "New Technique Brought to Films in 'The Power and the Glory,' with Spencer Tracy and Colleen Moore," *New York Times,* August 11, 1933, 13.

3. Donald Spoto, *Madcap: The Life of Preston Sturges* (Boston: Little, Brown, 1990), 151.

4. Pauline Kael, *The Citizen Kane Book* (New York: Bantam Books, 1971), 35–36, 50.

5. Ibid., 88.

6. Diane Jacobs, *Christmas in July: The Life and Art of Preston Sturges* (Berkeley: University of California Press, 1992), 123–124.

7. *Five Screenplays by Preston Sturges,* edited and with an introduction by Brian Henderson (Berkeley: University of California Press, 1986), 12.

8. Curtis, *Between Flops,* 80.

9. Spoto, *Madcap,* 155.

10. *Preston Sturges by Preston Sturges,* adapted and edited by Sandy Sturges (New York: Simon & Schuster, 1990), 274.

CREDITS

The Power and the Glory

1933

Producer:	Jesse L. Lasky
Director:	William K. Howard
Screenwriter:	Preston Sturges
Editor:	Paul Weatherwax
Cinematographer:	James Wong Howe
Music director:	Louis de Francesco
Art director:	Max Parker
Costumes:	Rita Kaufman

CAST

Tom Garner	Spencer Tracy
Sally	Colleen Moore
Henry	Ralph Morgan
Eve	Helen Vinson
Tom Garner Jr.	Clifford Jones
Mr. Borden	Henry Kolker
Henry's wife	Sarah Padden
Tom the Boy	Billy O'Brien
Henry the Boy	Cullen Johnson

Produced and released by Fox Film Corporation.
76 minutes. Black and white. No rating.

<u>THE POWER AND THE GLORY</u>

A narrative screen play
by
Preston Sturges

37

He suggests the prisoner
in the dock: not the son
come to bury his father.
He is twenty-three years
old. He is very handsome.
The young woman sits by
his side. She is thirty
years old. Very beautiful.
Very cold. Completely in-
different. She is dressed
severely but very smartly.
She looks at her lap, pulls
back her sleeve a little,
consults a diamond wrist
watch, puts the sleeve back
in place, and looks up again.
THE CAMERA begins to move.
It TRUCKS UP the aisle showing
a few of the hundreds gathered
in the cathedral. The people
in the front pews were very
prosperous. Those in back are
of humbler station. THE CAMERA
comes to rest on a small man
about fifty-five years old. He
is standing in back of the pews
next to the aisle. He is of the
bookkeeper type, if there is such
a type. His clothes are old but
well-brushed. His necktie was
already tied when he bought it.
He presses a derby hat to his
heart. His lips are quivering.
He is fighting back his tears.

CUT TO:

A-4   LONG SHOT..DOWN THE AISLE

This is over the shoulder of   SOUND: Organ.
the little man we have been looking
at. We see now the full magnificence
of the floral display. Tens of thousands
of dollars' worth of flowers have been
sent. This man must have been great
or else well-beloved. At least powerful.
The music rises in a tremendous crescendo.
The little man puts a handkerchief to his
nose, then, unable to contain his grief,
sobs, turns toward us, pauses a moment,
and staggers past the CAMERA.

CUT TO:

A-5   EXTERIOR..ANGLE SHOT..CATHEDRAL STEPS

We are looking up the steps at a small   SOUND: Street noises.
door. Through it comes the
little man. He puts his hat on askew,
blows his nose violently, then straightens   (Faint
his hat. The sound of the organ steals in   SOUND: (Organ.
upon us as a faint undertone to the street   (Music.
noises. The little man comes down the
steps and goes past us.

CUT TO:

A-6   FAÇADE OF A BUILDING

    We read "The Chicago &
    Great Western Railroad."
    It is chiselled into the
    stone in great Roman letters.   SOUND: Street noises.
    THE CAMERA ANGLES DOWN and
    picks up a flagpole jutting
    out from the building. On
    it a flag flies at half-mast.
    THE CAMERA ANGLES DOWN still
    further. It is now almost a
    VERTICAL SHOT. Twenty or thirty
    feet beneath us the little man
    appears. He pulls open a heavy
    glass door.

    CUT TO:

A-7   CLOSE SHOT..HEAVY GLASS DOOR..
    REVERSE

    The little man has opened the door.
    He comes into us. The door swings
    to behind him. As he comes near us
    we start TRUCKING ahead of him. His
    footsteps ring out sharply on the
    stone flagging of the empty corridor.
    Faintly we hear the organ music. The   SOUND: Faint organ
    little man turns sharply to the left.   music.
    We PAN with him. He enters a shiny
    bronze elevator. The gate clangs.

    CUT TO:

A-8   INTERIOR..ELEVATOR

    The little man and the aged elevator
    operator stand with their backs to
    us.

                    THE ELEVATOR MAN (turning)
                      It ain't over yet, is it,
                      Henry?

                    HENRY
                      I couldn't stay. I...I...
                      I knew him so long, you
                      know?

                  ELEVATOR OPERATOR
                    ~~Sure.~~ *Yeah? Well I knew*
                    him a long time too - and
He opens the gate. Henry   *I'm glad he croaked... the*
steps out.   *old b.....*

    CUT TO: *HENRY.*
                    Aw shut up!
A-9   ~~HENRY'S OFFICE~~

    The room is fairly dark.
    Henry comes into the picture.
    ~~████████████████████████~~
    ~~████████████████████████~~
    ~~████████████████████████~~
    ~~████████████████████████~~
    ~~████████████████████████~~
    ~~████████████████████████~~

                                (CONTINUED)

~~protooborg, then accosoo,~~
~~takes hold of a huge ledger,~~
~~carries it to his desk, slams~~
~~it down, and opens it to a~~
~~place marked with a strip of~~
~~paper. He picks up a pen,~~
~~examines the point, wipes it~~
~~on his back hair, and dips~~
~~it in the ink.~~ From the slip
of paper he begins copying
figures into his ledger. We
hear the scratching of the
pen. Then he sighs heavily,
looks up from his work and
far away. The organ music
steals in. It rises in
crescendo. Henry slams his
ledger closed, looks at us,
hesitates, takes a step forward, hesitates again, then
walks past us.

CUT TO:

SOUND: Scratching of pen

SOUND: Organ crescendos.

A-10   FOLLOWING SHOT..HENRY WALKING
        DOWN HALL

The organ music continues. It
is a very long hall with several
turnings. Henry's footsteps
~~shatterxikexxikmex~~ ring out.
Presently he stops before a
door marked "President". He
lifts his hand to knock, then,
remembering, lowers it again
and enters. From the doorway
he looks around the room and
we look around with him. It
is finished magnificently, as
magnificence was understood
in railroad circles in nineteen
hundred. Everything is very
expensive, very heavy, very
shiny. In a huge window there
stands a pedestal supporting
a bust. Henry crosses to it
and looks at it. It is bronze.
The rugged features show a man
in the prime of life. The jaw
is square, the mouth firm, the
eyebrows bushy, the nose prominent. The neck is thick and suggests great power. Little Henry
looks up into the g stern face
above him. He reaches out his
hand and pats the cheek.

SOUND: Organ music.

SOUND: FOOTsteps.

                    HENRY
            Goodbye, Tom.

He turns and starts back
toward us. As he passes the
desk he stops, picks up a
tintype in an old-fashioned
frame, and looks at it.
INSERT: SHOT of tintype. It
shows a railroad engineer standing below the cab of his engine.

                        (CONTINUED)

He is a fine-looking
big man. We recognize
the square chin, the bushy
brows, and the prominent
nose of the bust.
CUT BACK to Henry looking
at the tintype. He weighs
it in his hand for a moment,
then puts it in his inside
breast pocket and goes past
us.

CUT TO:

A-11   HALL..HENRY WALKING AWAY

Again his footsteps ring out   SOUND: Foot steps.
sharply and punctuate the
organ music. We do not   SOUND: Organ music.
follow him this time. The
hall is quite dark and Henry
disappears before the sound of
his footsteps has died out.
These come to us faintly, then
cease. The organ music fades
away.

***   FADE-OUT   ***

41

FADE IN:

B-1   CLOSE SHOT..HENRY..REAR VIEW

He is in his shirt sleeves
and a little apron hangs around
his neck. He is drying a dish.
He finishes and puts it down.
A woman's hand comes into the
picture and hands him a coffee
cup.

> THE WOMAN'S VOICE
> There...and you were
> very good not to break
> anything...for once.

THE CAMERA TRUCKS BACK re-
vealing Henry's wife. She
is a pleasant-looking woman
of fifty. She has strong
features.

> HENRY   (mildly)
> I don't break so much,
> I guess.

His wife empties the dish
pan, places it upside down
on the drainboard, spreads
the dish cloth on the bottom
of the pan.

> HIS WIFE
> Not so much now...but
> plenty in the beginning.

> HENRY   (ruefully)
> I've had quite a lot of
> practice.

> HIS WIFE (tartly)
> Well, if you were smarter,
> we could have had servants.

> HENRY
> I know...I'm not smart.

His wife takes him by the
shoulders and shakes him.

> HIS WIFE
> Don't be such a fool...
> don't you know when I'm
> joking? What would I
> want with help: I'm not
> a cripple. The only thing
> I ever wanted was you and
> a little house to live in
> and...and I got what I
> wanted. I've been happy.

> HENRY
> Honest?

> HIS WIFE
> You bet.

She kisses him on the cheek.

(CONTINUED)

                              HIS WIFE
                                   Would you like another
                                   cup of coffee? You
                                   shouldn't have it, but
                                   maybe...today...

                              HENRY
                                   I guess maybe I would.

                              HIS WIFE
                                   Go in the parlor and
                                   take a load off your
                                   mind. I'll bring it
                                   in to you.

                              HENRY
                                   All right.

          He takes off the little
          apron, hangs it on the a
          nail and goes out of the
          picture. His wife looks
          after him. Her expression
          changes to one full of sym-
          pathy. She shakes her head
          a little.

          CUT TO:

B-2   SHOT OF PARLOR THROUGH DOUBLE
          DOOR

          We see a little of the hall also
          with Henry's coat and derby hat
          hanging on a combination hatrack,
          mirror and umbrella stand made of
          quartered oak. The parlor is typical
          of a poor man's home. There is a small
          fireplace containing a coal grate.
          The coal grate is burning. The fireplace
          is flanked on one side with a rocking
          chair for the wife and on the other
          side with a morris chair for the husband.
          Beside the morris chair stands a table.
          On this there are a gilt reading lamp,
          with a fringed red shade, a pound tin
          of tobacco, and a little rack supporting
          two pipes. On the mantlepiece there are
          some photographs, a Japanese flower vase,
          and a small chime clock. The ticking is
          quite audible. A second after we come   SOUND: Clock
          into this picture the clock whirs, then   striking
          strikes seven. Henry appears, stands   seven.
          a moment with his back to us, then
          crosses to his coat and removes from
          it the tintype we saw before. He
          goes into the parlor, picks up a
          poker, stirs the coal fire, then
          sits down. He looks at the tintype,
          then looks into the fire. Very softly
          the organ music steals in Henry's   SOUND: Soft organ
          wife comes into the picture. She   music.
          stops beside him and holds out the
          cup of coffee. The organ music be-
          comes almost inaudible.

          CUT TO:

B-3   SHOT OF HENRY, HIS WIFE
AND FIREPLACE

Their positions are the same
as in the last scene, but
THE CAMERA is now directed
straight at the fireplace.
It shows this and the two chairs.
Henry takes the coffee from his
wife. He stirs it and murmurs:

> HENRY
> Thank you.

> HIS WIFE (pointing to the
>   tintype)
> What have you got
> there?

She leans over, picks up
the tintype, looks at it,
then throws it onto the
little table. She speaks
with bitterness:

> HIS WIFE   (bitterly)
> ~~I wouldn't be so blue~~
> ~~about that fellow~~...
> it's a good thing he did
> kill himself.

> HENRY
> Don't talk like that.

> HIS WIFE
> I'll talk any way I like
> when it comes to such
> people. He was a good-
> for-nothing.

She ~~xxxxxxx~~ sits in her
rocking chair, and rocks
crossly.

> HENRY
> You didn't understand him.

> HIS WIFE
> I understood him all right,
> and so did everybody else.
> The men he killed...four
> hundred in the big strike
> alone.

> HENRY   (petulantly)
> He didn't kill 'em. He
> had to protect the rail-
> road.

> HIS WIFE
> Tell that to their widows
> and children and see what
> they say.

Henry shrugs.

> HIS WIFE
> And ~~the~~ the way he
> treated his wife who

> (CONTINUED)

44

                                        HIS WIFE (cont'd)
                                             slaved for him and wore
                                             herself out and lost her
                                             prettiness, And then for
                                             a thank you, got kicked
                                             out to make room for
                                             somebody new...young and
                                             pretty.

                                        HENRY
                                             He didn't kick her out,
                                             it just happened, that's
                                             all, like everything else
                                             happened to him, things
                                             that don't happen to or-
                                             dinary people. He never
                                             was like ordinary people,
                                             and you can't judge him
                                             by ordinary standards.
                                             They wouldn't fit him.
                                             He was too...too big.

                                        HIS WIFE
                                             Oh, nonsense!

                                        HENRY
                                             It isn't nonsense. I
                                             ought to know. I knew him
                                             all my life...almost...
                                             Even when we were little
                                             boys, he was different.

          A VERY SLOW LAP DISSOLVE
          begins here. Almost im-
          perceptibly Henry's parlor
          fades and a view of the
          swimming hole Henry is talking
          about becomes clearer.

                                        HENRY
                                             Different from the others--
                                             as different as day is
                                             from night. He was bigger
                                             and stronger and he didn't
                                             know what fear meant.
                                             Maybe he was a show-off a
                                             little bit, but he always
                                             made good what he was
                                             showing.

          THE LAP DISSOLVE should
          be completed here:

          A lot of little boys   SOUND: Boys' voices
          ranging from seven to   yelling and laughing.
          twelve are playing around.
          In the background, the other
          side of the stream, there is
          a high rock jutting some twenty-
          five feet above the surface of the
          water. In front of this, there is
          a small rock, table-topped, about
          five feet from the surface. The
          boys dive from here.

          Cut to

CUT TO:

B-5   CLOSE SHOT..TABLE-TOPPED ROCK

Little Henry stands on this. He
is about eight years old. A
barefoot boy, dressed in a ragged
hickory shirt and ragged overalls.

                    NARRATOR'S VOICE
                        I was always kinda little,
                        and I didn't know how to
                        swim, but I used to go and
                        watch the other boys.

Little Henry jumps up and
down, laughs, and pounds his
knees in admiration at some
aquatic feat beneath him. Then
he turns his head and looks down
at someone climbing up the little
rock.

                    NARRATOR'S VOICE
                        Tom could do anything. He
                        was bigger than I was, but
                        only a year or so older.
                        It's funny that our friend-
                        ship began with a fight.

Tom climbs up on the rock.
He is a sturdy little boy,
handsome, well-muscled, and
beautifully built. He is
stark naked and dripping.

                    TOM   (breathlessly)
                        Come on in, it ain't cold.

                    LITTLE HENRY
                        I don't know how to swim.

                    TOM
                        ████████████. You don't
                        have to...all you got to
                        do is wiggle around and
                        splash ███ and you get
                        back to the rock all right.

                    LITTLE HENRY
                        I'd get drownded.

                    TOM
                        No you wouldn't. Come on.

He reaches for little
Henry who draws back from
the edge of the rock.

                    LITTLE HENRY
                        I don't wanta.

Tom takes his hand and little
Henry starts to cry.

                    TOM   (dragging him to the edge)
                        You gotta learn.

                        (CONTINUED)

LITTLE HENRY (at the top of his
                        lungs)
I don't wanta...I don't
wanta.

TOM
Yes you do too. ~~TXKXXYKNY~~
Skin outa your duds.

LITTLE HENRY (shrieking)
~~I don't wanta...I don't
wanta.~~ NO

TOM   (grasping him firmly)
All right...then go in
this way.

He throws him in the
water, then looks down
at him, ready to jump
in himself.

CUT TO:

B-6   VERTICAL SHOT FROM THE
         ROCK..LITTLE HENRY IN
         THE WATER

He is yelling bloody murder   SOUND: Yelling.
and screeching at the top of
his lungs. At the same time,
however, he splashes, squirms,
beats the water, and manages to
keep his head above it. Presently
instinct asserts itself and, still
yelling at the top of his lungs,
he swims dog-fashion to the shore.
As he touches bottom and stands up
in two feet of water, we

CUT TO:

B-7   ANGLE SHOT LOOKING UP AT TOM

The highlights and black shadows
of the bright sunlight should
prevent this shot from being at all
indecent. He is laughing hard at
little Henry's antics. Now he dives
gracefully and flashes past us. The
water splashes up and obscures our
view of the background.

CUT TO:

B-8   MEDIUM CLOSE SHOT..LITTLE HENRY

He is blubbering with rage and
fear. His eyes and ears are full
of water, his hair is glued down
over his face. He is trying to
get the water out of his eyes.
Tom runs into the picture.

TOM

There...that wasn't so
bad, was it? You done

(CONTINUED)

47

B-8   (CONTINUED)

                              TOM   (continued)
                                     pretty good.

         CUT TO:

B-9   CLOSEUP OF LITTLE HENRY'S FACE

         He parts the long hair, opens it
         like a pair of portieres, and
         glares at us venomously.

                            LITTLE HENRY
                                You tried to drownd me.

                            TOM'S VOICE
                                Don't be such a baby,
                                Henry.

                            LITTLE HENRY   (furiously)
                                I'll show ya if I'm a
                                baby...you tried to
                                drownd me...I'll show ya.

         He clamps his jaws shut. His
         face takes on a belligerent
         expression and he comes nearer
         the lens.

         CUT TO:

B-10   FULL LENGTH SHOT..THE TWO
         BOYS FACING EACHOTHER

         Tom is smiling amicably, but
         Henry is rage incarnate.

                            TOM
                                Come on, let's do it
                                again.

                            LITTLE HENRY   (at the top of his
                                                    lungs)
                                WHAT!

         In sheer desperation he takes
         a wild swing at Tom, catches
         him on the point of the jaw
         and knocks him flat. Then he
         doubles his fists, strikes an
         old-fashioned fighting pose, and
         dances up and down. The awful
         consequences of his act now be-
         come clear to him and he sobs
         aloud as he dances up and down.

         CUT TO:

B-11   CLOSE SHOT..TOM SITTING ON THE
         GRASS

         He rubs his jaw, looks at Henry
         speculatively, then starts to
         laugh.

                            TOM
                                What did you want to go
                                and do that for?

                              (CONTINUED)

48

                          LITTLE HENRY'S VOICE
                               I'll show ya. I'll show ya.

          He wails loudly. Tom
          starts laughing again
          and begins to rise.

          CUT TO:

B-12   CLOSEUP..HEAD OF ANOTHER
          LITTLE BOY

          He is looking at us in astonish-
          ment. His mouth hangs open and
          he is popeyed. After a second he
          swallows his saliva with difficulty,
          turns to one side, and yells:

                          LITTLE BOY
                               Hey, fellers, lookit!
                               Little Henry flattened
                               Tom. Hurry up!

          He dashes out of the picture.
          In the background thus made
          visible to us we see five or
          six little boys running toward
          us as fast as they can. One of
          them stumbles, falls flat, picks
          himself up again, and runs on.

          CUT TO:

B-13   MEDIUM CLOSE SHOT..TOM, LITTLE
          HENRY AND CIRCLE OF LITTLE BOYS

          Tom, laughing hard, gets to his
          feet. Little Henry jumps up and
          down and yells:

                          LITTLE HENRY
                               I'll show ya.

          He charges at Tom. There
          is a roar of encouragement   SOUND: Yells of boys.
          from the onlookers. Several
          phrases come through clearly:

                               1. Go on, Henry.
                               2. Flatten him, Tom.
                               3. He can't hurt you, Henry...
                                   not much.
                               4. Hit him in the slats, Tom.

          Little Henry swarms all over
          Tom. He throws a thousand
          punches, none of which have
          the slightest effect. Tom
          blocks them, rolls with the
          punches and slides them off
          his shoulders and elbows.
          He is grinning all the time
          and does not hit back. Little
          Henry is completely winded by

                                                (CONTINUED)

now. His arms fall to his
sides, he gasps for breath,
and between puffs manages:

>LITTLE HENRY (gasping for breath)
>There...that...that'll show
>ya.

>TOM   (amiably)
>You sure did...you're a
>good little scrapper,
>Henry.

A tough-looking boy about
fourteen speaks up:

>TOUGH BOY
>   (disgustedly)
>Aaaaaaaah! I could lick
>'im wid one hand.

He turns to little Henry.

>You wanta fight?

Little Henry looks at him in
horror.

>LITTLE HENRY
>I...I had a fight.

>TOM   (quietly)
>Let him alone.

>TOUGH BOY (to Little Henry)
>You didn't have no fight...
>Come on, if you're so good.

>TOM
>I said let 'im alone.

>TOUGH BOY
>Here.

He hits little Henry in the
face with the back of his hand.
Tom brings up a looping right
which smashes the big boy right
in the eye. He staggers back against
a tree, then charges forward bellowing
with rage. He is a good deal bigger than
Tom. A swell fight now takes place. Tom
hits very accurately and very hard. The
bigger boy hits very hard, but less accurately. He takes a good deal of punish-
ment. Both his eyes are blacked, and his
nose is bleeding and his lip is split.
He begins to flounder, then lands a lucky
blow which knocks Tom down. There is a
wild yell from the crowd. Tom, on all
fours, shakes his head to clear it, then
staggers to his feet. He retreats in a
circle. The big boy, scenting the kill,
tears after him. Tom, in full retreat,
shoots a right. The big boy stumbles but
keeps on. Tom shoots another right; the
big boy stumbles again but comes on rubber-

(CONTINUED)

B-13   (CONTINUED)

     legged. Tom shoots a right
     and a left. The big boy stops.
     Tom charges in. The big boy
     covers his face with his hands.
     Tom smashes him in the middle
     till he lowers his guard and
     lands a terrific uppercut on
     his jaw. The big boy falls
     flat on his face--out to the
     world. The other boys swarm
     around him.

          CUT TO:

B-14   CLOSE SHOT..TOM AND LITTLE HENRY

     Tom is nursing his hands, rubbing
     his knuckles.

                              LITTLE HENRY
                              I...I guess you coulda
                              licked me if you'd wanted
                              to.

                         TOM
                              Why of course I couldn't,
                              Henry, I couldn't do nothin'
                              with you at all...you're
                              a good scrapper.

                         LITTLE HENRY
                              So are you...Say...

                         TOM
                              What?

                         LITTLE HENRY
                              Will you teach me to swim?

     The picture begins to
     FADE slowly.

                              NARRATOR'S VOICE
                              That's how our friendship
                              began. It was a pretty
                              good one too, when you
     THE PICTURE FADES   figure how long it lasted.
     OUT.

     NOTE: Henry's Voice carries   He taught me to swim all
     through the scene changes. The right. You couldn't be
     Narrator's voice is especially   afraid of anything with
     useful at this time.   him there; you'd be ashamed.

B-15   CLOSE SHOT..TABLE-TOPPED ROCK..
     FADING IN VERY SLOWLY..TOM AND
     LITTLE HENRY

                              NARRATOR'S VOICE
                              I remember one day he almost
                              got killed. He was teach-

                         (CONTINUED)

51

NARRATOR'S VOICE (cont'd)
ing me to ~~dive~~, but I
was scared blue.

Tom goes to the edge of
the rock, puts his hands
palm to palm, and teeters
on the edge of the rock in
the standard diving position.

TOM
Come on, Henry.

LITTLE HENRY (flattened against
the back rock)
I don't wanta...I don't
wanta.

TOM
~~There isn't anything to be
scared of.~~ It's only
water. You can jump into
it from any place.

You couldn't be scared Henry

LITTLE HENRY
Oh no you can't. You
couldn't jump in from ~~away~~ *from*
~~up~~ there.

He points straight up to the
rock twenty feet above him.
Tom looks up at it then
speaks quietly:

TOM
Yes I could...I'll show ya.

Little Henry begins to
dance up and down.

LITTLE HENRY
No, no, don't do it! You'll
get hurted.

Tom begins to climb up the
face of the rock. THE CAMERA
ANGLES UP and follows his
progress.

NARRATOR'S VOICE
...But I couldn't stop him.
He was going to show me
and he did. He went up and
up and up...it was crazy.
Nobody'd ever dived from
there before. When he got
to the top, he looked kind
of small from where I was
and I guess we looked kind
of small to him too.

CUT TO:

B-16   SHOT OF SWIMMING HOLE FROM TOP
OF ROCK..POINT OF VIEW SHOT

THE CAMERA PANS AROUND, looks down
at little Henry who is dancing around

(CONTINUED)

                    nervously and then at a few
                    other boys who are looking up.
                    Suddenly and very loudly
                    we hear Tom's voice.

                                        TOM'S VOICE
                                    Here I come.

                    THE CAMERA follows the
                    path of the boy diving
                    into the water. This can
                    be done either with the
                    STEP-UP or by lowering
                    a camera on a rope. THE
                    CAMERA enters the water
                    and SHOOTS DOWN toward some
                    jagged rocks visible in
                    a slanting ray of sunshine.

                    CUT TO:

B-17   ANGLE SHOT..LITTLE HENRY AND
            WATER BENEATH HIM

                    He is looking intently at the
                    foamy spot where Tom disappeared.
                    We look at it over his shoulder.
                    After a moment he begins to scream:

                                        LITTLE HENRY
                                    Tom! Tom! Come up...Tom!
                                    Tom!

                    He looks across the swimming
                    hole.

                                    Help! Help! Tom is drownding.
                                    Help!

                    He dances up and down.
                    ANGLE UP to show some little
                    boys on the opposite side of
                    the water. They dive in and
                    splash toward us. THE CAMERA
                    ANGLES DOWN as they come nearer.
                    Little Henry points to the spot
                    where Tom disappeared and yells:

                                        LITTLE HENRY
                                    Right there! Right there!
                                    Go down and get 'im.

                    Two of the boys dive and swim
                    down under water.

                                    He's drownding...he's drownd-
                                    ing.

                    The boys reappear. They
                    speak breathlessly:

                                        FIRST BOY
                                    I...can't see nothin'.

                                        SECOND BOY
                                    's too deep.

                                        (CONTINUED)

53

B-17   (CONTINUED)

> LITTLE HENRY
> He's drownded.

He starts to sob.

CUT TO:

B-18   CLOSE VERTICAL SHOT..WATER

Very faintly at first we see
a white body coming toward us.
It breaks through the surface
and we see Tom with his head
thrown back fighting for air.
His eyes are closed and his
face wears an agonized expression.

CUT TO:

B-19   SAME ANGLE SHOT AS B-17

> LITTLE HENRY (yelling)
> Go down again! Go down
> again!

> FIRST BOY
> What's the use, I can't
> see nothin'.

> SECOND BOY   (suddenly)
> There he is!

All the boys in the water
race out of the picture.
THE CAMERA ANGLES UP and
PANS around to a spot
twenty feet away where
Tom is floating. Little
Henry runs to the extreme
edge of the rock, dances up
and down and yells:

> LITTLE HENRY
> Tom! Tom! Are you hurted?

Getting no answer he leans
still further out and yells:

> Tom!

He falls into the water.

CUT TO:

B-20   TOM LEANING AGAINST ROCK
                SURROUNDED BY OTHER BOYS

He looks white and quite ill.
His right hand is buried in
his left armpit.

> FIRST BOY
> Gee, you were lucky.

> TOM
> Yeah.

(CONTINUED)

Little Henry comes dashing
into the picture. He is soaking
wet and still snuffling.

> LITTLE HENRY
>> Are you all right? (snuffle)

> TOM
>> Yeah.

> LITTLE HENRY
>> (Snuffle) What happened?

> TOM
>> I caught my hand between two
>> rocks...I had a hard time
>> gettin' loose.

> LITTLE HENRY
>> Gee whiz! Do you want a
>> drink of water?

> TOM
>> No, thank you, Henry, I had
>> plenty of water.

> LITTLE HENRY
>> Gee whiz! I almost just
>> got drownded my own self...
>> I'm glad you're all right.

DISSOLVE TO:

B-21   FOLLOWING SHOT..TOM AND LITTLE HENRY

They are dressed now, walking down
the road toward the sunset. Their
bare feet kick up little clouds of
dust. Tom still has his right hand
under his left arm, although this
probably does not show much from the
rear. The two boys are talking, but we
cannot hear what they say: only the
murmur of voices.

> NARRATOR'S VOICE
>> We went home together. We
>> were chums. ▓▓▓▓. Summer
>> was ▓▓▓▓ over. School
>> ▓▓▓ starting ▓▓ next week.
>> I was sad because I wasn't
>> going to see ▓▓ much of Tom
>> any more. He didn't go to
>> school. His father said ▓▓
>> ▓▓▓▓▓▓▓▓▓▓▓▓▓ you
>> didn't need arithmetic to
>> feed hogs or reading and
>> writing to milk a cow. ▓▓▓
>> ▓▓▓▓▓▓▓▓▓...▓▓▓▓▓
>> ▓▓▓▓▓▓▓▓▓▓.
>> After a while I noticed ▓▓▓
>> Tom was kind of quiet. I
>> looked at him. His eyes
>> were full of tears.

CUT TO:

Little Henry stops, holds Tom
by the shoulders, and says:

> LITTLE HENRY
> What's the matter, Tommy?

> TOM (xxxfxiiyi)
> It's nothin'.

> LITTLE HENRY
> Yes it is. What is it?

> TOM
> It hurts me a little bit...
> where I caught my hand.

> LITTLE HENRY
> Let me see.

Tom pulls out his hand
and they both look at it.

> LITTLE HENRY
> Gee whiz!

INSERT: Very close shot of
hand. The fist is clenched. The
Back of the hand is terribly
bruised and blued. Running
diagonally across it there is
a big jagged cut, the shape of
a bolt of lightning. Little
Henry's hand comes into the
picture and lifts Tom's injured
hand gently. CUT BACK.
Little Henry is holding Tom's
hand.

> LITTLE HENRY
> Aw gee...that's turrible...
> wait a minute, I'll fix it.

He pulls his shirt tail out
of his overalls.

> TOM
> Don't do that.

> LITTLE HENRY
> Leave me alone.

He tears off his shirt tail,
folds it into a bandage,
then says:

> Wait a minute.

He goes to the side of the road
and THE CAMERA PANS with him.
He picks some big cool-looking
leaves from a bush, brings them
back. He chooses the biggest
leaf and spits on it.

> (CONTINUED)

                                        LITTLE HENRY
                                            That'll take the poison
                                            out.

He places the leaf,
spit down, on the bruised
hand, then arranges other
leaves alongside and over
this. He ties it all together
with his shirt tail and says:

                                        LITTLE HENRY
                                            Now...don't that feel better?

                                    TOM   TEM
                                            Sure, that's a lot better...
                                            thanks.

                                        LITTLE HENRY
                                            You're welcome...you better
                                            take my arm. I'll help
                                            you home.

Tom tries not to laugh.

                                    TOM
                                            All right, Henry.

The boys start toward us.

CUT TO:

B-23   LITTLE HENRY AND TOM
        WALKING AWAY

Little Henry has his arm
around Tom's waist. He
tries to support him. The
sun has almost set. The
shadows are very long.

                                        NARRATOR'S VOICE
                                            He was a brave kid and a
                                            brave man. A lot can happen
                                            in a man's life...plenty
                                            happened to him.

There is a fairly long pause.
The boys are quite far away now.
We hear the tree toads singing.   SOUND: Tree toads.

                                        NARRATOR'S VOICE
                                            ...plenty.

                    ****   FADE-OUT   ****

57

SEQUENCE "C"

FADE IN:

C-1   LONG SHOT..FLOOR OF THE NEW
YORK STOCK EXCHANGE

In the center of this shot there
is a wildly excited group surround-   SOUND: Men yelling.
ing one of the pillars. A terrific
din is going on.

LAP DISSOLVE TO:

C-2   CLOSE SHOT..THIS SAME GROUP

Favor one man, the specialist
in Santa CLARA stock. He
marks down his transactions on
a little card.
(AUTHOR'S NOTE: This stuff will
have to be checked; I don't
really know anything about it.
P.S.)

> SANTA FE MAN   (checking)
> Five hundred thirty-six and
> an eighth....five hundred
> thirty-six.

A man in the crowd nods.
Another man in the crowd
says:

> ANOTHER MAN
> Five hundred seven-eighths.

Santa Fe Man nods.
These transactions continue
until the stock is selling at
thirty-three. Then a page
boy comes into the picture
and taps the Santa Clara man
on the shoulder. He crosses
to a telephone and we PAN with
him. He speaks into the receiver.

CUT TO:

C-3   CLOSE SHOT..OFFICE OF THE PRESIDENT:
CHICAGO AND GREAT WESTERN RAILROAD

Henry is at the telephone. He is a   SOUND: Ticker.
little younger than the Henry we have
seen in the beginning of the picture.
He is about forty-five. Standing with
his back to us there is a huge man
reading the ticker which clicks busily.
He is in his shirt sleeves. The smoke
from a cigar curls over his head.

> HENRY (with his hand over mouthpiece
> It's New York.. He's on the wire.

> THE BIG MAN'S VOICE
> Tell him to hammer it down.

> HENRY (into the telephone)
(CONTINUED)   He says to hammer it down.

58

He listens for a moment, then
puts his hand over the mouthpiece
and turns to the big man.

> HENRY
> He says he __is__ hammering
> it down.

> THE BIG MAN'S VOICE
> Tell him to hammer it down
> harder.

> HENRY   (into the mouthpiece)
> He says to hammer it down
> harder.

After a pause, he puts his
hand over the mouthpiece and
looks around.

> HENRY
> He says he's doing the best
> he can.

> THE BIG MAN'S VOICE
> Tell him he's got to do a
> hell of a lot better than
> that or I'll kick his tail
> around the block.

Henry raises his eyebrows,
then speaks into the telephone:

> HENRY
> He says would you be kind
> enough to try a little
> harder.

He puts his hand over the
mouthpiece.

> He says allright.

> THE BIG MAN'S VOICE
> Tell him to start buying at
> thirty.

> HENRY   (into the mouthpiece)
> He says to start buying at
> thirty.

He puts his hand over the
mouthpiece and looks around.

> He says how much.

> THE BIG MAN'S VOICE
> As much as I can get...I
> want control.

> HENRY   (into the telephone)
> He says he wants control...
> All right.

He hangs up the receiver.

> THE BIG MAN'S VOICE
> What'd he say?

(CONTINUED)

                                              HENRY
                                     He said holy smoke.

        The big man chuckles.

        CUT TO:

C-4   LONG TABLE IN BOARD OF DIRECTORS'
        ROOM

        At the head of the table stands
        the chairman of the board. The
        directors sit at the sides of the
        table. The chairman is in the
        middle of a speech and apparently
        in the throes of great agitation.

                                              CHAIRMAN
                                     Gentlemen, this is insanity.
                                     We have more railroad now
                                     than we know what to do with...
                                     and he wants to buy a new
                                     one. The Reno & Santa Clara is
                                     a miserable little road. ~~It's
                                     been losing money for ten
                                     years...and its stations are
                                     in places that nobody would
                                     want to go to anyway, and
                                     its equipment is ready to
                                     fall apart.~~ It is nothing
                                     but a mountain of rust. He
                                     says it's a steal at nine
                                     million dollars, and I say
                                     he's...he's crazy...I'm
                                     against it.

        His whiskers vibrate.

                                     How about you, gentlemen?

        There is a chorus of assent;
        some lines come through.
                                     1.   I think it's ridiculous.
                                     2.   You're perfectly right,
                                          Elmer.
                                     3.   Foolhardy, foolhardy.
                                     4.   He's lost his judgment, if
                                          he ever had any.
                                     5.   I'll tell him "no" right to
                                          his face.
                                     6.   So will I.

                                              CHAIRMAN
                                     I'm glad to see you stand
                                     with me...

        Suddenly he stiffens and
        looks past us.

                                     ...Ah.

        The directors turn and look
        over their shoulders.

        CUT TO:

Framed in this stands the
huge man we have seen only
from the rear. His cigar is
clamped in his mouth. Under
his beetling brows his eyes
twinkle as he looks around
at the directors. He smiles a
little, then says:

                    THE BIG MAN
                Hello, boys.

We TRUCK BACK as he comes
forward and leans on the
back of his chair.

                Glad to see you all well...
                and happy.

He looks around at the
sour pusses of his directors.

                I called this special meet-
                ing because we've got a
                great opportunity...I want
                to buy a railroad...the
                Santa Clara.

Pandamonium breaks loose.
We hear the gentlemen
in chorus:

                1. Absolutely out of the question.
                2. I won't have it.
                3. It isn't worth two cents.
                4. Business is bad anyway.
                5. Etc.

~~The big man has been through
all this many times before.
Buying a railroad is a progressive
step that he has put through. It has
been done over the violent objections
of his directors. He looks at them
patiently. THE CAMERA PANS showing
the whole table. The chairman is on
his feet talking at the top of his
lungs: His words are lost in the general
din.~~ Suddenly there is a terrific
crash. The table almost ~~crashes~~   SOUND: Crash.
bounces and two inkwells are upset.
The directors look down to the president's SOUND: Another
end of the table. The crash is repeated.   crash.
INSERT: Very close shot: The fist of the
big man. It is a huge fist pressed down
on the mahogany. It raises once more
and crashes down. We hear the big man's
voice bellowing:

                    THE BIG MAN
                Quiet!...Don't make so much
                noise.

There is a dead silence. We have
time now to observe the big scar in
the shape of a bolt of lightning
on the back of the fist. The hand
relaxes and drums on the table.
CUT BACK TO:

C-5   (CONTINUED)

> The big man standing
> at the head of the table.

>> THE BIG MAN
>> Don't get so excited. This
>> isn't anything important.
>> Maybe I shouldn't have
>> bothered even to call you in..

> CUT TO:

C-6   CLOSE SHOT..CHAIRMAN

> He is looking at us popeyed.

>> CHAIRMAN
>> What? What? Nine million
>> dollars isn't important?
>> Then will you be kind enough
>> to tell me what IS important?

> CUT TO:

C-7   THE BIG MAN

> We might as well call
> him Tom from now on.

>> TOM

Yes — the railroad — money is NOT very important to me and when I die, I don't care if I leave fifty million dollars ... or only thirty million dollars. (laughter) We've got the finest road in the country right now but we need the Santa Clara to make it still finer. If I tell you we need it, it's because we need it ... if I tell you it's a good buy you ought to have sense enough to know it IS a good buy! I've forgotten more about railroads than most of you gentlemen will ever know

(Laughter)

(CONTINUED)

62

TOM (cont'd)
~~to hear... lot of bellyaching~~
~~about day. Tom sick and~~
~~tired of hearing you where~~
~~about economy everywhere~~
~~the brakeman needs a lantern~~
~~needs a new lantern or the~~
~~old Ninety-Nine needs a new~~
~~whistle~~. If you don't like
the way I'm running things,
speak up. There are plenty
~~of men willing to step into~~
~~my shoes and there are~~
plenty of railroads who
could use me. Now make it
snappy. You want the
Santa Clara or don't you?...
YOU!

THE CAMERA PANS TO
the man on his left.
He is a small shy-looking
man. He swallows hard and
quivers under Tom's gaze.
He looks around to the other
directors for support but none
is forthcoming. Eventually
in a small voice:

FIRST DIRECTOR
Yes.

TOM   (in a booming voice)
Yes what?

FIRST DIRECTOR
Yes, ~~sir~~. indeed.

THE CAMERA PANS to the
next man.

TOM'S VOICE
And you?

The second director swallows,
shrugs his shoulders.

SECOND DIRECTOR
I suppose so...oh yes.

THE CAMERA PANS to the
next director.

TOM'S VOICE
How about you?

THIRD DIRECTOR
By all means. I think the
Santa ~~Fe~~ is an excellent road.
...although I've never seen
it.

TOM'S VOICE
Thanks. And you?

FOURTH DIRECTOR
Why...I always was for it.

(CONTINUED)

THE CAMERA PANS to the
Chairman.

                              TOM'S VOICE
                                   What have you got to say,
                                   Elmer.

The chairman looks very
sour.   CHAIRMAN
                                   Oh all right if you feel
                                   that way about it.

                              TOM'S VOICE
                                   How about the rest of you
                                   boys?

                              THE CHAIRMAN (sourly)
                                   Let's save time. I'll take
                                   a vote. All those in favor
                                   say Aye.

There is a loud chorus of
Ayes.   SOUND: Chorus of "Aye".

                              THE CHAIRMAN
                                   Opposed?

There is not a sound.
THE CAMERA PANS slowly
over the rest of the
directors and comes back
to Tom. He beams at them
all.

                              TOM
                                   Thank you very much for your
                                   cooperation, gentlemen. I
                                   think that is all. Good
                                   afternoon

He starts to turn, then
looks back and says:

                                   Oh, one thing more,
                                   gentlemen...allow me to
                                   congratulate you...you
                                   bought the Santa Fe ten
                                   minutes ago.

He grins then turns and
walks out of the picture.

     CUT TO:

C-8   HENRY TYPING

We hear a door slam.
Tom comes into the   SOUND: Door slam.
picture. He is still
grinning.

                              HENRY   (nervously)
                                   What did they say?

                              TOM
                                   Oh, they were delighted.

                              HENRY
                                   Honest?

                                        (CONTINUED)

64

TOM

Oh yes. ~~Another cent. He soon goes up, only it needs ~~ ...By the way...
that stock will go up as
soon as it gets out we've
bought the road. Get ahold
of Emerson and buy ten
thousand for me and...uh...

He looks at Henry spec-
ulatively.

...a thousand for yourself.

HENRY

But...uh...I can't do it,
Tom. I haven't got the money.
I uh...I...

TOM

Shut up and do what I tell
you.

HENRY

But...but...

TOM

Go on now.

Henry looks frightened
to death and picks up
the receiver and says:

HENRY   (into phone)
Get me Emerson & Porter,
please.

Tom looks at him, laughs,
shakes his head, turns and
walks out of the picture.
Henry scowls after him.
The picture begins to FADE.

NARRATOR'S VOICE
That's how I got the money
to buy this house...I told
you I made it in Wall Street
and I did. I didn't tell you
Tom made me do it. I thought
you'd think better of...
what does it matter anyway.
He knew plenty about the
market, though he pretended
he didn't. It's funny when
you think he couldn't even
read and write when he was
twenty...had to sign his
name with a cross...it's
funny,

By now the picture has
FADED, the LAP DISSOLVE is
completed. Another picture has
taken its place.

FADE IN:

D-1   YOUNG HENRY WRITING A LETTER

He is dressed in the fashion
of 1900 His collar is ex-
tremely high. The lapels of
his coat are very small. His
hair is parted in the middle,
stiff with bear grease and
slicked straight down from the
top of his head. It shines
gloriously. There is the sus-
picion of a mustache under his
nose. He has a sheet of note
paper in front of him and he is
examining his pen point. He
pulls a piece of lint off it,
then wipes it on the back of his
head, examines it again, dips it
in the ink, revolves his wrist a
few times to loosen it, then with
a magnificent series of flourishes,
he commences. As we hear the first   SOUND: Pen scratches.
scratches we

CUT TO:

D-2   CLOSE SHOT..PAPER AND THE HAND WRITING

Buried in the midst of an unbelievable
maze of flourishes and curlicues we see
the following words:appear:

(AUTHOR'S NOTE:

    "Dear Friend Tom:-

        Well, Friend Tom, my train-
ing in Keokuk Business College is near-
ing completion and ere long, God willing,
I shall receive my diploma and launch
myself upon the seas of commercial life.
I think of you often and hark back with
gratification to the days of the old
swimming hole."

This comes at the bottom of the page.
It is blotted, and as the sheet is turned
over, we CUT back to:

Twice during the
writing of this
letter the hand,
having traced an
unbelievable
flourish at the end
of a word, will
pause, hesitate,
then go back and
add a little addi-
tional complication
to the previous
effort. P.S.)

D-3   YOUNG HENRY WRITING

He continues to write.

                  NARRATOR'S VOICE
                  In a way I was responsible
                  for Tom and Sally getting
                  married. I was away at
                  school. I wrote to
                  Tom. He couldn't read, but
                  I think it pleased him
                  anyway.

THE LAP DISSOLVE takes
place now.

He is a track walker. In his right
hand he carries the light, long-
handled hammer. At his belt hang a
couple of wrenches. ~~He is roughly
dressed, but his poor clothes do
not hide the magnificence of his
physique. He is very handsome and,
as a matter of fact, looks exactly
like the actor who plays the role.~~

NARRATOR'S VOICE
He was track walking for the
Great Western...he was a big
fellow.

Young Tom swings his long
hammer at each rail joint
to test its solidity. At the
second one he takes a wrench
from his belt, stoops over,
and tightens up the plate, then
continues toward us.

NARRATOR'S VOICE
Sally was teaching the little
mountain school. She was a
pretty kid, came of good stock
too...brave and honest.

THE POSTMAN'S VOICE
Hi, Tom.

Tom looks to one side of
us and waves his hammer.

TOM
Hi, Zeke.

THE POSTMAN'S VOICE
Got a letter fur ye.

TOM   (smiling)
Zat so? Now I wonder who all's
~~xxixt~~ wastin' paper on me.

PAN CAMERA as Tom walks over
to the postman's buggy. The
postman picks out the letter,
looks at it admiringly.

THE POSTMAN'
Pretty fancy writin' too...
elegant, ain't it?

He hands him the letter.

TOM
Thanks.

THE POSTMAN (slapping the reins)
Giddap, Molasses. Well,
s'long, Tom...don't take no
wooden money.
(He giggles and trots
out of the picture)

(CONTINUED)

                                    TOM
                                    S'long.

           He holds up his letter and
           looks at it hopelessly.
           He looks at it from several
           distances. It becomes no
           clearer. He opens his eyes
           wide, narrows them, then
           shakes his head, puts the
           letter in his pocket, then
           continues his walk. At the
           next rail joint he hits much
           harder than usual with his
           long-handled hammer.

           DISSOLVE TO:

D-5   THE PORCH OF THE MOUNTAIN
           SCHOOLHOUSE

           There is a babble of children's
           voices, then the door flies open.
           The children stream onto the
           porch followed by Sally, their
           teacher. She is a nice looking
           young girl, about twenty.

                                    SALLY
                                    All right...two o'clock...
                                    don't be late. Did you
                                    hear me, Willy?

                                    WILLY
                                    Yes, ma'am.

                                    SALLY
                                    And you too, Bobby.

                                    BOBBY
                                    Yes'm.

                                    SALLY
                                    Run along now.

           She waves the children
           off the porch with both
           hands. They all disappear
           except ~~a chubby little girl~~
           ~~of six who is having a hard~~
           ~~time undoing a newspaper parcel~~.
           Six little siders from 9
           to 4 who sit down and
           struggle with parcels of
           lunch.   SALLY
                                    What's the matter with you all
                                    Edie?

                                    EDIE
                                    We dassn't go home till supper-
                                    time.

                                    SALLY
                                    Why not, dear?

                                    (CONTINUED)

                        68

EDIE   (seriously) a new
We're having ~~another~~ baby...
gee, I hope it's a boy...
do you think it'll be a boy,
Miss Sally?

SALLY   (in some embarrassment)
Really, Edie, I...I haven't
the slightest idea.

EDIE

Well Papa says if it ain't
a boy he's gonna raise hell.

SALLY   (in horror)
EDIE!

EDIE

Yes'm.

SALLY   *Hold your tongue.*
~~Don't say that~~.

EDIE

Yes'm.

SALLY

Now eat your lunch...there...
I'll help you.

*She helps the five
little sisters then*

She ~~She~~ gets Edie started
on a large jam sandwich,
~~then~~ takes her own lunch
from a little paper and
starts to eat. She looks
at Edie disapprovingly, then
laughs in spite of herself.
A shadow falls on the lower
step. Sally looks up.

SALLY

Oh hello ~~there~~, Tom.

CUT TO:

D-6   REVERSE SHOT OF THIS GROUP..
EDIE AND SALLY FROM REAR..TOM
LEANING AGAINST BUILDING

TOM

How do, Miss Sally. Hello,
Edie.

EDIE

We're havin' a new baby up
to our house.

SALLY   (shocked)
Edie! Be quiet.

TOM

You already had it, honey...
your paw just yelled to me
when I come by.

(CONTINUED)

D-6   (CONTINUED)

                              EDIE   (all excitement)
                                      Was it a boy? ~~or a girl?~~

                              TOM   (laughing)
                                      It was twins, honey...two more
                                      girls.

Sally shrieks with
laughter. Tom laughs
too.

                              SALLY
                                      Sit down, Tom.

        CUT TO:

D-7   SALLY, EDIE, AND TOM ON
        THE SCHOOL STEPS

                              SALLY
                                      Will you have a piece of
                                      sandwich, Tom?

                              TOM
                                      No thanks, I just et down
                                      the line.

He jerks his thumb in that
direction. Then he adds:

                                      If I'd a known, I'd a waited.

                              SALLY   (embarrassedly)
                                      Oh...that would have been
                                      nice.

                              TOM   ~~Thanks~~ I uh...I
                                      just got another letter.

                              SALLY   (politely)
                                      Really. From whom?

                              TOM   (pulling the letter out of
                                           his pocket)
                                      To tell you the truth...I uh...
                                      I ain't looked yet.

He looks around nervously, then
tears the flap open, pulls out
the letter and holds the letter
off as might an old gentleman
who had mislaid his spectacles.
He pulls it very close to his nose,
tries a middle distance unsuccessfully,
then drops his hand, shakes his head,
chuckles, and says:

                              TOM
                                      Doggone I sure can't read
                                      THAT! writing.

He hands her the letter.

                                      Here...see what you can make
                                      of it.

                                           (CONTINUED)

                              70

Sally picks up the letter,
glances at it and says:

SALLY

What's the matter with that
writing? I think it's
very stylish. Of course
you can read it.

She tries to hand him back
the letter, Tom pushing it
back.

TOM

It hurts my eyes.

SALLY   (looking at it again)
I don't see why it should.
It's like copper plate.

TOM

Takes an expert to read that
stuff.

SALLY

Fiddlesticks! A child could
read it. Read that, Edie.

She holds the letter out in
front of the little girl whose
mouth is full of jam sandwich.
Edie reads obediently but quite
incoherently.

EDIE

"'Ear end om:-
    Ell, end Om, y aining
in eouk isness ollege is
earing ometion..."

Tom takes the letter away
from her gently.

TOM

That's just the way it looked
to me.

SALLY

Edie, I'm ashamed of you.

EDIE

I an't elp it. I ot oo much
andwich in y ouse.

TOM

Read it to me, will ya?

He hands her the letter.

SALLY

Surely.

TOM

Who's it from?

SALLY   (turning over the letter)
Somebody called Henry. Hasn't
he developed a beautiful

(CONTINUED)

71

                              SALLY (cont'd)
                                  handwriting.

                              TOM
                                  I guess so.

                              SALLY (reading)
                                  "Dear Friend Tom:-
                                      Well, Friend Tom, my
                                  training in Keokuk Business
                                  College is nearing comple-
                                  tion and ere long, God wil-
                                  ling, ~~I shall receive my
                                  diploma~~...". Tom ..

                              TOM
                                  Yes ma'am.

                              SALLY (very gently)
                                  Can't you read?

Tom looks away.

                              TOM
                                  Well...I can read some of
                                  the big letters, but that...
                                  that...

He jerks his thumb toward
the letter.

                                  ...them hen-scratches...
                                  nobody could read...only
                                  school teachers and such.

                              SALLY
                                  Tom.

                              TOM   (very uneasily)
                                  Yes ma'am?

                              SALLY
                                  Can you read at all?

                              TOM   (after a pause)
                                  No ma'am.

He looks away.

                              SALLY (after a pause)
                                  Can you write?

Tom doesn't answer. After
a moment Sally speaks again.

                                  Tom.

                              TOM
                                  Huh?

                              SALLY
                                  Can you write?

                              TOM
                                  No ma'am.
                                      (Suddenly he blurts out:)
                                  And I can't do no 'rithmetic

                                      (CONTINUED)

                              72

                              TOM   (cont'd)
                                      ██████, and I don't speak
                                      Greek, or Latin, or, or...
                                      Eyetalian, ████...now you
                                      know.

                              SALLY
                                      I don't either, but I can
                                      read and write and do arith-
                                      metic and...and...I'd be
                                      very glad to teach you what
                                      little I know.

                              TOM
                                      What would I want to learn
                                      fur?

                              SALLY
                                      I don't know...maybe to
                                      please me.

        Tom, pointing to the
        letter she still holds:

                              TOM
                                      Could...could you learn me
                                      to write like that?..like
                                      Henry?
                              SALLY
                                      I think so.

                              TOM
                                      Gee...would he be sore.

        CUT TO:

D-8   SHOT OF SCHOOL ROOM..SALLY   NIGHT
        AND TOM

        This shot is to FADE IN slowly
        so as to give the Narrator's
        voice time to capture the in-
        terest. Tom is sitting at a
        desk twelve sizes too small for
        him. He is having a hell of a
        time multiplying 920 x 368.
        Sally is sitting at the teacher's
        desk correcting papers.

                              THE NARRATOR'S VOICE
                                      ██████████████████████
                                      ██████████████████████
                                      ██████████████████████
                                      ██████████ They worked
                                      together every evening and
                                      Tom learned so quickly. I
                                      wondered sometimes if you
                                      couldn't teach people all
                                      they needed in a few months
                                      after they grew up and let
                                      them spend their childhood
                                      playing like puppy dogs.

                              TOM
                                      How much is eight times eight?

                                      (CONTINUED)

SALLY   (without looking up)
A hundred and **twenty-eight**.

TOM   (looking up indignantly)
No it isn't.

SALLY
The*n* figure it out for yoursel.

TOM   (furiously)
All right I WILL.
(after a moment)
There...

Sally rises, crosses, and
sits *o*n the bench beside him.
She checks his multiplication
and ma*r*ks it 8 with a little
circle around it.

TOM   (indignantly)
D*on*'t I get 10 on that?

SALLY   (coolly)
No, it isn't neat.

Tom pounds his fist down
on the table and stamps to
his feet and walks away.
Sally looks after him and
laughs.

CUT TO:

D-9   CLOSE SHOT ..SALLY AT THE DESK   *(blackboard*
flackboard)

SALLY
~~Stop spitting and~~ come here,
you big baby.

T*om slides into the* *seat*
beside her. Sally *takes*
a pen and paper and says:
Tom moves to her.

Now: Fingers straight,
wrist stiff, only the elbow
bending. Make me a ~~line~~ of
0's...like this. *this*

She does a series of beautiful
0s, ~~across the top of the sheet~~
~~then passes the sheet and pen to~~
~~Tom.~~ He *t*akes the ~~pen~~ in his
huge scarred fist, ~~clamps the paper~~
~~down tightly with his left hand,~~
sticks out his tongue a little, and
makes a line of 0's. He does everything wrong. His forearm is stationary.
He writes only with his fingers and his
wrist, which is the exact opposite of the
method Sally is teaching him. As he
finishes the line, Sally says:

SALLY
No no no. That's absolutely
wrong. Now relax. Now...

(CONTINUED)

74

D-9   (CONTINUED)

She puts her hand over his
and says:

                    SALLY
              I'll guide you.

Together they make a line
of beautiful ●'s. As they
start on the second line
we

DISSOLVE TO:

D-10   TOM AND SALLY WALKING UP A
        MOUNTAIN PATH AWAY FROM US

We TRUCK ALONG after   NARRATOR'S VOICE
them which will en-   It was bound to happen
hance the charm of the   sooner or later I guess.
scene besides being ex-   ~~don't know when he first~~
cellent exercize for the   ~~asked her to go walking~~...
director and camera men.   ~~I suppose he screwed his~~
                              ~~courage up one night when~~
                              ~~theyxwerextogatherxxxxxxxx~~
                              ~~during a lesson~~. All I know
                              is what she told me. He took
                              her walking one Sunday.
                              Naturally she wore her best
                              dress and kind of tight-fit-
                              ting shoes. After a while
                              they started up Old Baldhead.
                              As mountains go it isn't much,
                              but it's plenty for a hot
                              afternoon with tight shoes
                              on. At first she wondered
                              why he was taking her up it,
                              but he looked sort of grim,
                              so she went along without
                              asking questions. Her feet
                              bothered her a little but
                              she was game. By and by
                              they came to a little flat
                              place.

        CUT TO:

D-11   CLOSE SHOT..THE LITTLE
        FLAT PLACE

After a moment Tom appears
from below and climbs up on
it. He reaches down and
helps Sally. She looks a
little wilted. She sits down
on a rock and smoothes out her
dress. She folds her hands in
her lap, looks at Tom and awaits
the big moment.

                    NARRATOR'S VOICE
              Of course he was brave and all
              that, but there's some things
              any man is scared of and Tom
              was just like the rest of us.
He looks at her. He ~~swallows~~   He looked at her; he licked
~~hardland looks~~.away.   his lips a couple of times,
                              then he swallowed hard and

                                        (CONTINUED)

75

Sally looks at him, opens
her mouth as if to say
something, then closes it
again. Tom's pantomime
follows the narration.

NARRATOR'S VOICE   (cont'd)
looked away. Sally was
willing and even anxious to
help him, but there wasn't
anything she could do. After
a while he looked back at her,
opened his mouth a few times
like a goldfish, and said:
"Sally." She gripped the
rock beside her and said:
"Yes, Tom."   He took her
by the hand and said: "Come
on."

Tom says: "Come on". Sally
and Tom climb out of the
picture.

So they climbed up the
mountain some more.

CUT TO:

D-12   FOLLOWING SHOT.. TOM AND
          SALLY CLIMBING.

NARRATOR'S VOICE
She began to think perhaps
he was crazy. and
she didn't like him nearly
so much as she did at the
beginning of the walk, but
what with the tight shoes and
all, she couldn't think very
clearly. So she followed
along and hoped for the best.
It was steaming hot, she said.

Tom mops his brow and
takes his coat off.

Even Tom began to mop his
head and she felt like lying
down and dying. But a woman
will go a long way to get the
man she wants, so she followed
him up the mountain. By and
by they came to another
flat place.

CUT TO:

D-13   CLOSE SHOT..THE OTHER FLAT
          PLACE

Tom and Sally come into the
picture. There is no rock to
sit upon this time, so Sally
stands up and looks at her
feet pensively. Tom looks more
nervous than ever.

NARRATOR'S VOICE
Tom tried again. He looked
at her, then he got scared
and looked away. Then he
looked back at her and made
the big effort. His eyes
xxxxxxxxxxxxxxxxxxxxxx
almost popped out of his head
and his jaw muscles stood
out like whipcord. He opened
his mouth but nothing came

(CONTINUED)

76

                              NARRATOR'S VOICE (cont'd)
                                   out. So he took her hand
                                   and led her up the mountain.

      CUT TO:

D-14   TOM AND SALLY CLIMBING UP
         THE MOUNTAIN

                              NARRATOR'S VOICE
                                   They were both feeling pretty
                                   blue by now. Sally was
                                   stumbling every once in a
                                   while. The afternoon wasn't
                                   what you'd call a success.
                                   Sally didn't care much what
                                   happened any more, but Tom
                                   was too worried to notice
                                   anything. By and by they
                                   came to the top of the moun-
                                   tain.

      CUT TO:

D-15   THE TOP OF THE MOUNTAIN

      Tom, looking very nervous,
      appears. Sally staggers
      into the picture a moment
      after. Almost bleary-eyed
      she looks around for a place
      to sit. She collapses onto a
      little rock. Tom sits beside
      her.

                              NARRATOR'S VOICE
                                   There wasn't any higher to go,
                                   so something HAD to happen.
                                   They looked around at the view
      THE CAMERA PANS and looks   and it sure was a pretty sight.
      at the view.

                                   On one side was the valley
                                   they'd just come from with
                                   its little houses and the
                                   railroad tracks, straight
                                   and shiny, reaching away beyond
                                   the hills. On the other side
                                   were the real mountains and
                                   Sally thanked the Lord he
                                   hadn't taken her up one of
                                   those. The sun was almost set;
                                   the mist was rolling up. the
                                   mountain. It got to be chilly;
      THE CAMERA PANS back to   something had to be done.
      Tom and Sally.

                                   So he looked at her with a
                                   terrible expression on his
                                   face and his hands opened and
                                   closed, then he screwed his
                                   eyes shut, counted one, two,
                                   three, and said: "Will you
      We see Tom speaking.   marry me?" And she said: "Of
                                   course I will, darling" and

                              (CONTINUED)

                    77

NARRATOR'S VOICE   (cont'd)
they kissed eachother a
little scared. And then
she said: "But Tom...couldn't
you have asked me at the
FOOT of the mountain?" But
they were pretty happy just the
same and they stayed happy
for quite a while too. She
used to kick a little bit,
but she stuck by him.

***   FADE-OUT   ***

FADE IN:

E-1   CLOSE SHOT..OFFICE OF THE PRESIDENT:
       GREAT WESTERN RAILROAD..TOM SIGNING
       STOCK CERTIFICATES

He signs each certificate with a
beautiful flourish and we recognize
the Spencerian method. Simultaneously
with the FADE-IN comes the voice of
the Narrator.

                    NARRATOR'S VOICE
                When Tom bought the Santa
              Clara that time, he got more
                than he figured on. The
                Santa Clara had a president
                and the president had a
                daughter...

Henry comes into the picture.
He jerks over his shoulder with
his thumb and says:

                    HENRY
                He's here.

                    TOM
                Who?

                    HENRY
                The president of the Santa Clara

                    TOM   (sneeringly)
                Well well...so Mr. Borden
                is calling on ME, huh?
                This is a great honor.

He sticks a cigar in the corner
of his mouth and lights it.

                He didn't lose any time,
                did he?

                    HENRY (sympathetically)
                I suppose...I suppose he's
                worried about his job.

                    TOM   (harshly)
                Yeah? Well he's got a reason
                to. What he don't know about
                railroads is plenty...the
                old sissy.

He smiles pleasantly,
blows out a cloud of smoke,
and speaks very gently:

                He kept me out of a club
                once...guess he thought I
                was too common.

                    HENRY (quite ill at ease)
                Shall I show him in?

                    TOM   (harshly)
(CONTINUED)   Let him wait. He kept me

79

TOM   (cont'd)
         waiting for two weeks once.

HENRY   (looking away)
         Yes, sir.

He exits. Tom,noticing
his disapproval,calls
after him:

TOM   ~~Now~~ Horseradish !

He returns to signing his
stock certificates. After
signing a couple, he looks
in the direction Henry has
gone, then, almost surreptitiously, examines his
finger-nails. Not satisfied
he removes a pen-knife from
his vest pocket and cleans
them.

      CUT TO:

E-2   HENRY'S SECRETARIAL OFFICE..
         MEDIUM CLOSE SHOT..RICHARD
         BORDEN AND HIS DAUGHTER,EVE

They are sitting on a leather
sofa. Borden is an aristocratic-
man looking man about sixty years
old. His clothes are somewhat
old-fashioned, but extremely well-
cut. His face is drawn. His eyes
are restless. At first glance,
Eve is a raving beauty. On closer
examination her mouth seems a
little hard. She is the woman we
saw in the cathedral in the first
scene. She is about twenty-seven,
extremely well-dressed. They are
talking.

MR. BORDEN
         You've got to help.

EVE
         Sh.

She looks up as Henry comes
into the picture.

HENRY
         Mr. Garner will see you in
         a few minutes, Mr. Borden.
         He's engaged at the moment.

Mr. Borden flashes a great
display of teeth and speaks

rapidly:

MR. BORDEN
         Oh yes, surely, surely. Thank
         you very much.

                  (CONTINUED)

                                        HENRY
                                    Not at all.

        He crosses to his desk
        and we PAN with him. He
        sits down, arranges some
        papers, then turns his
        head and looks at Borden
        and his daughter.

        CUT TO:

E-3   MEDIUM LONG SHOT..MR. BORDEN
           AND EVE

        They are busy talking but are
        too far away for us to hear
        more than a murmur of voices.

                                        NARRATOR'S VOICE
                                    I felt sorry for that old
                                    fellow. Tom was a good
                                    friend, but a tough enemy.
                                    I couldn't figure out what
                                    the girl was doing there. He
                                    seemed to be asking her to
                                    do something and she looked
                                    like she didn't care much
                                    for the job. After a while
                                    she seemed to say: "Oh,
                                    all right", and I guess
                                    Borden was smarter than I
                                    gave him credit for. She
                                    sure was a beautiful woman...
                                    you couldn't blame Tom much.

        The buzzer sounds twice.   SOUND: Buzzer.
        Henry comes into the picture.

                                        HENRY
                                    Will you come in now.

                                    MR. BORDEN (rising)
                                    Oh yes. Surely, surely.
                                        (to Eve)
                                    Come along, dear.
                                        (to Henry)
                                    This is my daughter, heh heh
                                    heh.

        Eve rises, precedes her
        father and Henry. They cross.
        Henry opens a big door. They
        exit.

        CUT TO:

He has one foot on the desk
and is glaring in the direction
of the door. Suddenly his expression changes to one of con-
sternation. He takes his foot
off the desk, blinks his eyes
a couple of times, then rises
reluctantly. Eve, Mr. Borden,
and Henry come into the picture.
Henry closes the door after them,
remaining in the office. He
starts to cross to a desk in the
corner.

                    BORDEN   (effusively)
                        Hello there, Tom. Glad to
                        see you.

He shakes him warmly by the
hand.

                    TOM
                        Hello.

                    BORDEN
                        This is my daughter, Eve...
                        Mr. Garner...Mrs. Thurston.

Eve looks right into his
eyes, then smiles a little
and gives him her hand.

                    EVE
                        How do you do...this is very
                        nice. I've heard a great
                        deal about you...you don't
                        seem so ferocious as they
                        say.

Tom is quite ill at ease
with this woman. Her voice
is pitched low. She drawls
certain words. He chuckles
a little nervously.

                    TOM
                        I guess I'm not so...so
                        terrible as all that.
                            (He chuckles again).

                    BORDEN
                        Eve was taking me to lunch
                        and we happened to be passing
                        by,...I thought perhaps you'd
                        join us.

                    TOM   (on the point of refusal)
                        Thanks but...

                    EVE

                            (CONTINUED)

TOM   (after a pause)
         Well, I guess I can get
         away all right.

Suddenly he turns to
Borden.

         Say...you know what happened
         this morning, don't you?...
         you know who owns Santa Clara

BORDEN
         Oh yes...I know.

EVE
         Come along, I'm starving.

Tom takes his hat, then
calls to Henry.

TOM   (to Henry)
         I'll be back at three.

Tom, Eve, and Borden exit.
Henry looks after them,
scratches the back of his
head, then closes the door.
He frowns.

         NARRATOR'S VOICE
         Right then and there I knew
         there was trouble coming.

A DISSOLVE begins here
that will end up with a
SHOT of Henry typing in
his own office.

         I don't know why I knew it,
         but I felt scared like you
         do sometimes before a storm.

The clicking of the type-
writer comes faintly as the   SOUND: Faint clicking of
new scene FADES IN.   typewriter.

E-5   HENRY TYPING IN HIS OFFICE

         NARRATOR'S VOICE
         He didn't come back till
         nearly four o'clock and he
         looked like the cat that et
         the canary...it's marvellous
         what a young female can do .,
         ~~the spoiled man~~.

The buzzer sounds once.   SOUND: Buzzer.
Henry rises, picks up a
sheaf of papers, crosses to
the door. We PAN with him.
He opens the door.

CUT TO:

Tom is marching up and down,
his hands clasped behind him.
He is smoking a Corona Corona.
Henry enters. Tom speaks
boisterously:

                    TOM
                         Hello there, sourpuss...
                         anything new.

                    HENRY
                         Just these.

He puts the papers on the
desk.

                    TOM
                         Have a cigar?

He pulls a Corona Corona
out of his breast pocket
and points it at Henry.
Henry takes it.

                    HENRY
                         Thanks...I'll smoke it tonight
                         after supper.

He picks up a piece of paper
from the desk, then wraps it
up carefully.

                    TOM
                         All right.

He pulls another cigar out
of his pocket.

                         Then you can smoke this one
                         now.

                    HENRY   (surprised)
                         Thank you.

Tom strikes a match and
holds it out for him.
Henry puffs.

                    TOM
                         You know...that fellow Borden
                         isn't so bad. I don't see
                         why he shouldn't run the Santa
                         Fe. What do you think?

                    HENRY   (laughing)
                         It's all right with me.

                    TOM
                         Pretty girl he's got there.

He shakes his head.

                    Had a tough time of

                         (CONTINUED)

84

                                    HENRY   (pricking up his ears)
                                            How's that?

                            TOM
                                    Married ~~this~~ some fellow when she
                                    was too young to know any
                                    better, poor kid. I guess
                                    he was pretty much of a
                                    scoundrel all right...cost
                                    her father a lot of money to
                                    get rid of him.

He shakes his head again.

                                    She sure is pretty. Say...

                            HENRY   (suspiciously)
                                    What?

                            TOM
                                    Did you notice her voice?

                            HENRY
                                    I heard it, yes.

                            TOM
                                    Like music.

The DISSOLVE begins here.

                            NARRATOR'S VOICE
                                    That was quite a day. First
                                    we bought the Santa Claus, then
                                    we told the directors where
                                    to get off, then we met Eve...
                                    but that wasn't all.

The DISSOLVE is finished.

E-7   LONG SHOT (POINT OF VIEW)..
        HENRY AT HIS DESK IN HIS OWN
        OFFICE
        _____

        We TRUCK down to Henry. Suddenly
        he looks up at us. He looks as-
        tonished.

                            HENRY
                                    Tommy!

He jumps to his feet.

                                    I'm glad to see you but...
                                    what are you doing here?

        CUT TO:

E-8   CLOSE SHOT..HENRY AND TOMMY
        STANDING BESIDE HENRY'S DESK
        _____

        They shake hands. Tommy is
        an unusually handsome boy of
        twenty, probably blond. He is
        the young man we saw in the
        cathedral.

                                                (CONTINUED)

> TOMMY
> > Hello, Henry.
>
> HENRY
> > Why aren't you in New Haven...
> > are you sick?
>
> TOMMY
> > I got kicked out.
>
> HENRY
> > Holy mackerel!

Tommy looks toward
the adjoining office.

> TOMMY
> > Is the old man in there?
>
> HENRY
> > Yes.
>
> TOMMY
> > Is he in a good humor?
>
> HENRY
> > He sure is. You picked the
> > right day for this.
> > (He laughs)
> > Get in quick before he
> > changes.

Tommy starts, then looks
back at Henry, smiles a
little.

> TOMMY
> > Gee, I'm scared.

DISSOLVE TO:

E-9   TOMMY IN ARMCHAIR

The chair is in front of
a window and the sunlight
streams in on his white face.

> TOMMY
> > I know what you mean, Father,
> > but...it's hard to make you
> > see it. You never went to
> > college, and...

He shrugs his shoulders.

> > I didn't do any more than
> > anybody else...I just got
> > caught, that's all. I got
> > a tough break.

PAN to Tom looking down at
his son. He has a cigar clamped
in the corner of his mouth. He
shakes his head and scowls.

> (CONTINUED)

86

TOM

> Bad business...bad business.
> When I think how I had to
> sweat to get an education...
> and what your mother went
> through.
>> (he pauses)
> If there's one thing I despise
> it's a man who can't hold
> his liquor.

TOMMY

> I can drink plenty.

TOM

> Yeah? Well let's see how
> much you can drink on fifteen
> dollars a week.

He crosses to his desk
and picks up a telephone.

> Get me MacIntosh.

TOMMY

> What do you mean?

TOM
>> (into telephone)
> MacIntosh?...What do our
> junior bookkeepers get?...
> Oh, sixteen, huh?
>> (Aside, to his son:)
> Lucky, huh?
>> (into telephone again)
> A young friend of mine is
> looking for a job. I can't
> recommend him very highly
> but still, I'd appreciate
> it......Fine. He'll be there
> at nine tomorrow morning.
> And remember this: Don't show
> him any favoritism whatso-
> ever because he's a friend of
> mine. His name is Thomas
> Garner, Junior. Goodbye.

He hangs up. PAN to
Tommy. He is looking at
his father evilly. His face
is full of hatred.

TOM

> Now go home and see your
> mother...and if I were you,
> I wouldn't brag about my
> drinking.

Tommy rises. His face is
working with fury.

TOM

> And don't look at ME that
> th way, boy...you're giving
> away too much weight. Now
> beat it.

DISSOLVE TO:

E-10   CLOSE SHOT..TOMMY AND
              SALLY SITTING ON A COUCH

Sally has changed considerably
since we saw her last. Her
features are ravaged by time.
She is dressed expensively but
not very smartly. She holds
her son's hand and looks very
angry.

NARRATOR'S VOICE
    I heard Sally was
    pretty sore...she got
    a little testy...as
    she grew older...

                        SALLY
              That's the most disgusting
              thing I've ever heard of.
              The idea of your becoming
              a bookkeeper!

              TOMMY
              At sixteen dollars a week!

                        SALLY
              Or at any other price.

              TOMMY   (whiningly)
              Especially at my age, Mother...
              I ought to be taking exercize
              and having fun. You can't
              have any fun when you're old.

                        SALLY
              Well...you can't have much.

A door slams. Sally
turns and looks at us.
Her face is very hard.

CUT TO:

SOUND: Slam of door.

E-11   TOM WITH HIS BACK TO THE DOOR

His hand is still on the knob.
He looks puzzled for a moment,
then raises his eyebrows in
mild amusement and chuckles.

                        TOM
              What are you looking at me
              THAT way for?

He takes a step toward us.

CUT TO:

E-12   SALLY AND TOMMY

Sally rises to her feet and
walks toward Tom. THE CAMERA
PANS to include Tom. They
come to a standstill.

                        SALLY
              I will not have my son
              treated in that way. Do you
              understand?

Tom's expression hardens
a little.

                        TOM
              Now wait a minute, Sally.

          (CONTINUED)

88

SALLY   (at the top of her lungs)
~~There's nothing to wait for!~~ *No, I won't*
I've seen you handle men be-
fore and you're not going to
~~handle Tommy~~ *treat him* the way you
~~handled them.~~ *treated them).*

TOM

Oh bunk!

SALLY

Bunk nothing. Just because
you didn't have any fun when
you were young, you don't
want anyone else to have any.
You and your theories. Everybody thinks you're so smart...
you never would have got any-
wheres if it wasn't for me
and you know it.

TOM

What's that got to do with
this.

SALLY

Just that I won't have it,
that's all.

TOM

Listen, Sally. You've spoiled
him. You ought to have sense
enough to see it. You've
treated him like a baby all his
life.

He points in the direction
of Tommy.

And now look at him--irres-
ponsible, useless, kicked out
of college,~~for a pretty~~
/ *Stet* ~~silly mess.~~ I'd like to
be proud of him...I'm ashamed
of him.

SALLY   (in a fury)
Oh you are, are you? That's
a fine thing to say: Ashamed
of your own son. ~~You make me~~
~~sick. I wish I'd never met~~
~~you. To think I've wasted~~
~~my life on it.~~

TOM

~~Have it your own way.~~ *alright* I'll
stay at the club ~~tonight~~ *for*
a few days

If you are ashamed of yourself

He turns.

SALLY

~~All right,~~ and you can stay
as long as you like too.

Tom exits and slams
the door after him.
Sally crosses and sits beside her son. She looks
toward the door.

(CONTINUED)

SALLY
> For all I care.

TOMMY   (putting his arm around her)
> That's telling him, Mother...
> thanks.

SALLY   (beginning to whimper)
> Oh Tommy...what I have to
> put up with.
>   (she sniffles)

TOMMY
> There...there.

***   FADE-OUT   ***

FADE IN:

F-1   MEDIUM LONG SHOT..A LITTLE
        SHACK IN THE MOUNTAINS

        It is a very poor man's home.
        The time is dusk and we see
        the windows lit from within.
        Smoke is curling from the
        chimney. We start TRUCKING
        toward this house. ~~The~~
        ~~Narrator's Voice fades in~~
        ~~timed also with the~~
        ~~corruption from the last~~
        ~~sequence~~ The Narrator's
        Voice fades in with the shot.

                            NARRATOR'S VOICE
                              Maybe Sally was right at
                              that...Tom might be a
                              track walker yet, ~~still and~~
                              happy and satisfied, if
                              it wasn't for her. I guess
                              women have a lot to do with
                              men's ambition. I never
                              heard of any great men that
                              were bachelors. Still...
                              I dunno.

        THE CAMERA is quite close
        to the house now.

        CUT TO:

F-2   TOM AND SALLY IN THE
        KITCHEN

        These are young Tom and young
        Sally, of course. They are
        seated at a kitchen table cov-
        ered with a red and white oil-
        cloth. Tom is rolling a cigarette.
        Sally is looking off into space.
        She looks a little worried. In
        front of Tom sits a cup full of
        coffee with a spoon in it. Tom,
        busy with his cigarette:

                          TOM
                            You sure cook nice, honey.

        Sally doesn't answer. Tom
        finishes his cigarette and
        lights a match, then looks
        at his wife.

                          TOM
                            What's the matter?

                          SALLY
                            Oh, nothing.

        Tom looks concerned.

                          TOM
                            Unhappy?

                        (CONTINUED)

                                SALLY   (smiling at him)
                                         Of course not, dear. Some-
                                         times I worry,...I suppose
                                         it's because I love you/

The match burns Tom's
fingers. He chuckles, strikes
~~light~~another match, lights
his cigarette, blows out a
happy cloud of smoke, then
speaks:

                                TOM
                                         What are you worried about?

                                SALLY
                                         The future.

Tom looks greatly puzzled.

                                TOM
                                         What's the matter with it?

                                SALLY
                                         Do you want to be a track
                                         walker all your life?

                                TOM
                                         Why not?

Sally gives him a dirty
look, then rises, picks
up a couple of dishes and
speaks with irritation:

                                SALLY
                                         Of course if you don't see it,
                                         there's nothing more for me
                                         to say.

She shrugs her shoulders
and walks out of the picture.
Tom twists his head and
looks after her.

                                TOM
                                         What's the matter with being
                                         a track walker? We got
                                         plenty to eat. We own this
                                         here house. The work is
                                         easy and I get in some good
                                         fishing on the side. What's
                                         the matter with it?

His head follows her as
she comes back into the
picture. Sally leans her
two fists on the table.

                                SALLY
                                         Haven't you any ambition?

                                TOM
                                         To do what?

                                (CONTINUED)

92

                    SALLY
                         To rise up in the world.

Tom considers this for
a moment and scratches his
head.

                    TOM
                         I dunno as I'd mind...but
                         there's a lot of worry goes
                         along with it.

Sally's eyes shine.

                    SALLY
                         Just think, Tom, foreman, and
                         then yard master, maybe
                         superintendent some day. We
                         could have good clothes and
                         a better house and...and...
                         maybe even a horse and car-
                         riage.

Tom looks at her pensively.

                    TOM
                         You'd like all that stuff,
                         huh?

                    SALLY
                         Of course I would.

Tom looks away.

                    TOM
                         I guess you married the
                         wrong feller.

                    SALLY   (with fire)
                         No I didn't? You've got it
                         in you, Tom, I know you have.
                         You can do anything you want
                         if you'll just want to. Will
                         you try to be somebody, Tom?

Tom shrugs his shoulders.

                    TOM
                         I guess so.

Sally is all animation now.

                    SALLY
                         Good! Oh I'm so happy...First
                         of all you have to get an
                         education?

                    TOM   (angrily)
                         What the hell do I want with
                         MORE education.

                    SALLY   (laughing)
                         You need plenty more.

She comes over and plays
with his hair.

                              (CONTINUED)

                              93

SALLY

You must go to Chicago and
study...maybe engineering...
I don't know yet...we'll find
out what'll help you the most.

TOM

What'll I use for money?

SALLY

I've got it all figured out.
When you leave, they'll need
somebody else. They'll have
to get another track walker,
won't they?

Tom senses what is coming.

TOM

Yes, but...

SALLY

I can walk track. Now shut
your mouth. I know everything
you're going to say. Mr.
Robinson likes us. I know he'd
like to help us get along.
Just because a woman never did
it doesn't mean a woman couldn't
do it. You said yourself it
was easy work.

TOM

But...but...

SALLY   (almost in tears)
Please, honey, do it for me.
Say you will. Make me happy.

Tom is full of indignation.
He is spluttering.

TOM

I never heard of such a thing.
Why it's...it's...A woman
supporting a man...Huh!
Anyway, there ain't a chance
of it. Robinson would laugh
you out of his office.

SALLY   (very quietly)
Oh no he wouldn't...I asked
him yesterday.

TOM

WHAT?

SALLY

He said yes...that it was a
very good idea.

CUT TO:

94

F-3   CLOSE SHOT..THE PRO-
       FESSOR IN FRONT OF HIS
       BLACKBOARD

        The board is covered with
        figures demonstrating some
        problem or other having to
        do with engineering. There
        might also be a drawing of a
        steel girder with arrows in-
        dicating the various stresses
        which act upon it.

                THE PROFESSOR:
                    That is all for today,
                    gentlemen. Thank you.

        He returns to his desk. We
        hear the babble of the stu-   SOUND: Students' voices(male)
        dents' voices.

        CUT TO:

F-4   TOM GATHERING HIS PAPERS TO-
       GETHER

        We see also the students around
        him doing the same thing. Tom
        is dressed very poorly but the
        other young men are dressed in
        the height of fashion of 1900.
        One of the young men approaches.

                THE YOUNG MAN
                    Oh Garner, you're alone here
                    in the city, aren't you?

                TOM
                    Yes.

                THE YOUNG MAN
                    Jack and I wondered if you'd
                    like to have supper with us
                    and then play a little pool
                    or something afterwards.

                TOM   (smiling)
                    I sure would like to. Thanks
                    just the same, but I only just
                    got time to grab a bite some-
                    where...I'm going to night
                    school too.

        The other young man has
         approached.

                JACK
                    My gracious.

                TOM   (chuckling)
                    I haven't much time to learn,
                    so I gotta work fast. Thanks
                    just the same...see you to-
                    morrow.

        He picks up his books
        and exits.

               (CONTINUED)

THE YOUNG MAN   (shaking his head)
                  Amazing.

JACK
                  Amazing? My dear boy, he's
                  a menace. What chance is
                  there for a loafer like me
                  when there are people like
                  that in the world.

CUT TO:

F-5   TOM STANDING IN FRONT
           OF A SALOON, IT IS SNOWING.

           He reaches in his pocket
           pulls out three one-dollar
           bills and some change. His
           lips move as he calculates.
           He says: "Room", silently.
           He puts two of the one-
           dollar bills in his left
           hand pocket. Then he says:
           "Tuition". He puts another
           dollar bill and a fifty-cent
           piece in his left-hand pocket.
           He says: "Carfare". He puts
           five dimes and two nickels in
           his left-hand pocket. He looks
           at what he has left in his hand
           and weighs it speculatively, then
           turns and goes into the saloon.

CUT TO:

F-6   TOM AT THE BAR

           Over his wide shoulders we
           see the bartender appear. Tom
           slaps down his nickel. The
           bartender draws a foaming schooner
           of beer, knocks the top off with
           a stick, shoves it across and rings
           up the nickel. Tom picks up
           the schooner, looks at it,   SOUND: Cash register.
           then hands it back to him.

                       TOM
                             Take a little of that collar
                             off please.

           The bartender gives him a
           dirty look, then puts a
           little more beer in the schooner
           and shoves it back.

                       TOM
                             Thanks.

           He takes a fistful of
           pretzels, shakes some pepper
           sauce into his beer and starts
           his meal. Presently he turns
           his head, looks down the length
           of the room and sees a huge

                                      (CONTINUED)

counter with a sign above it
marked "Free Lunch." Behind
this counter presides a colored
man. Tom sticks the rest of the
pretzels in his mouth, grabs his
beer, and wanders down to the
free lunch counter.

CUT TO:

F-7   SHOT UP THE COUNTER..TOM ON ONE
SIDE, COLORED MAN ON OTHER

Tom looks hungrily at the wonder-
ful display, then points to a lump
of corned beef and says:

                TOM
                      Gimme some of that.

The colored man gives him a
medium-sized sandwich of it.

                      Thanks.

He wolfs it down and takes
a small swallow of the beer
he is nursing along. Tom
points to a ham.

                TOM
                      And some of that.

The colored man looks at
the schooner of beer sig-
nificantly and hands him
a ham sandwich which he also
wolfs and washed down with a
sip of beer. Tom points to a
dish full of marinated herring
and says:

                TOM
                      I'll tackle one of those.

The colored man opens his eyes
wide, points to the schooner of
beer and opens his mouth to
speak. Tom beats him to it and
says in a hard voice:

                TOM
                      Were you goin' to say some-
                      thing?

              THE COLORED MAN
              Naw suh, I wasn't goin' to
              say nothin'.

He hands Tom a herring on a
plate with a fork. Tom rolls
it up and makes one mouthful
of it. The colored man looks at
him in astonishment.

                      (CONTINUED)

Tom, with his mouth
full, points to the dish
of herrings.

> THE COLORED MAN (in astonishment)
> You want another one?

Tom holds up two fingers.

> THE COLORED MAN (meekly)
> Yas suh.

He puts two herrings on
the plate and speaks with
a trace of irony:

> You like a few potatoes on
> the side?

Tom nods his head. The
colored man closes his
eyes in pain, puts three
large potatoes on the dish
and hands it to him. As
Tom washes down one of the
potatoes with a sip of beer
the colored man gives a high
sign to the bartender and points
to Tom. Tom turns at this moment.
The colored man pretends to be
scratching his head. INSERT:
The bartender nodding his head in
our direction. He turns, picks
up a bung-starter and comes out
under the bar. Return to Tom
and the colored man. The bartender comes into the picture
and looks at Tom evilly. Tom has
his mouth full.

> THE BARTENDER
> Sure an' what do you think
> ye're doin'?

Tom continues chewing, reaches
up with his left hand, taps the
word "Free" on the Free Lunch sign,
then holds his schooner of beer
aloft.

> THE BARTENDER (furiously)
> Listen, you bum, that's been
> tried before.

He reaches his bung-starter
aloft and starts to bring it
down. Tom's left hand flashes
out, catches his wrist, and
squeezes it. HE DOES NOT TWIST
IT. Tom continues to squeeze.
A look of agony comes on the
bartender's face, his hand loosens,
and the bung-starter clatters to the
floor.

> THE BARTENDER
> Quit it, leggo me arm!

(CONTINUED)

98

> Tom finishes chewing,
> swishes the beer around in
> the bottom of the schooner,
> and pours it down his throat.
> He sets the schooner down on
> the free lunch counter, he
> clenches his right fist, then
> turns to the bartender.

                    TOM
                         You called me a bum just now.

               THE BARTENDER
                    I didn't mean it.

                    TOM
                         Don't let it happen again...
                         now get back to your work.

> He drops the bartender's
> hand. The bartender mutters:

               THE BARTENDER
                    If I was a little younger...

                    TOM
                         If you was a little younger
                         I wouldn't let you off so
                         easy.

               THE BARTENDER
                    Bah!

> He goes out of the picture.
> Tom points to the floor and
> calls after him:

                    TOM
                         Don't forget your hammer.

> He turns and laughs to
> the colored man who is
> feeling none too secure.

               THE COLORED MAN
                    Kin I fix you a little dessert?

                    TOM
                         No thanks, I had plenty.

> He picks up his books.

                         So long...you got nice food
                         here.

               THE COLORED MAN (with forced
                                     amiability)
                    Come in again some time.

                    TOM
                         I will.

> He exits.

> DISSOLVE TO:

It is quite dark and represents a cut in the mountains.
We hear the wind howling in the
distance. The snow is flying
by horizontally.

>   NARRATOR'S VOICE
>   Tom always laughed about that
>   bartender...they got to be
>   good friends later on. He
>   was pretty lonely there in
>   Chicago, but he sure worked
>   hard.

In the distance we hear a
hammer hitting the rail.   SOUND: Faint hammering on
                                                 rail.

>   NARRATOR'S VOICE
>   Sally sent him all she could
>   spare. I guess neither one
>   of them et very much during
>   that year.

We hear the sound of the
hammer again, and we see   SOUND: Hammer on rails.
a lantern bobbing up and
down as it approaches.

>   NARRATOR'S VOICE
>   Track-walking is easy in
>   summer, but in winter it's
>   something else again.

The lantern is quite near
now. We hear the hammer
clang on the rail, then   SOUND: Hammer clanging on
faintly the crunch of   rails.
boots through the snow.   Crunch of snow.
A figure dressed as a man
comes into view. It staggers
a little bit. As it gets up
to us we recognize Sally, blue
with cold. She swings the hammer
but instead of the sharp clang
expected, we hear a double tinny
noise made by a loose plate. She
gets down on her knees, scoops
away the snow, examines the plate,
then takes a big wrench from her
belt and tightens the nuts that
the cold has loosened. She stands
up again, taps the rail once more,
then staggers past us. We PAN
and watch her disappear in the dark-
ness. After she has disappeared, we   SOUND: Hammer on
hear her test the rail once more.   rail.

            ****   FADE-OUT   ****

FADE IN:

G-1 SHOT A VERY SMART RESTAURANT..
     LUNCHTIME

THE CAMERA PANS slowly, comes to
rest eventually on Tom and Eve,
then TRUCKS down to a CLOSEUP.
The Narrator's Voice continues
until the closeup.

                    NARRATOR'S VOICE
               That Borden girl sure took
               old Tom over the jumps. Maybe
               she liked him a little bit...
               I dunno. He was handsome and
               even when he was old he was
               young somehow. It got so
               he saw her nearly every day--
               sometimes twice a day--for one
               excuse or another. Maybe it
               was fun for her, but with him...
               it was madness. Everybody
               knew it too...except Sally.

THE CAMERA has now arrived
at a CLOSEUP.

                    TOM
               I've reached the end of the
               rope, Eve. I don't know
               what to do. It's like a
               physical illness. I can't
               breathe properly when I'm
               away from you. And whenever
               my phone rings I think it
               may be you, and my heart
               starts pounding. It's ter-
               rible and it's wrong, and it
               shouldn't be, but I love you
               more than any man ever loved
               a woman.

                    EVE
               I'm glad.

                    TOM
               You shouldn't be.

                    EVE
               What are you going to do about
               it?

                    TOM
               I don't know.

                    EVE
               Have you discussed divorce
               with Mrs. Garner.

                    TOM   (impulsively)
               I couldn't divorce Sally.

                    EVE   (coolly)
               You're not asking me to be-

                         (CONTINUED)

101

                                        EVE   (cont'd)
                                               come your mistress, I hope.

                                        TOM
                                               Of course not.

                                        EVE
                                               Well...

                                        TOM
                                               I don't know.

Eve rises and picks up
her bag.

                                        EVE
                                               Well...call me up some day...
                                               when you've made up your mind.

                                        TOM   (also on his feet)
                                               Eve...

                                        EVE
                                               Goodbye.

On the way out she bows
to several friends.

        CUT TO:

G-2   TOM BEHIND HIS DESK

Henry comes into the picture.
He puts a basket of letters
on Tom's desk, then looks down
at him. Tom is unconscious of
Henry's presence. He stares off
into space unhappily.

                                        HENRY
                                               Your missus is here.

Tom doesn't answer.

                                        HENRY
                                               Tom.

Tom looks around vaguely:

                                        TOM
                                               Huh?

                                        HENRY
                                               Your missus is here. Shall
                                               I bring her in?

                                        TOM
                                               Oh...sure...bring her in.

Henry exits. Tom scowls
after him, then, with an
effort, pulls himself to-
gether. Sally comes into

                                        (CONTINUED)

the office.

                    SALLY
                         Hello, Tom.

                    TOM
                         Hello, Sally. What's on
                         your mind?

                    SALLY
                         Can you spare me a few
                         minutes?

                    TOM
                         Of course I can. Sit down.

Sally leans against the
desk and looks down at
him.

                    SALLY
                         I want you to take me to
                         Europe.

                    TOM
                         Why?

                    SALLY
                         Because we need it. There's
                         something the matter with us,
                         Tom, with you and with me,
                         and more with me than with
                         you. I've noticed the way
                         you were the last few months.
                         First I thought it was your
                         fault. Then I had a good
                         look at myself--not in the
                         mirror--but in the mind. It
                         was quite a shock to see what
                         I'm like. I'm a disagreeable
                         old woman, Tom--bad-tempered,
                         and everything else that goes
                         with it. I wouldn't blame
                         you if you never spoke to me
                         again. ████████████████████
                         ████████████████████████████
                         █████████████████.But I
                         wont be that way any more...
                         Take me away for a little whil
                         Tom, someplace where we can
                         be alone together...someplace
                         where we can...become friends
                         again. You've built so many
                         miles of railroad...and every
                         mile has taken you further
                         away from me...I've missed you

                    TOM
                         Sally...

                         (CONTINUED.)

103

                                    SALLY
                                          Yes, honey.

                                    TOM
                                          A terrible thing has happened. ...
                                          I never kept anything from you
                                          and I'm not going to begin now.

                                    SALLY
                                          What is it, Tom?

                                    TOM
                                          I'm in love.

Sally looks down in her
lap.

                                    TOM
                                          I didn't think such a thing
                                          could happen. I tried not
                                          to. It dadn't do me any good.
                                          ...What are we going to do
                                          about it?

Sally doesn't answer.

                                    TOM   (more cheerfully)
                                          Maybe your idea of a trip
                                          IS good. Sure, that's it.
                                          We'll go off somewhere and...
                                          and...

                                    SALLY   (in a monotone)
                                          And have you thinkin' about
                                          her all the time.

                                    TOM
                                          I wouldn't be thinking about
                                          her, honey. Ixx I'd like to
                                          forget about her. You know
                                          that's true.

He reaches for the
telephone. Ixxixixi
Rxx

                                          I'll tell Henry to make the
                                          arrangements. We'll go to
                                          Paris, that's where we'll go...
                                          we'll cut up and have a hell
                                          of a time.

Sally puts her hand on his
and prevents him from lifting
up the receiver. She speaks
with great understanding as
if she were reasoning with herself.

                                    SALLY
                                          Why shouldn't you be in love
                                          and have fun and be young and
                                          do what you want to just once
                                          before you die...

Tom looks at her suspiciously.

                                                  (CONTINUED)

                                    104

                              TOM
                                   What's the matter with you,
                                   Sally, don't talk that way.

                         SALLY   (as if to herself)
                                   I never let you have any fun.
                                   I made you work and grind
                                   and push up--not because you
                                   wanted to...because I wanted
                                   you to. I wanted the power
                                   and the money...you wanted
                                   to go fishing.

                              TOM
                                   Sally, don't talk that way.
                                   You sound crazy.

Sally rises and looks at
him.

                         SALLY
                                   Have her...have her...take
                                   her away and spend all your
                                   millions on her. God God
                                   bless you, Tom. God bless
                                   you both. I hope she makes
                                   you happier than I did.

She walks out of the office.
Tom runs after her, catches
her in the door.

                              TOM
                                   Sally.

                         SALLY
                                   Let me go.

She wrenches her hand away.

CUT TO:

G-3   THE BIG DOOR..CHICAGO AND
           GREAT WESTERN BUILDING

A sad-looking woman   NARRATOR'S VOICE
is selling violets on   I didn't see it myself,
the steps of the building.   thank God, but the flower
A hungry-looking little   woman did. She got in plenty
girl stands beside her.   of trouble too, explaining
                             how she got the bag. Sally
Sally's actions follow   came out like a woman in a
the narration.   dream. She started down the
                             steps, then stopped, went
                             back to the flower woman,
                             handed her the bag and said:
                             "Here's some money for you
                             and the little girl...I
                             hate it." Then she went
                             down the steps. Her car
                             pulled up and her chauffeur
                             jumped out, but she told him
                             she wouldn't need him any
                             more and sent him home. Then
                             she stood for a little while
                             on the curb. She turned
                             and looked up at the big
                             building, maybe at Tom's

                              (CONTINUED)

                              NARRATOR'S VOICE (cont'd)
                                   offices...I dunno. Then
                                   she started to cross the
                                   street. I guess she wasn't
                                   used to traffic any more, she'd
                                   had her own car so long.
                                   The flower woman screamed and
                                   the motorman rang his bell
                                   and jammed his brakes on so
                                   hard he knocked all the
                                   people on the floor. But you
                                   can't stop a street car as
                                   quick as all that. She was a
                                   fine woman.

              ****   FADE-OUT   ****

FADE IN:

H-1   PANARAMIC SHOTS OF A
        GREAT RAILROAD BRIDGE
        IN CONSTRUCTION

                              NARRATOR'S VOICE
                              I don't know how man rise
                              up in the world. They don't
                              seem to do anything spec-
                              tacular but they get there
                              just the same. It doesn't
                              take so long either...maybe
                              the most of us are so dumb
                              it's easy for them...I dunno.
                business   Tom knew his job and he could
                              handle men. His first job
                              was the Missouri Bridge...
                              it was a swell bridge.

        CUT TO:

H-2   MECHANIC IN CHARGE OF
        A HUGE STEAM DERRICK

He is at his post surrounded
with levers and pressure
gauges. Sally comes into the
picture. She is dressed in a
short skirt and laced boots
that come almost to the knee.
On top of this she wears a
mackinaw and over it all a
little apron.

                              SALLY
                              Hello, Mr. Mulligan. Do you
                              know where my husband is?
                              MULLIGAN
                              Yes'm. He's up top...been
                              up there all mornin'.

                              SALLY   his
                              He's so in love with this/old
                              bridge that he can't think
                              of anything else.

                              MULLIGAN
                              She sure is a fine bridge.

                              SALLY
                              Yes, but he's got to eat
                              just the same. His dinner's
                              been spoiling for fifteen
                              minutes. Will you send me
                              up?

Mulligan points in astonishment.

                              MULLIGAN
                              Up there?

                              SALLY
                              Certaihly up there. If he
                              can go up, I can.

                              MULLIGAN   (scratching his head)
                              Well I don't know about that

(CONTINUED)

107

                              MULLIGAN   (cont'd)
                                 Mrs. Garner. I never heard
                                 of a woman goin' up before.
                                 I wouldn't want him to fire
                                 me now.

                              SALLY
                                 Nonsense.

                              MULLIGAN
                                 Well if I send ye up, ye'll
                                 be sure an' say ye made me
                                 do it now...ye made me do
                                 it aginst me better judgment.

                              SALLY   (laughingly)
                                 I will, Mr. Mulligan.

                              MULLIGAN
                                 Then up ye go, Mrs. Garner.

              CUT TO:

H-3   SALLY STANDING ON
              A SHORT STEEL GIRDER

              Her back is to us. She
              holds on to the cable
              sling passed over the
              huge hook. In the
              background we see Mr. Mul-
              ligan in his little house
              behind the winding drums.
              Sally stamps her foot and
              waves at Mulligan.

                              SALLY
                                 Hurry up, his dinner is
                                 burning.

              Mulligan toots his whistle.   SOUND: Whistle.
              Sally starts upward. We
              ANGLE THE CAMERA and follow
              her ascent. When she has
              gone up about a hundred feet
              we

              DISSOLVE TO:

H-4   THE PATIO OF TOM'S HOUSE..
              TOM AND TOMMY

              The old man and his son are
              seated there, small coffee cups
              beside them. A butler offers a
              box of cigars. Tom takes one, then
              xxd looks at his son.

                              TOM
                                 Cigar?

                              TOMMY
                                 No thanks.

              He lights a cigarette

                                       (CONTINUED)

which he takes from a gold
case. The butler lights Tom's
cigar, then exits. Tom blows
out a cloud of smoke, looks at
his son a little nervously, and
speaks:

                    TOM
                         I'm going to be married next
                         month...quietly of course.

               TOMMY   (after a pause)
                         Ixkapaxyantiixhaxyaxyxhappyx
                         Are you?

               TOM
                         Yes.

               TOMMY
                         You might have...waited a
                         little longer.

               TOM   (belligerently)
                         What good would that do?

Tommy shrugs his shoulders.

                    TOMMY
                         Nothing really.

Tom looks at his son speculatively for a moment,
then speaks gently:

                    TOM
                         There's no use feeling that
                         way about it, boy. You and
                         I...ought to be friends.

He looks away uneasily.

                         I hoped maybe you'd come and
                         live with us.

Tommy smiles bitterly.

                    TOMMY
                         Sure...why not?

               TOM
                         That's the way to talk. And
                         listen, we won't talk any
                         more about bookkeeping. Have
                         a good time. We only live
                         once. I guess I can earn as
                         much as you can spend, huh?
                         What do you say?

Tommy jumps to his feet
and takes his father's hand.

                    TOMMY
                         Aw gee, Father, that's swell.

                         (CONTINUED)

                              109

Tom puts his arm around his
son's shoulder and pats him.

                              TOM
                         You're a good kid at that.

The picture begins to
FADE.

                              NARRATOR'S VOICE
                         He was born in the shadow of
                         the bridge... and the riveters
                         sang his lullabies.

        DISSOLVE TO:

H-5   A LITTLE PLATFORM
        HIGH UP ON THE BRIDGE..
        TOM AND HIS FOREMAN

        Tom also wears knee-high
        laced boots and such an
        outfit as a field engineer
        would wear. His foreman is
        dressed in overalls. They
        are examining a blueprint.

                              TOM
                         We're a week ahead now...
                         with luck we'll be in by
                         April. Those girders come? ·

                              FOREMAN
                         Yeah, they come down this
                         mornin'.

                              TOM
                         Then hustle up and finish that
                         span.

                              FOREMAN
                         I can't hustle the men more
                         than I been doin'.

                              TOM
                         They're going to hustle
                         plenty more. I ain't going'
                         to be caught by the thaw
                         whether they like it or not,
                         do you get me?

                              FOREMAN   (raising his eyebrows)
                         Oh sure.

                              SOUND: Intermittent
                                      rivetting.

NOTE:
I forgot to mention
that two steel cables
a foot apart are visible
just in back of the little
platform. They are vertical
and come in at the top of the
frame and disappear behind the
platform. One has been going
up and the other has been going
down during this scene. Sally

                              (CONTINUED)

comes up into view,
standing on the little
girder held by the twin
cables. The little girder
stops at the platform level.

> SALLY   (crossly)
> Hurry up, your dinner's
> burning!

> TOM
> What?

He glares at her.

> What do you mean by riding up
> on that thing...who let you
> do it? I'll break Mulligan's
> neck for this.

> SALLY
> I made him do it; it wasn't
> his fault. Come on, get
> aboard.

Tom looks at the foreman
for sympathy, but finds
him suppressing a chuckle.
Tom gets on the girder,
then speaks to the foreman.

> TOM
> You comin' down?

The foreman takes a
sandwich out of his pocket.

> FOREMAN
> I might as well eat up here...
> the air's nice.

He gives a high sign to
Mulligan on the ground, waving
downward, then blows a whistle.   SOUND: Whistle.
Tom and Sally begin to descend.

CUT TO:

H-6   MOVING SHOT FOLLOWING TOM AND
             SALLY DOWN

They are quite close to us. We
see the bridge and, far below,
the river. The background must be
sharp.

> TOM
> I never heard of such a
> thing.

> SALLY
> Oh stuff and nonsense.

She looks around.

> Pretty, isn't it?

(CONTINUED)

111

                                        TOM   (crossly)
                                                Sure it's pretty.

He relaxes a little
and smacks his lips.

                                                What have we got for dinner,
                                                honey? I'm kinda hungry at
                                                that.

                                        SALLY

                                                Something special...something
                                                very special.

                                        TOM   (looking worried)
                                                Why? Is this a holiday or
                                                somethin'? Holy Moses, I
                                                didn't forget our anniversary
                                                again, did I?

                                        SALLY   (smiling)
                                                No, not that.

                                        TOM

                                                What is it then?

Sally moistens her lips
and looks a little scared.

                                        SALLY

                                                We're going to have a baby.

                                        TOM   (At the top of his lungs)
                                                WHAT?

He throws his arms
wide and yells:

                                        SALLY

Having let go the
cable sling above him,
he almost falls off the
girder. He drops astride
the girder and holds it with
his knees.

                                        SALLY   (frightened to death)
                                                Oh my God!

She gets down cautiously
and sits astride the girder
also.

                                        TOM

                                                Gee, that's great...will it
                                                be a boy or a girl?

                                        SALLY

                                                I don't know, darling.

                                        TOM

                                                Why didn't you tell me before?

                                        SALLY

                                                I didn't know.

                                                (CONTINUED)

                                    112

He takes her hands, then
kisses them impulsively.

                    TOM
                         They'll never stop me now,
                         honey.

                    SALLY
                         What do you mean?

                    TOM
                         I'll make so much money for
                         you and the kid, We'll buy
                         the Great Western and give
                         it to him to play with.

                    SALLY
                         Suppose it's a girl.

                    TOM   (seriously)
                         Now don't spoil everything.

Tom moves closer to
her and takes her in
his arms.

                         Oh Sally, I love you so, ~~I'm~~
                         ~~so grateful to you~~. I'd be
                         a bum without you, but to-
                         gether...there's nothing we
                         can't do.

Sally buries her head in
his shoulders The girder
comes gently to the ground.
Two or three steel workers
look at this touching scene
in astonishment. Tom and
Sally are oblivious to
everything.

                    SALLY
                         My Tom.

                    TOM
                         My darling.

Mr. Mulligan comes into the
picture.

                    MULLIGAN
                         Your dinner's burnin' up,
                         Mrs. Garner. I can smell it
                         from here.

Sally looks around hastily,
then runs out of the picture.
The steel workers are chuckling   SOUND: Chuckling.
audibly. Tom rises and looks at
them evilly.

                    TOM
                         What the hell are you doing
                         here? Haven't you got any

                         (CONTINUED)

113

                                        TOM   (cont'd)
                                                   work to do?

                                        MULLIGAN
                                                   We knocked off for chow.

                                        TOM   (ferociously)
                                                   Then go and eat before I
                                                   knock you off proper.

         He isn't really angry
         though and he can't
         contain the good news
         much longer. He motions
         Mulligan to him and says:

                                        TOM

                                                   Come here.

         Mulligan crosses to him.
         Tom looks around cautiously,
         then cups his hands, puts
         them against Mulligan's ear,
         and whispers something into
         the cup. Mulligan raises his
         eyebrows in pleased surprise.

                                        MULLIGAN
                                                   Well that sure is fine. Xx
                                                   xxxkxxxxixxhyxthxxhxxxx I
         He shakes him by the hand.   know how you feel. I felt
                                                   the same way meself.

         Tom's face falls and he
         speaks with disappointment.

                                        TOM

                                                   Oh, you've got one?

                                        MULLIGAN
                                                   Eleven, my boy, eleven...
                                                   goin' on twelve.

         Tom looks very sour.

                                        TOM

                                                   Aaaah!

         He stamps out of the
         picture.

                 DISSOLVE TO:—

                    ****   ******   ****

                 H—4

                    dissolve to

H-6 BIS   COMBINATION SITTING ROOM-
              DINING ROOM-OFFICE IN TOM'S
              CABIN AT CONSTRUCTION CAMP..
              MULLIGAN

We do not see Tom but we hear   SOUND: Footsteps.
him pacing up and down the room.
Mulligan's eyes follow him twice
across the room.

                    MULLIGAN
                      Sit down, Mr. Garner,
                      you're wearin' out the
                      carpet.

Tom comes into the picture.

                  TOM
                    I can't sit down,I'm too
                    nervous.

                  MULLIGAN (complacently)
                    You'll get used to it.

                  TOM
                    Do you suppose she's all
                    right?

                  MULLIGAN
                    Certainly she's all right.
                    It's nothing for a woman.
                    Have a drink.

With a shaking hand,
Tom picks up a whiskey
bottle and pours a drink.
Half of it misses the glass
and goes on the table. He
lifts the glass to his mouth.
Just as he starts to drink,
we hear the doctor's voice.

                  DOCTOR'S VOICE
                    It's a boy, Tom.

Tom chokes a little on
his drink and puts down
the glass, then turns
slowly.

CUT TO:

H-6A   TRUCKING SHOT..CLOSEUP
           TOM'S FACE

He is walking toward us.
He starts to smile, then
his lips tremble, he wipes
a tear out of his eye and
laughs nervously.

DISSOLVE TO:

H-6B   TOM LOOKING INTO A
         CRIB

His face works with emotion.
Silently His lips form the
words: "My son." He turns
slowly.

CUT TO:

H-6C   TOM STANDING BESIDE SALLY'S
         BED

Her face is very white and her
eyes seem unusually big and
dark. She smiles at him, but
doesn't speak. Tom sinks to his
knees, takes her hand, and speaks
gently:

                         TOM
                         My son...my son. I've
                         got a son. Oh Sally, they'll
                         never stop me now. Thank
                         you...

DISSOLVE TO:

H-7 ----

ANGLE DOWN over clergyman's
shoulder. Tom, Eve, Tommy,
and Henry. The clergyman
is mumbling away but we hear
the voice of the Narrator.

NARRATOR'S VOICE
It was strange to see a son
acting as his father's best
man, but it was so soon after
Sally's accident, it was done
very quietly. I was the only
other person.

EVE
I do.

Check up on this,
I've only been mar-
ried twice and I
don't remember. P.S.

THE CLERGYMAN
I hereby pronounce you man
and wife...whom God hath
joined together let no man
put asunder.

Tom and Eve kiss and
everybody shakes hands.

LAP DISSOLVE BEGINS.

THE NARRATOR'S VOICE
They say trouble comes in
bunches. Tom hadn't been
married a week when the fun
began   ~~trouble started~~ down in Illinois.

THE DISSOLVE IS COMPLETED
HERE.

H-8   STOCK SHOT: A WAREHOUSE
        BURNING AT NIGHT

NARRATOR'S VOICE
The Aurora yard men were on
strike...but the freight had
to move so we sent down some
strike-breakers. The boys
didn't like that, so they
burned the warehouse...there
just happened to be a few
strike-breakers inside...And
when they came out somebody
started firing.

CUT TO:

H-9   STRIKE BREAKERS RUNNING OUT
        OF FLAMING WAREHOUSE

Some policemen come out with
them. A shot is fired. A
strike-breaker clutches his
belly, spins, and falls. A
policeman pulls his revolver
and fires. A fusillade is
fired; two strike-breakers
and a policeman fall. The
others run back into the

SOUND: Shot.

SOUND: Shot.

(CONTINUED)

burning warehouse. ANGLE
UP to show the roof of the
warehouse emitting huge
flames. ANGLE DOWN again
to the warehouse door. It
opens. A policeman appears,
~~Eujindxkim~~ silhouetted against   SOUND: Shot.
a flickering light. A shot is
fired. A fusillade comes from
the door of the warehouse. We
ANGLE UP again to the roof to
the accompaniment of the answering fusillade from the strikers.
The roof falls in releasing a wall
of flame and sparks which drift
down in front of the lens like
burning snow.

                              NARRATOR'S VOICE
                              There weren't so many killed
                              but it started the big
                              strike. The brotherhood
                              went on a sympathy strike;
CHECK THIS. P.S.   the brakemen and the trainmen
                              too. It was a swell chance
                              for somebody so the I.W.W.'s
                              jumped in and then the REAL
                              trouble started. Tom was
                              down there for ~~three~~ weeks...
                              he spent his honeymoon alone.

            DISSOLVE TO:

H-10   THE LIVING ROOM OF TOM'S
            HOUSE..EVE AND TOMMY

            The radio is playing sweet music.
            Eve, wearing a dinner dress, sits
            languidly on a sofa. Tommy
            wears a dinner jacket. He is
            sitting in a big chair reading the
            paper. He peeks at Eve around the
            paper. She is drumming on the
            arm of the couch with her fingers.

                         EVE   (petulantly)
                              This is the damnedest honey-
                              moon I've ever heard of. Who
                              does he think I am--~~something~~
                              ~~or something?~~

                         TOMMY   (lowering the paper)
                                     and laughing)
                              That's what you get for
                              marrying a railroad man.

                         EVE
                              My FATHER is a railroad man...
                              he didn't go off like this
                              for weeks on end.

                         TOMMY   (mildly)
                              Maybe he didn't tend to bus-
                              iness so much.

                         EVE   (furiously)
                              He tended to business all righ'

                                   (CONTINUED)

118

TOMMY

Well...my father owns his
railroad now.

EVE   (looking down at her hands)
That's true.

Tommy jumps to his feet,
drops his paper, and
crosses to her.

TOMMY   (consolingly)
I'm sorry. Anyway your
father is still the president.

EVE   (laughing bitterly)
Yes. We fixed that up,
didn't we?

TOMMY

What do you mean?

EVE

Nothing.

TOMMY   (after a pause)
It was only a little railroad anyway.

EVE   (vexed)
I guess it wasn't so little
as all that.

TOMMY

Of course it wasn't...

He takes her hand.

Let's don't fight...we ought
to be good friends.

Eve looks at him a
little strangely for a
moment, then speaks:

EVE

Why not?

Tommy looks at her in
puzzlement.

Would you like to take me
dancing?

TOMMY

Why...why...why sure.

EVE

Do you dance well?

TOMMY

All right I guess.

Eve rises, stands close
to Tommy, puts her arm around

(CONTINUED)

his neck, stretches
out her left hand to
his right hand, and
says:

                              EVE
                         Let me see.

DISSOLVE TO:

H-11   INTERIOR OF A WAREHOUSE..STRIKERS' MEETING

A platform has been erected
at one end of the big shed.
About a thousand railroad
men are assembled here.
They sit on benches made by
laying planks across boxes
of merchandise. The shed is
dimly lit except for the
speaker's platform. On the
back edge of this platform
sit a dozen of the leaders.
In front of them stands a
wild-looking man. He is
speaking to the accompaniment of fiery gestures. His
voice comes faintly and as he
makes his points, the crowd
hurrays loudly, interrupting
the voice of the Narrator.
As the Narrator speaks the
CAMERA PANS and picks out a
few characteristic faces; then
it returns to the orator.

                         NARRATOR'S VOICE
                         After about four weeks the
                         wobblies were running the
                         whole shebang. They talked
                         foolish but the men were so
                         sore by then they'd listen
                         to anything. They began to
                         hate Tom though most of them
                         had known him all their lives
                         and they figured what they'd
                         do to him if they ever laid
                         their hands on him. They
                         were going to string him up
                         and tear him apart and plenty
                         of other things. He was a
                         blood-sucker, an oppressor
                         of the poor, and all like
                         that...that was the night
                         he walked in on 'em.

CUT TO:

H-12   INTERIOR OF AN AUTOMOBILE

Tom and a burly private detective sit in the back seat.
Another detective sits beside
the chauffeur. We ANGLE DOWN
on the four of them in the

                                   (CONTINUED)

moving car. We hear
the noise of the engine
and the occasional blast   SOUND: Noise of engine, and
of the horn.   honking of horn.

                        TOM
                        I want you boys to wait out-
                        side.

                FIRST DETECTIVE
                        You're crazy, Mr. Garner,
                        you can't go in there alone.

                SECOND DETECTIVE
                        Listen, Boss, they'll tear
                        you apart.

                        TOM
                        In a pig's eye, son, in a
                        pig's eye.

The car comes to a halt.
The chauffeur jumps out
and runs around the back of
the car and opens the door.

                FIRST DETECTIVE
                        Take ONE of us with you,
                        Mr. Garner.

Tom, getting out of the
car:

                        TOM
                        Nonsense.

                SECOND DETECTIVE (holding out
                                      a revolver)
                        Here...for God's sake.

                        TOM
                        Boloney.

He disappears.

CUT TO:

H-13   DOORWAY LEADING INTO
        WAREHOUSE..SENTRY

A big brakeman is standing
guard with a shotgun. Suddenly he lifts the gun to
the port position and calls:

                        SENTRY
                        Halt.

We hear the crunching of   SOUND: Crunching of
gravel, then Tom comes into   gravel.
the picture and walks up to
the brakeman. The latter
peers at him in astonishment.

                        (CONTINUED)

121

                                        SENTRY
                                    You can't go in there,
                                    Mr. Garner.

        Tom does not even halt
        in his stride. As he
        passes the Sentry, he
        calls:

                            TOM
                                Go peddle your papers, you
                                fathead.

        He opens the door and
        steps inside the warehouse.

        CUT TO:

H-14   CLOSE SHOT..THE ORATOR ON
        THE PLATFORM

        He is almost foaming at the
        mouth. He yells at the
        top of his lungs:

                                    THE ORATOR
                                    ...the jobs belong to you,
                                    and the railroad and the
                                    ground under the railroad.
                                    Tom Garner thinks he owns
                                    the railroad, but he's going
                                    to find out different. You
                                    work and slave and give him
                                    the best years of your life
                                    and what does he give you in
                                    return? STARVATION WAGES--
                                    just enough to keep you alive.
                                    He's a dirty bum and a crook
                                    and a slave-driver. If I
                                    could lay my hands on him, I'd
                                    ...

        He looks past us in
        puzzlement. He peers into
        the darkness, shading his
        eyes.

                                        ...I'd...I'd...

        CUT TO:

H-15   LONG SHOT DOWN THE AISLE..
        TRUCKING

        Far down stands the orator
        on his platform. Just in front
        of us stands Tom with his back
        to us.

                            TOM   (loudly)
                                    You'd what?

        There is a gasp of
        surprise. All the men
        turn and look back at Tom.

                                        (CONTINUED)

122

He starts down the
aisle. We TRUCK down
with him.

CUT TO:

H-16   CLOSE SHOT..THE ORATOR
              ON THE PLATFORM

His face registers amazement.
He follows the progress of
Tom down the aisle. Tom
climbs the steps onto the
platform and comes into the
picture. He walks over to the
orator who backs away a little
nervously. Tom points to a chair
at the back wall.

                    TOM
                         Sit down, horse-face, you've
                         talked enough.

                    ORATOR   (indignantly)
                         What do you mean by...

Tom steps forward, takes
him by the arm, escorts
him to the chair, and puts
him into it gently. He
pats him on the head, then
turns and speaks very quietly:

                    TOM
                         Listen, boys. You've
                         started something you can't
                         finish...you've got a bear
                         by the tail. I've listened
                         to all the conferences,
                         meetings and threats I'm
                         going to listen to. This is
                         the end...I've got a bellyful.
                         Nobody runs this railroad but
                         me. You bozoz can work...or
                         you can quit. Twelve o'clock
                         is the deadline.

He looks at his watch.

                         You've got fifty minutes...
                         so make up your minds. This
                         isn't a private fight. The
                         storekeepers are waiting for
                         goods, men and women are
                         waiting for food and babies
                         are waiting for milk...they
                         won't have to wait any longer.
                         THIS RAILROAD RUNS TONIGHT.
                         Five thousand men are coming
                         down from Chicago, they'll be
                         here at twelve o'clock. A
                         thousand state militia are
                         moving in to keep order.

He looks around.

                              (CONTINUED)

123

                                              TOM (cont'd)
                                                   I hope there won't be any
                                                   trouble...but if you're
                                                   looking for it...you'll
                                                   find it. That's all.

         He turns and calls to
         the orator.

                                              Come here, you.

         The orator comes forward
         scowling.

                                              Now tell 'em what you were
                                              going to do to me when you
                                              met me face to face. So long.

         He steps off the
         platform.

         CUT TO:

H-17   LONG SHOT DOWN THE
         AISLE

         Tom walks up until he
         has passed us.

                                         NARRATOR'S VOICE
                                              But they wouldn't listen to
                                              him. They thought they
                                              could force his hand.
                                              They were wrong. Four hundred
                                              and six men were killed...
                                              maybe it was his fault...I
                                              don't know.

         DISSOLVE TO:

H-18   HENRY'S LIVING ROOM..
         HENRY AND HIS WIFE SIT
         ON EITHER SIDE OF
         THE FIRE

                                         HENRY'S WIFE
                                              Of course it was his fault.

                                              (CONTINUED)

                                   HENRY'S WIFE   (cont'd)
                                        Everybody said so.

                                   HENRY
                                        I never felt that way...
                                        Tom didn't either. He was
                                        happy as a lark for a couple
                                        of years after the strike...
                                        his conscience was clear.

                                   HENRY'S WIFE
                                        Then why did he kill himself?

                                   HENRY   (after a pause)
                                        I don't know.

                                   HENRY'S WIFE (triumphantly)
                                        Of course you don't...because
                                        I'm right. It was his con-
                                        science bothered him...about
                                        Sally and how mean he was to
                                        his son and the widows and
                                        children of all those men...
                                        that's why he killed himself
                                        and you know it too.

                                   HENRY   (doggedly)
                                        It isn't so.

                                   HENRY'S WIFE (angrily)
                                        You make me tired the way you
                                        stick up for that man. He
                                        was ignorant and no good...
                                        a bully...a slave-driver...
                                        rotten to his wife, and then
                                        a suicide.

                                   HENRY   (furiously)
                                        You know so much, huh?

                                   HENRY'S WIFE
                                        Then why did he kill himself
                                        if I'm wrong?

                                   HENRY   (very quietly)
                                        He didn't kill himself.

                                   HENRY'S WIFE
                                        What?

                                   HENRY
                                        I never told you...it was too
                                        rotten, but you think you know
                                        so much.

          THE DISSOLVE BEGINS.

                                        He died on his wedding anni-
                                        versary. You didn't know that,
                                        did you, you who know so much.
          THE DISSOLVE IS COMPLETED.

                                     125

FADE IN:

I-1   TOM SITTING AT HIS DESK

He looks very happy and is
paring an apple with his pocket
knife. Henry comes into the
office.

                  TOM   (gaily)
                  Hello, Bullswool...you want a
                  piece of apple?

                  HENRY

                  No thankw. Say, Tom. You
                  didn't forget what day today
                  is, did you?...I mean, 'cause
                  you didn't mention it.

                  TOM

                  Tuesday, ain't it?

                  HENRY   (laughing, and shaking his
                            head)
                  You're a fine husband. This
                  is your wedding anniversary.

Tom jumps to his feet.

                  TOM

                  Holy smoke! I forgot all about
                  it!

He looks at his watch.

                  I've just got time before the
                  Board meeting...almost. Let
                  'em wait a little. I'll run
                  up to the house and pretend
                  I knew it all the time.

He grabs his hat, pats
Henry on the shoulder; he
exits, yelling:

                  Thanks, Henry, you're a life
                  saver.

              DISSOLVE TO:

I-2   FASHIONABLE JEWELERS' SHOP

This is shot from the rear
showing the door, the display
cases, and the street outside.
A Rolls Royce town car pulls
up to the curb, Tom jumps out
without assistance from the
chauffeur, runs into the shop.
As he enters he yells:

                  TOM

                  I want to get something quick.

              (CONTINUED)

                              TOM   (cont'd)
                                   What does Mrs. Garner like,
                                   do you know?

The proprietor rushes   THE PROPRIETOR
forward.   Yes, Mr. Garner, I know
                                   exactly. She was in three
                                   days ago and admired them.

                              TOM   (looking at his watch)
                                   All right, let's have it.

The jeweler swallows
hard, reaches into a
case with great care, and
lifts out a magnificent
necklace of black pearls.
Tom takes them and looks
at them suspiciously.

                         TOM

                                   What's the matter with 'em,
                                   they look all smoky?

The jeweler swallows
hard again.

                         THE JEWELER
                                   They are black pearls,
                                   Mr. Garner.

                              TOM

                                   Oh. How much are they,
                                   are they cheap?

                         THE JEWELER
                                   For such pearls, yes, Mr.
                                   Garner, very cheap.
                                        (He swallows)
                                   Thirty-five thousand.

                         TOM

                                   I'll give you twenty-seven,
                                   take it or leave it.

The jeweler opens his   XXXXXX
mouth wide, swallows
his saliva, licks his
lips.

                         THE JEWELER
                                   I'll take it, thank you.

                         TOM

                                   Fine. Put 'em on the bill.
                                   So long.

He picks up the pearls
and sticks them in his
pocket. He starts out.

                         THE JEWELER
                                   Don't you want the case?

                         TOM

                                   Haven't time.

                                   (CONTINUED)

I-2   (CONTINUED)

            He runs out of the store.
            Through the glass door we
            see him stop beside an old
            man peddling little fuzzy
            monkeys that dangle up and
            down on the ends of elastics.

            CUT TO:

I-3   CLOSE SHOT..TOM AND THE
             PEDDLAR

                                    Tom   (putting out his hand)
                                             Give me one of those.

            He reaches in his pocket,
            pulls out a roll, cannot
            find anything smaller
            than a five-dollar bill.
            He puts it in the peddler's
            hand and takes the fuzzy
            monkey.

                                    THE OLD PEDDLAR
                                             No change, mister, for so
                                             big.

                                    TOM

                                             Never mind...good luck to you.

            He runs and jumps into
            his car, slams the door
            after him. The big car
            pulls away. The peddlar
            looks after him in amaze-
            ment.

            DISSOLVE TO:

I-4   EVE'S BEDROOM..EVE AND BABY

            Eve wears a lace tea gown and
            looks very beautiful. She is
            telephoning. Near her feet her
            baby plays on a soft woollen
            coverlet stretched xxxxxxx
            xxxxxxxxx on the floor.

                                    EVE   (at the telephone)
                                             ...of course I missed you.
                                             Why don't you come and have
                                             tea with me, darling?

            PAN to doorway. Tom
            appears. He is smiling
            happily. He pulls the
            necklace out of his pocket.
            He holds it with both hands.
            From his left hand hangs also
            the fuzzy monkey.

                                    EVE

                                             He won't be home till dinner.

                                    (CONTINUED)

128

                                   EVE
                                        (cont'd)
                                        ...He has a directors' meet-
                                        ing.

Tom chuckles silently,
then advances on
tiptoe.

                                   EVE

                                        He's right here on the floor
                                        beside me like a little blond
                                        angel...
                                                (she speaks very softly)
                                        ...he looks just like you.

Tomxsmiles
Tom's smile freezes on
his face. It changes to
an expression of horror.

                                   EVE

                                        Goodbye, dear...don't be
                                        long.

She hangs up the receiver,
rises, sees Tom out of the
corner of her eyes, clutches
her heart, and turns slowly.

                                   TOM

                                        Who were you talking to?

Eve licks her lips.

                                   EVE

                                        Why uh...why uh...why I was
                                        talking to Amy Johnson...
                                        a girl I went to school with.
                                        I wanted her to come to tea...
                                        but she couldn't come.

                                   TOM

                                        You said: "Don't be long."

                                   EVE
                                        (smiling nervously)
                                        Of course. I meant don't be
                                        long till you call me again.
                                        Isn't that perfectly natural?

                                   TOM
                                        (looking away)
                                        Sure...sure.

Eve swallows hard,
then looks at the pearls
and speaks happily:

                                   EVE

                                        But darling, what's that?

                                   TOM
                                        (in a monotone)
                                        Oh.

He turns slowly and
looks at her.

                                        (CONTINUED)

                              TOM
                                   For you.

He forces a smile.

                                   This is our wedding anniver-
                                   sary. I suppose you thought
                                   I'd forgotten, but I hadn't.

                              EVE   (in ecstasies)
                                   You sweet lamb. They're
                                   beautiful, Tom.

She puts them on, then
kisses him.

                                   Thank you.

                              TOM
                                   You're welcome.

Like a man in a daze he
holds out the fuzzy monkey.

                                   This is for Buster.

                              ~~EVE~~x   ~~(taking the monkey)~~x
Eve takes the monkey
and puts it in front
of the baby.

                              EVE
                                   Say thank you to Daddy.

There is an awkward
silence, then Tom
looks at his watch.

                              TOM
                                   I've got a meeting...I've
                                   got to go.

                              EVE
                                   Goodbye, dear. You were
                                   sweet to bring this to me.
                                   be home early.

                              TOM
                                   Yes.

He turns, then pauses
in the doorway.

                                   What was her name...your
                                   friend?

                              EVE   (palely)
                                   Johnson, dear, Amy Johnson.

                              TOM
                                   Oh yes...like to meet her
                                   some time. Goodbye.

He exits. Eve clutches
her heart. She closes
her eyes.

DISSOLVE TO:

I-5   TOM IN HIS AUTOMOBILE

He stares ahead, his mouth   SOUND: Street noises.
hangs open a little. We   Purr of the engine
hear the street noises,   Triple notes of
the purr of the engine ,   a French horn.
and, occasionally, the triple
~~shaka~~ notes of the French
horn. After a moment Tom
presses his big scarred hand
over his eyes, then he removes
it, forces himself to laugh,
and shakes his head trying to
dispell the horrible thoughts
he has entertained.

DISSOLVE TO:

I-6   FULL SHOT..THE BOARD OF
         DIRECTORS' ROOM

We ANGLE DOWN on this
from the height of the ceiling.
We see the whole table and
all the directors. At the far
end sits Tom. At the near end
Elmer, the chairman, is on his
feet talking.

                         ELMER
                    I particularly wanted to take
                    up the freight rate on pig
                    iron, gentlemen.

CUT TO:

I-7   VERY CLOSE SHOT..TOM

Elmer's voice comes ~~faintly~~.
We hear it as it sounds to
Tom whose mind is wandering.

                    ELMER'S VOICE (faintly)
                    Trainloads from Nevada to
                    Wyoming...Gondolas on the
                    other hand...ballast by way
                    of the Canal...Colorado also
                    but mostly Michigan and Wis-
                    consin.
During this, Tom's
eyes have looked away.
They wander around the
room insanely, then
look up at us and glow
dully with astonishment.

CUT TO:

I-8   VERY CLOSE SHOT..ELMER
         SPEAKING

He also looks mildly insane.
His eyes seem very big and
rolly.

                         ELMER
                    ...But if we ship it a whole
                    trainful at a time, this is not
                    the case...because he's right

                         (CONTINUED)

131

                                    ELMER   (cont'd)
                                        here on the floor beside me...
                                        like a little blond angel...

Elmer leans forward
and speaks confidentially--
really a whisper:

                                        ...he looks just like you.

There is a terrific crash.
The whole table bounces.   SOUND: Crash.

CUT TO:

I-9   CLOSE SHOT..TOM ON HIS FEET

His huge fist is still pressed
on the table. An inkwell is
knocked over in front of him.
He looks around wildly. The
directors near him stare in
amazement. Little by little
he relaxes. Jerkily he ~~raxex~~
raises his left hand to his
eyes, holds it there a second,
then speaks quite normally.

                                    ~~ELMER~~
                                    TOM
                                        Excuse me, Elmer, I didn't
                                        hear what you said.

He sits down slowly, leans
forward, and looks at Elmer
dully.

                                        Go on.

His mouth hangs open.

                                    ELMER'S VOICE
                                        I was saying, Tom, that it
                                        seems to me, if we hauled
                                        pig iron in whole trains in-
                                        stead...

Tom's eyes waver. He
begins looking around the
room again like a hunted
man.

                                    ELMER'S VOICE   (faintly)
                                        ...from Nevada ~~fxxxxWx~~ to
                                        Wyoming...ballast by way of
                                        the Canal instead of...
                                        of course I will concede...
                                        but mostly Colorado, not to
                                        mention Michigan and...

A horrible cry is heard.
Tom yells with blood in his
throat.

                                    TOM
                                        NO NO!

                                        (CONTINUED)

He buries his head in
his hands.

                    TOM

            Oh God, no...don't let it
            be.

He lifts his head and
stares at the directors,
then rises.

                    TOM

            I'm ill...you'll have to
            forgive me...I want to go
            home. Henry, Henry. Where's
            Henry? Where is he?

Henry comes into the
picture and puts his
arm around him.

            I want to go home, Henry.
            Take me home. I'm not
            feeling well.

Very weakly he waves his
hands to the directors.

            Have to forgive me...sorry...
            not feeling well.

He starts out of the room.
Huge, but looking very old,
his arm is around Henry's
shoulder. Henry holds him
around the waist and tries
to support him. The CAMERA
FOLLOWS them out of the room.

DISSOLVE TO:

I-10   THE HUGE LIVING ROOM IN TOM'S
        HOUSE
        ────────────────────────

Double doors open wide. Tom
staggers into the room helped
by Henry on one side and his
butler on the other.

                    HENRY

            You ought to go to bed, Tom.

                    TOM

            No.

He points to his desk.
They lead him to it. He
sits in the chair. The
left side of his mouth
trembles a little. He
clutches the arms of his
chair. INSERT: Henry
whispering in the butler's
ear.

                    HENRY (whispering)
            Get the doctor immediately.

                    (CONTINUED)

I-10   (CONTINUED)

       RETURN to Tom at his
       desk. Henry stretches
       forth his hand gently
       and pats his shoulder.

                        HENRY
                          You'll feel better in a
                          little while. It's the heat
                          I guess.

                        TOM   (in a monotone)
                          Where's my wife?

                        HENRY
                          They've gone to get her.

                        TOM
                          Want to see her.

       He smiles at Henry
       cunningly.

                          You know why?

                        HENRY
                          No, Tom.

       Tom winks at him.

                        TOM
                          Secret.

       CUT TO:

I-11   DOORWAY

       Eve is framed there.
       She looks frightened to
       death. She calls out to
       us:

                        EVE
                          Tom, what's the matter?

       She comes forward slowly.
       She goes past the CAMERA.
       W
       CUT TO:

I-12   TOM AT THE DESK

       With a terrific effort he
       rises and looks at us ter-
       ribly. Then a smile of
       cunning appears.

                        TOM
                          Where's little boy?

       Eve comes into the
       picture.

                        EVE
                          He's in bed, dear.

                        (CONTINUED)

                                                     EVE   (cont'd)
                  ...Please sit down. The
                  doctor's coming right away.

                                      TOM

                  Want to see little boy.

He smiles.

                  Not much time.

He raises his arm.

                  Help me.

He puts his arm around
Eve. Henry goes to the
other side. Tom waves him
away.

                                      TOM

                  No...only want my wife...good
                  little wife.

They go slowly out of
the room. Tom's left
foot drags a little.
A moment after they
disappear, Henry follows
slowly.

DISSOLVE TO:

I-13   THE BABY SLEEPING IN HIS
              CRIB.

He clutches the fuzzy monkey.
PAN to doorway. Tom, supported
by Eve, drags into the room. Eve
looks terribly afraid. Tom is
smiling cunningly. He leans against
the wall, pushes Eve in in front of
him, then pushes the door, which does
not quite close.

CUT TO:

I-14   CLOSE SHOT..TOM'S FACE

He is leering at us. The
smile hardens, the lips
draw back and his expression
becomes ferocious. Then the
smile returns. He whispers:

                                      TOM   (whispering)
                  Who does he look like?

CUT TO:

I-15   SHOT OF THE ROOM

In the foreground Eve stands
next to the crib. In the

(CONTINUED)

background Tom leans against
the wall. He comes forward
now unsteadily and
leans on the foot of the crib;
with his free hand, the
right one, he points to the
child and repeats:

                    TOM
                         Who...who does he look like?
                         Quick.

                    EVE   (clutching her throat)
                         No, no.

Tom leans over the crib.
His huge hand is working.
It comes near the child's
throad.

                    TOM   (raucously)
                         Who?

                    EVE   (falling to her knees)
                         I won't tell you...I can't...
                         kill me if you want to...I
                         can't tell you.

Tom takes the child by
the throat. He yells:

                    TOM
                         WHO?

                    EVE.   (screaming)
                         Don't! I'll tell you. Oh
                         God, I couldn't help it.
                         I'm young, I fell in love. Oh
                         God.

She lowers her head and
says more gently:

                         Oh God...it was Tommy.

Her head sinks almost to
the floor. Tom stares at
her in horror. He looks
into the crib, then down
at Eve. His face works
spasmodically. He staggers
over to her and looks down
at her. His expression
changes to one of revulsion.
Very weakly he kicks her.
She rolls over on her face. He
tries to spit on her, but his
mouth is dry. He turns back
to the crib, looks down in it.
His great hands begin to work.

CUT TO:

I-16   THE HALL OUTSIDE THE
        NURSERY

        Henry stands just near the
        door. He looks horror-stricken.
        Suddenly he looks up.

        CUT TO:

I-17   TOMMY HURRYING DOWN THE HALL

                                TOMMY
                        What's the matter, Henry?
                        I hear the old man is ill.

        CUT TO:

I-18   HENRY

        Henry looks at him and
        swallows. He cannot speak.

        CUT TO:

I-19   TOM LEANING OVER THE CRIB

        INSERT SHOT of the Baby.
        He moves in his sleep, then
        opens his eyes, smiles at us,
        and says:

                        BABY
                    Da da.

        CUT BACK TO:

I-20   · TOM

        He straightens up, looks around
        vaguely and waves backward with
        his hands. He staggers, almost
        falls, clutches at the doorknob.
        The door flies open revealing
        Henry and Tommy. Tom points at
        Tommy.

                        TOM
                    Want to see you.

        DISSOLVE TO:

I-21   TOM'S BEDROOM

        We are shooting toward the
        window, away from the door.
        Tom and Tommy stagger past
        us. Tom has his arm on Tommy's
        shoulder but his fist clutches
        the cloth of his son's coat
        so that he seems to be holding
        on to him rather than supported
        by him. As they go past a highboy,
        Tom stops. Tommy has to stop also.
        Tom pulls open the top drawer. His
        hand fumbles for a minute, then comes
        out with a big Colt revolver.

                        (CONTINUED)

                        137

I-2   (CONTINUED)

                              TOMMY   (trying to get away)
                                       What are you going to do?

                              TOM   (bringing the gun up to
                                          Tommy's heart)
                                       You know...what I'm going to
                                       do.

        CUT TO:

I-22   REVERSE SHOT OF THIS
        SHOOTING AT THE DOOR

        Tom's left hand holds Tommy
        in an iron grip. His right
        fist pushes the revolver at
        Tommy's heart. Tommy is
        almost paralyzed with fright.
        He backs away slowly. Tom
        follows, staggering. He
        glares into his son's eyes.

                              TOMMY
                              No...no...father...please.

        Tom laughs bitterly.

                              TOM
                              My son.

        Tommy backs up against the
        wall.

                              TOMMY
                              No.

        Tom's lips draw back in
        a snarl. His big hand
        starts to close on the re-
        volver. His jaw muscles
        work. Suddenly he says:

                              TOM
                              Wait...I'll give you one
                              chance.

        He smiles cunningly and
        repeats:

                              ...one chance.

        He pauses, gloating over
        his idea.

                              You've done everything else
                              to me, now...

        He turns the gun around,
        pressing the barrel against
        his own heart and offering
        the handle to Tommy.

                              Pull.

        Tommy shrieks hysterically.

                                       (CONTINUED)

                         138

                        TOMMY
                              No!

                    TOM
                              Pull...that...trigger.

        Tommy's eyes start from
        his head in horror. His
        hand closes over the re-
        volver. His grip begins
        to tighten. Tom leans very
        close to him and leers into
        his face.

        CUT TO:

I-23   HENRY STANDING IN THE HALL

        There is an explosion. He
        turns, runs across the hall,   SOUND: Explosion.
        throws open the door, and
        enters.

        CUT TO:

I-24   TOM SWAYING ON HIS FEET

        The force of the explosion
        has knocked him back about
        three feet. Tommy is limp
        against the wall. The smoking
        revolver dangles from his
        fingers. With a supreme effort
        Tom steps forward, takes the
        gun from his son's hand and
        holds it in his own. With his
        left hand he tightens the fingers
        xxxxxxxxx of his right hand around
        it. His knees buckle. He clutches
        the edge of his bed and falls into
        a kneeling position beside it.
        Henry runs into the picture, throws
        himself on his knees beside Tom.

                        HENRY
                              Tom,.Tom...Tommy.

        Slowly Tom rolls his great
        head over. He leers up at
        Henry and whispers:

                    TOM   (whispering)
                              Suicide.

        Then his eyes close.
        After a moment, he
        speaks:

                    TOM
                              My son...my son.

        He chuckles evilly.

                              (CONTINUED)

> TOM
>
> I've got a son.

DISSOLVE TO:

I-25   YOUNG TOM KNEELING BESIDE
SALLY'S BED

He holds her hand between
his two big paws and kisses
it hysterically. His voice
is full of exultation.

> TOM
>
> My son...my son...I've got
> a son. Oh Sally, they'll
> never stop me now. We'll
> own the world. Thank you,
> God, thank you for your
> kindness.

He looks up and a little
toward us. The scene
begins to FADE, leaving
only a beam of light
on young Tom's face. He
is radiant with joy and
tears of emotion stream
down his cheeks.

> TOM
>
> Our Father, Who art in
> heaven, hallowed be Thy
> name, Thy kingdom come,
> Thy will be done, for Thine
> is the power and the glory.
> Amen.

The organ playing
Schubert's Ave Maria steals
in at the beginning of this
prayer. It becomes louder
as the light fades. The
light is gone entirely at
the word Amen. Immediately
thereafter the music reaches
its greatest volume.

*****   THE END   *****

Started December 6th 1932
Finished January 16th 1933
Preston Sturges spoke
Bianca Gilchrist wrote.

Easy Living

"Hey, What's the Big Idea?"

Easy Living was the first Sturges film I ever saw, long before I really knew who Sturges was. I laughed till it hurt, and I promised myself two things: to find out more about Jean Arthur, who won me over with her talent for farce while still coming through as a gutsy woman with beauty, brains, and spirit; and to find out more about that Sturges guy who wrote the script. I was still in college, but I was already beginning to realize that those script credits mattered as much if not more than the name of the director.

This script, with its zany blend of farce, satire, and comedy, represents Sturges at his carefree best. Sturges clearly had fun writing it and in pushing it forward. He notes that when he handed his producer, Maurice Revnes, the script, Revnes told him that "1936 was not the time for comedies and [he] wanted to abandon the whole project. I disagreed. Any time was a good time for comedies."[1] Sturges then shopped it to Mitchell Leisen, who shared his enthusiasm, and the film was made with a fine cast headed up by the luminous Jean Arthur as Mary Smith, Edward Arnold as the bumbling billionaire J. B. Ball, and Ray Milland as the misfit millionaire son who falls for Mary.

And yet when *Easy Living* appeared in 1937 the critics were less than kind at worst, and only lukewarm in their praise at best. Frank S. Nugent wrote in the *New York Times:* "Sturges throws a Kolinsky coat around Cinderella and lets slapstick take its course. It's a fairly exhausting course, too, with more involvements than we care to mention, with its cast frequently overwhelmed by its Sennett touches."[2] *Variety* focused on the studio rather than Sturges, identifying Paramount as the home of "slapstick farce" since its success with *My Man Godfrey* (1936) and suggesting that *Easy Living* was but a poor imitation of that popular comedy. The reviewer went on to say, "Disconcerting is the fact that the studio spared neither expense nor talent, in its efforts to make something good out of something that was second-rate when it started."[3]

But the film has grown in stature over the years. Pauline Kael, for instance, represents the view of many today when she calls *Easy Living* "one of the most pleasurable of the romantic slapstick comedies of the 30's and full of surprises."[4] Indeed, there is much to praise in the production and acting, including the incredible sets, which almost steal the film. Yet it is in the script reprinted here that we see the spark that ignited the project.

Synopsis

From a story by Vera Caspary, dated April 10, 1937.
    Note that this script is written in the format that has been the "standard" since roughly the end of the 1940s.

Sequence A (32 pages)

New York banker J. B. Ball (with J. B., of course, sounding a lot like J. P. . . . Morgan!) is at breakfast approving household bills to be paid. Thus a major double theme for the film is established: money and food. A black cat had earlier crossed his path in the upstairs hallway on the way to the dining room. His son Johnny is at the table, and a strong argument between them follows, which leads J.B. to shout, "Until I was twenty-six I was as dumb as you are." The son storms out of the paternal home to make his own way in the world. J.B. now goes on the warpath when he sees his wife, Jenny, has bought yet another sable coat. This new quarrel and chase lead them to the roof of their New York residence, where J.B. tosses the coat off the balcony in his anger.

Cut to Mary Smith riding an open-roofed double-decker bus when the sable coat lands on her head. The famous two-liner follows as she calls out, "Hey, what's the big idea?" "Kismet," replies the turbaned Hindu seated behind her.

The sequence builds as Mary gets off the bus and goes door to door trying to return the coat. She meets J.B., who gives her a ride, supposedly to return the coat, and they become involved in a funny discussion of compound interest. She complains that the falling coat damaged her hat, so J.B. orders his car to a fancy hat shop where she is invited to choose a hat to match the coat, the gift of which she accepts because she does not recognize its value. Afterward she says goodbye and realizes she doesn't even know her benefactor's name.

We now see Mary going to work at the magazine office of *The Boys' Constant Companion,* which is staffed by old ladies. She is fired for being late—and wearing a sable coat to boot (think of the gossip!)—and for lying, since her story sounds so invented. Mary's response is to lay waste to the office, including a portrait on the wall of "The Typical American Boy," which she busts over the manager's head.

Sequence B (7 pages)

Ball is in his office. Louis Louis, "a small foreigner," is fighting for a few more days in which to pay the note on the Hotel Louis. J.B. gives him a week,

Mary Smith (Jean Arthur) bends the ear of J. B. Ball (Edward Arnold), the "Bull of Broad Street," in *Easy Living.* Courtesy The Academy of Motion Picture Arts and Sciences.

after which he will close the hotel. Meanwhile, the clerk from the hat shop, misinterpreting the purchase, confides to Louis that he has the dope on the "Bull of Broad Street." Ball, the clerk suggests, has acquired a young female companion for his declining years: Mary Smith.

Sequence C (31 pages)

Johnny is on the street reading the want ads. And so is Mary, who bumps into him—literally. Cut to Mary arriving at her apartment only to find that she owes her week's rent, seven dollars that she doesn't have. Then she receives a telegram from the Hotel Louis. She goes to the hotel and is met by Louis, who says, "You look exactly like I t'ought . . . only a hundred percent better." There is total misunderstanding on both sides as he leads her to a suite he insists she should live in. This is the longest scene in the script as Louis Louis, described as looking like "Mickey Mouse," shows off each room. Finally Mary is alone in the enormous suite.

Cut to Mary at an automat, where Johnny has found work as the busboy. As he cheerfully plays the "where have I seen you before?" game with her it be-

A suddenly wealthy Mary Smith (Jean Arthur) romantically eyes a suddenly impover-
ished Johnny Ball (Ray Milland) in a New York automat in *Easy Living.* Courtesy The
Academy of Motion Picture Arts and Sciences.

comes clear that she has no money and is very hungry. He suggests he can open
a few of the automat windows and shove her food, and she replies, "Don't go
around putting ideas in people's mouths."

What follows is the beginning of romance and the full flowering of slapstick
farce as all the automat doors fly open and a comic Mardi Gras erupts aimed at
free food. This is definitely capitalism turned upside down, with street bums
rushing in for a free meal along with the regular businessmen. Johnny finds himself in trouble with the house detective, and after a fight in which he is fired he
rescues Mary from the chaos.

On the street Johnny and Mary walk and talk. She is impressed that he lost his
job over her and decides to take him up to her, as she puts it, "Lark in the Park."
In the meantime her luggage, including her grandmother's trunk, has arrived.

Sequence D (19 pages)

J.B. is angry because he has learned his wife has left for Florida. With his
wife and son both gone, he decides to move into the Hotel Louis for a spell, un-
aware that Louis Louis has installed Mary in the Imperial Suite.

Cut to Mary's suite, where she and Johnny are trying to figure out how to use the huge "shell" bathtub. Of course the water starts shooting at them from all angles, bringing them together in a festive baptism.

J.B. arrives at the hotel, calling Louis Louis "You greasy little hamburger." Meanwhile Johnny and Mary talk; still neither realizes who the other is.

Sequence E (16 pages)

Montage of gossip as newspapers hint that, with Mary and J.B. both staying at the Hotel Louis, something juicy must be afoot. Suddenly the hotel is *the* place to be. Louis says, "De beauty of success is you don't got to be polite."

Meanwhile every merchant in town is calling to offer Mary gifts, including a Saxon car with two chauffeurs. Even maharajas are moving into the hotel. In the midst of all of this, Johnny is looking for a job with the frustrated line, "There must be *something* for somebody who can't do anything," and Mary draws closer to him in a charming attempt to comfort him.

At this point a Mr. E. J. Hulgar arrives from his stock company to sound Mary out on the direction of the stock market: up or down. She, of course, is clueless, but Hulgar thinks he is getting valuable inside information from J. B. Ball himself. Mary consults with Johnny, who knows no more than she, and then, with confidence, tells Hulgar that the market is going down. Hulgar leaves on the double.

Sequence F (11 pages)

We open with a cross-cut between the rival offices of J.B. and Hulgar, where brokers are trying frantically to understand why the stock market has gone crazy since Hulgar acted on Mary's advice. As J.B. says to his partners, "What does it mean, gentlemen, when steel scrap is scarcer than hens' teeth?"

J.B. now dictates a letter, the ticker tape humming in the background in counterpoint. Comic confusion breaks out as J.B. tries to finish the letter while dealing with a number of phone calls to investors everywhere.

Cut to Mary in her suite, completely bewildered by all the gifts that have poured in from everywhere. Hulgar calls to get more advice, explaining that she has just won $18,000 for her help. Mary hangs up and hugs Johnny.

Meanwhile, the stock market is fluctuating wildly, and J.B. is caught in the middle of it all. He soon learns that his wife wants a divorce and that his company has just about gone bankrupt. In short, total disaster!

Sequence G (4 pages)

(Missing from the script are shots G-1 through G-8, which set up Hulgar arriving to ask more market advice from Mary.)

With a mouth full of food, Johnny is juggling phone calls in the Imperial Suite when Mary asks him if steel stocks will go up or down. He says up but, when questioned further, votes for down. When she asks how he knows which answer to give, he announces that his father is J. B. Ball, the "Bull of Broad Street." Mary is still clueless, though, since she has never heard Ball's name before.

Mary wants some reassurance that the market is not just unfathomably chaotic, and Johnny gravely offers the following logic: "The market follows the weather like a dog follows a cat . . . I've made a deep study of it." Mary then rushes to tell Hulgar that steel is going down.

Sequence H (10 pages)

We cut to J.B. in his office, seeing a man who is a thorough professional and expert on the market—which, unbeknownst to him, has just become even more irrational than usual. All of J.B.'s "reasoning," however, is sound.

J.B.

(Yelling)

> What do you mean, "down"? . . . I tell you steel is going up . . . it has to. Bank clearings are up sixteen decimal one per cent . . . the railroads have got to buy new equipment (unless they're going to make the passengers walk.) Timken is on three shifts . . . Ohio Wire and Steel . . .

With a cross-cut, we see Hulgar about to make a killing by investing in the stock going down.

Back in J.B.'s office, chaos rules. His partners begin arriving (including one directly from the barbershop with the apron still around him), the ticker tape is spurting out a mile a minute, and in the midst of it all J.B. tries to dictate a letter to Mary about the interest-yield math problem with which they began their encounter originally.

We now have three-way cross-cutting as we switch rapidly between Hulgar, J.B., and Mary in her suite receiving lavish gifts from a jeweler. Johnny is still reading the want ads; he is attracted to one in particular: "Learn dentistry at home—practice on your friends."

Mary, in "kind of a daze," invites Johnny to come with her to buy a dog. She then explains that they have just made $18,000 and throws her arms around his neck.

Meanwhile, at the Stock Exchange, "pandemonium seems to be loose."

As the sequence ends, it appears J.B. and partners are in bankruptcy. Mary's comic anarchy has reached its zenith.

(There is no Sequence I. Several of Sturges's scripts in fact end with *H*, but where they continue on, *I* is often not used, probably because of the potential for confusion with the number one.)

Sequence J (28 pages)

This is the concluding act. It starts with Johnny and Mary coming out of a pet shop with an "enormous English sheepdog," a goldfish, and a parrot. They encounter a newspaper boy hawking papers that proclaim a stock market crash. Johnny alludes to the crash of '29, then stops in horror when he reads that the Ball Company is "tottering."

Johnny takes off to find out what has happened. Cut to Ball's office, where his partners are panicking. Now Mrs. Ball returns claiming she will forgive J.B. all his sins, including the rumors about the girl in the Hotel Louis. J.B. has no time to sort this out, for his son arrives too. Thus the family reunites as all comes crashing down around them. When Johnny reveals that he has been staying at the Hotel Louis, his parents stare at him as if *he* were the object of all the rumors.

Back at the hotel, Mary and Louis Louis are trying to figure things out. She winds up giving Louis a double slap for the implications he makes about her behavior. In what is perhaps the longest "slow burn" in the movies, Mary begins to understand what has happened since the coat fell on her.

Mary looks down at the fur and up at Louis.

MARY

(Frightened)

But if this is, is . . . sable, why then he must have . . . made a mistake. You wouldn't give a coat like this to a stranger, would you?

Louis is in for an education, too, for he gave Mary the Imperial Suite for seven dollars a week, thinking she was J.B.'s female "friend."

J.B., having heard Johnny's story, now calls Louis Louis, who tries to explain to J.B. that Mary is "a phoney from Phoneyville." Louis Louis does a double take when J.B. wants to see her.

Meanwhile, Mary has shown up at J.B.'s outer office in an attempt to return the coat now that she knows its value. Mary, still having no grasp of the workings of the stock market, promises J.B. she can make it rise again. It's just a matter of a call to Hulgar.

Now, fortunes are reversed. Mary discovers that Johnny is J.B.'s son, but he understands that she didn't know this before. Mary also smooths things over with Mrs. Ball. She returns the coat to Mrs. Ball, saying, "I wish you'd explain to your son I don't accept sables from gentlemen."

Mary is free again, walking out onto the street. Except that Ball has sent the police to find her. This leads to the final scene where she is brought together with everyone, including Louis Louis, J.B., and Johnny. All misunderstandings clear up as the stocks rise, Johnny calls out to sell more, and we understand that father has accepted son. The final fade comes as Mary "smiles into Johnny's eyes."

Turning Adaptation Inside Out

In the Introduction we saw how Sturges reversed the character, and thus the plot and implications, of the original story written by Vera Caspary. Sturges is quite blunt: "Miss Caspary's little story of deceit and disillusion was set aside, but the title was a good one."[5] Out of a serious tale in which a young woman steals a fur coat, Sturges created a much lighter story about an innocent who has not a clue that the coat that falls upon her is indeed a valuable fur. The two treatments do have one thing in common: in both, "the girl's life changed completely."[6]

There are other innovations as well. Sturges's Johnny starts out wanting nothing to do with his father's money. By script's end, however, he has transformed, discovering that he is quite good at playing the market, which wins him Mary's love. Both Mary and Johnny now have everything—a fairy tale indeed.

Caspary's original story is much darker. Here Mary Winslow falls for Vic, a poor junior executive struggling to make it. In the end, after Mary has stolen the coat, been exposed, and been forced to give up the coat, she realizes it is better to be with the man she loves, no matter how poor, than to live the lies she had been living—a message quite different from Sturges's celebration of capital leading to love. Caspary also peppers her story, which she states "may be played in two ways: as ironic comedy or ironic tragedy," with such moralisms as "Easy living is often uneasily maintained."[7]

Sturges, however, was not interested in delivering such high-toned morals; rather, his aim was to create a joyful free-for-all romp of a satirical comedy that never breaks its witty slapstick-filled pace and mood.

Romantic Comedy Meets a Wall Street Satire: "Any Time Was a Good Time for Comedies"

In many ways *Easy Living* is the comic-satiric version of *The Power and the Glory,* with its strong dose of romantic screwball comedy. Again we witness Sturges's delight in keeping his comedy going at a nutty, frantic pace and maintaining a light, bright tone without any of the troubling implications conjured up in *The Power and the Glory,* where both American capitalism and romance end badly.

On the satirical level, *Easy Living* perhaps surpasses any of Sturges's other scripts in its nutty treatment of American capital, as when the clueless Mary Smith confronts Mr. Hulgar two-thirds of the way through this farce. Sturges's portrayal of the role of chance in the market, which had such a somber effect in *The Power and the Glory,* becomes purely ridiculous here as Hulgar assumes that Mary is the mistress of the Bull of Broad Street and that she thus has the latest hot tips.

One can hardly imagine a conversation more at cross-purposes than this segment of Mary and Hulgar's exchange:

HULGAR

(Staccato)

I want to make you some money. The best way is in steel. Is it going up or is it going down . . . that's all we have to know. I'd like to make you a <u>lot</u> of money.

MARY

(Amiably and vaguely)

Well, that's certainly very nice of you. Go ahead.

HULGAR

Go ahead and what?

MARY

Go ahead and . . . what ever it is.

HULGAR

(Frowning slightly)

It's the "whatever it is" I came to see you about. Shall I buy or shall I sell?

MARY

Why don't you just use your own judgment?

HULGAR

(Quickly)

That's the last thing in the world I want to use.

It's a wonderfully loopy scene, especially charged as it is with comic sexual tension. And it is the kind of moment, like so many of Sturges's best, that got recirculated in later films in slightly differing forms. Certainly the scene in which Gerrie and the Weenie King discuss money and beauty in *The Palm Beach Story* comes immediately to mind.

But Sturges does not leave his satire there. He pushes it to yet another level as he has Mary turn to Johnny and discover that he thinks the market will do poorly because of poor weather!

Easy Living is also a fairy-tale romantic comedy. Mary Smith is the simple, innocent gal who winds up with the disenchanted son, Johnny. Sturges's delightful ability to catch a budding romance in just a few lines and gestures is clear in Sequence E, even in the midst of all the Wall Street confusion. Johnny, the real rich boy, is reading the want ads in Mary's dreamland hotel suite, which is full of gifts. He has about given up the whole battle and has just uttered his great line, "There must be *something* for somebody who can't do anything." The scene goes like this:

JOHNNY

I guess I'm pretty dumb at that.

149

MARY

(Taking his hand impulsively)

Of course you're not, Johnny . . . you're just a little under-
developed . . . I mean, it's only temporary.
(She adds this last hastily and smiles apologetically)
I mean, some people develop sooner than others, but once the
others develop, they're just as well developed as the first ones,
don't you see? It's like you take a chicken. Now a chicken reaches
maturity at . . . at, well whatever it is, but on the other hand a
horse . . . takes much longer.

JOHNNY

(Nicely)

You feel I am of the horse type.

MARY

I think I'm kind of dumb myself.

JOHNNY

But very sweet.

He holds her hand tightly.

MARY

Am I?
(She smiles at him and seems to come a little closer)

Sturges does not press his luck by turning these moments into long kisses or
emotional outpourings. Rather, he keeps the fairy-tale quality of the whole story
intact, and that goes for the romance as well.

The film follows the script surprisingly closely, giving us a parody of a happy
ending as Mary gets Johnny and a new wealthy life of . . . easy living. Sturges's
swift comic reversals of fortune in this tale, of course, completely undermine
any "realism" or seriousness the film might have had. We don't believe the ending, but we *enjoy* it nevertheless. This is Sturges's talent, in part: to create in us,
the audience, a double response of critical, satirical laughter and pure pleasure
in the "sending up" of romantic endings.

Some changes occur in the actual film, but in almost every case they turn out
simply to amplify the comedy already established in this revised final script.
For example, the script ends with it being implied, but not stated, that Johnny
and Mary are now together and that Johnny will wind up helping Dad increase
his fortune. The film pushes this wedding of capital and romance even further
into the realm of fantasy. We see J.B. standing on the balcony with Mrs. Ball.
As the rising stock market figures are called out, J.B. shouts down for Johnny
to come work for him. At this point Johnny grabs Mary and tells her she has a
job too—"Cooking my breakfast!" This is long before women's lib, of course,
and Mary seems thrilled with this prospect. We cut to Mrs. Ball looking very

pleased with J.B. But then he spies the same coat that caused all the problems in the first place. He grabs it and heaves it once more over the balcony, and it lands, yes, on yet another unsuspecting female.

Again we come full circle. When Mary sees the upset girl looking around, she grabs her man's arm and leads him off, saying, "Johnny, this is where we came in!" Although this is even richer than the script, the point is, the script is so full of comedy that we can see how easily this final ending grew out of the written blueprint. No one, after all, set Sturges's script aside, as he did Vera Caspary's original tale.

NOTES

1. *Preston Sturges by Preston Sturges,* adapted and edited by Sandy Sturges (New York: Simon & Schuster, 1990), 283.

2. Frank S. Nugent, *"Easy Living," New York Times,* July 8, 1937, 20.

3. *"Easy Living," Variety,* July 2, 1937, 46.

4. Pauline Kael, *"Easy Living* Reviews," *Microsoft Cinemania 97* (CD-ROM), Microsoft Corporation, 1996.

5. *Preston Sturges,* 283.

6. Vera Caspary, "Easy Living: An Original Screen Story," May 1, 1935, UCLA Special Film Collection, 34.

7. Ibid., 34–35.

CREDITS

Easy Living

Released July 7, 1937

Producer:	Arthur Hornblow Jr.
Director:	Mitchell Leisen
Screenwriter:	Preston Sturges
Story by:	Vera Caspary
Cinematographer:	Ted Tetzlaff
Editor:	Doane Harrison
Music by:	Boris Morros
Art design by:	Hans Dreier and Ernst Fegte
Set designer:	A. E. Freudeman

CAST

Mary Smith	Jean Arthur
J. B. Ball	Edward Arnold
Johnny Ball	Ray Milland
Mr. Louis Louis	Luis Alberni
Mrs. Ball	Mary Nash
Van Buren	Franklin Pangborn
Mr. Gurney	Barlowe Borland
Wallace Whistling	William Demarest
E. F. Hulgar	Andrew Tombes

A Paramount release. 86 minutes.
Black and white.

Prod. 1138

EASY LIVING

FINAL REVISED SCRIPT

April 10, 1937

<u>SEQUENCE "A"</u>

AFTER THE MAIN TITLES:
FADE IN:

A-1   ANGLE SHOT - DOWN ON J.B.'S VALET AND LEGS

The valet picks lint off the striped trousers. A
spattered foot taps angrily. THE CAMERA ANGLES UP and
we see J.B. from the rear. He is scowling at a newspaper.

A-2   INSERT: CARTOON IN NEWSPAPER

This is a caricature of J.B. as a bull in a frock coat,
waving a silk hat in greeting. The caption is: "The
Bull Returns from Abroad."

A-3   FULL SHOT - ON J.B.

> J.B.
> (Snorting)
> Wise guy!

> VALET
> (Finishing)
> Yes, sir...thank you, sir...good
> morning, sir.

J.B. throws the newspaper aside and walks out of the
SHOT.

> J.B.
> Same to you.

A-4   TWO MEN SERVANTS - <u>IN THE HALLWAY</u>

One is exercising a vacuum cleaner, the other washing
a wall.

> THE SERVANTS
> Good morning, sir.

> J.B.
> (Appearing in the
> picture)
> Morning.

He starts by, pauses and points to a discoloration,
then continues. The servant looks at it near-sightedly
and nods his head.

A-5   THE HALLWAY - TWO MAID SERVANTS

They are washing windows at the stair-head.

                        THE MAID SERVANTS
                   Good morning, sir.

                        J.B.
                   (Appearing)
                   Morning, morning.

He nearly stumbles as a black cat crosses his path.

                        J.B.
                   (Pointing)
                   Shouldn't let cats in here s'bad
                   luck.

He looks back at the cat and misses the top step.
The maid servants scream as he slips.

A-6   SHOT OF THE STAIRS AND J.B. HURTLING PAST

A-7   LOW CAMERA SHOT UP AT THREE SERVANTS

They react violently to the bumps we hear.

A-8   SHOT FROM BEHIND THE STAIRS

We hear a series of bumps and J.B.'s feet shoot into
view. Immediately his son, Johnny, appears, looks
slightly surprised, and says:

                        JOHNNY
                   Good morning, father, could I
                   see you for a moment?

A-9   CLOSE SHOT - J.B. SITTING AT THE FOOT OF THE STAIRS

                        J.B.
                   (Furiously)
                   Well, I'm not hiding behind
                   anything, am I?

        DISSOLVE TO:

A-10   A PILE OF BILLS

A hand takes the top one off and passes it out of
the picture at the rate of one a second.

4-9-37   (Continued)

A-10
                    J.B.'S VOICE
          What was the matter with the old
          garbage can?

                    BUTLER'S VOICE
                (Nearer the microphone)
          Somebody stole it, Mr. Ball.

A-11   J.B., JOHNNY, AND BUTLER <u>AT BREAKFAST TABLE</u>

        J.B. continues to sip coffee and okay bills through
        scene.

                    J.B.
          Nothing is safe.
                (To Johnny)
          I thought I just bought you a car
          a couple of months ago.

                    JOHNNY
                (Uneasily)
          I turned it in as a down payment
          on the Lugatti....and they're get-
          ting a little restless.

                    J.B.
          Tell the chef the world is not
          made of butter.
                (To his son savagely)
          You turned in a free and clear
          paid-up American car on a foreign
          jalloppe?
                (To the secretary)
          You tell him to try lard.

                    BUTLER
                (Worried)
          Well now, Mr. Ball, the chef says
          that...

                    J.B.
          Tell him you can fry a very nice
          egg in lard.
                (He takes another bill)
          Tell him I said so.

                    BUTLER
          Very good, Mister Ball.

4-9-37   (Continued)

A-11   JOHNNY
                          (Rising to his feet)
                    I think you're being slightly
                    offensive, father.

                              J.B.
                          (Rising to his feet)
                    You call that "slightly offensive,
                    father," do you?
                          (Grabbing Johnny by
                           the lapel)
                    If any man called me a loafer and a
                    parlor snake I'd knock his block off
                    if it was my own grandfather.

                          JOHNNY
                          (Right in his
                           father's teeth)
                    We don't do that to our grand-
                    fathers these days.

                              J.B.
                    What your grandfather would have
                    done to you is nobody's business.
                          (He narrows his eyes)
                    I remember one time I was about your
                    age and I'd been out all night play-
                    ing...
                          (He clears his throat
                           hastily, glares at
                           his son)
                    I'll put a thousand in your account.
                          (To Butler)
                    ...and tell that chef...

                          JOHNNY
                          (In a small voice)
                    Don't bother.

                              J.B.
                          (Turning)
                    Hunh?

                          JOHNNY
                          (Stonily)
                    I said, "Don't bother." I am very
                    grateful for the room and board,
                    but not at these prices...
                          (He rises stiffly)
                    ...the cooking isn't good enough.

4-9-37   (Continued)

                            J.B.
                     (To his son)
I've told you nine thousand times
DON'T BUY ON TIME PAYMENTS...I
should think a cat would understand
that.

                         BUTLER
He certainly should.

                            J.B.
                     (To his son)
I'll show you why - how much was
the car?

                        JOHNNY
                     (Uneasily)
Well, uh...eleven thousand dollars.

                            J.B.
                     (Rigidly)
Eleven thousand dollars!

                        JOHNNY
Of course that includes the re-
painting, and...and making it just
like new...

                            J.B.
                     (Hypnotized)
Making it just like new!

                        JOHNNY
                     (Hastily)
Well, you see, father, the new ones
are very hard to...

                            J.B.
                     (Exploding)
Eleven thousand dollars for a second-
hand Spiggoty!

                        JOHNNY
                     (Beginning to get
                      angry)
Now wait a minute!

                            J.B.
                     (Yelling)
I've waited for twenty years...to
find out I'm the father of a butter-
fly! A big mutton-head!

A-11   J.B.
                         (Stunned)
                  The cooking isn't good enough!
                         (He turns to Butler)
                  You tell that chef...

                              JOHNNY
                  And I'll tell you something else
                  that isn't good enough - it's be-
                  ing a banker's son; everybody
                  thinking you're a fool who couldn't
                  earn a nickel on his own. A nincom-
                  poop living on his father's charity.
                  A...a...

                              J.B.
                  Oh, pooh! I was a banker's son,
                  and until I was twenty-six I was
                  as dumb as you are.
                         (Reminiscently)
                  ...till one day the fat all fell off
                  my brains, and from then on...how
                  old are you?

                              JOHNNY
                         (Coldly)
                  Old enough to earn a good living
                  without any help from you...or your
                  sneering friends.
                         (He throws his check-
                           book on the table)
                  I'm going to make you eat your words.

                              J.B.
                         (Without much force)
                  That's all you'll be eating.

                              JOHNNY
                  Possibly.

                              J.B.
                  Probably.

                              JOHNNY
                  Right!
                         (He turns on his heel
                           and starts around the
                           table)

                              J.B.
                  Right.
                         (After a moment he holds
                           up the checkbook)
                  Hadn't you better take this along
                  just in...?
4-9-37   (Continued)

A-11   His head follows Johnny around, and we hear a door
        slam to which J.B. reacts. Now he looks at his
        Butler for sympathy, then wets his pencil and picks
        up the last bill. His eyes nearly pop out of his head.

                          J.B.
                    What's this?

                          BUTLER
                    Madam asked me to give it to you, sir.

        J.B. crashes his fist down on the breakfast table and
        upsets the coffee pot. Bill in hand he rises to his
        feet.

A-12   MRS. BALL AT DRESSING TABLE - NEGLIGEE

        We see her in the mirror rouging her lips. The lip-
        stick skids across her face at a loud bang.

A-13   FULL SHOT - MRS. BALL'S BATHROOM

        A mirror in the background moves and J.B. hurries in
        and bumps his face into a mirror. He looks around,
        holds out a protecting hand, and hurries toward his
        wife.

                          J.B.
                        (Yelling)
                    What do you mean by buying
                    another sable cloak?

A-14   TWO SHOT - J.B. AND MRS. BALL

                          MRS. BALL
                    Well, I have to keep warm, don't I?
                    Or do you expect me to put news-
                    papers between my...

                          J.B.
                        (Shouting this down)
                    Warm? You ought to be sizzling.
                        (He shakes the bill
                        under her nose)
                    Have you any idea how many dollars
                    fifty-eight thousand dollars is?

                          MRS. BALL
                    Are.

4-9-37   (Continued)

162

A-14   J.B.
                    Very funny...very funny, but I'll
                    tell you something that isn't so
                    funny - we're so close to being
                    broke I can feel the wolf snapping
                    at my pants...and they're <u>last year's</u>
                    <u>pants!</u> Here I am practicing every
                    economy, I have just come back in a
                    miserable little cabin you could
                    hardly swing a cat in, and I find you...

                          MRS. BALL
                    You get seasick in big cabins.

                          J.B.
                    Don't cloud the issue. Why did you
                    buy another sable cloak?

                          MRS. BALL
                        (A little nervously)
                    Well, I...I...you want me to look
                    well, don't you? After all, the
                    wife of the fourth biggest banker
                    in the...

                          J.B.
                    Third biggest...What's the matter
                    with the fur coats you've got?

                          MRS. BALL
                        (Quite nervous now)
                    I haven't any to speak of, and
                    they're out of style.

                          J.B.
                        (Restraining himself)
                    How can <u>fur</u> be out of <u>style</u>?
                    A 'possum is the same today as it
                    was in nineteen six.

                          MRS. BALL
                        (Desperately)
                    The <u>cut</u> is different.

                          J.B.
                        (Exasperated)
                    All right, give a couple of them a
                    <u>haircut</u>...and you can take this one
                    back at the same time.

A-15   CLOSE SHOT - MRS. BALL

                          MRS. BALL
                    I'd rather <u>die</u> than humiliate
                    myself in front of Mr. Zickle.
4-9-37

                              163

A-16   J.B. - PAST MRS. BALL

                         J.B.
              Then I'll humiliate myself.
              Where is it?

                    MRS. BALL
                       (Defiantly)
              I won't tell you.

                         J.B.
              You're being a little childish,
              Jenny. All I have to do is...

He turns and slides the door of a clothes closet full
of fur coats.

                         J.B.
              Holy smoke!

A-17   J.B. AND MRS. BALL IN PROFILE IN FRONT OF CLOSET

                         J.B.
              You'd better give it to me before
              I lose my temper. Is this it?
                       (He points to a coat
                        of white fur)

                    MRS. BALL
              Yes.

                         J.B.
              In a pig's nose it is.

He reaches for another coat, and as he does so he
turns and watches his wife. She continues to look at
the coats nervously.

                         J.B.
              I'll bet this is it.

                    MRS. BALL
              That's right.

                         J.B.
              Unhunh. I suppose these are sable
              too.

As his hand reaches the middle of the rack, Mrs. Ball
gets more and more nervous.

4-9-37   (Continued)

164

A-17   MRS. BALL
                         (Laughing nervously)
                    As far as you're concerned they are.

                              J.B.
                         (Barking suddenly)
                    How about this one?

                              MRS. BALL
                    That's K-Kolinsky.

Suddenly she looks at him suspiciously, but he drops
his hands to his sides and speaks "hamily".

                              J.B.
                    I guess you got me, Jenny.

                              MRS. BALL
                         (With satisfaction)
                    You're not as smart as people think.

                              J.B.
                         (With heavy melancholy)
                    That's right, that's right. I'll
                    just take this Kolinsky...
                         (He reaches up and
                          grabs it)
                    ...as a sort of consola...

Mrs. Ball snatches the coat away from him like a
tigress.

                              MRS. BALL
                    You give me that coat.

She runs out of the bathroom and slams the door after
her. J.B. follows.

A-18   MRS. BALL IN HER BEDROOM

She braces herself against the bathroom door and
feels for a key. The coat gets in her way.

                              J.B.'S VOICE
                    Open that door.

                              MRS. BALL
                         (Breathing hard)
                    You'll play tricks on me, will you?...

The door bangs open an inch, but Mrs. Ball bounces it
shut. Suddenly she looks off RIGHT then runs on tip-
toe out of the room.

4-9-37

A-19   J.B. - IN THE BATHROOM

He glares at the door, then steps back and hunches
his shoulder.

                    J.B.
                 (Breathlessly)
            This is getting a little -
                 (Puff, puff)
            ...ridiculous.

He grits his teeth and hurls himself against the free
door. As he flies through it -

A-20   MRS. BALL'S BEDROOM

J.B. bursts into the room headlong, knocks over a
breakfast tray on a stand and catapults onto the bed.
His collar comes undone as he scrambles to his feet.

A-21   A DOORWAY IN THE HALL

Mrs. Ball bursts out of this at full gallop, slamming
the door behind her. Suddenly she stops dead, coat
in arms.

A-22   SERVANTS IN HALLWAY

In the foreground of a very long hall we see a house-
man washing the walls. Near him another man is polishing a doorknob. At the other end of the hall a
maid is promenading a Bissell. The two men look back
at us in astonishment.

                 THE HOUSEMAN
            Good morning, madam.

A-23   MRS. BALL IN FRONT OF DOORWAY

                 MRS. BALL
            Good morning, Joseph.

She steals a look over her shoulder then walks primly
past the CAMERA. As she leaves the picture, the door
flies open and J.B. leaps into the picture, collar
undone and necktie flying. He skids to a stop and
scowls past the CAMERA.

4-9-37

A-24   THE SERVANTS IN THE HALLWAY

They are looking more astonished than ever.

                    THE HOUSEMAN
              Good morning, sir.

J.B. enters the picture at a brisk walk.

                    J.B.
              Good morning, Jasper...Justin...
              whatever it is.

A-25   TRUCKING SHOT...AHEAD OF THE BALLS

She clutches the coat to her bosom. J.B. is puffing
along fifteen feet behind and gaining visibly.

                    J.B.
                (With false sweetness)
              Could I speak with you a moment,
              my love?

                    MRS. BALL
                (Putting on a little speed)
              In a little while, my sweet.

The servants stare after them in astonishment, and
a maid comes into view.

                    MRS. BALL
              Good morning, Esther.

                    THE MAID
              Good morning, madam...good morning,
              sir.

                    J.B.
              Hey!

This last as Mrs. Ball darts out of the picture.
J.B. throws a look over his shoulder, then leaps
after her. The servants are agog.

A-26   FLASHES OF IRON STAIRS

First Mrs. Ball, then J.B., then Mrs. Ball. J.B.
slips.

4-9-37

A-27   <u>STAIRHEAD ON THE ROOF...PAST A LAUNDRESS</u>

There are sheets all over the place. Mrs. Ball hops
out of the stairhead and puts her finger to her lips.
She disappears between two rows of sheets. J.B.
appears blowing hard.

> J.B.
> Did Mrs. Ball come up here?

> THE LAUNDRESS
> (Very nervously)
> Why, uh, uh, no, sir.

> J.B.
> That's funny.
> (But suddenly he barks:)
> Are you sure she told you to
> say that?

> THE LAUNDRESS
> Yes, sir...I mean...

A-28   MEDIUM CLOSE...J.B.

> J.B.
> I know what you mean.

He looks around, and his eyes rivet on the lower
edge of a drying sheet. He tip-toes over to it and
lifts it up. His wife's feet run out of the picture.
As J.B. follows - we follow with some blind man's
buff and near accidents ending in:

A-29   <u>A CORNER OF THE ROOF</u> - TRANSPARENCY

We see the park in the distance. Mrs. Ball limps
into the picture and halts: the doe at bay. J.B.
crunches his way across the gravel and confronts
her. He pants.

> J.B.
> (Fixing his collar)
> All right...now that you've made
> a spectacle of us both..
> (He holds his hand out for the
> coat)

4-9-37   (Continued)

A-29
                    MRS. BALL
                 (Desperately)
            But I tell you, Mr. Zickle won't
            take it back...He told me so...
            it was specially grown in Russia.

                    J.B.
                 (Stonily)
            Hand it over.

                    MRS. BALL
            But you can't get your money
            back, Juney. You'll have to
            pay for it. There simply isn't
            a thing...

                    J.B.
            Give me that coat!

Mrs. Ball looks at it as if it were a sick child.
Suddenly she snuffles and passes it over.

                    MRS. BALL
            All right, now that you've got
            it, what are you going to do
            with it, eat it?

J.B. looks at it a moment, then stiffens.

                    J.B.
            I'll show you what I'll do
            with it.

He gives Mrs. Ball one more glare, then raises
the coat high over his head. Mrs. Ball screams.
J.B. hurls the coat over the parapet. Mrs. Ball
groans and leans out.

                    J.B.
            Remember that for the next
            time.

A-30   VIEW DOWN ON FIFTH AVENUE (UPPER SIXTIES)

The falling coat will probably not pick up, but
we see considerable traffic studded with busses.

4-9-37   (Continued)

A-31   TOP OF MOVING BUS..LOOKING FORWARD..MARY SMITH
        (TRANSPARENCY)

        On the rear seat sits a turbaned Hindu reading a
        book. In front of him sits Mary Smith, a pretty
        young woman, modestly dressed, her hat is jauntily
        topped by a long feather. Her face is serene; she
        enjoys the day. The seat ahead of her is empty, but
        the rest of the bus is well filled. The coat falls
        over Mary's head and she screams a muffled scream.
        The other passengers stare as she comes out from
        under the coat. Her feather is broken and hanging in
        front of her face. She turns around and glares
        indignantly at the Hindu.

                         MARY
                    What's the big idea?

A-32   CLOSE SHOT..HINDU - PAST MARY - (TRANSPARENCY)

        Startled, the Hindu looks up and points to his book.

                         HINDU
                    Kismet!

        He smiles a toothy smile and returns to his studies.
        Mary looks at him in puzzlement, then at the coat,
        then up at the buildings. Suddenly she reaches out
        and rings the buzzer. She rises and starts back.

A-33   THE BUS STAIRS - (TRANSPARENCY)

        Mary comes down them as the bus stops. She gets
        off and looks vaguely across the street. Her
        feather tickles her nose and she throws it up
        angrily.

A-34   J.B. AND BUTLER IN FRONT HALL

        J.B. comes down the last few stairs and hustles
        into his overcoat. He claps a derby on his head.
        The butler swings open a door and speaks cheerfully.

                         BUTLER
                    Pleasant day, sir.

                         J.B.
                    (Through clenched teeth)
                    You said it.

        He passes out the door.

4-9-37

A-35   AREAWAY IN FRONT OF J.B.'S HOUSE

J.B. appears in the doorway. Suddenly he turns his
head and gives a startled look to the right.

A-36   A FURIOUS CHEF APPROACHING...PAST J.B.

He jabs a double-fingered hand toward J.B. and speaks
belligerently.

>   CHEF
>   Listen to me, you.

>   J.B.
>   (Stupefied)
>   What!

A-37   MRS. BALL'S BEDROOM FROM OUTSIDE THE WINDOW

Mrs. Ball appears looking very angry. She sticks
her head out the window and looks straight down.
Now she hurries inside and appears a second later
with a large goldfish globe in her arms.

A-38   TWO SHOT. J.B. AND THE CHEF

>   CHEF
>   (Belligerently)
>   You tell me to fry in lard?

>   J.B.
>   What about it?

>   CHEF
>   You go fry yourself in lard,
>   you dirty capitalist.

He throws a wadded apron in J.B.'s face. We hear a
whistling sound, a tinkle of glass, and the chef is
soaking wet, with a fish doing flip-flops on the top
of his cap. J.B. opens his mouth wide and starts
bellowing with laughter.

DISSOLVE TO:

4-9-37

171

A-39   THE DOORWAY OF A FIFTH AVENUE RESIDENCE...(MARY AND
        A BUTLER)

        Mary comes into shot and rings doorbell.

A-40   J.B.'S LINCOLN AT CURB

        J.B. Still chuckling comes into shot. His chauffeur
        holds open the door as J.B. is about to get in. He
        sees something off.

A-41   MARY AT DOORWAY OF HOUSE NEXT DOOR

                            BUTLER
                 No, Miss. Not here.

                            MARY
                 Thanks.

        She looks at her watch and turns to next building.
        J.B. steps into the picture and touches her on
        the shoulder. As she looks at him startled,
        CUT TO:

A-42   TWO-SHOT..MARY AND J.B.

                            J.B.
                 Where'd you find it?

        Mary starts to offer him the coat then snatches
        it back.

                            MARY
                        (Suspiciously)
                 How do I know it's yours? Find
                 what?

                            J.B.
                        (Pointing to the coat)
                 See if it doesn't say "A.B.
                 Zickel & Co."

        Like a cautious player examining a poker hand, Mary
        looks inside the coat.

                            J.B.
                 You earn your own living?

4-9-37   (Continued)

A-42   MARY
                      (Relaxing and looking
                        up)
                 That's it all right...What?
                 Of course I do.
                      (Then scowling)
                 But I don't see that it's any
                 of your bus...Look what you
                 did to my hat!

                           J.B.
                      (Interrupting)
                 You got a fur coat?

                           MARY
                      (Displeased)
                 No I have not, but I still don't...

                           J.B.
                      (Staccato)
                 That's where you're wrong. You
                 got <u>that</u> one. Happy birthday.

He waves his hand and steps toward the curb just
as his car pulls up.

                           MARY
                      (Spacing the words)
                 Just a minute, Santy Claus!

                           J.B.
                      (Turning, startled)
                 Hunh?

                           MARY
                 What's the matter with it,
                 is it hot?

                           J.B.
                      (Innocently)
                 I don't know, I never wore one.

                           MARY
                 What kind of fur is it?

                           J.B.
                      (Getting a little tired of this)
                 Zebra. Anything else you'd like to know?

                           MARY
                      (Bridling)
                 Yes! I'd like to know where you get
                 off to...

4-9-37   (Continued)

                           173

                              J.B.
                    (Silencing her by the
                     quality of his voice)
                Let me give you a little piece of
                advice, young lady. Don't be too
                wise. Don't think you know all
                the answers. Sometimes nice things
                do happen to people...Very nice
                things! Remember that.

She looks away for a moment, then back at J.B.
She smiles charmingly.

                              MARY
                Well then, could you lend me
                ten cents?

                              J.B.
                    (Surprised)
                Uh...why certainly.

                              MARY
                    (Watching him in
                     growing surprise)
                This is pay-day and when I got off
                I forgot I didn't have another d...

She watches him a moment and he gives her an
embarrassed look.

                              MARY
                Of course, if you're short, it
                doesn't really ma....

                              J.B.
                    (Almost crossly)
                Don't be...
                    (Now he gets an idea)
                Oh, you mean to take the bus.
                    (Indicating his car)
                What's the matter with this bus?

Mary's suspicions are renewed.

                              J.B.
                    (Overpoweringly)
                Hop in! Hop in!

She hops in.

DISSOLVE TO:

A-43   INTERIOR LINCOLN..J.B. AND MARY (TRANSPARENCY)

                              J.B.
                The Boys' What?

                              MARY
                The Boys' Constant Companion.
                It's a magazine...for boys.
                              J.B.
4-9-37   I never heard of it.   (Continued)

                              174

>   MARY
>   (A little crossly)
>   It's got a million readers.

>   J.B.
>   (With satisfaction)
>   It hasn't got me.

He looks at her a moment, then lifts the speaking
tube.

>   J.B.
>   Stop at a hat shop.

>   MARY
>   (Nervously)
>   It's terribly sweet of you but I
>   really haven't the time and the
>   coat more than makes up for...for...

>   J.B.
>   (With inward amusement)
>   Listen: if I can keep waiting what's
>   waiting for me, the Boys's Constant
>   Reminder can wait a few minutes also.

>   MARY
>   Companion...Boys' Constant Companion.

>   J.B.
>   Companion.

>   MARY
>   (Brightly)
>   You know, I was going to buy a fur
>   coat...You can get them two dollars
>   a week and one percent on the balance.

>   J.B.
>   You mean one percent a month?

>   MARY
>   Yes. Isn't it wonderful how they
>   do it for so little?

>   J.B.
>   (Indignantly)
>   So little! That's twenty-five per-
>   cent a year.

A-43   MARY
                          (Smiling gently)
                    One percent a month is <u>twelve</u>
                    percent a year.

                               J.B.
                          (Smiling falsely)
                    Of course you don't know who I
                    am, but I'm very good at computing
                    interest.

                               MARY
                          (With a little less
                           warmth in her smile)
                    I'm sure you are, but having passed
                    through high school myself, I think
                    I can say that one percent a month
                    is...

                               J.B.
                          (Forcing a smile)
                    Just a moment: You owe a hundred
                    dollars which you are paying off at
                    two dollars a week or eight dollars
                    sixty-six and two-thirds cents a
                    month.

                               MARY
                          (Through pinched lips)
                    You mean eight dollars a month.

                    She forces a smile and explains.

                               MARY
                    There are four weeks in a month.

                               J.B.
                          (Ferociously)
                    There are four and one-<u>third</u> weeks
                    in a month, Madam. Otherwise there'd
                    be only forty-eight weeks in a year.

                               MARY
                    You mean Leap Year!

                               J.B.
                          (Yelling)
                    If I meant Leap Year I'd...look...
                    At the end of six months you've paid
                    off fifty-two dollars but you're still
                    paying...

                               MARY
                          (Brightly)
                    Twelve percent.

4-9-37   (Continued)

                         J.B.
                 (Without stopping)
         At the end of forty-nine weeks
         you've paid everything except
         two dollars so you're paying
         SIX HUNDRED PERCENT !

                         MARY
                 (Patiently)
         You don't seem to understand that
         twelve times one can't possibly be
         six hundred. Twelve times one is
         twelve. I don't want to be rude,
         but I should think even a small
         child...

                         J.B.
         Let's forget all about it.

                         MARY
         Right !

                         J.B.
         Right !

He gives her a quick look, being reminded of his son,
then starts in pantomime, to persuade an imaginary
opponent. Mary examines the fur. Suddenly both lift
their heads, look at each other simultaneously and
open their mouths to speak. They think better of it
and look away.

                         MARY
                 (After a moment)
         This isn't mink, is it?

                         J.B.
                 (Absorbed)
         Huh? I should say it isn't.

Now he looks up.

                         J.B.
         It's...it's...Levinsky.
                 (He starts figuring again)

                         MARY
                 (Awed)
         You mean Kolinsky?
                 (Gently)
         You shouldn't give away a real
         Kolinsky coat.

                              J.B.
                    Look....I'll put it another way:
                    A farmer borrowed one hundred cows...

        CUT TO:

A-44   SIDEWALK IN FRONT OF VAN BUREN'S SHOP

        J.B.'s car comes to a stop and J.B. and Mary, carrying
        the coat get out.
                              J.B.
                         (Triumphantly)
                    Now....how much did the farmer pay?

                              MARY
                         (Almost embarrassed)
                    Twelve cows.

        J.B. looks at the Doorman for sympathy, slaps his
        hand against his sides and follows Mary.

        DISSOLVE TO:

A-45   J.B., SALESWOMAN AND MARY IN A CONE-SHAPED HAT

        J.B. looks sourly at the hat.

                              MARY
                    Don't you like this one either?

                              J.B.
                    I do not. It looks like a salt
                    shaker.

A-46   MARY - SALESWOMAN AND MR. VAN BUREN - OVER J.B.

        This is the first we have seen of Mr. Van Buren who
        is prim and middle-aged.
                              VAN BUREN
                         (Vexed)
                    We consider it very rekerky!

                              J.B.
                         (Rising and look-
                          ing around)
                    That's the trouble with it.

        Suddenly he spies something.

        4-9-37   (Continued)

A-46   J.B.
            Here ! What's this?

He starts out of the picture.

                  VAN BUREN
                  (Chidingly)
            Ah, ah, ah ! We prefer to...
                  (Hurrying forward)
            ...handle them ourselves.

A-47   A SHOWCASE - J.B.

The showcase contains a magnificent cloth-of-gold hat
with a sable wrapped around it. J.B. leans into the
case and grabs it.

                  J.B.
                  (Looking around)
            Ah, ah, ah! yourself !

He straightens and turns.

A-48   J.B. - APPROACHING - OVER MARY

                  J.B.
                  (Handing her the hat)
            Try this.

As Mary puts it on, Van Buren hurries into the picture.

                  VAN BUREN
            That, of course, is genuine...

                  J.B.
                  (Mimicking his manner)
            Ah ah ah!
                  (To Mary)
            Try it with the coat.

He holds the coat for her and steps back.

A-49   MARY AND HER REFLECTION

She takes a step nearer the mirror and stops to gape
at such magnificence.

A-50   CLOSE SHOT - J.B.

He chuckles.
                  J.B.
            Now you're talking.

A-50   The CAMERA PANS onto the saleswoman whose eyes are
        bulging. The CAMERA CONTINUES on to Mr. Van Buren
        whose mouth is hanging open and from there to a
        CLOSE SHOT OF MARY. Her lips are trembling.

A-51   J.B. AND MARY AND VAN BUREN

        J.B. looks in pockets, then:

                        J.B.
                  (Taking out a card)
              I haven't got any money with me.

        He hands Van Buren the card.

                        J.B.
              Send me the bill.

                        VAN BUREN
                  (Slightly worried)
              Why uh...

        He does a double take at the card, then smiles a
        knowing and confidential smile of supreme delight.

                        MARY
              Could I have my old hat in a bag?

                        VAN BUREN
                  (Horrified)
              A bag? My dear! We'll send it to
              you in a Rolls Rerce!

        He takes out a pencil.

                        VAN BUREN
              And the name?

                        MARY
              Mary Smith...34 West 112th.

                        VAN BUREN
              ...a hundred and twelfth. A bag!

        He explodes in giggles.

                        J.B.
              Come on. I've got to get to work.
        He starts out.

4-9-37   (Continued)

A-51   MARY
                       (Coming to)
                  You and me both...Goodbye!.

           She follows J.B.

A-52   VAN BUREN AND SALESWOMAN

                           VAN BUREN
                       (Bowing low)
                  Goodbye, goodbye, goodbye!

                           SALESWOMAN
                       (After a moment)
                  Did you get that coat?

                           VAN BUREN
                       (Archly)
                  My dear...you don't seem to realize:
                  That was the BULL OF BROAD STREET!

           DISSOLVE TO:

A-53   INT. CAR - MARY - ON SIDEWALK

                           MARY
                       (Taking his hand)
                  Goodbye!

                           J.B.
                       (Gruffly)
                  Goodbye, goodbye! Keep the moths
                  out of Levinsky!

                           MARY
                       (Laughing)
                  I will...and I don't know how to
                  thank...
                       (The car pulls away)
                       (Suddenly)
                  You didn't tell me your name!

           She looks after it, blinks, looks down at the coat,
           then shrugs, turns, and hurries toward the door of
           the building behind her.

           DISSOLVE TO:

A-54   MAIN OFFICES - BOYS' CONSTANT COMPANION

           A door at the far end opens and Mary hurries in.

A-54   CLOSE TRUCKING SHOT - MARY

           The CAMERA PRECEDES her as she hurries along. The
           clerks and stenographers turn as she passes and absorb
           her coat with stupefied expressions.

4-9-37   (Continued)

A-56   CLOSE SHOT- HEAD STENOGRAPHER

She is a middle-aged, sour-faced lady. She looks up
vaguely, then at her wristwatch, then up at Mary.
Now, for the first time, she sees the coat. Her
mouth falls open.

A-57   TRUCKING SHOT - AHEAD OF MARY

She smiles nervously and reaches her desk. She hangs
the coat on a hanger, places the hat over it on the
tree, gives the coat a last loving pat, and sits at
her machine. There she puts on some paper cuffs,
puts a little oil on her machine, and runs the carriage back and forth a couple of times. Now she
rolls some paper into the machine and lifts her hands
to type. A shadow falls over her and she turns,
frightened. The head stenographer looks down at
her unsympathetically.

                    MISS SWERF
          The manager would like to
          see you, Miss Smith.

                    MARY
               (Looking up in dismay)
          Oh.
               (Slowly she starts to rise)

DISSOLVE TO:

A-58   MR. VAN BUREN - AT TELEPHONE

                    VAN BUREN
                 (Gloating)
          And who do you think was
          with her?

A-59   ANOTHER GENTLEMAN MILLINER

In his right hand he holds the telephone, in his
left a small flowered bonnet which he revolves and
considers. Suddenly he comes to life.

                    MILLINER
          NO!

A-60   MR. VAN BUREN - AT TELEPHONE

                    VAN BUREN
                 (Happily)
          But YES!
4-9-37   (Continued)

A-61   GENTLEMAN MILLINER

                    MILLINER
                (Intently)
            What's her name, Albert?

A-62   VAN BUREN - AT TELEPHONE

                    VAN BUREN
                (Looking around)
            If you'll SWEAR not to breathe
            a word of it to a soul, Osric,
            and let me copy that velvet
            pillbox with the cellophane
            snapdragon...

DISSOLVE TO:

A-63   THE MANAGER'S OFFICE OF THE BOYS' CONSTANT COMPANION

A chilly looking manager sits behind his desk. Mary,
worried, stands opposite. Miss Swerf looks out the
window and as if she smelt something unpleasant.

                    THE MANAGER
                (Reluctantly)
            Miss Smith - it appears, that you
            arrived late for work this morning
            in a garment we do not quite under-
            stand.

                    MARY
                (Relieved)
            Oh, you mean the fur coat!

                    THE MANAGER
            Precisely. You receive, I
            believe, twenty-two dollars a
            week, which is ample for your
            needs, but leaves us puzzled
            in the matter of fur coats.

                    MARY
                (Laughing)
            Oh! It hit me on the head on
            the 5th Avenue bus and then the
            old gentleman who dropped it told
            me to keep it and got me a hat to
            go with it because he broke the
            feather on my old one, that's all.

The manager and Miss Swerf exchange an amused glance.

4-9-37   (Continued)

THE MANAGER
        (Purringly)
And who was this philanthropist?

MARY
He didn't tell me his name.

THE MANAGER
        (Sadly)
Ah ha! And you ask us to
believe, Miss Smith, that a
complete stranger having dropped
a valuable mink coat...

MARY
        (Quickly)
It isn't mink! It's Kolinsky.

THE MANAGER
Mink OR Kolinsky, whatever that is...

MISS SWERF
It's mink.

MARY
        (Angrily)
It is not mink!

THE MANAGER
        (Raising a hand)
It doesn't really matter. The
thing that does matter is that
you wish us to believe...

MARY
        (Quickly)
It is a little unusual and I
suppose if somebody told me...

THE MANAGER
        (Interrupting)
It's most unusual. So unusual
in fact that....

MISS SWERF
This is a boys' magazine, you know.

MARY
        (Indignantly)
What about it?

4-9-37

(Continued)

A-63   THE MANAGER
                        The Boys' Constant Companion
                        regrets that it will no longer
                        require your...

                              MARY
                            (Desperately)
                        Wait a minute ! I didn't want
                        you to know I was so extravagant
                        and it was foolish of me to...to...
                        I guess I don't make up very good
                        stories...I bought it out of my
                        savings...but I thought that you'd
                        think...That's why I was late.

                              THE MANAGER
                            (Purringly)
                        And where did you buy it?

    Mary stiffens, tries to look at the label in the
    coat, then suddenly says:

                              MARY
                        Zickel's.

    She glares at the manager.

                              THE MANAGER
                        And how much did you pay for it?

    He reaches for the phone book and turns to the
    back of it.

                              MARY
                        I don't see why I should have to...

                              MISS SWERF
                            (Cutting in)
                        That coat cost four hundred
                        dollars if it cost a...

                              MARY
                        It did not ! It cost...a hun-
                        red and sixty-two... seventy-
                        nine.

                              THE MANAGER
                            (Reaching for the phone
                             book)
                        Now we're getting somewhere.

    He turns to the Z's.

4-9-37   (Continued)

A-63

                    MARY
               (Nervously)
          It may not have cost exactly a
          hundred and sixty-two seventy-nine...
          I never bought a fur coat before
          and naturally I was excited and...
          and....

     During this time the manager has been dialing a
     number.

                    THE MANAGER
               (Into phone)
          Did you sell a Kolinsky coat
          this morning for...

                    MARY
          Anybody's apt to make a mistake.
          There were all sorts of prices and...

                    THE MANAGER
               (Through Mary's speech)
          ...one hundred and sixty-two
          dollars and seventy-nine cents?
          ...YOU DID NOT!...NOTHING UNDER
          FIVE HUNDRED! Thank you very much
          indeed.
               (He hangs up the telephone)
          I believe that's all, Miss Smith.
          As I said before, the ethical
          requirements of the Boys' Constant
          Companion...

                    MARY
               (In tears)
          Well, it DID hit me on the head.

     She walks to the door and the CAMERA PANS with her.
     Now she turns and looks back angrily.

                    MARY
          And the old gentleman DID tell
          me to keep it and DIDN'T tell me
          his name and he DID get me a hat
          and you're just an evil-minded...

A-64   MISS SWERF AND THE MANAGER

     Miss Swerf laughs archly.

                    MISS SWERF
          Ha ha.

4-9-37

A-65   MARY - BY THE DOOR

Infuriated by the laugh and the injustice of the
situation, she picks up a vase full of flowers,
takes two steps and hurls it.

A-66   MISS SWERF AND THE MANAGER

The manager springs to his feet. Miss Swerf tries
to duck and falls backwards over a waste paper
basket. The flowers smash on the wall above her and
she is deluged with water. Mary hurries into the
SHOT, picks up a dictaphone and hits the manager over
the head with it. Now she rips the telephone off the
wall and, using it as a hammer, breaks the glass top
of the desk, smashes the electric clock, knocks the
lamp onto the floor and throws the inkwell at the
wall.

A-67   A PICTURE ON THE WALL

This represents the typical American Boy, smiling
happily. Mary hurries into the picture and unhooks
the typical American Boy.

A-68   THE MANAGER AND MISS SWERF HIDING BEHIND THE DESK

Mary steps into the SHOT, breaks the American Boy
over the manager's head, throws her paper cuffs at
Miss Swerf and hurries out.

A-69   THE OUTER OFFICE

To the astonishment of the other clerks, Mary runs
sobbing to her desk. The CAMERA PANS with her. She
grabs her fur coat and hat, snatches up her bag,
and runs out.

FADE OUT:

END OF SEQUENCE "A"

4-9-37

SEQUENCE "B"

FADE IN:

B-1 OUTER OFFICES - J.B. BALL & COMPANY

An elevator door opens and the lethargic staff galvan-
izes into action as J. B. appears and strides toward
us.

B-2 TRUCKING SHOT AHEAD OF J.B.

He pauses momentarily, turns a hastily opened ledger
around so that the columns read the right way, gives
the clerk a quick look and passes on. He yells out of
the picture:

      J.B.
    Get me Mrs. Ball...Good
    morning!

He reaches his desk, and an old colored porter who
takes his hat and overcoat and pins a carnation in
his buttonhole. His secretary, Lillian, enters.

      LILLIAN
    Mrs. Ball has already left
    the house...

      J.B.
    All right. Never mind.

      LILLIAN
    She's left for Florida...she
    said you don't need fur coats in
    Florida. She said all you need
    in Florida is a bathing suit and
    an amiable...

      J.B.
    (Shutting her up)
    All right! All right! Any-
    body waiting?

      LILLIAN
    Mr. Louis is here, Mr. Ball.

      J.B.
    (Vaguely)
  Who?

      LILLIAN
    Louis Louis...you know, the
    Hotel Louis.

4-9-37   (Continued)

B-2

                                    J.B.
                               (Bloodthirstily)
                         Oh he is, is he? Well, send
                         him in!

B-3   CLOSE SHOT - LOUIS OUTSIDE J.B.'S DOOR

       He is a small foreigner in an astrakhan collar and a
       derby. Lillian appears around the door.

                                  LILLIAN
                               (Whispering)
                          Go in.

       Louis yanks a rabbit's foot out of his pocket, rubs
       it vigorously, swallows once, replaces the luck
       piece, closes his eyes tight and plunges forward.

B-4   DOOR OF J. B.'S OFFICE

       It bursts open and Louis pops in, beaming. He bows
       low and removes his derby.

                                   LOUIS
                               (With false jocularity)
                         Wal, Mr. B., the bonds is due
                         today and here I am!

       He laughs merrily, closes the door behind him and
       takes a step forward.

                         Johnny-on-the-spots!

B-5   J.B. OVER LOUIS

                                    J.B.
                         Fine! Then you don't have to
                         bother me. It's the window down-
                         stairs called LOANS...it's the
                         big one.

B-6   LOUIS - OVER J.B.

                                   LOUIS
                               (Ingratiatingly)
                         Mr. B.! You and me get along
                         like Mike and Ike.
                               (He holds up two fingers)
                         Why should I wisit dot loan shark?

B-6

                    J.B.
                (Exasperated)
            Did you come here to pay or
            what?

                    LOUIS
                (With conviction)
            Yas.
                (Then with less conviction)
            I come here to pay my respects
            and in the whole world of financials
            there's nobody I respect more...

B-7   J.B. - OVER LOUIS

                    J.B.
            Listen you! You're a year
            behind on your first mortgage,
            you're two years behind on your
            second mortgage, you're three
            years behind on...

B-8   LOUIS - OVER J.B.

                    LOUIS
                (Holding up a hand)
            What do I know about such things?
            De Hotel Louis must succeed because
            it's de bast: Tink on my roast
            weal a la J. B. Ball, my pig's
            feet sauce Diablo, my wenison
            winaigrette... How can such a
            hotel...

B-9   J.B. OVER LOUIS

                    J.B.
                (Interrupting)
            Everybody knows you're the
            finest cook in the world...
            that's why you don't know any-
            thing about business. The sooner
            you get back in a kitchen, the better
            off you'll be. You're forclosed!
            I'm doing you a favor.

B-10   LOUIS - OVER J.B.

                    LOUIS
            Gimme six months, Mr. B.

4-9-37   (Continued)

B-10
                              J.B.
                    Not on your tintype.

                              LOUIS
                    Gimme six weeks.

                              J.B.
                           (Reluctantly)
                    I'll give you a week.

                              LOUIS
                           (With fire)
                    What good is a week?

B-11   J.B. - OVER LOUIS

                              J.B.
                           (Roaring)
                    All right I WON'T GIVE YOU
                    a week!

B-12   LOUIS - OVER J.B.

                              LOUIS
                           (Desperately)
                    All right, I'll TAKE a week!...
                    Goodbye, I got to hurry.

          He puts on his derby.

                              J.B.
                           (Puzzled)
                    What're you going to do?

                              LOUIS
                           (Scatter-brained)
                    I don't know, but I only got
                    a week to do it in.

          He rushes out and the CAMERA TRUCKS IN to a CLOSE
          SHOT of J.B. He glares after Louis and mutters to
          himself.

                              J.B.
                    Roast weal a la...

          His voice trails off and he pushes the lever on the
          Dictophone.

                              LILLIAN'S VOICE
                           (Tinnily)
                    Yes, Mr. Ball.

4-9-37   (Continued)

191

B-12

J.B.
~~Get me a ham sandwich and a
cup of coffee.~~

DISSOLVE TO:

B-13   LOW CAMERA SHOT - AT THE DOORMAN OF THE HOTEL LOUIS

The word; "Louis" is plainly marked on his cap. The
CAMERA IS ALREADY TILTING BACK as we come into the
shot. We MOVE UP the doorman's buttons and look
straight up at the imposing twin towers which branch
out menacingly.

B-14   HIGH CAMERA SHOT - DOWN ON LOUIS

He shakes his head.

B-15   CLOSEUP - HIGH CAMERA ON LOUIS

> LOUIS
> How can such a phenonument be
> a flap?

He makes a helpless gesture.

B-16   VAN BUREN - <u>IN THE DOORWAY OF HIS SHOP</u>

He sees Louis, shades his eyes like an Indian to
make sure, then steps forward happily.

> VAN BUREN
> Louis!

B-17   CLOSE SHOT - LOUIS (TRANSPARENCY)

Behind him we see the traffic of Park Avenue. He
sees the approaching Van Buren and scowls.

> LOUIS
> (Rudely)
> Vot?

Van Buren hurries into the shot and grabs Louis'
lapel.

4-9-37

(Continued)

                        VAN BUREN
                    (Triumphantly)
                Who do you suppose was in my
                salong this moring?

                        LOUIS
                    (Harshly)
                Vot do I suppose was in your
                saloon? Vot I need is someting
                in my saloon...someting like a
                conwention.

                        VAN BUREN
                    (Slightly disappointed)
                You'll NEVER guess, Louis.

                        LOUIS
                    (Bored)
                All right, I'll play you one
                riddle...who?

                        VAN BUREN
                The Bull of Broad Street!

                        LOUIS
                    (Blankly)
                De Vot?

                        VAN BUREN
                The Bull of Broad Street...
                with a chicken!

                        LOUIS
                    (Shrugging)
                Bull, chickens...

        He starts to shrug again, then the other's meaning
        hits him like a hammer. He grabs his lapels.

                        LOUIS
                You don't mean de Ball from
                Bull Street, you dumbbell?

                        VAN BUREN
                But that's what I've been...

                        LOUIS
                    (Joyously)
                Vit a tvoip?

                        VAN BUREN
                With a ...dancing partner.

                              LOUIS
                          (Excitedly)
                    You got de dope? De dame's
                    name?, de hangout, etcetela,
                    etcetela?

                              VAN BUREN
                          (Happy at last)
                    I have! But I haven't the
                    slightest intention of parting
                    with a single scrap of it.

                              LOUIS
                          (Seizing him in a
                           vice-like grip)
                    Listen, wan...
                          (Van Buren struggles to
                           loosen himself to no
                           avail)
                    ...vit a little corruption from
                    you...corfu shall not rang next
                    veek!

                    END OF SEQUENCE "B"

4-9-37

SEQUENCE   "C"

FADE IN:

C-1   INSERT: NEW YORK NEWSPAPER WANT AD SECTION

We read the column headings - "HELP WANTED MALE"

DISSOLVE TO:

C-2   CLOSE UP INSERT:

> "Wanted - Cook. Must have
> short order experience -
> Bon Ton Cafe $80."

CAMERA PULLS BACK TO

C-3   A SUBWAY KIOSK

We are shooting at the side containing the news
stand. Facing us are two tramps reading the want
ads. Behind them and with his back to us, Johnny
is also reading the want ads.

> FIRST TRAMP
> (Indicating the paper)
> Can you see me bending over a
> hot stove for eighty Samelkas?

> SECOND TRAMP
> (Prophetically and with
> a slight accent)
> Wait till it comes their turn to
> bend over.

C-4   REVERSE SHOT FROM INTERIOR NEWS STAND

We recognize Johnny lighting a cigarette. He is not
accustomed to reading want ads and has some trouble
in finding the right places to read. Now he wets
his thumb and turns over to the next page. Mary
comes angrily into the shot. She throws down three
cents, picks up a newspaper and opens it violently.
They both read the ads for a moment, then turn
rapidly and bump into each other as they start in
opposite directions. As they bump Johnny's new
cigarette falls to the street.

4-10-37   (Continued)

C-4   MARY
                          (Crossly)
                   Why don't you...

                             JOHNNY
                   I'm sorry.

He tips his hat, and they pass out of the picture.
The first tramp turns and picks up the cigarette. He
looks at it disgustedly, then throws it on the ground.

                          FIRST TRAMP
                          (Scornfully)
                   Cork tips!

                          SECOND TRAMP
                          (Prophetically)
                   They'll find out!

C-5   DAYLIGHT - MOVING SHOT - MARY'S FEET

        The buckles twinkle as she marches along briskly.

        DISSOLVE TO:

C-6   NIGHT - MARY'S FEET - MOVING SHOT

        The shoes are dusty, and the feet walk along slowly.
        They seem discouraged.

C-7   STAIR LANDING - A ROOMING HOUSE

        A dog is scratching himself on a cocoa mat. A child
        is wailing in the distance. Mary comes wearily up
        the dimly-lit stairs. She turns toward us and goes
        past the CAMERA.

C-8   A HALL BEDROOM

        The door opens and we see Mary silhouetted against
        the light from the hall. She switches on the light,
        comes in, closes and locks the door behind her. She
        takes off the hat and the coat, puts them on the bed
        and looks at them with some enmity. She takes a
        step toward the window and her eye focuses on some-
        thing on the bureau. She frowns.

4-10-37

C-9   CLOSE SHOT - <u>A RENT BILL STUCK IN THE CORNER OF THE</u>
        <u>MIRROR</u>

        We read: "1 week & breakfist...$7.00". Underneath
        in a scrawly handwriting, we read: "Please."
        Underneath that we read: "And no kiding".

C-10   CLOSE SHOT - MARY

        As she looks at the bill she turns her head slightly
        and looks frightened. We hear the slow tramp of
        feet up the stairs.

C-11   MARY - <u>IN THE MIDDLE OF THE ROOM</u>

        She hurries to the door and switches out the light.
        We see her faintly in the darkness. We hear a knock
        on the door.

        SOUND: KNOCK ON DOOR. REPEATED, THEN MORE LOUDLY.

        After a moment the knock is repeated. Now we hear a
        very loud knock, followed by the landlady's voice:

                        LANDLADY'S VOICE
                Miss Smith.

        Now we hear steps moving away. After a moment the
        light is switched on again. Mary exhales with relief
        and crosses to the bureau. The CAMERA PANS with her.
        She takes out an old handbag and starts looking
        through it. She pauses, turns toward the window and
        sniffs.

C-12   <u>A GAS COOKER ON A WALL BRACKET IN ANOTHER APARTMENT</u>

        This is the type of apparatus made to fit on a light
        fixture. On the cooker sits a frying pan. In the
        frying pan sit some liver and onions.

C-13   MARY - WITH THE HANDBAG IN HER HAND

        She licks her lips, then goes through the rest of
        her handbag unsuccessfully. She puts it back in
        the drawer and fixes a look on something on the
        bureau.

C-14   CLOSE SHOT - <u>A PIG BANK ON THE BUREAU</u>
        The pig is decorated with roses.

C-15   MARY - LOOKING AT THE PIG BANK
        She reaches for it, hesitates and knocks on the
        bureau three times.

4-10-37   (Continued)

197

C-15   SOUND: THREE KNOCKS ON BUREAU

Now she puts her hand on it, pauses and closes her
eyes for a second. She shakes the pig bank and is
rewarded by a pleasant clicking.

SOUND: CLICKING NOISE.

She tries to shake the coin out into her hand. This
doesn't seem to work. She tries to spoon it out with
a nail-file. No success. Now, after a moment's
speculation, she sits the little pig on the edge
of the dresser, takes off her shoe and takes a whack
at it. She misses it but makes a beautiful dent in
the edge of the dresser, which she repairs with
spit. She tries again, hits the pig and the clay
flies all over the room. The coin disappears. She
looks for it, first standing up, then on her knees.
The CAMERA PANS with her. She looks under the bed,
then works her way to the door.

C-16   CLOSE SHOT - MARY ON HER KNEES

Suddenly she smiles - and the smile turns into a
frown.

C-17   <u>THE FLOOR AND PART OF THE BOTTOM OF THE DOOR</u>

A shiny dime lies two inches from the door. Next
to it lies a telegram, not quite under. Mary's
hand comes into the picture and picks them both up.

C-18   MARY ON HER KNEES

She examines the coin carefully, then bites it. She
tears open the telegram. As she looks at it in
puzzlement.

C-19   A WESTERN UNION BLANK

On it we read:

                MISS MARY SMITH
                34 WEST 112TH STREET
                NEW YORK, N.Y.

                CAN I SEE YOU AT ONCE
                QUESTION MARK URGENT
                EXCLAMATION POINT

                     (Signed) LOUIS LOUIS
                               HOTEL LOUIS
                               PARK AVENUE
        DISSOLVE TO:

4-10-37

C-20   <u>MR. LOUIS' OFFICE IN THE HOTEL LOUIS</u>

This is the type of office hidden behind the
reception desk in large hotels. Its walls are
partitions over which peep some hotel palms. The
office is occupied by Mr. Louis who is pacing up and
down like a lion, and Mr. Gurney, his Scottish bookkeeper. Mr. Gurney sits next to a desk and does
finger exercises on its glass top.

                    LOUIS
          Vun veek...
               (He knocks on wood)
          Vot can you do in vun veek?

                    GURNEY
               (Heavily)
          The world only took a week.

                    LOUIS
          Don't boin me up, vill you,
          Goiney? If you can do miracles,
          just a suggestion; shake down
          de Valdorf, de Plaza, de Ritz
          and leave us opp -- like a
          cendle!

He sticks one finger in the air. Now the room
shakes violently and we hear a tremendous rumbling
sound. Louis clutches a filing cabinet and looks
fearfully toward Gurney.

                    LOUIS
               (Yelling)
          Vot's dat?

                    GURNEY
               (Wearily)
          The subway.

Louis laughs greenly and proceeds.

                    LOUIS
          Ever since I seen dot
          picture....

A bellboy comes in quietly and stops behind him.

                    THE BELLBOY
          Sir....

4-10-37   (Continued)

C-20   Louis jumps as if he had been jabbed with a pitchfork
         then turns indignantly.

                          LOUIS
                       (Furiously)
                  How many times I told you don't creep!

                          THE BELLBOY
                  There's a Miss Smith to see you, Mr.
                  Louis.

                          LOUIS
                       (Electrified)
                  Vell, vy don't you say so...?
                       (He shoves him aside)
                  Get out of my way!

         He takes a step toward the door, then stops and pats
         the seat of his trousers. He turns to Gurney.

                          LOUIS
                  Vere's my tail coat?

                          GURNEY
                  Here.

         Gurney takes a cutaway off a hanger and holds it out
         for Louis.

                          LOUIS
                       (Peeling off his coat:
                        to bellboy)
                  Get me a flower!

         The bellboy jumps out of the room and Louis struggles
         into the cutaway and buttons the first button into the
         second hole.

                          GURNEY
                       (Starting to unbutton
                        him; sadly)
                  How can you think of girls at a
                  time like this?

                          LOUIS
                       (Indignantly)
                  Goils? She's de goil-friend of our
                  foist, second and toid mortgage!
                  Vot's de matter vit you?

         He glares at Gurney and buttons the third button into
         the second buttonhole.

                          GURNEY
                  Hunh?

4-10-37   (Continued)

C-20   He starts to unbutton the third button.

                            LOUIS
                    She got to live here! Vit his own...
                    Vit Smitty in de house, not even a
                    MONSTER could foreclose!

        The bellboy hurries in with an Easter lily.

                            LOUIS (Continuing)
                            (Furiously)
                    Vot's de matter vit you! You tink
                    I'm a stiff? Put it back in de icebox!

        He turns to Gurney and seizes his hand.

                    Mitt me, Goiney...dis is de last
                    cheese in de trap!

        He turns and hurries out.

C-21   THE LOBBY - CLOSE SHOT - MARY - IN A LOUIS XIV ARM
        CHAIR

        She looks around at the splendour.

C-22   VERY HIGH CAMERA SHOT

        This is SHOOTING DOWN past a crystal chandelier. This
        shot should give the impression of a very high lobby
        and obviate the use of a glass shot. Mary is very
        small below us. Louis walks into the shot, coat-tails
        flying. He hurries toward her, stops a moment to
        pluck a flower from a vase, and continues toward her,
        adjusting the flower in his buttonhole. As he reaches
        her -

C-23   CLOSE SHOT - MARY IN THE ARMCHAIR

        Louis takes the last step into the picture.

                            LOUIS
                    Mis Smit?

                            MARY
                    Yes.

                            LOUIS
                    A pleasure.
                        (He bows deeply and beams
                        at her fur coat)

4-10-37   (Continued)

                                201

LOUIS
                       (Continued)
                   You must excuse my liberty in sending
                   you a telegram.

         He smirks, scrapes. Mary looks slightly dazed.

                   You look exactly like I t'ought...
                   only a hundred percent better.

                         MARY
                   Well - thanks. I don't know how you
                   heard of me, but I'm sure we'd get
                   along all right. I'm fast and...

                         LOUIS
                       (Interrupting)
                   Miss Smit, I'm a man like dis! I
                   don't beat around de bush to come in
                   de back door. I tell you dis is vere
                   you belong and dis is vere you got to
                   be.

                         MARY
                   Well, I'm perfectly willing. I don't
                   ask very much and...

                         LOUIS
                       (With force)
                   You don't have to ask NUTTING. Ve
                   anticilpate!...anything you vant
                   you push de bell it's dere before
                   you take off de finger. Look!

         He jerks on a bell-pull behind her which comes off in
         his hands. He smiles bravely and says:

                   New! I'm telling you, my dear
                   young lady, until you lived in de
                   Hotel Louis...YOU AIN'T!

                         MARY
                       (In surprise)
                   Do I have to live here?

                         LOUIS
                   I insist! Do me a favor, will you?
                   Take a peek.

                         MARY
                       (Frowning slightly)
                   What at?

                         LOUIS
                       (Lifting her to her feet)
                   Please.
         PAN TO ELEVATOR.
4-10-37   DISSOLVE TO:

C-24   <u>INSIDE OF IMPERIAL SUITE DOOR</u>

The door swings open and Louis bows Mary in. She
stops and looks in puzzlement. He comes in after her
and closes the door.

C-25   TRUCKING SHOT - BEHIND LOUIS AND MARY

They walk ahead of us. We see a long vista of open
doors.

                    LOUIS
                 (Pointing)
        Foyer...foist reception room...
        second reception room...washroom...

He jerks open a door and a ladder falls out and hits
him on the head.

        For hanging pictures.
                 (He puts the ladder
                  back in the closet,
                  rubs his head and
                  continues)
        Informal saloon, formal saloon,
        dining room...gymnaselum...plunge --

                    MARY
                 (Pointing)
        What's that?

                    LOUIS
        A camel.

He mounts it, pushes a switch and the appartus revolves its saddle.

        You vant a horse?

He pushes another switch and bobs up and down violently.

        S-some fuh-huh-huh-huh-hun, huh?

They pass to the next room, which is covered with
mirrors.

                 (He points to a
                  door)
        Foist bedroom, second bedroom...
        YOUR bedroom...

They have now reached the end of the suite and a
magnificent chamber.

4-10-37   (Continued)

                            MARY
                          (Puzzled)
                   My bedroom?

                            LOUIS
                     (With a wide gesture)
                   Couldn't you be cozy here?

                            MARY
                       (Still puzzled)
                   It's cozy all right, but I don't
                   think I understand exactly...
                   How much would you pay me?

                            LOUIS
                   How much would I pay you? For vot?

                            MARY
                   Well, for whatever it is?

                            LOUIS
                       (Pointing toward the
                          suite)
                   Don't you think you should pay me
                   a little something?

                            MARY
                   For what?

                            LOUIS
                       (With a trace of indigna-
                          tion)
                   For what! For what I just showed
                   you: de bedrooms, de svimming pool,
                   de horse...de...de...

                            MARY
                   Wait a minute.
                       (She gives him a long
                          look)
                   Are you trying to rent me this...
                   little number?

                            LOUIS
                       (With emphasis)
                   Exactly!

                            MARY
                   Is that why you sent for me?

C-25   LOUIS
                      Soltenly.

          Mary starts to laugh.

                              MARY
                      I think you got the wrong Smith.

                              LOUIS
                          (Pulling his lip)
                      You tink so?

                              MARY
                          (Giggling)
                      I'm sure of it.

                              LOUIS
                      Mary Smit?

                              MARY
                      Yes.

                              LOUIS
                      A hundred and tvelf? - Vest?

                              MARY
                      Yes.

                              LOUIS
                      You bought a hat dis morning?

                              MARY
                      Yes.

                              LOUIS
                          (Relaxing)
                      You're de right Smit.

                              MARY
                      But I don't see...

                              LOUIS
                          (With emphasis)
                      Dis is vere you belong. A beautiful
                      goil like you got to have a back-
                      ground. Dis...
                          (He indicates)
                      ...is vot you call a background!

                              MARY
                      I should say it is.

4-10-37   (Continued)

                                .

LOUIS

No matter vere you look you von't
find anudder background goes so
far back.

He makes a sweeping gesture.

MARY
(Embarrassed)

I guess that's right, but you
don't seem to understand. I
couldn't afford even the...the...
I couldn't afford any of it.

LOUIS

Dot's vot you tink, my dear lady,
But I'm telling you confidential;
de management vill make concessions.

MARY
(Embarrassed)

That's very sweet of you, Mr.
Louis, but...

LOUIS
(Significantly)

Ve vill meet you more dan halfway.

MARY
(Shaking her head)

Even if you came the whole way,
Mr. Lou .....

LOUIS
(Interrupting her)

Listen!
(He smiles a confi-
dential smile)
Vot are you paying now?

MARY
(Quietly)

Seven dollars.

LOUIS
(Thinking she has
misunderstood)

I said vot are you paying...?
I mean - rent.

MARY

Seven dollars.

4-10-37   (Continued)

                    LOUIS
                (Like a parrot)
            Seven dollars.
                (He looks down the per-
                spective and back at her;
                very rapidly)
            Seven? One two tree four five
            six SEVEN?

                    MARY (Matter-of-fact)
            With breakfast... one egg.

                    LOUIS
                (Waving this aside)
            Vun eggs or tree eggs...seven
            dollars!
                (He looks down the vista
                again. Shakes a finger
                at her)
            You ain't got no svimming pool at
            dat price.

                    MARY
                (Suppressing a laugh)
            I have not.

Louis clasps his hands behind his back and walks up
and down like Mickey Mouse.

                    LOUIS
                (Muttering)
            Seven dollars...seven times seven
            is fifty-six...minus de breakfast...

He stops in front of Mary.

            My dear young lady, could you make
            it...

                    MARY
                (Gently)
            Not seven times seven, Mr. Louis,
            one times seven...seven dollars a
            week.

                    LOUIS
            A WEEK!

                    MARY
                (Apologetically)
            With breakfast.

4-10-37   (Continued)

                        207

> LOUIS
> (Numbly)
> Vun egg!
> (He walks up and down,
>   gesticulating to himself)
> Seven dollars a week...vit a
> gymnaselum!

As he passes her, he looks at her reproachfully
and points a finger at her.

> LOUIS
> You drive a hard bargain, my
> dear young lady.
> (He shakes his head)
> Seven dollars a veek!

> MARY
> But Mr. Louis, I...don't...

> LOUIS
> (Nervously)
> It's yours.

> MARY
> But Mr. Louis....

> LOUIS
> (Rapidly)
> It's YOURS! You vant breakfast?
> You got it.

> MARY
> But...

> LOUIS
> (Interrupting)
> I vant you here. Two eggs!
> Ostrich eggs. Vot do I care?
> Ve'll send a truck and move
> you immediate.

> MARY
> But... but I owe for the week!

> LOUIS
> Ve'll pay it!

Mary looks at him a long moment.

4-10-37   (Continued)

C-25
                Vy - Why?

Louis looks at her speculatively before answering.

                    LOUIS
                I'll tell you: I don't beat
                around de back door and come
                in de coal chute. Come here.

He takes her by the arm and leads her over to a
window.

C-26   LOW CAMERA SHOT - <u>AT A TWINKLING TOWER</u> PAST LOUIS
AND MARY

                        LOUIS
                You see dem lights going on
                and off? Dot's bellboys!
                Dey run up and down de switches
                people shouldn't know my hotel is
                a fizzle...strictly confidential.

                    MARY
                Oh, I'm sorry. Mr. Louis.

                    LOUIS
                    (Shrugging)
                Vit you here, I got anyvay some
                <u>legitimate</u> lights in my tower.

                    MARY
                    (Smiling slowly)
                Oh!

                    LOUIS
                    (Holding up a finger)
                You could do me also vun
                little favor.

                    MARY
                    (Puzzled)
                What?

                    LOUIS
                    (Very confidentially)
                De next time you see Mr. Ball...

                    MARY
                    (Interrupting)
                Mr. Who?

4-10-37   (Continued)

C-26
                              LOUIS
                           (Contrite)
                    Excuse me.
                           (He bows)
                    I shouldn't mention names.
                    De next time you see...dot
                    soitain party...vidout de name...
                    vill you tell him vot a
                    beautiful layout ve got here?
                    Vill you tell him vot classy
                    soiwice ve give? Vill you
                    tell him under no soicumstances
                    you vill not move?

                              MARY
                    Tell who?

                              LOUIS
                    Dot party.

                              MARY
                    Where?

                              LOUIS
                    Verever it does the most
                    good.

                              MARY
                           (Beginning to
                            understand)
                    Oh, you mean you want me to
                    boost your hotel.

                              LOUIS
                    De exact woid! It vould have
                    took me ten years. Boost
                    it in de right place.... and
                    soon.

                              MARY
                    I'll do my best, Mr. Louis

                              LOUIS
                    And loud.

                              MARY
                    And loud.

          Louis steps outside and looks back around the
          door.

4-10-37   (Continued)

C-26   LOUIS
                  And how.

                            MARY
                  And how.

                            LOUIS
                          (Happily)
                  Hotsie-tootsie.

He beams and closes the door. The CAMERA MOVES into
a CLOSE SHOT on Mary. She looks around speculatively
a moment then closes her eyes for a count of three.
Now she opens them and looks around quickly. She looks
inquisitively at something out of the picture.

C-27   MODERNISTIC BATHROOM

Mary enters and switches on the light. As she does so
a radio begins to play pleasant music. She looks
around happily and tests the water in the wash basin.
It is real water. Now she crosses to the tub, looks
down into it, and twists a faucet. A spray of water
shoots up and hits her in the face. She laughs and
reaches for a towel and starts to dry herself. As she
does this, the music stops and we hear a silky
announcer's voice.

                          ANNOUNCER
                  And now, ladies and gentlemen of the
                  radio audience, I hope you're good and
                  hungry because I'm going to give you
                  Careful Carrie's recipe for little
                  thin brown crispy buttered griddle
                  cakes with crackling little pig
                  sausages and Colonial syrup....

During this announcement Mary has lowered the towel
and stared transfixed at the radio. She has swallowed
her saliva a couple of times and licked her lips
nervously.

                          ANNOUNCER
                  To one cup of wind-blown, feather-
                  fuzzy, silk-strained....

Mary reaches forward desperately and twists the radio
knob viciously. A woman announcer's voice with a
southern accent replaces the previous announcer.

                          WOMAN ANNOUNCER
                  ... a crusty golden brown. Now
                  you all takes the ham and places
                  it in .....

4-10-37   (Continued)

C-27   More desperate than ever Mary twists the knob.

                         A VERY POWERFUL ANNOUNCER
                    The cheese to choose! Remember these
                    four points: Strength, aroma, power
                    and light...

         Mary seizes the knob and turns it back and forth. We
         hear a medley of different announcers:

                    .....like mother used to make...

                    .....the size of a walnut, add....

                    .....and bake until.....

                    .....with a beaker of Fireside Ale
                    in the hand and a song....

                    .....with mustard. Then roll your
                    feet in breadcrumbs.....

         Mary gives up. She puts her hands over her ears and
         hurries out.

         DISSOLVE TO:

C-28   INT. AUTOMAT - CLOSE SHOT AT CHANGE COUNTER

         Mary's hand puts down a dime, and the cashier slides
         over two nickels. Mary's hand reaches for them.

C-29   MARY

         She finishes picking up the nickels.

                         MARY
                    Thanks.

         She moves away, and the cashier gets an eye-full of
         the coat.

C-30   THE SOUP SLOTS

         They are marked: "One Nickel". Mary comes into the
         picture, chooses "Beef Soup and Cracker Special". The
         slot flies open. She reaches under the counter for
         a spoon and takes the soup and moves on. CAMERA
         TRUCKS with her. She stops at the beverage spiggots,
         puts a glass under one of them and her remaining
         nickel in the "Milk" slot. The milk starts squirting

         4-10-37   (Continued)

C-30   out of the next spiggot. Hastily Mary moves her glass
        over. She is short-changed slightly on the milk and
        gives the metal partition a whack to squeeze out a
        little more. We hear some machinery fall in the back-
        ground. Mary looks around nervously, then picks up
        her milk and moves out of the picture.

C-31   FAT MAN - AT TABLE

        He is not only fat but untidy-looking. He wears a
        derby hat and is busy wolfing his food. Mary comes
        into the picture and puts her soup and milk on a
        standup table. The fat man tips his derby, replaces
        it on his head and continues eating. Mary notices
        him for the first time. She looks disapprovingly at
        the collection of dishes in front of him.

G-32   THE FAT MAN - PAST MARY

        The table before him is strewn with empty dishes of
        different sizes. On his right are two cups of coffee
        one empty. He is busy polishing gravy from his
        plate. He swallows the piece of bread, pushes the
        plate to one side and makes a pile of all the empty
        plates in front of him. Now he reaches for a double
        order of ice-cream.

C-33   MARY - PAST THE FAT MAN

        Still watching him disapprovingly she starts to eat
        her soup and sip the milk. As she gets a spoonful
        of soup halfway to her mouth, the Fat Man hiccoughs
        and tips his hat. Mary puts the spoon back in her
        plate. The Fat Man takes one more lick of his ice
        cream, downs the cup of coffee, tips his hat and de-
        parts. Mary looks at the debris he has left on the
        table. A busboy moves into the picture and starts
        piling the things together.

                        MARY
                  (Shaking her head)
                  If I hadn't seen it I wouldn't
                  have believed it.

C-34   BUSBOY - PAST MARY

        The busboy is Johnny. He wears an over-size white
        overseas cap made smaller by a safety pin in the back.

        4-10-37   (Continued)

213

C-34   JOHNNY
                     I've seen a lot of things today
                     I never would have believed.
                          (Now a little more
                          interest comes
                          into his eye)
                     Haven't we met?

C-35   MARY - PAST JOHNNY

                          MARY
                          (Sarcastically)
                     I don't think so. I didn't get
                     to the Waiters' Ball this year.

C-36   JOHNNY - PAST MARY

         He laughs.
                          JOHNNY
                     I know I've seen you some place.
                     You weren't at the Princeton
                     Prom, were you?

C-37   MARY - PAST JOHNNY

                          MARY
                     No. It couldn't have been at Mrs.
                     Astor's on Tuesday, could it?

                          JOHNNY
                          (Simply)
                     I wasn't there.

                          MARY
                     You missed a lovely evening.
                          (She starts to giggle)

                          JOHNNY
                     Were you in Palm Beach in February?

                          MARY
                          (With mock seriousness)
                     Not in February. You weren't in
                     Saint Moritz for Christmas, were you?

C-38   JOHNNY - PAST MARY

                          JOHNNY
                     I couldn't get away.

C-39   MARY - PAST JOHNNY
                          MARY
                     That's funny, I couldn't either..
                     so I guess we never met.

         She puts the last spoonful of soup in her mouth and
         sips her milk primly.

C-40   JOHNNY - PAST MARY

                          JOHNNY
                I know I've seen you some place.

          He starts piling his dishes on a tray.

                     (Conversationally)
                I hear the beefsteak pie is mag-
                nificent...six nickels. With a
                grapefruit salad, three nickels,
                you'd have a meal fit for a queen.

C-41   MARY - PAST JOHNNY

                          MARY
                     (Looking up resentfully)
                Will you shut up?

C-42   JOHNNY - PAST MARY

          He is surprised and apologetic.

                          JOHNNY
                I'm terribly sorry. It just seemed
                to me that part of my duties would
                be to suggest.....

C-43   MARY - PAST JOHNNY

                          MARY
                     (Crossly)
                Well, if you can suggest where to get
                the nine nickels, I'll follow your sug-
                gestion. If you can't don't go around
                putting ideas in people's mouths.

C-44   JOHNNY - PAST MARY

                          JOHNNY
                Oh, you mean you haven't...I mean...
                uh....uh....

          He is so embarrassed he doesn't know what to say. He
          opens his mouth a couple of times, raises his eybrows
          then grins a sickly grin. Now he finishes loading his
          tray, picks it up and moves away. The CAMERA TRUCKS
          ALONG beside him. As he walks he turns back to steal
          a look at Mary and bumps into a departing customer.
          By a miracle, nothing is spilled. Johnny looks back
          at the customer and says:
                          JOHNNY
                I'm sorry.

          4-10-37

C-45   <u>THE DIRTY DISH CHUTE</u>

Johnny comes into the picture and slides his try into
the aperture. Now he looks back across the room speculatively. He feels in his trouser pockets, but, finding nothing, removes his hand. Suddenly his eyes
narrow. He starts out of the picture.

C-46   <u>MARY - AT THE TABLE</u>

She finishes the milk and scoops a little piece of
piecrust off the plate. Johnny comes up behind her.
He looks around nervously, then takes a towel and
starts polishing her table.

                    MARY
              (Looking up disapprovingly)
         Are <u>you</u> in again?

                    JOHNNY
              (Out of the side of his
               mouth, indistinctly)
         Listen.

He looks around once more before continuing.

                    MARY
         What?

                    JOHNNY
              (Still indistinctly)
         Look: You go over to the hot dish
         window and pick out what you like,
         see? And....

                    MARY
              (Frowning)
         The hotchkiss window? What's the
         matter, you got something wrong
         with your teeth?

                    JOHNNY
         Sh!
              (He looks around
               again like a
               conspirator)
         The <u>hot dish</u> window. You pick out
         what you like and I'll go around in
         back and work the gag. I'm allowed
         in the back.

                    MARY
              (In a low voice)
         What are you trying to do - land us
         all in the jug?

                    JOHNNY
              (Shaking his head)
         I'll put the nickels in when I get
         paid and you can pay me back sometime.

4-10-37   (Continued)

C-46   MARY
                    Some time in Saint Moritz.
                    I'm not so hungry as all that.

                              JOHNNY
                    Don't be a sucker, that beef pie
                    is a wow.

                              MARY
                            (Weakening)
                    Suppose they see you?

                              JOHNNY
                    I'll say the door was stuck. Go
                    on..I'll be behind the grapefruit.

          He gives her a reassuring pat and hurries away. Mary
          looks around nervously, then rises and tilts her chair
          forward to hold her place. Now, whistling noiseless-
          ly and still looking from right to left, she wanders
          toward the fruit salad windows.

C-47   MARY WALKING AWAY FROM US

          She is about eight feet from the fruit salads. Now
          she looks at them inquisitively. She starts to reach
          toward one of the doors, then puts her hand down to
          her side again and looks back past us. With a sharp
          click one of the doors flies open.
          SOUND: CLICK

          Slightly startled, Mary looks back at it, then over
          her shoulder once more before reaching for it. As
          she takes it, she bends down to look through the com-
          partment. She smiles nervously.

C-48   JOHNNY - IN THE SPACE BEHIND THE FRUIT SALADS

          He is also bending over and smiling. Now he points
          away from us down toward the hot dishes.

C-49   CLOSE SHOT - MARY, LOOKING THROUGH THE COMPARTMENT
                              MARY
                            (In a whisper)
                    Is it all right?

                              JOHNNY
                            (Laughing)
                    Everything's hunky-dory....
                    I'll meet you at the beef-
                    pies.

          4-10-37   (Continued)

C-49   He points again and starts away from us. The CAMERA
        ANGLES UP to a sort of turret set in the wall about
        eight feet up. What we see of the turret is globula
        Through it project two shiny lenses on tubes like
        opera glasses. The turret turns slowly and the opera
        glasses seem to follow Johnny's progress behind the
        partition. The CAMERA ANGLES DOWN again as Johnny
        stops behind the beef pies.

C-50   CLOSE SHOT - MARY - IN FRONT OF THE BEEF PIES

        She points a finger at one and says, soundlessly: "I
        this one all right?"

C-51   CLOSE SHOT - JOHNNY

        He holds up his hand and says:

                          JOHNNY
                       (Soundlessly)
                    Just a minute.

        He examines the beef pie critically then shakes his
        head and waggles his finger: "No, no, no."

                          JOHNNY
                    Too small.

        He moves his nose near the next one and nods his head
        slowly downward to say it is all right.

C-52   CLOSE SHOT - MARY - IN FRONT OF THE BEEF PIES

        She nods all right also, and smiles and points at it

C-53   CLOSE SHOT - THE GLOBULAR TURRET

        The opera glasses move down and up once as if saying
        "all right".

C-54   MEDIUM CLOSE - JOHNNY

        He pulls up his right sleeve and reaches his hand in
        the compartment, being careful to avoid the piecrust.
        He fiddles for a second, then we hear a click.

        SOUND: CLICK

        Johnny takes his hand out of the compartment, looks
        down through it and smiles.

4-10-37

C-55   SHOT - <u>THROUGH THE COMPARTMENT</u> - AT MARY

        She smiles, removes the beef pie and waves.

C-56   MEDIUM CLOSE - JOHNNY WAVING THROUGH THE COMPARTMENT

        A heavy hand drops on his shoulder. His face falls
        and he straightens up and looks behind him.

C-57   JOHNNY AND THE AUTOMAT "DICK"

        This turns out to be the Fat Man who was sitting at
        Mary's table. He is now chewing on a toothpick,
        standing half in and half out of a swinging door with
        a bull's-eye on it.

                          THE DICK
                Come on.

                          JOHNNY
                The uh... the... the...the...
                     (He points weakly)
                ...the...the...door isn't working.

                          THE DICK
                Neither are you, buddy. Come on.

        He starts to drag him down the passageway.

                          JOHNNY
                     (Holding back)
                Quit shoving.

                          THE DICK
                Don't get hard, buddy...I ain't
                as soft as I look.

                          JOHNNY
                     (Working himself into
                      a position)
                That's what <u>you</u> think.

                          THE DICK
                That's what <u>I</u> think.

        He starts to reach for a black-jack and Johnny sinks
        a terrible punch into his midriff.

                          THE DICK
                Ouf! You will, will you, you...
                     (He lets out a terrible
                      hiccough, then springs
                      on Johnny)

4-10-37

C-58   MARY - AT HER TABLE

She is eating her beef pie rather fast. She reaches
for a forkful of the grapefruit salad, and pauses
with it in midair at the sound of a terrible crash.
She stiffens and looks around nervously. Some
customers near her do the same. The crash that
comes now is ten times bigger.

SOUND: CRASH

C-59   JOHNNY AND THE DICK - ON THE FLOOR

They are nearly buried in knives, forks, coffee pots
and crockery, fighting vigorously. The dick tries to
get to his feet and in grasping for something, his
hand pulls a lever.

C-60   A COUPLE OF BUMS STANDING AT THE TOOTHPICK TABLE

Behind them stretches a long vista of food compart-
ments. With a loud click all the doors in view fly
open and remain open, vibrating slightly. The first
bum turns his head, then clutches the second bum.
and points excitedly.

                        THE FIRST BUM
          Horace!

C-61   THE DICK AND JOHNNY WRESTLING - IN THE DEBRIS

The dick's feet tangle up in a couple more levers.

C-62   THE BEVERAGE PANEL

Simultaneously, tea, steaming coffee, milk, grape-
juice and orange juice start hissing their way into
the world. From a large spiggot next to them blobs
of ice-cream come plunking out.

C-63   THE CUSTOMERS NEAREST THE BEVERAGE PANEL

An old gentleman looks, adjusts his pince-nez, then
picks up his cup and hurries forward. Somebody yells

                        SOMEBODY
          Hey!

and all the customers in sight hurry toward us.

4-10-37

C-64   THE CASHIER - <u>IN HIS CHANGE BOOTH</u>

He looks around in astonishment as people hurry by
him without stopping for nickels.

C-65   <u>EXT. OF THE AUTOMAT</u>

The door flies open and a bum hurries out, turkey
leg in hand. He puts his fingers between his teeth
and whistles stridently.

SOUND: WHISTLE

C-66   MARY - <u>AT HER TABLE</u>

She is trying to finish her beef pie and see what's
going on at the same time. More and more people are
hurrying past her. Somebody fights his way toward
her and we recognize Johnny in his shirt sleeves. He
struggles into his coat and leads her out.

LAP DISSOLVE:

C-67   TRUCKING SHOT - AHEAD OF JOHNNY AND MARY ON <u>PARK</u>
<u>AVENUE</u> (NIGHT)

Mary stops and takes his arm.

>   MARY
>   (Distressed)
>   Then you lost your job?

>   JOHNNY
>   There wasn't any future in
>   it, anyway.

They continue walking.

>   You slave for twenty years and
>   you're <u>still</u> behind the nut salad.

>   MARY
>   It's too bad, just the same.
>   Have you got any money saved up?

>   JOHNNY
>   Well, un..uh...no.

4-10-37   (Continued)

C-67

MARY
Now you see? You ought to save
your money while you're working,
and then when you're "resting"
you can eat.

JOHNNY
(Suppressing a smile)
Like you.

MARY
(Frowning)
No, not like me...but when you
get hungry no bus boy is going
to lose his job trying to feed you.

JOHNNY
There's something to that.

MARY
More than meets the eye.

They walk along in silence for a few steps. Presently
Mary speaks.

MARY
(Looking straight ahead)
You got a place to sleep?

JOHNNY
(Taken by surprise)
Oh, uh...oh...sure.

MARY
(Distrustfully)
Where?

JOHNNY
(Pointing vaguely in
several directions)
Why, uh...uh...uh...?

MARY
(Cutting him short)
I get it...A LARK IN THE PARK!

JOHNNY
(Philosophically)
Well, suppose a fellow did,..

4-10-37

(Continued)

C-67   MARY
                        (Interrupting)
                    You'd better come up to the Louis
                    and talk it over.

                             JOHNNY
                        (Astonished)
                    The Louis?

                             MARY
                        (With finality)
                    The Louis.

                             JOHNNY
                        (Almost indignantly)
                    Then what were you doing in the
                    Automat?

                             MARY
                        (Looking straight
                            ahead)
                    Eating.

          DISSOLVE TO:

C-68   TRUCKING SHOT-AHEAD OF MARY AND JOHNNY IN MARY'S
          SUITE

          Mary is leading Johnny toward us.

                             MARY
                        (In a mock grand
                            manner)
                    Formal reception room...informal
                    reception room...

          She puts her hand on a doorknob.

                    ... beer saloon ...

          She opens the door. The same ladder falls out
          and hits Johnny on the head.

                    That's for hanging pictures.
                    I'm sorry...Dining room...
                    gymnasium as I live and breathe...
                    and plunge.

                             JOHNNY
                    And what?

          4-10-37   (Continued)

C-68   MARY
                 Swimming hole to you....first
                 bedroom, second bedroom, my
                 bedroom.

She looks down suddenly.

C-69   A LITTLE PILE OF LUGGAGE <u>IN THE MIDDLE OF THE FLOOR</u>

         This consists of two straw suitcases, an oilcloth
         hatbox, several laundry boxes wrapped in string, her
         grandmother's trunk with a round top, a book and a
         Coney Island Kewpie Doll lamp, also a pair of galoshes
         and an umbrella.

C-70   MARY AND JOHNNY - LOOKING DOWN AT THE LUGGAGE

                           MARY
                 Well, that certainly looks
                 rich in here.

Johnny is looking around at the room. Now he turns
and looks at her a moment before speaking.

                          JOHNNY
                 Just once more; <u>Why</u> did he
                 want you to live here?

                           MARY
                 He said: because the lights
                 in his towers were illegal...
                 but with me living here it
                 would be all right... or something
                 like that.
                          (She sits down on
                           her suitcase)

Johnny looks at her for a moment, then sits down
beside her.

                          JOHNNY
                 Are you <u>sure</u> he didn't say
                 anything else?

                           MARY
                 Nothing, except I was to put in
                 a good word for the place with
                 anybody I met, and you're the
                 first person I met, and I brought
                 you right over.

Johnny shakes his head and looks at the floor.

4-10-37   (Continued)

                        MARY
                    (Making a great
                     effort)
            First he said something about
            telling a Mr. Somebody something
            or other...then he said he shouldn't
            mention names, and he was sorry
            he'd said it or something.

                        JOHNNY
            Who?

                        MARY
            Mr. Louis.

                        JOHNNY
            No. No! Whose name did he mention
            and then say he shouldn't?

                        MARY
            Oh.
                    (She thinks a moment
                     then announces:)
            Bull!

                        JOHNNY
            That's funny....my name is "Ball."

                        MARY
            That's funnier still.

                        JOHNNY
            What?

                        MARY
            That was it.

They turn and look at each other a little eerily.

FADE OUT:

            END OF SEQUENCE "C"

                        225

SEQUENCE "D"

FADE IN:

D-1   CLOSEUP - J.B.'S BUTLER <u>IN A HALLWAY</u>

He is lit from the next room into which he peeks with
a worried expression. Now he leans forward and frowns.

D-2   J.B. - PAST THE BUTLER

He is in his library in front of the fireplace, ap-
parently engaged in destroying his collection of
books. As he tears a cover off a book -

D-3   CLOSE SHOT - J.B.

He completes the movement of tearing the cover off the
book. Now he tears the other cover off, places the
covers together, tears them in four, and throws them
in the fireplace. He now tears the body of the book
into pamphlets, tears these into strips and throws the
whole caboodle into the fireplace. He picks up the
hearth brush, sweeps the hearth clean of debris and
puts the hearth brush in the fire also and rises to
his feet.

D-4   THE BUTLER - <u>IN THE HALLWAY</u>

He watches his master with deep concern. Now he
straightens as J.B. approaches.

>   BUTLER
>   To bed so early, sir?

>   J.B.
>   (Coming into the shot)
>   Yes, have you any objections?

>   BUTLER
>   There's nothing like it, sir...
>   for a dull night.

J.B. grunts and goes by, then stops and turns around.

>   J.B.
>   How many trunks did she take?

4-22-37   (Continued)

                    BUTLER
                (Sadly)
Twelve trunks, seventeen suitcases, three jewel boxes and an
umbrella.

                    J.B.
                (Surprised)
What does she want with an umbrella
in Florida?

                    BUTLER
We thought it ill-advised, sir.
Will that be all, sir?

                    J.B.
                (Looking away)
Mr. Johnny home yet?

                    BUTLER
No, sir.

                    J.B.
                (Savagely)
How many trunks did he take?

                    BUTLER
He took nothing, sir...nothing at
all.

                    J.B.
Fathead!

                    BUTLER
                (Coldly)
Sir?

                    J.B.
                (Raising his voice)
I said: My son is a fathead!

                    BUTLER
Indeed, sir; it had escaped us,
sir. Will that be all, sir?

                    J.B.
                (Taughtingly)
Yes, sir....I mean no sir.

                    BUTLER
Sir?

4-22-37   (Continued)

D-4   J.B.
                  You pack me a bag and bring
                  it down to the Club. This
                  place is clammy!

                           BUTLER
                  Yes, sir.

                           J.B.
                        (Triumphantly)
                  No, sir! I've changed my mind.
                  That's deader than this is.
                  You bring that bag to the Ritz.

                           BUTLER
                  Very good, sir.

                           J.B.
                  No.

                           BUTLER
                  Sir?

                           J.B.
                  You bring it to the Louis.

                           BUTLER
                  Sir?

                           J.B.
                        (Yelling)
                  The Louis, the Louis, the Hotel
                  Louis!
                        (He chuckles)
                  Louis will drop dead.

          DISSOLVE TO:

D-5   MARY AND JOHNNY - IN THE MIDDLE OF THE BATHTUB IN
          THE IMPERIAL SUITE

          They are looking around inquisitively.

                           MARY
                        (Apparently answer-
                         ing a question)
                  I think he said "to wash"....but
                  I don't know what you'd wash in
                  a thing like this.

          4-22-37   (Continued)

D-5   JOHNNY
                    Maybe an elephant.

                             MARY
                    Besides, it hasn't got any faucets.

Now Johnny looks down and frowns.

D-6   INSERT - THE FISH FAUCETS

D-7   CLOSE SHOT - JOHNNY LOOKING AT THEM

        He reaches down and twists one gingerly. Nothing
        happens. He twists it further and nothing happens.
        He leaves it crossways and tries the next one. Nothing
        happens. He tries the next one, then moves over to
        the other side and tries those with a beginning irrita-
        tion. As he reaches the last fish, Mary sticks her
        head in the picture and he leans over and speaks to her.

                             JOHNNY
                    I thought for a moment these
                    might have something to....

        He twists the last fish and everything starts at once.
        Water hisses at them from all sides and all levels.

D-8   SERIES OF SHOTS - JOHNNY AND MARY BEING SQUIRTED

        Johnny struggles with the fish and eventually turns off
        the water. As they stand and look at each other like
        a pair of drowned cats, the buzzer rings.

D-9   VAN BUREN - IN THE CORRIDOR

        He takes his finger off the button. He looks like a
        walking dry goods store. He carries a bunch of dresses
        in his arms, an assortment of handbags are looped over
        his wrists, and several hats are piled on his head.
        Now we hear the door open. Van Buren rehearses a quick
        smile, then smiles. His smile freezes somewhat.

D-10   CLOSE SHOT - MARY PEEKING AROUND THE DOOR

        We see very little of her, but what we see is very wet.

                             MARY
                    What is it?....Oh, hello.

        4-22-37

D-11   TWO SHOT - VAN BUREN AND MARY

                         VAN BUREN
               Just pour yourself into these,
               dear, and fall in a faint. I
               never try to sell anything...
               I never try to persuade the...
                    (He falters and
                     looks down)
               prospect or...

          Mary follows his gaze and looks around the door and
          down. The CAMERA PANS DOWN to the bottom of the door.
          A beautiful pool is spreading out onto the floor of the
          hall.

          DISSOLVE TO:

D-12   LOUIS - PAST WALLACE - IN LOUIS' OFFICE

          Louis wears a dinner jacket with a black and white
          satin tie.

                         LOUIS
                    (Shouting indignantly)
               Vot do you mean you don't? You
               carried planty lies in your colyum
               Vallace, and in de second place
               it's de troot, and in the toid
               place she lives right here in de
               Hotel Louis....
                    (He points a finger at
                     heaven and adds,)
               De rondeloo of de Bong Tong.

D-13   WALLACE - PAST LOUIS

                         WALLACE
                    (Severely)
               I don't know who you've got living
               here, but I tell you the old man
               don't buy fur coats for dames! If
               anybody knew it would be me wouldn't
               it?

D-14   LOUIS - PAST WALLACE

                         LOUIS
                    (Passionately)
               I tell you she is and he does
               but you don't.

          4-22-37   (Continued)

                              230

                         WALLACE
                       (Furiously)
            I don't what?

                         LOUIS
                        (Pained)
            You just don't know vot's going on.

                         WALLACE
                   (Stabbed to the heart)
            I don't know what's going on!

                         LOUIS
            You just ain't up to date.

                         WALLACE
                    (Not believing
                       his ears)
            I just ain't up to.....

                         LOUIS
                  (Interrupting him)
            You lost your gripe.

                         WALLACE
                      (Exploding)
            Listen, you greasy little Hamburger!

They immediately seize each other by the collar, and
there is a breathless struggle, punctuated by efforts
to trip each other and to stamp on each others feet.
Each successful stamp is celebrated by an "Ouch!"
from Wallace and an "Ai!" from Louis. The door flies
open and Mr. Gurney hurries in.

                         GURNEY
            Mr. Ball is at the desk, Mr. Louis.

                         LOUIS
                    (Thunderstruck)
            Mr. B!

Slowly he takes his hands off Wallace. Now, catching
him off his guard, he gives Wallace a swift kick in
the shins. He cackles at him and threatens him with
a punch, then turns to Gurney.

                         LOUIS
                      (Fearfully)
            Vot does he vant?

He threatens Wallace with another punch as he sees the
latter creeping up on him.

4-22-37   (Continued)

D-14   GURNEY
                      A room and a bath.

                              LOUIS
                           (Hypnotized)
                      A room and a bat!
                           (He breaks into a
                            smile and speaks
                            ecstatically)
                      Goiney.....it woiked!

                             WALLACE
                           (Sourly)
                      You boys must think I was born
                      yesterday.

As Louis swings on him, we hear:

                           J.B.'S VOICE
                           (Shouting
                      Hey!

They turn and listen with mixed emotions.

                           J.B.'S VOICE
                      How long does it take to get
                      a room in this shebang?

Wallace looks dumbfounded.

D-15 J.B. - FROM BEHIND HOTEL COUNTER

The old man looks around furiously.

                              J.B.
                           (Yelling)
                      No wonder you don't do any business!

He starts pounding on a service bell. On the third
bang Louis flies into the picture. He is also on the
far side of the counter.
                              LOUIS
                           (Ecstatically)
                      Mister B! Are you a sight for
                      eye sores!

                              J.B.
                           (Scowling)
                      Hunh? Give me a room with a bath.

                              LOUIS
                           (Importantly)
                      A room vit a bat.
                           (He sticks his fingers in his
                            mouth and looks toward the key rack)

                                232

D-15   LOUIS
                     (Continued)
               Now let me see...de Imperal soot
               is naturally already occupied...
               heh, heh, heh...
                     (He turns and winks
                      at Mr. Ball)

D-16   CLOSE SHOT - J.B.

        He reacts unpleasantly to the wink, then looks behind
        him to see if it was for somebody else.

D-17   J.B. AND LOUIS - PAST GURNEY'S HEAD

                        LOUIS
                    (Stretching out
                     his hand)
               Give me de keys to the Royal.

                        J.B.
                    (Irritatedly)
               I don't want a royal...I just
               want a room with a bath.

                        LOUIS
                    (Shrugging his
                     shoulders)
               All right! Give me de Prince
               of Pilsen soot!

                        J.B.
                    (Raising his voice)
               I don't want the Prince's soot...
               I want a room with a bath!

                        LOUIS
                    (Expecting J.B. to
                     understand)
               But it couldn't be in de
               tower, den.

                        J.B.
                    (Furiously)
               What do I want to be in a
               tower for?

4-22-37   (Continued)

D-17   LOUIS
                        (Completely be-
                          wildered)
                    You don't vant to be near the
                    Imperal soot?

                              J.B.
                        (Still furiously)
                    What for?

Louis gives him a long look, then shrugs his shoulders
and reaches his hand out toward Gurney.

                              LOUIS
                        (Resignedly)
                    Give me a plain double room.

                              J.B.
                        (Louder than ever)
                    WITH BATH!

                              LOUIS
                        (Losing his temper for
                          a second)
                    Naturally, vit bat. You think
                    ve use de rain barrel?

He immediately looks very contrite, bows and says:

                              LOUIS
                    Only a joke.

He takes the keys from Gurney's hand and points out
of the picture.

                              LOUIS
                    After you, Mister B.

J.B. walks out of the shot. Louis lingers for an
instant.

                              LOUIS
                        (To Gurney)
                    Raise all the prices five
                    dollars...I don't vant no
                    rabble around here.

Saying which, he shapes his mouth for a Bronx cheer
and looks up at the top of the partition.

4-22-37

D-18   WALLACE - AT THE TOP OF THE PARTITION

Between the clock and amongst the palms we see his
phizz looking displeased. THE SCORE AT THIS POINT
THINS OUT TO A SINGLE DEEP CLARINET NOTE. His head
disappears.

D-19   REVERSE SHOT - WALLACE ON PARTITION

This is from inside the office. He climbs down onto a
table and picks up a telephone without waiting to reach
the floor. As he dials a number,

D-20   MOVING SHOT - AHEAD OF J.B.

Louis hurries up and falls in step.

                    LOUIS
        It's an unexpected surprise to
        have you, Mister B.

                    J.B.
                (Sardonically)
        I just moved in for the funeral.

                    LOUIS
        Yea...but de last corpse laughs de
        longest.

D-21   WALLACE - AT THE TELEPHONE

                    WALLACE
                (Into telephone)
        Kill the Sprickels blessed event
        and lead off with: What leading international
        financier...Make that: Flash!
        What leading international financier...

D-22   THE ELEVATORS

Louis precedes J.B. into the picture and reaches for
the elevator bell. As he does so, the elevator door
opens, and Mary appears en negligee.

                    MARY
        Oh, Mister Louis, I was just looking
        for you.

4-22-37

D-23   CLOSE SHOT...LOUIS

His face is a mixture of glee, anticipation, and
amusement. He seems to be signaling to Mary to look
to his right.

D-24   CLOSE SHOT...MARY

She stares past us in puzzlement for a moment, then
looks slowly to her left.

> MARY
> (Surprised)
> Why, hello...Santy Claus !!

D-25   J.B., LOUIS, AND MARY

J.B. stares at Mary for a second before recognizing
her.

> J.B.
> (Chuckling)
> How are you getting along?

D-26   CLOSE SHOT...FACE ON...J.B., MARY,AND LOUIS BETWEEN
THEM

Louis now does some very bad acting.

> LOUIS
> You know each other, hunh?
> Vell, vell, vell.

> J.B.
> (Somewhat perplexed)
> You live here?

> MARY
> Oh, yes...Mr. Louis made me a
> special rate.

> LOUIS
> (Without pleasure)
> Vit breakfast.

> J.B.
> (With relief)
> Oh.

4-22-37   (Continued)

                         MARY
                    (To Louis)
               That's what I wanted to see
               you about, Mr. Louis...would
               it be all right if I had the
               breakfast now?

                         LOUIS
                    (Astonished)
               You mean <u>now</u>?

                         J.B.
                    (Diffidently)
               Don't you think <u>supper</u> would be
               a better idea?

                         MARY
               I don't think I'm entitled to
               supper.

                         LOUIS
                    (Stupefied)
               Entitled!
                    (He laughs raucously
                     and slaps J.B. on
                     the stomach)
               Is she entitled!

          J.B. takes out his watch to see if the crystal is
          broken.

                         LOUIS
                    (To Mary)
               You name it, and ve'll wrastle
               it up.
                    (He snaps his
                     fingers to some-
                     body out of the
                     picture and calls:)
               Oinest!

                         MARY
                    (Slightly embarrassed)
               That's awfully kind of you, Mr.
               Louis, but...

          A headwaiter complete with menu hurries into the
          picture.

                         LOUIS
                    (To the headwaiter)
               Take an order.

                      LOUIS (Cont'd)
                    (To Mary)
Vot you should have is you should
have a little snack of lobster
Financier...

                      J.B.
                    (Interrupting)
Breast of guinea hen on Westphalian
ham.

                      LOUIS
                    (Nodding
                      enthusiastically)
Breast of guinea hen naturally,
vot am I tinking...and a little
orange and avocado salad.

                      J.B.
                    (Sharply)
Endive and beet root...and don't
forget the truffles with the hen.

                      LOUIS
                    (Dejectedly)
Endive and beet root and a bottle
of nineteen twenty-tree Mumm, don't
you tink?

                      J.B.
                    (Without hesitation)
No I do not. I'd give her George
Goulet, nineteen-nineteen.

                      LOUIS
                    (Bridling)
Vit guinea hen?

                      J.B.
You heard me.

                      LOUIS
                    (Dejectedly)
And a bumb surprise on de end.

                      J.B.
                    (Severely)
Give her some Port Salut cheese
and a lemon water ice.

                    THE HEADWAITER
Yes, sir.

                              LOUIS
                          (To Mary)
                    You're good and hungry, yes?

                              MARY
                    Well, yes, I..I...

                              LOUIS
                          (With decision)
                    Soive for two in the Imperal
                    Soot... and snappy!

          He indicates the elevator to Mary and J.B.

          DISSOLVE TO:

D-27   EXTERIOR - ELEVATOR'S NINTH FLOOR

          The doors open, and J. B. and Louis step out.

                              J.B.
                          (To Mary)
                    Glad to have seen you again.
                    Good night.

                              MARY
                    Good night.
                          (She turns to Louis)
                    And thank you for the supper,
                    Mr. Louis.

                              LOUIS
                    S'entirely mutual. Nightie-night.

          The elevator doors close.

                              J.B.
                          (Frowning)
                    What's that young lady's name?

                              LOUIS
                          (Repeating)
                    Vot's dat young lady's...
                          (He throws a glance full
                            of admiration at J.B.)
                    Miss Mary Smitt.

                              J.B.
                    Miss Mary Smith?

                              LOUIS
                    Exactly!

D-27

                                J.B.
                        I thought it was Jones.

                                LOUIS
                        Vot a diplomat!
                            (He fumbles once,
                            then falls in step
                            with J.B.)

            DISSOLVE TO:

D-28   MEDIUM CLOSE - JOHNNY'S SUIT ON A CLOTHES LINE ON THE
        TERRACE OUTSIDE THE IMPERIAL SUITE LIVING ROOM -
        (NIGHT)

        The suit is dripping. The CAMERA which is inside the
        living room, PULLS BACK, OVER THE SOFA AND BETWEEN
        Johnny and Mary without showing them, and ONTO THE
        remains of a magnificent supper: empty champagne
        bottle, fruits, nuts, flowers, bomb surprise, etc.

                                JOHNNY'S VOICE
                        That's one of the finest suppers I
                        ever supped...

        The CAMERA TRUCKS BACK AND PANS UP, revealing Johnny
        and Mary behind the supper table. She wears a Van
        Buren creation, and Johnny is wrapped in a voluminous
        white turkish towel bath robe. He has another towel
        around his neck as a scarf.

                                JOHNNY (Continued)
                        I mean I ever..that's right,
                        supped.

                                MARY
                        'Salmost too marvelous.
                            (She flops over sidewise)

        Johnny does likewise, then turns over on his side to
        see her better. This brings his back in view. We
        TRUCK IN TO A CLOSE TWO SHOT. On his back we read:

                        "Stolen from the Hotel Louis"

                                JOHNNY
                        We used to have a chef years ago
                        who could make that guinea hen like
                        that. That's one of my father's
                        favorite dishes...poor old father.

4-22-37

                                240

D-29   OVERHEAD SHOT - JOHNNY AND MARY

                        MARY
            I guess he must have been pretty
            rich at one time.

                        JOHNNY
                    (Puzzled)
            Who?

                        MARY
            Your father...I mean to have a
            chef and all like that.

                        JOHNNY
            Oh...oh, yes.

                        MARY
            Has he been dead long?

                        JOHNNY
            The chef? I don't think so.
            He just went back to Bulgaria
            or Montenegro or whatever it...

                        MARY
                    (Interrupting)
            I mean your father. Has he
            been dead long?

                        JOHNNY
                    (Surprised)
            Did I say he was dead?

                        MARY
            Well, you said, "poor old father."

                        JOHNNY
            Well, you don't have to be
            dead to be "poor old father"...
            you don't even have to be poor.

                        MARY
            I suppose you don't have to be
            old either.

                        JOHNNY
            Not so terribly.

                        MARY
            Then I wouldn't go around saying
            "poor old father" and squeezing
            sympathy out of people.

4-22-37   (Continued)

                              JOHNNY
                         (A little desperately)
                    I wasn't trying to squeeze any
                    sym...I mean, I should think a
                    fellow has a right to think of
                    his parents once in a while, so
                    when I said: "poor...old..."

                              MARY
                         (Interrupting)
                    What are you going to look for...

                              JOHNNY
                    Huh? I said: "poor...old...fa...

                              MARY
                    ...in the morning? What kind of
                    a job?

                              JOHNNY
                    What kind of a...oh! I don't
                    know. What would you suggest?

                              MARY
                    I should think I'd aim a little
                    higher. At least it wouldn't
                    do any harm to try. Can't you
                    do anything besides wait on table?

                              JOHNNY
                    I can't wait on table. I just
                    know how to take the dishes off!

                              MARY
                    Didn't you study to be something?

                              JOHNNY
                    Something like what?

                              MARY
                    Something like a...dentist or
                    something.

                              JOHNNY
                    No.

                              MARY
                         (Acidly)
                    How did you intend to while away
                    the hours when you grew up?

D-29

                        JOHNNY
            I didn't have to study for that.
            In training, I have whiled an
            hour in twenty-six minutes flat.
            It was always my dream to do it
            in twenty-five. I remember at
            school there was a boy called
            Overdunk who had unusually long
            legs and...

                        MARY
            Oh, shut up.

                        JOHNNY
            It wasn't Overdunk, it was
            Underdunk.

Johnny chuckles at her, turns slightly on his side
and arranges himself more comfortably. Mary closes
her eyes. Johnny looks at her interestedly.

                        JOHNNY
            I'm glad you came into the
            Automat.

                        MARY
                 (Sleepily)
            So am I.

Johnny edges a little closer.

D-30   J.B. - IN BED

He has a big cigar in his mouth. He talks into the
telephone. A book lies across his stomach.

                        J.B.
                 (Into telephone)
            That's right. AND the Westphalian
            ham AND the Goulet nineteen nineteen.
            Talking about it made me hungry...

D-31   LOUIS - AT THE TELEPHONE

His face is full of admiration.

                        LOUIS
                 (Shaking his head)
            Vot a diplomat!

4-22-37

D-32   JOHNNY AND MARY - ON THE COUCH

                    JOHNNY
         Good night.

He leans over and gives Mary a long kiss on the lips
to which she responds dreamily and pleasantly. As
he draws back for breath, she comes to suddenly. Her
eyes snap open and she looks at him indignantly.

                    MARY
        SAY!

D-33   LOUIS - AT THE DESK DOWNSTAIRS

He puts the telephone down and shoves it away from
him. His face is still full of admiration. A house
detective in an iron hat sticks his ugly puss in the
picture and speaks out of the side of his mouth.

                 THE HOUSE DICK
        Listen, boss, that new dame's got
        a guy in her soot.

                    LOUIS
              (Explosively)
        Who ast you vot time it is?

FADE OUT:

                END OF SEQUENCE "D"

4-22-37

<u>SEQUENCE "E"</u>

FADE IN:

E-1   <u>A NEWSPAPER PRESS</u> IN FULL BLAST

The copies riffle out in the usual way.

DISSOLVE TO:

E-2   <u>A NEWSPAPER TRUCK</u>

It is piled high with bundles of newspapers. We hear
its motor running. On the side of the truck is pasted
a card which reads:

> "Featuring -
> I Cover the Back Door
> by
> Wallace Wisling"

Another bundle is thrown on, and the truck pulls away.

E-3   <u>SHOTS FROM MOVING NEWSPAPER TRUCK</u> - NIGHT

We see interesting flashes of the New York skyline as
the truck whizzes up Broadway, drumping bundles as it
goes.

DISSOLVE TO:

E-4   A PRETTY BLONDE CHORINE <u>IN A TWIN BED</u>

Her face is screwed up to hear better.

> CHORINE
> Over to where?

E-5   A PRETTY BRUNETTE CHORINE - <u>IN AN INVISIBLE BATH TUB</u>

She lowers a newspaper and shouts past the CAMERA.

> BRUNETTE
> I thaid: over to the Louis... itth
> thimply thwarming with bankerth.

DISSOLVE TO:

E-6   A MIDDLE-AGED COUPLE - <u>IN A HOTEL BED ROOM</u>

The wife is greasing her face and the husband is bending over untying his shoes. The husband straightens
up and speaks indignantly:

4-22-37   (Continued)

E-6

                    THE HUSBAND
          What's the matter with this hotel?

                     THE WIFE
                  (A la Mary Boland)
          It isn't fashionable, dear. You will
          notice that when J.B. Ball wants to
          piccadillo he doesn't pick it here.
          He goes over to the.......

E-7   NIGHT SHOT - (MINIATURE) HOTEL LOUIS

        The two great towers rise in unlighted gloom except
        for the dim lights of Mary's suite. THE MUSIC HOLDS
        AN ORGAN POINT, THEN SOUNDS A LIVELY NOTE as a light
        flashes on in the tower. After a second we hear THREE
        CHEERFUL ASCENDING NOTES, and three lights run up the
        tower. Now to musical accompaniment the lights zig-
        zag from the left to the right tower. THE MUSIC
        STRIKES AN ORGAN POINT and we

        DISSOLVE TO:

E-8   SERVANTS' DINING ROOM IN THE BALL MANSION

        A tableful of servants is listening agog to the
        butler hidden behind a newspaper.

                     THE BUTLER
          "Flash! What leading international
          financier has gone pfoot with his
          wife over a beautiful gell, and
          followed her over to the Hotel
          Louis - question mark!"

        The Butler lowers his newspaper and speaks lugubriousl;

                     THE BUTLER
          Many things are clear today which
          previously were murky.

        DISSOLVE TO:

E-9   NIGHT SHOT - (MINIATURE) - HOTEL LOUIS

        More and more lights twinkle on to the gay music. When
        the towers are lit up like Christmas trees, the stars
        in the background fade out, night changes to day, we
        see the Hotel Louis in the bright sunlight, and the
        MUSIC BECOMES EXALTANT.

E-10   HIGH CAMERA SHOT - TAXI CABS AND PRIVATE CARS IN
        FRONT OF THE HOTEL LOUIS

        They blow their horns raucously as the doorman scurrie
        up and down. Now TO A MARCH, SOMETHING LIKE "THE MARCH
        OF THE TOREADORS", we CUT TO:

4-22-37

E-11   LOUIS, GURNEY, AND SOME EXTRAS AT THE HOTEL DESK
        Feature CHORINES and the MIDDLE-AGED COUPLE

        Louis is in front of and Gurney behind the desk. They
        are each telephoning. The head of the queue waits
        impatiently. Gurney looks at his key-rack, then speaks
        into the telephone:

                          GURNEY
        How big a suite do you want, madam?

                          LOUIS
                    (Butting in on Gurney's
                    business)
        Vot do you mean: How big of a soot?
        She takes vot ve give.
                    (Now he snarls into
                    his own telephone)
        Ve don't give out de names from de
        customers. Vot kind of a dump do
        you tink dis is?
                    (After which he looks around
                    cautiously, then adds in a
                    low voice:)
        Mary Smitt.

        He hangs up, and the phone immediately rings.

                          THE HEAD OF THE LINE
                    (Irascribly)
        Here, here. When a man takes the
        trouble to.....

                          LOUIS
                    (Shutting him up with
                    a gesture)
        Please, yes?
                    (Now he barks into the
                    telephone:)
        De two dollar room? You'd haff to
        be a dwarf.

        He slams the phone down and chuckles to the Head of
        the Line.

                          LOUIS (Cont'd)
        De beauty of success is you don't
        got to be polite.
                    (He snatches up the
                    ringing phone)
        Vell? Who are you and vot do you
        vant?

E-12   MRS. BALL - IN A MOVING OBSERVATION CAR

        She is at the telephone. The scenery is flashing by
        behind her. She has a newspaper in her hand.

4-22-37   (Continued)

E-12
<blockquote>
MRS. BALL
(Icily)
I am Mrs. J. B. Ball, and I want
some information.
</blockquote>

E-13   THE HORRIFIED LOUIS - <u>AT THE TELEPHONE</u>

He opens his mouth to speak, licks his lips nervously,
then gives out with:

<blockquote>
LOUIS
I'm sorry, lady, you got de wrong
Louis!
(He hangs up and mops
his forehead)
</blockquote>
The bell rings again.

DISSOLVE TO:

E-14   <u>MARY'S BED</u>

We see a vague protuberance in the middle, but no
Mary. The phone is ringing. After a moment Mary
appears between the enormous pillows. She reaches
for an alarm clock on a table beside the bed, shoves
it under the mattress and disappears between the
pillows. The phone rings again. Mary reappears slowly,
blinks her eyes and gives the room a quadruple take-it.
The phone rings once more. Mary reaches for it
gingerly.

<blockquote>
MARY
(Into telephone)
Yes...yes,--this is me...the
what of what?
</blockquote>

E-15   A VERY REFINED GENELTMAN AT A DESK IN FRONT OF A
<u>MAGNIFICENT CAR</u>

<blockquote>
GENTLEMAN
The V-Sixteen Company of America,
Miss Smith.
</blockquote>

E-16   CLOSE SHOT - <u>MARY SITTING UP IN BED</u>

<blockquote>
MARY
(Into telephone)
You'd like to what. Have I
ever what?
(She yawns a loud yawn)
</blockquote>

4-22-37   (Continued)

                    MARY (Cont'd)
          Excuse me...Of course I've never
          driven one...we had a Saxon...yes,
          I guess it is different but...Well,
          what do you want to do that for?
          I'll take your word for it that it...
          Even if I did want it, what would
          I use for...
                    (Defeated, she shrugs
                     her shoulders)
          All right...all right... You can
          put two chauffeurs on it if it
          makes you happy...Pink! ... I said
          any color you like. All right,
          good-bye.

She hangs up and stares at the phone. Now she starts
to get out of bed. She puts on a dressing gown. The
phone rings.

SOUND: TELEPHONE BELL

                    MARY
                 (Picking up the
                  telephone gingerly)
          Yes.... this is Miss Smith....
          Fine, how did you sleep? Who?
          You'll have to say it again....
          Cart what?...Carray's..Yes, I've
          got it...No...no, I'm sorry but
          I haven't...You make what?...Oh,
          well that's fine but I don't want
          any jewelry.

Another phone starts to ring. Mary looks over desperately and sees there is a second phone beside the
bed. She unhooks it and puts it to her ear.

                    MARY
                 (Into second phone)
          Hello, yes...
                 (Into first phone)
          But how do you know I'm honest?
          Suppose I run away with them?
                 (Into second phone)
          I've already got a fur coat.
                 (Into first phone)
          Look, I just got up and I want
          to take a bath.
                 (Into second phone)
          I said I want to take a bath!
                 (Into first phone with
                  a little impatience)
          All right, but give me a chance to
          wake up.

E-16
> MARY (Cont'd)(Into second phone)
> I SAID I WANT TO BRUSH MY TEETH.

A third telephone starts to ring. She looks toward it
open-mouthed.

> MARY (Cont'd)
> (Into first telephone)
> All right.
> (Into second phone)
> ALL RIGHT.
> (Shouting across the room
> at the third telephone)
> ALL <u>RIGHT</u>!

She hangs up the two telephones and holds her temples.
The first telephone starts to ring. She looks at it
indignantly. As she opens her mouth to cuss it, the
second telephone starts to ring. As she turns to this,
the third telephone chimes in with its bass jangle. Now
a buzzer rings. Mary puts her hands over her ears. We
hear a sharp knocking on the door. Mary takes her hands
down. Looks helplessly at the door and crosses to it.
THE CAMERA PANS with her. She opens the door six inches
and peers out. She steps back in amazement as a six-
foot basket of flowers is pushed into her. As she looks
at this open-mouthed, two hands appear and give her a
pile of a hundred assorted letters and telegrams. She
closes the door slowly and the telephones stop ringing.
There is an immediate knock on the door. Mary opens the
door and a white flower box about seven feet long is
pushed in at her. She holds this in her arms patheti-
cally. She closes the door again.

> MARY
> (Closing the door)
> Thanks.

The instant the door is closed there comes a rap from
the door leading to the rest of the suite. Almost in
tears Mary turns toward it.

E-17   THE DOOR - OPENING

Johnny appears, his arms full of telegrams, letters
and flowers. He wears a bewildered expression..
Another phone starts ringing.

E-18   MARY - PAST JOHNNY

> MARY
> (Yelling)
> Answer that, will you.

Johnny dumps his armful into Mary's arms. He picks
up a telephone.

> JOHNNY
> (Into phone in a phoney
> Cockney accent)
> This is the Smith resident..I'll see
> if the mistress is at 'ome, madam.

4-22-37

E-18   He puts his hand over the transmitter and grins at Mary.

                              MARY
                        (Raising her voice to
                         be heard)
                  Tell her I'm canning some fruit.

                              JOHNNY
                        (Into telephone)
                  The mistress has left for the 'unt,
                  madam..no, no, the 'unt..the riding
                  of 'ounds on an 'orse.. I said: an
                  'orse..an equine! Very good, madam.

         He hangs up and reaches for another ringing phone.
         Mary hurries out of the room.

         DISSOLVE TO:

E-19   LOUIS - IN HIS LOBBY - FULL OF PEOPLE

         His hands are clasped behind his back and he is teetering
         back and forth happily, like a rocking chair. He stands
         fairly near the hotel desk. There are scenes of great
         activity around him. Suddenly he narrows his eyes and
         looks outside the picture, suspiciously.

E-20   A MAHARAJAH FOLLOWED BY THREE VEILED WIVES

         They are followed by many employees with luggage.

E-21   LOUIS

         Still looking out of the picture, his expression becomes
         even more suspicious. He turns toward the hotel desk,
         does a quick thumbs-down, and starts out of the picture.
         The CAMERA PANS with him. A passing gentleman button-
         holes him. This gentleman is of the nervous type who
         returns to a door he has just locked to make sure he
         has locked it.

                              GENTLEMAN
                  Are you positive this is the
                  Hotel Louis?

                              LOUIS
                        (Sharply and without
                         stopping)
                  You vant to see my boit certificate?
                  De line forms on de left.
                        (He indicates the place and
                         continues his stroll)

         We hear an elevator door rumble open. Louis turns
         his head sharply then beams in recognition.

4-22-37

E-22   THE ELEVATOR DOORS OPENING

     J.B. strides out, and the CAMERA TRUCKS AHEAD of him.
     Louis hurries into the shot and falls in step on the
     second try.

> LOUIS
> (Confidentially)
> Good morning.

> J.B.
> How are you?

     Louis gives him a wink and moves the flower from his
     own buttonhole to J.B.'s. In doing this he pulls him
     down a little by the lapel.

> LOUIS
> (Mysteriously)
> Dat coitain party called up, but
> I give her a bum steer.

> J.B.
> (Puzzled)
> What?

> LOUIS
> (Even more mysteriously)
> De storm and strife just give me a
> buzz but I got her completely
> mystified.

> J.B.
> (Pointing to himself)
> Me too.

     He gives Louis an impatient look and walks out of
     the picture.

> LOUIS
> (Full of admiration)
> Vot a diplomat.

E-23   A LARGE DOORMAN STANDING BY J.B.'S AUTOMOBILE

     He throws open the door and speaks funereally.

> DOORMAN
> Good morning, sir.

4-22-37

E-24   INTERIOR - <u>J.B.'S CAR</u>

This is a landeaulet, and the rear quarter is open
to the beautiful morning. J.B. gets into the car
and passes the doorman a coin.

                    DOORMAN
                  (Solemnly)
          Yes, sir. Thank you, sir.

Unsmilingly he gives J.B. a wink. The car pulls
away and J.B. turns in astonishment and tries to
look back at the doorman. Now he looks ahead again
with a puzzled expression on his face. After a
moment something catches his eye. He looks out of
the picture, smiles and nods "Good morning."

E-25   AUTOMOBILE SHOT - THE PRESIDENT OF THE FIRST NATIONAL
        BANK

He is a rural type in sideburns and a Rolls-Royce.
He smiles a toothy smile, then points to his morning
paper and gives J.B. a terrific wink.

E-26   CLOSE SHOT - J.B. <u>IN HIS AUTOMOBILE</u>

He has a terrific take-it, then looks forward in
puzzlement.

DISSOLVE TO:

E-27   CLOSE SHOT - HELP WANTED COLUMN

Under the heading: "Help Wanted - Female" we read:
among other ads:

                "Cocktail waitress, twelve
                dollars and tips. Must have
                curves."

                    MARY'S VOICE
                  (Reading)
          "Cocktail waitress, twelve dollars
          and tips. Must have curves."

E-28   MARY AND JOHNNY - <u>AT THE BREAKFAST TABLE IN THE
        GRAND SALON</u>

They are dressed to go out. Each has a newspaper.
Behind them we see flowers in boxes and in pots.

4-22-37   (Continued)

                        253

The table is covered with the remains of breakfast
and advertising letters and telegrams.

> JOHNNY
> (Looking up)
> Well, you've got 'em, haven't you?

> MARY
> (Reading)
> "Attractive girl over eighteen
> that will dive from ten-foot pole."

> JOHNNY
> (Reading from his paper)
> "Raise giant frogs...biddies lay
> ten thousand eggs."

> MARY
> Stop joking.

> JOHNNY
> (Innocently)
> Who's joking?

Mary looks at him for a moment suspiciously, then
returns to her paper and reads solemnly:

> MARY
> "Companion for mild mental case
> in exchange for refined surroundings."

> JOHNNY
> (Solemnly)
> "Let us teach you tattooing."

Mary looks up quickly, but Johnny seems to be on the
level.

> JOHNNY
> (Reading)
> "Stuff small animals for profit
> and pleasure...very life-like."

> MARY
> (Challengingly)
> Where?

Johnny turns his paper around and points it out
for her.

                         JOHNNY
          There must be something for somebody
          who can't do anything.

                         MARY
                     (Reading)
          "Attractive widow with small
          capital would like to meet gentle-
          man with sense of humor."

Johnny laughs. Mary joins him in spite of herself.

                         JOHNNY
          I guess I'm pretty dumb at that.

                         MARY
                     (Taking his hand impul-
                      sively)
          Of course you're not, Johnny...
          you're just a little under-developed...
          I mean, it's only temporary.
                     (She adds this last hastily
                      and smiled apologetically)
          I mean, some people develop sooner than
          others, but once the others develop, they're
          just as well developed as the first ones,
          don't you see? It's like you take a
          chicken. Now a chicken reaches maturity
          at...at, well whatever it is, but on the
          other hand a horse...takes much longer.

                         JOHNNY
                     (Nicely)
          You feel I am of the horse type.

                         MARY
          I think I'm kind of dumb myself.

                         JOHNNY
          But very sweet.

He holds her hand tightly.

                         MARY
          Am I?
                     (She smiles at him and
                      seems to come a little
                      closer)

The buzzer rings. Mary rises disappointedly.

E-29   THE FOYER OF MARY'S SUITE

Mary comes into the picture and reaches for the doorknob. No sooner has she touched it, than Mr. Hulgar
is inside, closing the door behind him.

                    MR. HULGAR
                 (Rapidly)
            E. J. Hulgar and Company, stock-
            brokers, all principal cities.

                    MARY
                 (Stupefied)
            What?

                    HULGAR
                 (Staccato)
            I want to make you some money.
            The best way is in steel. Is
            it going up or is it going down...
            that's all we have to know. I'd
            like to make you a lot of money.

                    MARY
                 (Amiably and vaguely)
            Well, that's certainly very nice of
            you. Go ahead.

                    HULGAR
            Go ahead and what?

                    MARY
            Go ahead and...whatever it is.

                    HULGAR
                 (Frowning slightly)
            It's the "whatever it is" I came
            to see you about. Shall I buy or
            shall I sell?

                    MARY
            Why don't you just use your own
            judgment?

                    HULGAR
                 (Quickly)
            That's the last thing in the
            world I want to use.
                 (He looks all around
                  the room before con-
                  tinuing)
            But if you could find out how he feels
            about it...if you could sort of worm
            it out of him, then we'd have something.

                      MARY
Who?

                      HULGAR
Him.

                      MARY
What?

                      HULGAR
        (After looking all around)
Allbay.

                      MARY
Who?

Hulgar seizes her shoulders and whispers in her ear.
She looks first astonished and then amused.

                      MARY
Well, I'll go right in and ask
him, but I don't think he knows
anything about it.

Hulgar steps back in horror.

                      HULGAR
He's here?

                      MARY
        (Innocently)
He's having his breakfast.

                      HULGAR
        (Nearly trembling)
I..I'll wait in the hall.

                      MARY
Why?

                      HULGAR
        (Retreating)
Don't mention my name.

                      MARY
        (Reassuringly)
I don't even remember it.

Hulgar pauses for a slight take-it, then backs out.
Mary looks at him a moment, then turns toward the salon.

E-30   JOHNNY - <u>AT THE BREAKFAST TABLE</u>

He is reading the paper. He looks up as Mary comes into
the shot, then reads:

                    JOHNNY
            "Sponge rubber neckties...look
            like leather...wear like iron."

                    MARY
            A man in the hall wants to know
            how you feel about steel.

                    JOHNNY
                (Vaguely)
            Steel neckties?

                    MARY
            Just plain steel.

                    JOHNNY
            Oh, steel.

                    MARY
            Yes.

                    JOHNNY
                (Scowling importantly)
            It's going down.

                    MARY
                (Frowning also)
            How do you know?

                    JOHNNY
                (Amiably)
            All right, make it "up."

                    MARY
            Listen, goofy, this is important.

The phone rings and Johnny claps it to his ear.

                    JOHNNY
                (In a very deep voice)
            Hammell's Funeral Parlor...I'll
            connect you with our chief embalmer,
            madam...telephone, Mr. Zerp.
                (He hangs up)
            Where was I? Oh! My father was
            saying something about steel. He was
            saying, if you compare the price of raw
            pig with...

4-22-37   (Continued)

E-30

> MARY
> (Interrupting him)
> Phooey!

> JOHNNY
> Pig iron..pig iron..with the coke
> shipment of..of..well, the coke
> shipments and divided the total by...
> (I'm not very good at mathematics)
> ..it would be plain to a child of
> six, oh no, that was rubber..I think
> he said a child of three.

> MARY
> Well, which way is it going?

> JOHNNY
> (Emphatically)
> It's going down.
> (He points out the window)
> Every time it looks like rain the
> market goes down...like a dog follows
> a cat.

> MARY
> Are you sure?

> JOHNNY
> (Scowling importantly)
> I've made a deep study of it.

> MARY
> (Doubtfully)
> Well, all right.
> (She exits)

The phone rings and Johnny picks it up while still
scowling after Mary.

> JOHNNY
> (With a thick German accent)
> Hallo, dis is de ackvarium...ya, de
> fish house.

E-31   MR. HULGAR - PACING THE HALL

He turns nervously at the sound of a door opening.

E-32   MARY STANDING IN THE DOORWAY

> MARY
> He says it's going down.

4-22-37

E-33   MEDIUM CLOSE - MR. HULGAR PAST MARY

He rises onto the balls of his feet as if he were going
to take off.

                    MR. HULGAR
              (Beaming)
          Down?

                    MARY
          Down.

                    MR. HULGAR
          Holy smoke!

He hurries away and disappears around a bend in the
hall. Mary turns toward us, looks back once over her
shoulder, then raises her eyebrows and goes past the
CAMERA.

FADE OUT:

                    END OF SEQUENCE "E"

SEQUENCE "F"

FADE IN:

F-1 J.B. - STANDING BEHIND <u>HIS DESK</u>

He stands next to a ticker. Facing him are two of
his partners. The third sits on the window sill
tying ticker tape into Chrysanthemum bows.

       J.B.
      (Forcefully)
    ...that steel is going up!
    It's the chance we've been
    waiting for. Steel is going
    up! Why is pig iron soaring?
    Why are ore shipment so heavy?
    What does it mean, gentlemen,
    when steel scrap is scarcer
    than hens' teeth?

DISSOLVE TO:

F-2 CLOSE SHOT - HULGAR IN HIS <u>WIRE ROOM</u>

He bends over an operator and speaks rapidly to the
accompaniment of the clicking instrument.

       HULGAR
    ...that steel is due for a big
    drop, double exclamation point,
    this is the greatest opportunity
    the clients of E. J. Hulgar and
    Company have ever had to participate
    in advance information from the
    world's greatest expert on steel,
    triple exclamation point. Further
    more,...

DISSOLVE TO:

F-3 J.B. AND PARTNERS - <u>IN HIS OFFICE</u>

       J.B.
    ...sixteen decimal one per cent?
     (He pounds his desk)
    It means, <u>steel</u> <u>is</u> <u>going</u> <u>up</u>!
    There isn't any way for it to go
    but <u>up</u>. A child of <u>two</u> could
    understand <u>that</u>.

      PARTNER NO. TWO
    I hope you're twenty million dollars
    right...because that's how much you
4-22-37 could be wrong.   (Continued)

F-3   J.B.
                   Forget it. Go on out and play golf.

          The three partners start out of the room.

F-4   THE PARTNERS GOING OUT <u>THE OPEN DOOR</u>

          Lillian stands by the open door waiting. As he
          passes thru, the third partner does a quick half-hitch
          on the doorknob with the ticker-tape he carries in
          his hand. Lillian closes the door and comes toward us.

                            LILLIAN
                   The financial delegation from Ecuador
                   is waiting, Mr. Ball.

F-5   J.B....PAST LILLIAN

          She stops beside his desk.

                            J.B.
                   All right.

                            LILLIAN
                   And Mr. Salmon from London, and Mr.
                   Jonas, and Mr. Metzger, and Lord...

                            J.B.
                        (Without any pauses whatsoever)
                   Take a letter: Miss Mary Smith care
                   of the Boys' Whatever-it-is make that
                   the Hotel Louis Park Avenue New York
                   New York my dear Miss Smith make that
                   my dear Mary...
                        (He looks at the ceiling for
                         inspiration)

                            LILLIAN
                        (After a moment)
                   "My dear Mary..."

                            J.B.
                        (Scowling)
                   Don't rush me...now where was I?

                            LILLIAN
                   "My dear Mary..."

                            J.B.
                   Oh. My dear Mary: A school boy
                   called Jones, make his name Willie...

4-22-37   (Continued)

                              LILLIAN
                 Willie Jones.

                              J.B.
                          (Crossly)
                 No, no, just Willie. A schoolboy
                 called Willie I want this on plain
                 paper..have we got any plain paper?

                              LILLIAN
                 If we haven't we'll get it.

                              J.B.
                          (Thoughtfully)
                 A schoolboy called Willie Jones...

                              LILLIAN
                 Just Willie.

                              J.B.
                          (A little sharply)
                 I said his name was Jones...needed
                 one hundred marbles for the purpose
                 of playing a game of maggies.

                              LILLIAN
                          (Gently)
                 Aggies.

                              J.B.
                 Whatever it is.

        The ticker begins to click, and J.B. reaches for the
        tape automatically.

                              J.B.
                 You got that?

                              LILLIAN
                          (With mild resentment)
                 Of course I have.

                              J.B.
                 Good!
                          (He looks vaguely at the tape)
                 His friend Henry, on the other hand...
                          (He frowns slightly and puts on
                           his pince-nez as the ticker
                           starts to spurt)
                 His friend Henry, on the other hand...
                 steel's too low buy a thousand at the
                 market.

                          LILLIAN
                (Pushing a switch on the Dictaphone)
            One thousand steel!

                          J.B.
            Tell Hyde to come in here.
            On the other hand, his friend Henry.

    The ticker starts to spurt faster.

            Buy five and tell that fellow to
            keep on the...another five.

                          LILLIAN
                    (Into Dictaphone)
            Ten more and watch it.

                          J.B.
                    (With an eye on the ticker)
            Did you ring for Hyde?

                          LILLIAN
            Yes, sir.

                          J.B.
            Get me Keech and Company.
            His friend Jack on the other hand...

                          LILLIAN
            His name was Henry.

                          J.B.
                    (Belligerently)
            What do you mean his name was...

                          LILLIAN
                    (Handing him a phone)
            Keech and Company.

                          J.B.
                    (At the telephone)
            I want to speak to the Colonel.
                    (To Lillian)
            I thought his name was Jack.
                    (Looking at the tape)
            Somebody's trying to pull a fast
            one over there. Well, if they
            think they're going to kid me,
            they're...
                    (Into telephone)
            Hello, Keech, this is Ball...Buy me
            fifty steel...yes, fifty thousand...
            right!
                    (To Lillian)
            Where's Hyde?

F-5   LILLIAN
                    He's in the barber shop.

                             J.B.
                    He's always in the barber shop.
                    You tell that fat head that...

         Mr. Hyde hurries into the picture. He wears a barber's
         apron, and his head is covered with lather.

                             HYDE
                          (Excitedly)
                    Yes?

                             J.B.
                          (Yelling)
                    This is a fine time to fool with your hair!
                    Get down on the floor and buy steel! If
                    you paid a little more attention to the
                    market and a little less to...BUY ANOTHER
                    FIFTY!

                             LILLIAN
                        (Into Dictaphone)
                    Fifty more.

F-6   CLOSE SHOT - <u>TICKER</u>

         It ticks furiously.

         DISSOLVE TO:

F-7   LONG SHOT - <u>THE LIVING ROOM OF MARY'S SUITE</u>

         In the foreground a jeweler is laying out his wares,
         and it is through his arms that we see that the rest
         of the room has quite a few people in it. In the
         middle we recognize Mary looking pretty much bewildered

F-8   MARY AND MR. VAN BUREN

         Mary is looking around a little goggle-eyed.

F-9   A BEAUTIFUL MODEL WALKING BY

         She is dressed in satin and is a well-developed girl.

F-10   VAN BUREN AND MARY

                             VAN BUREN
                        (Looking after the model)
                    Just a minor mood: the Can-Can.

                             THE JEWELER
                        (Coming into the shot)
                    Madame, if you please, telephone.

                             MARY
                        (To Van Buren)
4-22-37   Excuse me.

F-11   HULGAR - IN A GLASS PHONE BOOTH MARKED "ELWYN F.
        HULGAR & COMPANY"

        Behind him we see the wild activity of a broker's
        office on a heavy day.

                        HULGAR
                Hello, Hello, HELLO!

        He beams at this last one, then adds cautiously:

                Are we alone? I mean, can you
                talk?... Good. Well, you've
                just made...

F-12   MARY - AT A TELEPHONE

        This is somewhere away from the gang in the living
        room.

                        MARY
                ...eighteen thousand dollars!
                What do you mean, eighteen thou-
                sand dollars?

F-13   HULGAR - IN THE PHONE BOOTH

                        HULGAR
                That's right: two times nine.
                    (He chuckles)
                Call me right away if you get
                any more news.

        He turns his head at an enthusiastic roar which
        penetrates the phone booth.

                Goodbye.

        He hangs up and runs out to see what's happening.

F-14   MARY AT THE TELEPHONE

                        MARY
                    (In a dead voice)
                How much did you say?

        She pushes the receiver up and down a couple of
        times, then hangs up.

4-22-37

266

F-15   THE LIVING ROOM FULL OF PEOPLE

They spring to attention as Mary enters. They prof-
fer their wares.

F-16   VAN BUREN, A MODEL, AND MARY

The model is wearing something very swell, which Mr.
Van Buren indicates:

> VAN BUREN
> Can't you see yourself in this?
> You'd be simply beyond the beyond.

> MARY
> (Passing thru the shot)
> Eighteen thousand.

> VAN BUREN
> What?

> MARY
> That's what he said.

She passes out of the picture.

F-17   JOHNNY READING THE NEWSPAPER

He looks up, smiles happily, then reads from the
paper:

> JOHNNY
> I think I've found it..."Learn
> dentistry at home -- practice
> on your friends."

F-18   MARY - PAST JOHNNY

She looks at him for about two seconds before speaking.

> MARY
> Let's go out and buy a dog.

> JOHNNY
> Are you talking to me?

He looks around past the CAMERA, then back at Mary.

4-22-37   (Continued)

F-18
>   MARY
>   One of those great big woolly ones,
>   with the bangs over the eyes.

F-19   JOHNNY

He looks around behind him to the other side, then
back at Mary.

>   JOHNNY
>   (Slightly worried)
>   Mary!

He snaps his fingers at her.

>   Mary, can you see me?

F-20   MARY - PAST JOHNNY

Johnny rises and takes her in his arms.

>   MARY
>   I suppose they're terrible if they
>   catch fleas...they must multiply
>   so, but I've got to have one any-
>   way, I've wanted it all my life.

>   JOHNNY
>   (Really worried)
>   Mary!

>   MARY
>   (In a small voice)
>   We've just made eighteen thousand
>   dollars...that's nine thousand apiece.

She bursts into tears and throws her arms around
his neck.

DISSOLVE TO:

F-21   HIGH CAMERA SHOT - DOWN ON FLOOR OF N.Y. STOCK EX-
        CHANGE

Pandemonium seems to be loose. SOUND: ROAR

4-22-37

F-22   MR. HYDE <u>NEAR THE STEEL POST</u>

He stands on a chair yelling at the top of his lungs and making signs. We can't hear what he says, however. He is in his shirt-sleeves and his hair is snarled with soap. It seems to be standing on end.

SOUND: ROAR

F-23   J. B. <u>BY THE TICKER</u>

> J.B.
> And fifty!

> LILLIAN'S VOICE
> Fifty more!

F-24   J.B.'S PARTNERS

These are three anxious-looking gents about J.B.'s age.

> J.B.'S VOICE
> And twenty.

> LILLIAN'S VOICE
> Twenty more.

The partners wince - then go into a huddle.

> J.B.'S VOICE
> Get me Keech and Company.

The partners break up the huddle -- turn and look past us.

> FIRST PARTNER
> As your partners, J.B., we ... uh ...

> J.B.'S VOICE
> Hello, Keech?

> SECOND PARTNER
> (Desperately)
> We don't want to buy any more
> steel!

F-25   J.B. - PAST THE PARTNERS

> J.B.
> (Into telephone)
> J.B.... All right - buy as much
> as you can swing.

4-22-37   (Continued)

                         FIRST PARTNER
                      (Stepping forward)
                  We feel it is unwise...

                         SECOND PARTNER
                  We absolutely refuse to buy any
                  more steel!

                         THIRD PARTNER
                  You'll put us all in bankruptcy.

                         J.B.
                      (Glaring at them)
                  You're in bankruptcy now...you
                  fathead! The only thing will
                  save you is steel!

F-26   J.B., LILLIAN, AND PARTNERS

                         PARTNERS (Simultaneously)
                  (1) Wh-wh-what?
                  (2) How can you...
                  (3) My poor wife...!

                         LILLIAN
                      (Into telephone in the background)
                  Well, he's very busy right now, but
                  I'll give him the message. All right...
                  all right...

                         J.B.
                      (To his partners)
                  Go and sit down some place.
                      (To Lillian)
                  Thirty more and get me Noyes and
                  Company.

                         LILLIAN
                      (Into telephone)
                  Noyes and Company.
                      (Looking up)
                  That was Mrs. Ball's lawyers,
                  Spitz and O'Neil.
                      (Into telephone)
                  Buy thirty.

                         J.B.
                  What do they want?. Twenty more.

                         LILLIAN
                  Twenty more. Mrs. Ball is divorc-
                  ing you.

                           J.B.
                Holy smoke...and ten.

                         LILLIAN
                    (In the distance)
                And ten.

           FADE OUT:

                 END OF SEQUENCE "F"

G-9   <u>JOHNNY AT THE BREAKFAST TABLE</u>

He is putting some jam on a piece of thickly buttered
toast. The phone rings, and he claps it to his ear.

                    JOHNNY
                (In a very deep
                 funereal voice)
            Cartwell's Funeral Parlor....
            Miss who?... Just a moment,
            madam, I'll connect you with
            our chief embalmer.

He hangs up and fills his mouth with toast. Mary
comes into the shot.

                    MARY
            How do you feel about steel?

Johnny shakes his head solemnly in the negative.

                    MARY
            What does that mean?

Johnny does "thumbs down".

                    MARY
            You mean it's going down?

                    JOHNNY
            Unhunh.

He takes a swallow of coffee.

                    MARY
            How do <u>you</u> know?

                    JOHNNY
            All right, make it "up."

                    MARY
            Listen, goofy, this is important.

The telephone rings.

                    JOHNNY
            I'm sorry, madam, our em-
            ployees are not permitted
            to answer the phone during busi-
            ness hours...No, I'm sorry, madam.
                (He adds this last sternly
                 and hangs up.)

4-3-37   (Continued)

MARY
Is there any reason why you
should know anything about steel?

JOHNNY
(Trying to remember)
Well, my father was saying something about it, if I could
just remem....

MARY
Does he know anything about it?

JOHNNY
(With forced modesty)
My father is J.B. Ball.

MARY
(Vaguely)
Is that so? What does he do?

JOHNNY
(A little crossly)
What does he do! You never heard
of J. B. Ball?

MARY
(Also a little cross)
No, I never heard of J. B. Ball.

JOHNNY
(Louder)
You never heard of the Bull
of Broadstreet?

MARY
(Loudly)
No! What is he, a wrestler?

JOHNNY
(Very much subdued)
Well, anyway...he was saying, if
you compare the price of raw pig
iron with the average stock clear-
ances for the year...I forget the
exact year..and divided the total
by the common whatever it is I'm
not very good at mathematics...it
would be plain to a child of six
oh, no, that was rubber...I think
he said a child of three.

4-3-37

(Continued)

                         MARY
               Can't you remember what he
               said about steel?

                         JOHNNY
               I guess he didn't mention
               steel.

                         MARY
               Well, what do you think about it?

                         JOHNNY
               I think it's going down...way down.

He takes a bite of toast.

                         MARY
               Why should it.

                         JOHNNY
               Why shouldn't it?

He swallows with difficulty and points to the ceilin

                         JOHNNY
               It's a nasty day...looks like
               rain...everybody's depressed..
               down goes the market!
                    (He takes a swig of
                       coffee)
               On the other hand, you take
               a sunny day... everybody's
               cheerful...the market goes
               up...S'perfectly natural.

                         MARY
                    (A little doubtfully)
               Then you're sure?

                         JOHNNY
                    (Gravely)
               Positive! The market follows the
               weather like a dog follows a cat...
               I've made a deep study of it.
                    (He looks at her solemnly)

                         MARY
               Thanks.

She turns and hurries out. Johnny claps his hand
to his mouth to prevent himself from laughing out
loud. The telephone rings.

4-3-37   (Continued)

                    JOHNNY
               (Into telephone with
                with a thick German accent)
          Hallo, dis is de akvahrium - de
          fish moosayum, ya...
               (He continues in a normal
                voice)
          Oh, her car is waiting, thanks.

G-10   MR. HULGAR - PACING THE HALL

        He turns nervously at the sound of a door opening.

G-11   MARY STANDING IN THE DOORWAY

                    MARY
          He says he's positive it's
          going down.

G-12   MEDIUM CLOSE - MR. HULGAR PAST MARY

        He rises onto the balls of his feet as if he were
        going to take off.

                    MR. HULGAR
               (Beaming)
          Down?

                    MARY
          Down.

                    MR. HULGAR
          That's all I wanted to know.

        He hurries away and disappears around a bend in the
        hall. Mary turns toward us, looks back once over
        her shoulder, then raises her eyebrows and goes
        past the CAMERA.

        FADE OUT:

                    END OF SEQUENCE "G"

4-3-37

EASY LIVING

SEQUENCE "H"

FADE IN:

H-1   J. B. - STANDING BEHIND HIS DESK

He stands next to an old-fashioned ticker. Facing him
are two of his partners. The third sits on the window-
sill tying ticker tape into double bows.

                    J.B.
                (Yelling)
        What do you mean, "down"?... I tell
        you steel is going up...it has to.
        Bank clearings are up sixteen decimal
        one per cent...the railroads have
        got to buy new equipment (unless they're
        going to make the passengers walk.)
        Timken is on three shifts...Ohio
        Wire and Steel...

                SECOND PARTNER
                (Desperately)
        But look at the terrible chance
        we're taking, J.B....

                    J.B.
                (Interrupting)
        We've got to take long chances.
        Nothing but a long chance will
        make up for our losses. With a
        ten point rise...

    DISSOLVE TO:

H-2   CLOSE SHOT - HULGAR IN HIS WIRE ROOM

He bends over an operator and speaks rapidly to the
accompaniment of the clicking instruments.

                HULGAR
        ...that it's due for a drop. This
        is the greatest opportunity the
        clients of E. J. Hulgar and Company
        have ever had to participate in
        advance information Period Steel is
        going down double exlamation point
        says the world's greatest expert
        on steel, and....

    DISSOLVE TO:

4-3-37

H-3   J.B. AND PARTNERS - <u>IN HIS OFFICE</u>

                           J.B.
          That's why we're in up to our
          necks! It's the chance I've
          been waiting for! Why is pig
          iron soaring? Why are ore ship-
          ments so heavy? What does it
          mean when steel scrap is scarcer
          than hens' teeth?
                (He pounds on his desk)
          It means, <u>steel is going</u> up! It
          can't go any way <u>but up. A</u> child
          of <u>two</u> could understand <u>that</u>.

                       PARTNERS ONE AND TWO
                  (Lugubriously)
              I hope you're right.....

                           J.B.
          Forget it. Go on out and play
          golf.

The three partners start out of the room.

H-4   THE PARTNERS <u>GOING OUT THE OPEN DOOR</u>

Lillian stands by the open door waiting. As he passes
thru, the third partner does a quick half-hitch on the
doorknob with the ticker-tape he carries in his hand.
Lillian closes the door and comes toward us.

                       LILLIAN
              The financial delegation from
              Ecuador is waiting, Mr. Ball.

H-5   J.B....PAST LILLIAN

She stops beside his desk.

                       J.B.
              All right.

                       LILLIAN
              And Mr. Salmon from London, and
              Mr. Jonas, and Mr. Metzger and
              Lord ....

4-3-37   (Continued)

      J.B.
     (Without any pauses
      whatsoever)
Take a letter: Miss Mary Smith
care of the Boys' Whatever-it-
is make that the Hotel Louis Park
Avenue New York New York my dear
Miss Smith make that my dear Mary...
     (He looks at the ceiling
      for inspiration)

      LILLIAN
     (After a moment)
"My dear Mary...."

      J.B.
     (Scowling)
Don't rush me..now where was I?

      LILLIAN
"My dear Mary...."

      J.B.
Oh. My dear Mary: A school boy
called Jones, make his name Willie,

      LILLIAN
Willie Jones.

      J.B.
     (Crossly)
No, no, just Willie. A schoolboy
called Willie I want this on
plain paper...have we got any
plain paper?

      LILLIAN
If we haven't we'll get it.

      J.B.
     (Thoughtfully)
A schoolboy called Willie Jones...

      LILLIAN
Just Willie.

      J.B.
     (A little sharply)
I said his name was Jones...needed
one hundred marbles for the purpose
of playing a game of maggies.

      LILLIAN
     (Gently)
Aggies.

4-3-37   (Continued)

                                   J.B.
                         Whatever it is.

          The ticker begins to click, and J.B. reaches for the
          tape automatically.

                                   J.B.
                         You got that?

                                 LILLIAN
                            (With mild resentment)
                         Of course I have.

                                   J.B.
                         Good!
                            (He looks vaguely at the
                            tape)
                         His friend Henry, on the other hand...
                            (He frowns slightly and puts on
                            his pince-nez as the ticker
                            starts to spurt)
                         His friend Henry, on the other hand...
                         steels too low buy a thousand at the
                         market.

                                 LILLIAN
                            (Pushing a switch on the
                            Dictophone)
                         Buy one steel.

                                   J.B.
                         Tell Hyde to come in here. On the
                         other hand, his friend Henry ...

          The ticker starts to spurt faster.

                         Buy five and tell that fellow to
                         keep on the...another five.

                                 LILLIAN
                            (Into Dictophone)
                         Ten more and watch it.

                                   J.B.
                            (With an eye on the
                            ticker)
                         Did you ring for Hyde?

                                 LILLIAN
                         Yes, sir.

                                   J.B.
                         Get me Keech and Company. His
                         friend Jack on the other hand....

4-2-37   (Continued)

                              LILLIAN
                    His name was Henry.

                              J.B.
                         (Belligerently)
                    What do you mean his name was....

                              LILLIAN
                         (Handing him a phone)
                    Keech and Company.

                              J.B.
                         (At the telephone)
                    I want to speak to the Colonel.
                         (To Lillian)
                    I thought his name was Jack.
                         (Looking at the tape)
                    Somebody's trying to pull a fast
                    one over there. Well, if they think
                    they're going to kid me, they're...
                         (Into telephone)
                    Hello, Keech, this is Ball. Buy me
                    fifty steel...yes, fifty thousand...
                    right!
                         (To Lillian)
                    Where's Hyde?

                              LILLIAN
                    He's in the barber shop.

                              J.B.
                    He's always in the barber shop.
                    You tell that fat head that....

          Mr. Hyde hurries into the picture. He wears a barber's
          apron, and his head is covered with lather.

                              HYDE
                         (Excitedly)
                    Yes?

                              J.B.
                         (Yelling)
                    This is a fine time to fool with your
                    hair! Get down on the floor and buy
                    steel! If you paid a little more
                    attention to the market and a little
                    less to... BUY ANOTHER FIFTY!

                              LILLIAN
                         (Into dictophone)
                    Fifty more.

          4-3-37

H-6   CLOSE SHOT - <u>TICKER</u>

It ticks furiously.

DISSOLVE TO:

H-7   HULGAR - <u>IN A GLASS PHONE BOOTH</u> MARKED "ELWYN J. HULGAR
& COMPANY"

Behind him we see the wild activity of a broker's
office on a heavy day.

> HULGAR
> Hello, Hello, HELLO!

He beams at this last one, then adds, cautiously:

> Are we alone? I mean, can
> you talk?... Good. Well,
> you've just made....

H-8   MARY - <u>AT A TELEPHONE</u> - IN <u>THE GRAND SALON OF HER</u>
<u>SUITE</u>

A jeweler is silently laying out his wares near her
and the rest of the room has quite a few people in
it.

> MARY
> ...eighteen thousand dollars!
> What do you mean, eighteen
> thousand dollars?

H-9   HULGAR - <u>IN THE PHONE BOOTH</u>

> HULGAR.
> That's right: two times nine.
> (He chuckles)
> Call me right away if you get
> any more news.

He turns his head at an enthusiastic roar which
penetrates the phone booth.

> Goodbye.

He hangs up and runs out to see what's happening.

4-3-37

H-10   MARY AT THE TELEPHONE

                        MARY
                   (In a dead voice)
                   How much did you say?

She pushes the receiver up and down a couple of times,
then hangs up.

H-11   THE LIVING ROOM FULL OF PEOPLE

They spring to attention as Mary has finished her call.

H-12   VAN BUREN, A MODEL, THE JEWELER AND MARY

The model is wearing something very swell, which Mr.
Van Buren indicates:

                        VAN BUREN
                   Can't you see yourself in this?
                   You'd be beyond the beyond.

                        THE JEWELER
                   (Handling about a half
                    a million dollars worth
                    of gems)
                   I'll leave these here .... just
                   try them out..

                        MARY
                   (Passing thru the shot)
                   Eighteen thousand.

                        VAN BUREN
                   What?

                        MARY
                   That's what he said.

She passes out of the picture.

H-13   JOHNNY READING THE NEWSPAPER

He looks up, smiles happily, then reads the paper:

                        JOHNNY
                   I think I've found it..."Learn
                   dentistry at home -- practice
                   on your friends."

4-3-37

H-14   MARY - PAST JOHNNY

She looks at him for about two seconds before speaking. She is in a kind of a daze. An $18,000 daze.

> MARY
> Let's go out and buy a dog.

> JOHNNY
> Are you talking to me?

He looks around past the CAMERA, then back at Mary.

> MARY
> One of those great big woolly ones,
> with the bangs over the eyes.

H-15   JOHNNY

He looks around behind him to the other side, then
back at Mary.

> JOHNNY
> (Slightly worried)
> Mary!

H-16   MARY - PAST JOHNNY

Johnny rises and takes her in his arms.

> MARY
> I suppose they're terrible if
> they catch fleas,...they must
> multiply so, but I've got to
> have one anyway, I've wanted it
> all my life.

> JOHNNY
> (Really worried)
> Mary!

> MARY
> (In a small voice)
> We've just made eighteen thousand
> dollars...that's nine thousand
> apiece.

She bursts into tears and trows her arms around his
neck. All the others in the room regard the scene
with some amazement.

DISSOLVE TO:

4-3-37

H-17   HIGH CAMERA SHOT - DOWN ON <u>FLOOR OF N.Y. STOCK</u>
        <u>EXCHANGE</u>

Pandemonium seems to be loose.

SOUND: ROAR

H-18   MR. HYDE <u>NEAR THE STEEL POST</u>

He stands on a chair yelling at the top of his lungs
and making signs. We can't hear what he says, however.
He is in his shirt-sleeves and his hair is snarled
with soap. He seems to be standing on end.

SOUND: ROAR.

H-19   J.B. <u>BY THE TICKER</u>

                        J.B.
            And fifty!

                    LILLIAN'S VOICE
            Fifty more!

H-20   J.B.'S PARTNERS

These are three anxious-looking gents about J.B.'s
age.

                    J.B.'S VOICE
            And twenty.

                    LILLIAN'S VOICE
            Twenty more.

The partners wince - then go into a huddle.

                    J.B'S VOICE
            Get me Keoch and Company.

The partners break up the huddle -- turn and look
past us.

                    FIRST PARTNER
            As your partners, J.B., we ... uh ...

                    J.B.'S VOICE
            Hello, Keoch?

                    SECOND PARTNER
                (Desperately)
            We don't want to buy any more steel!

4-3-37

284

H-21   J.B. - PAST THE PARTNERS

                          J.B.
                    (Into telephone)
               J.B....All right - buy as much
               as you can swing.

                      FIRST PARTNER
                    (Stepping forward)
               We feel it is unwise....

                       SECOND PARTNER
               We absolutely refuse to buy any
               more steel!

                      THIRD PARTNER
               You'll put us all in bankruptcy.

                          J.B.
                    (Glaring at them)
               You're in bankruptcy now ... you
               fathead! The only thing will save
               you is steel!

J-22   J.B.'S PARTNERS - PAST J.B.

                        PARTNERS
                    (Simultaneously)
               (1) Wh-wh-what?
               (2) How can you ...
               (3) My poor wife....!

                          J.B.
               Go and sit down some place.
                    (To Lillian)
               Thirty more -- and get me
               Noyes and Company.

                      LILLIAN'S VOICE
                    (Coolly)
               Buy thirty.

FADE OUT:

                   END OF SEQUENCE "H"

4-3-37

<u>SEQUENCE "J"</u>

FADE IN:

J-1 A CHAUFFEUR - <u>AT THE WHEEL OF MARY'S CAR</u>

He is looking across the sidewalk in perplexity.

J-2 <u>THE FRONT OF A LARGE PET SHOP</u>

Mary appears with an enormous English sheepdog flanked
by Johnny who carries a goldfish globe with fish and a
parrot in a travelling cage. Mary beams at him but he
looks a little sheepish.

      NEWSBOY'S VOICE
    WUXTRY! WUXTRY!

J-3 NEWSBOY - <u>ON THE SIDEWALK</u>

He is selling papers fast.

      NEWSBOY
    Wuxtry! Wuxtry! Stock market
    crashes. Wuxtry...that's a
    nickel, mister.

J-4 JOHNNY AND MARY - <u>IN FRONT OF MARY'S AUTOMOBILE</u>

The chauffeur is trying to open the door and keep away
from the sheep dog at the same time.

      NEWSBOY'S VOICE
    Wuxtry!

Johnny looks PAST THE CAMERA toward the newsboy.

      JOHNNY
    Probably my old man pulling a fast
    one...oh, I forgot, you never heard
    of my old man.
      MARY
    Hunh?

4-3-37   (Continued)

J-4   She looks toward the newsboy also. Now the latter
       gallops into the picture and shouts up at them:

                          NEWSBOY
                       (Breathlessly)
                  Fortunes vanish!...market crash woist
                  since twenty-nine!

                          JOHNNY
                  Let me see that.

       He gives the parrot and the goldfish to the chauffeur
       then feels for a coin and speaks with amusement:

                          JOHNNY
                  What do _you_ know about twenty-nine?

                          NEWSBOY
                       (Indignantly)
                  I coulda hoid about it, couldn't I?

       Johnny realizes he hasn't any coin.

                          JOHNNY
                  Never mind, I guess I haven't any...
                       (Suddenly)
                  Let me see that!

       He grabs the paper from the boy's hand and stares at
       it.

                          MARY
                  What's the matter?

J-5   CLOSEUP - HEADLINES

       In the midst of a lot of stuff about the market we
       see the paragraph that has caught Johnny's eye. It
       reads: "Ball and Company Tottering".

                  It is rumored that the firm of J.E.
                  Ball and Company, for more than fifty
                  years leaders in the world of finance..."

J-6   JOHNNY, MARY, THE NEWSBOY, THE CHAUFFEUR AND THE
       ANIMALS

                          JOHNNY
                       (Harshly)
                  Where's the subway?

4-3-37   (Continued)

J-6   Tho newsboy starts to point.

> JOHNNY
> (Continued)
> Give me a nickel.

> MARY
> (Worried)
> What's the matter, Johnny? Where
> are you going? Don't you want the
> car?

The newsboy holds up a nickel and Johnny snatches
it.

> JOHNNY
> Subway's faster...I'll see you
> later, Mary.

He runs out of the picture.

> NEWSBOY
> (Looking at his hand)
> Hey!

> MARY
> (Severely)
> Shut up, I'll get you your money.

She turns to the chauffeur.

> MARY
> (Continued)
> Have you got a nickel, Mr. Hornby?

> HORNBY
> I believe I 'ave, madam.
> (Then severely to the
> newsboy)
> 'Ere!

He loads the goldfish and the parrot onto the newsboy,
then reaches for a purse.

DISSOLVE TO:

4-3-37

J-7   J.B., PARTNERS AND LILLIAN

This is in the old man's office. The ticker is clicking furiously but nobody watches it. Lillian sits
with her back to us. Across the desk sits the old man
and behind his two of his partners are perched on the
windowsil like old crows. A third partner is near
the ticker making cat's cradles with the tape. Lillian
hands him a phone.

> LILLIAN
> Mr. Hyde.

> J.B.
> Yes, Lester.

J-8   MR. HYDE - <u>IN A BOOTH</u>

He is completely exhausted; his forehead covered with
sweat, his eyes wild, his hair rigid. Outside we hear
the roar of the exchange.

SOUND: ROAR

> HYDE
> (Panting)
> S'no use, J.B., we can't turn it...
> looks as if everybody in the
> country's selling.

He tries to run his fingers through his hair, looks
furiously at his hand and ejaculates:

> GAW -!!!

J-9   J.B., PARTNERS AND LILLIAN

> J.B.
> (Into phone)
> Take it easy, take it easy. You
> did the best you could.

He hands the phone back to Lillian, reaches for the
tape and says:

> We might buy....

His partners looks at him fearfully.

4-3-37   (Continued)

J-9   J.B.
                         (Continued)
                      Never mind.

He looks at his partners.

                      Why don't you birds go out and
                      eat?

Solemnly the three partners file out. J.B. turns to
Lillian.

                          J.B.
                         (Continued)
                      You, too, Lillian. You can send
                      me in a sandwich.

                          LILLIAN
                         (Rising)
                      I have it outside for you, Mr.
                      Ball.

She walks out of the SHOT. J.B. gets up and looks
out the window. After a moment we hear a door close.

                          J.B.
                         (Without looking
                          around)
                      Just put it on the desk.

Mrs. Ball walks into the picture carrying a tray with
a sandwich and a glass of milk. She puts it on the
desk. Her back is to us. She looks at him for a
moment, then sniffles. His expression softens when
he sees who it is.

                          MRS. BALL
                      Juny...

She takes a step forward and he takes her in his arms.
As she cries he pats her on the back.

                          J.B.
                      There, there, there. My gracious.

                          MRS. BALL
                         (Emotionally)
                      You know I'd scrub floors for you,
                      Juny. I'd do anything...

J.B. gives her a mildly amused look.

4-3-37   (Continued)

                         J.B.
          We've been through tighter squeaks
          than this, Jenny - and you haven't
          scrubbed any floors yet.

                         MRS. BALL
                    (Emotionally)
          But I would.

                         J.B.
                    (Soothingly)
          Of course you would...and probably
          do a very nice job of it.

                         MRS. BALL
          And I forgive you everything, Juny...
          even the...the...girl in the Hotel
          Louis.

J.B. gives her a slight frown.

                         J.B.
          I'm afraid you've got me mixed up
          with somebody else, Jenny. I hap-
          pened to spend the night in Louis'
          Hotel...

Mrs. Ball looks away a little dramatically.

                         MRS. BALL
          Oh, I don't expect you to admit it...
          After all, you are a handsome forceful
          man, and I...am not exactly the debutante
          you married.

                         J.B.
          Now wait a minute, Jenny. I've got
          enough trouble without...

There is a knock on the door.

SOUND: KNOCK

                         J.B.
                    (Continued - crossly)
          Come in...
                    (He scowls)
          HAH! The prodigal!

4-3-37

J-10   JOHNNY - COMING <u>IN DOORWAY</u>

                        JOHNNY
                   (In some embar-
                    rassment)
                Hello, Father...Hello, Mother.

J-11   MRS. BALL AND J.B. - PAST JOHNNY

        as Johnny goes toward them:

                        J.B.
                   (Sardonically)
                You didn't happen to bring along
                a lot of that money you were going
                to make, did you?

        Mrs. Ball puts her arms around Johnny's neck.

                        MRS. BALL
                My poor, poor boy.

                        JOHNNY
                If there's anything I can do to
                help...

                        J.B.
                Anything but floor-scrubbing, your
                Mother has already spoken for that.

                        MRS. BALL
                How can you be so heartless, Juny?

                        J.B.
                I'm not heartless, I'm just laying
                out the work.

                        JOHNNY
                I'm sorry I left the way I did
                yesterday. I hope you weren't
                worried, Mother.

                        MRS. BALL
                You left! Then you don't know...
                about your Father and myself.

                        J.B.
                   (Trying to turn
                    the conversation)
                Where'd you spend the night?

4-3-37   (Continued)

J-11   JOHNNY
                     At the Hotel Louis.

J.B. turns and stares at his son; Mrs. Ball stares at
h<u>im</u>. Johnny turns and stares at his mother, then at
<u>his</u> father...

DISSOLVE TO:

J-12   <u>THE LOBBY OF THE HOTEL LOUIS</u>

Gurney is behind the desk and Van Buren in front of it.
They are sharing the newspaper. Louis is pacing up
and down in front of the desk like a caged lion. His
hands are behind his back most of the time, but occasionally he points to the ceiling, then slaps his side.

                        LOUIS
             Just ven everyting vas going nice.

He stamps up and down.

                        GURNEY
                     (Reluctantly)
             Every cloud has a silver lining.

                        LOUIS
                     (Furiously)
             Never mind de weather...ve got
             enough to worry about.

                      MARY'S VOICE
             Hello.

They turn as the dog starts barking.

J-13   MARY FOLLOWED BY HORNBY AND A BELLBOY

She soothes the dog that is barking at Louis. The
parrot cackles mirthlessly. Louis hurries into the
shot.

J-14   TWO SHOT - LOUIS AND MARY

                        LOUIS
                  (In a stage whisper)
             You seen de papers?

                        MARY
             I just saw the headlines.

4-3-37   (Continued)

                    LOUIS
                (Dramatically)
It says dat coitain party is
tottering....and every time he
totters I teeter.

                    MARY
                (Sympathetically)
You mean something's happened to
your hotel?

                    LOUIS
                (With finality)
If he's in de soup, de Louis is
phlooy.

                    MARY
                (Blankly)
If who's in the soup?

                    LOUIS
                (With a trace of
                  impatience)
De party vot give you de sables.
Ve're alone, dear....let's cut
de comedy.

                    MARY
                (Blankly)
What sables? I haven't any sables.
                (She laughs)

                    LOUIS
                (To Van Buren)
I'm doing her a friendship and she
wants to play puss in a corner.
                (He swings on Mary)
Vot do you call dis.....horse?

                    MARY
This is Kolinsky.

                    LOUIS
                (Vulgarly)
You and me boat.

                    MARY
                (Beginning to get
                angry)
If you don't believe me, ask
Mr. Van Buren.
                (She points out of
                the picture)

4-3-37

J-15   VAN BUREN

                        VAN BUREN
                 If it's all the same to you, I'll
                 just stay on the sidelines.

J-16   MARY AND LOUIS

                        LOUIS
                   (Pointing to Van Buren)
                 He's de vun vot told me.

        Mary looks slowly toward Van Buren.

J-17   CLOSE SHOT - VAN BUREN

        He looks away unhappily.

J-18   MARY AND LOUIS

        Mary looks down at the fur and up at Louis.

                        MARY
                   (Frightened)
                 But if this is, is.....sable,
                 why then he must have....made
                 a mistake. You wouldn't give a
                 coat like this to a stranger,
                 would you?

J-19   VAN BUREN

                        VAN BUREN
                   (Horrified)
                 Who, me?

J-20   MARY AND LOUIS

                        LOUIS
                 Never!

        After a pause Mary turns to Louis.

                        MARY
                 Do you happen to know the name
                 of the gentleman who helped you
                 order my supper last night?

        4-3-37   (Continued)

J-20
                              LOUIS
                          (Disgustedly)
                    Don't go too far, vill you? Ven
                    I give you de Imperal Soot for a
                    buck a day vit breakfast, don't
                    tell me you don't even know J.B.
                    Ball by name, vill you?

                              MARY
                    Wait a minute: You thought I
                    was a....close friend of his?

                              LOUIS
                          (Insolently)
                    Vell?

                              MARY
                    You thought he gave me a .....
                    sable coat?

                              LOUIS
                    Vell?

          Mary hauls off and gives him the world's hardest slap
          in the face. As Louis looks at her in stupefaction,
          she gives it to him back-hand on the other side of
          his face. Louis immediately hauls off to hit her
          back. The dog barks at him furiously. Mary turns
          on her heel and rushes out of the shot.

                              LOUIS
                          (After a moment)
                    Get out of my hotel.

          DISSOLVE TO:

J-21   CLOSE SHOT - J.B. - (LOOKING VERY BELLIGERENT)

          This is in his office.

                              J.B.
                          (Bellowing)
                    You said steel was going down
                    because the weather was bad!

J-22   JOHNNY IN A CHAIR - HIS FATHER LEANING OVER HIM

          A little way back we see Mrs. Ball.

                              JOHNNY
                          (Squirming)
                    I was only joking, Father.

          4-3-37   (Continued)

                    J.B.
                 (Yelling)
     But you can't make jokes about
     steel when your name is Ball!
     For Heaven's sake, don't you
     realize your responsibility?
     Don't you know that rumors rule
     the market? Where did you
     leave this girl?

                    JOHNNY
     In front of a pet shop.

                    J.B.
     What's the name of it?

                    JOHNNY
     I don't remember.

J.B. turns to Mrs. Ball and makes a hopeless gesture.

                    J.B.
     There's your son for you.
          (Then turning to
           Johnny sarcastically)
     Do you by any remote possibility
     remember the girl's name?

                    JOHNNY
                 (Exasperated)
     Mary Smith -- if that'll do you
     any good.

                    J.B.
                 (Stupefied)
     Huh? Mary Smith! You mean at the
     Hotel Louis?

                    JOHNNY
                 (Stupefied in turn)
     How did you know she was at the
     Hotel Louis?

                    MRS. BALL
                 (Coolly)
     I thought the whole world knew it.

J.B. lifts a telephone receiver, pauses for a second,
gives his wife a take-it, looks once at his son,
then snarls into the phone:

                    J.B.
     Get me the Hotel Louis.

DISSOLVE TO:
4-3-37

                        297

J-23   MEDIUM CLOSE - LOUIS

He stands by the desk. Gurney hands him the telephone.

                        LOUIS
                    (Still boiling)
            De noive....
                    (Into telephone)
            Hallo?
                    (Then very amiably)
            Hallo, Mr. B. I seen de papers.
            You know how I feel. Anyting I
            got is....Who? Dot vun! You
            know vot I found out? She vas a
            phoney from Phoneyville. She
            pretended all de while she was
            your little palsie-walsie, and
            just now, after she et me out of
            house and....Vat? I trun her
            out....lock, stock, and
                    (Now he becomes
                    very unhappy)
            Vell, now, vait a minute. Vot?
            But Mr. B. Vell, who was to...
            but.....but.... Vell, I'll try,
            but....but...
                    (He reacts violently to
                    a click on the other
                    end)

                        GURNEY
            What's the matter?

                        LOUIS
                    (Quietly)
            De cook is goosed.
                    (He hangs up)

        DISSOLVE TO:

J-24   J.B.'s DESK

J.B., Mrs. Ball, Johnny and Lillian have each a telephone in hand.

                        J.B.
                    (Roaring)
            What do you mean, you fired her?)
            Is this the Boys' Constant What-)SIMULTAN-
            you-call-it?   ) EOUSLY

                        JOHNNY   )
                  (Between snatches of   )
                  telephone conversation -   )
                  looks at his father with   )
                  a peculiar expression)   )
            She told me she never even heard   )
            of you.   )
)
                        MRS. BALL   )   SIMULTAN-
                  (Into telephone)   )   EOUSLY
            V-Sixteen Company of America? Can   )
            you give me the license number of...)   )
)
                        JOHNNY   )
                  (Wearily)   )
            It was a pet shop that had rabbits   )
            and goldfish and dogs and parrots   )
            and...and...and it was a pet shop.   )

                        LILLIAN
                  (Into telephone)
                  (Note: This must
                  be heard clearly)
            Hello.....police department? Give
            me Captain Jackson of the Traffic
            Squad, I want a V-16 picked up....
            Hello, Captain Jackson, I'm speak-
            ing for Mr. J.B. Ball.....

      CUT TO:

INT. OUTER OFFICE OF J.B. BALL

      Mary is arguing with the second or third assistant
      secretary.

                        SECRETARY
            I'm very sorry......

                        MARY
            But I tell you I've got to see him.
            It's terribly important. He's made
            a very expensive mistake.

                        SECRETARY
            Why don't you write him a nice, long
            letter?

                        MARY
            Listen, sister, I'm giving you fair
            warning ----
                  (She picks up the
                  inkwell)
      4-3-37

J-26   INT. J.B.'s OFFICE

Johnny, Mrs. Ball and J.B. are all talking simultaneously into phones -

                    JOHNNY
                (Into phone)
            Do you sell gold fish. Well,
            what do you sell?

                    MRS. BALL
                (Into phone)
            Repeat that, please, J-B-N what?

                    J.B.
                (Yelling into
                 phone)
            What do I care about your morals?

J-27   J.B.'s OFFICE

The dictaphone buzzes - Lillian takes it. Now for
the first time Lillian loses her equanimity. She
rises and yells:

                    LILLIAN
                (Yelling)
            WHAT? ... WHO?

She puts her hand to her heart and relaxes. She hands
the dictaphone to J.B. and speaks quietly.

                    LILLIAN
                (Quietly - to J.B.)
            Here she is.

J-28   MARY - IN OUTER OFFICE

She speaks excitedly into telephone that the secretary
hands her.

                    MARY
            Hello, Mr. Ball, this is Mary
            Smith. Do you remember me,
            the girl you gave the Kolinsky
            coat to?

4-3-37

J-29   J.B. - WITH JOHNNY BESIDE HIM

                        J.B.
              I hope to tell you I remember
              you. Where are you?

Johnny's expression becomes peculiar.

J-30   MARY - AT PHONE

                        MARY
                      (Rapidly)
              You made a mistake, it wasn't
              Kolinsky - it was sable, if you
              know what that is, and it's worth
              a lot of money so I hurried right
              down and...what? I'm right out-
              side but they won't let me in.

J-31   J.B. - AT PHONE - (JOHNNY AND LILLIAN IN BACKGROUND)

                        J.B.
                  ....THEY'LL LET YOU IN!

J.B. slams down the phone and all dash to door.

J-32   INT. OUTER OFFICE - THE DOOR TO J.B.'s OFFICE

It flies open and J.B., Lillian, Johnny and Mrs. Ball
dash by.

                        MARY
                   (Without stopping)
              Hello, Mr. Ball. Hello, Johnny.

                        MRS. BALL
                   (Quietly to Johnny)
              My new coat.

J-33   J.B. - PAST MARY

J.B. strides up to Mary.

4-3-37   (Continued)

J-33
                                J. B.
                              (Rapidly)
                    Mary, did you tell anybody this:
                    Mr. Ball said steel was going down?

J-34   MARY - PAST J.B.

                                MARY
                    Why, yes, didn't you want it to?

                                J.B.
                    Want it to! Of course I didn't
                    want it to!

                                MARY
                    I'm terribly sorry - did you want
                    it to go up?

                                J.B.
                    More than you'll ever know.

                                MARY
                              (As if it were nothing)
                    Well, I can fix that -

                                J.B.
                    Hunh!
                              (He looks around -
                               then back at Mary)

                                MARY
                    Have you got a telephone?

                                J.B.
                    Have I got a telephone -

          They walk toward us and the CAMERA TRUCKS AHEAD of
          them.

                                MARY
                    If I can only remember his name -
                    he's a little man with a carnation -
                    he rhymes with something...
                              (She snaps her fingers)
                    Vul - Hulgar! All principal cities -
                    Where's the phone book?

          DISSOLVE TO:

J-35   HULGAR - IN PHONE BOOTH

                                HULGAR
                              (In a whisper)
                    Yes, this is me.

4-3-37   (Continued)

J-36   MARY - <u>AT PHONE IN J.B.'S OFFICE</u>

J.B. lands near the phone.

> MARY
> (In a whisper)
> Well, this is me - and listen:
> Steel is going up - do you hear me?

J-37   HULGAR - <u>IN PHONE BOOTH</u>

> HULGAR
> (Excitedly - in whisper)
> Holy smoke! We'd better cover
> right away then -

J-38   MARY - <u>AT PHONE</u>

> MARY
> (In whisper)
> Get <u>plenty</u> of covers because Mr. "B" -
> you can guess who that is - has got
> it...
> (She looks up helplessly)

J.B. holds a card in front of her.

> He's got it...cornered - do you know
> what that means?

J-39   HULGAR - <u>IN PHONE BOOTH</u>

> HULGAR
> (In a panic)
> Holy mackerel! Are you sh-sure?

J-40   MARY - <u>AT PHONE</u>

> MARY
> (In whisper)
> I'm positive...
> (She laughs silently)
> Don't forget to tell the principal
> cities...

She hangs up.

> J.B.
> It can't work -

> MARY
> It worked this morning -

4-3-37

J-41   MEDIUM CLOSE - <u>THE TICKER</u>

It is clicking spasmodically. J.B. and Mary come
into the picture - J.B. picks up the tape and scowls
at it - Mary looks at it blankly -

                    MARY
            Which one is it?

                    J.B.
                (Pointing)
            That one -

They watch it a moment - suddenly the ticker has a
little spurt - J.B. becomes tense. Mary beams.

                    MARY
                (Pointing)
            Oh, look!

                    J.B.
                (Yelling)
            Where's Hyde?

                    LILLIAN'S VOICE
            He's in the barber...

J-42   A BARBER SHOP

A stock exchange messenger is leaning over a figure
being lathered by the barber.   Mr. Hyde springs out
of the chair, and we get one glimpse of him with a
towel tight over his head and his face covered with
lather. He runs out, followed by the messenger.

J-43   THE THREE PARTNERS - AT LUNCH

Suddenly they look past us, rise, wipe their mouths
and hurry past CAMERA.

J-44   HIGH CAMERA - <u>ON STOCK EXCHANGE FLOOR</u>

There is more excitement than ever.

J-45   MR. HYDE - <u>ON EXCHANGE FLOOR</u>

He has discarded the barber's apron - He is fighting
his way toward us through a crowd of excited men - A
messenger runs up to him and gives him some sheafs of

4-3-37   (Continued)

304

J-45   paper - Mr. Hyde tries to speak, gets soap in his
        mouth, wipes it hurriedly off his face and gets some
        in his eye. We leave him looking like a pirate with
        the towel on his head -

J-46   J.B., MARY AND THE THREE PARTNERS - <u>AT THE TICKER</u>

        J.B. seems his old self, with a big cigar in his
        mouth.

                          J.B.
                Buy twenty!

                          LILLIAN'S VOICE
                Twenty more!

                          THIRD PARTNER
                          (Happily)
                Why don't you buy fifty?
                          (He starts making a very
                           complicated sailor's knot
                           with ticker tape)

        Mary looks at them all happily - Now she moves to the
        next window and the CAMERA PANS WITH HER. This
        brings Johnny into the SHOT - He is sitting dejected-
        ly on the window sill.

                          MARY
                Hello - I didn't get a chance to
                say it before.

                          JOHNNY
                          (Unhappily)
                Hello, Mary...
                          (He nods out of the
                           picture)
                This is my mother.

        Mary turns and smiles.

J-47   MEDIUM CLOSE - MRS. BALL

                          MRS. BALL
                          (Tragically)
                How do you do, my dear. What a
                <u>lovely</u> coat.

4-3-37

J-48   MARY AND JOHNNY
                            MARY
                     (Puzzled by the manner)
                I guess it is all right - I thought
                it was Kolinsky, but Mr. Ball must
                have made a mistake when he gave it
                to me.

J-49   MEDIUM CLOSE - MRS. BALL

                          MRS. BALL
                I hardly think he did -
                     (Suddenly she buries her
                      face in her handkerchief)

J-50   MARY AND JOHNNY

        Mary takes a step forward impulsively, then looks at
        Johnny.

                          JOHNNY
                     (Quietly)
                You told me you didn't know my
                father, Mary.

                       J.B.'S VOICE
                     (Triumphantly)
                SIXTY-TWO!

                     THIRD PARTNER'S VOICE
                     (Weakly)
                Hooray!

        Mary looks over her shoulder at the noise - then
        back at Johnny.

                          MARY
                I didn't know he was your <u>father</u>,
                Johnny - I mean when you asked me
                if I knew Mr. Ball I said "No" be-
                cause...
                     (Now she looks from Mrs.
                      Ball to Johnny - suddenly
                      she frowns and speaks in-
                      dignantly)
                What <u>is</u> this?
                     (Suddenly she understands)
                Oh!
                     (Then looking at Johnny almost
                      pleadingly)
                Oh, no!

4-3-37   (Continued)

306

                (She looks from one
                to the other, then
                at the sleeve of the
                coat)
Why...everybody must have thought
so! - That's why - of course!
                (She turns toward
                Mrs. Ball)
I don't blame you for hating me,
Mrs. Ball, and I don't blame you
for believing it - if I loved a
man and... and...
                (She turns slowly
                to Johnny)
- but why this big lug, who prac-
tically spent the week-end with
me - who answered the phone for
me -
                (Her lips begin
                to tremble)
- that I thought was my friend -
why HE should believe it - that's
a different story -

             J.B.'S VOICE
SIXTY-SIX!

             THIRD PARTNER'S VOICE
Hooray!

             MARY
And as far as I'm concerned, Mr.
J.B. Ball, Junior, you can...

J-51   J.B. AND PARTNERS - AT TICKER

             J.B.
SIXTY-SEVEN!
             (He looks toward Mary)
What's going on over there?

             THIRD PARTNER
Hooray!

4-3-37

J-52   MARY AND JOHNNY - PAST J.B.

Mary comes toward us - as she does so, she takes off
the coat, then the hat.

> MARY
> Here's your coat and hat...
> (She slams them in
> the arms of the
> third partner)
> I wish you'd explain to your son
> I don't accept sables from gentlemen --

J-53   CLOSE SHOT - J.B.

> J.B.
> (Ticker tape in
> hand)
> What's that?
> (He looks down at
> the tape rigidly)
> Another ten!
> (He looks back
> at Mary)
> What did you say?

> LILLIAN'S VOICE
> Buy ten!

J-54   CLOSE SHOT - MARY

She goes out, slamming the door.

J-55   JOHNNY AND MRS. BALL

His mother is a little distance behind him - he comes
forward rapidly.

> JOHNNY
> Mary!

His mother looks worried.

J-56   CLOSE SHOT - J.B. AND PARTNERS

Ticker tape in hand, he glances toward his son.

4-3-37   (Continued)

J-56   J.B.
                           (Yelling)
                    What have you done now? If I
                    didn't have to stick by this --
                    Buy twenty!

                         SECOND PARTNER
                    When do we start selling?

                              J.B.
                    At a hundred.
                           (To his son)
                    Go get that girl and don't come
                    back without her!

J-57   SIDEWALK IN FRONT OF BALL AND COMPANY

        We see Mary's beautiful V-16 at the curb. Mary comes
        flying out the door, gallops down the steps and jumps
        into the car and slams the door. The car zips away -
        as it does so, Johnny comes running out. He stops at
        the curb and looks helplessly in the direction taken
        by Mary. He turns at a voice.

                         LOUIS' VOICE
                           (Nervously)
                    Hello!

J-58   LOUIS - PAST JOHNNY

        Louis comes down the bank steps he had started to
        climb. He is magnificently arrayed in an overcoat -
        with a brown fur collar, white-topped button shoes
        and a small silk hat -

                            LOUIS
                       (Nervously playing a part)
                    Hallo, Mr. Junior! Va've you
                    been hiding hourself?

                            JOHNNY
                         (Depressed)
                    I've been around -

                            LOUIS
                    Vy don't you come see my new hotel?
                    I'm doing such a business -- I'm
                    just going to inform Mr. B.

4-3-37   (Continued)

J-58   JOHNNY
                     He was there last night -

                              LOUIS
                            (Horrified)
                     SH!
                            (He looks all
                            around)

                              JOHNNY
                     So was I -

                              LOUIS
                            (Stupefied)
                     Hunh -

We hear a police siren and both men turn their heads.

J-59   HIGH CAMERA SHOT - ON POLICE ESCORT

        We see Mary's easily recognizable V-16 flanked by a
        dozen motor cops doing fifty miles an hour.

        SOUND: SIREN.

J-60   AUTOMOBILE SHOT - LOW CAMERA AHEAD OF POLICE ESCORT

        The engines roar and the sirens shriek.

        SOUND: MOTORS AND SIRENS.

J-61   INT. V-16

                              MARY
                     But I haven't done anything -
                     Why should you arrest me and...
                     and...

                              CAPTAIN
                     I'm just followin' orders, lady -

J-62   AUTOMOBILE SHOT - BEHIND POLICE ESCORT

        We follow it a moment then take a corner on two wheels.

        SOUND: MOTORS AND SIREN.

4-3-37

J-63   LOW CAMERA SHOT - CLOSE ON J.B., LILLIAN AND PARTNERS -
        LOOKING DOWN THROUGH OPEN WINDOW.

                        J.B.
                What's that?

                        LILLIAN
                    (Weakly)
                I must have forgotten to call
                off the police - for Miss Smith.

                        J.B.
                Oh -
                        (He roars with
                        laughter)

                        LILLIAN
                    (Dejected)
                It's the first thing I've ever
                forgotten!

                        J.B.
                    (Pleased)
                S'about time!

J-64   JOHNNY AND LOUIS - AT CURB

        We hear the sirens and motorcycles coming nearer -
        Their heads turn, open-mouthed, with the arriving
        procession. Now the whole escort comes between the
        CAMERA and the two characters. Mary jumps out of the
        V-16 into Johnny's arms -

J-65   CLOSE SHOT - JOHNNY AND MARY

        Behind them stands a stupefied Louis.

                        MARY
                    (Sobbing and
                    hysterical)
                They arrested me, Johnny - Tell
                them I didn't do anything - you
                saw me give the coat back and all
                the jewels are hidden under the
                horse - you know where, Mr. Louis -

                        LOUIS
                Huh? You mean de camel?

        The old police captain comes into the shot.

4-3-37   (Continued)

> MARY
> (Quite hysterical)
> You know I haven't done anything
> wrong, Johnny - don't let them
> put me in prison -

> CAPTAIN
> Where's Mr. Ball?

> LOUIS
> Right dere in front of you!

The captain turns toward Johnny -- J.B. hurries into
the shot.

> J.B.
> Here I am!

> CAPTAIN
> (Crossly)
> Well - which is which?

> J.B.
> (Yelling)
> Well, which one do you want?

> CAPTAIN
> (Aroused)
> Which one of yez wanted _her_ so bad...
> and so quick?

> JOHNNY
> Me.

> CAPTAIN
> ...I guess maybe there's been
> some kind o' misunderstandin' -

> JOHNNY
> There _has_ been - a _little_ one -

> MARY
> (Looking up at him)
> Not so little as you think -

J-66   LOW CAMERA SHOT - UP AT THE THIRD PARTNER _ON WINDOW
LEDGE

He balances himself outside the window. Through
cupped hands he croaks -

J-66   THIRD PARTNER
                    STEEL A HUNDRED AND FIVE!

He nearly loses his balance.

J-67   MARY, JOHNNY, J.B., LOUIS AND OTHER POLICEMEN

        Suddenly a peculiar look comes over Johnny's face.
        He looks up and puts his hand to his mouth.

                              JOHNNY (Yelling)
                    Sell fifty!

        We hear a distant "Hooray!"

                              J.B.
                         (Astonished)
                    Hooray is right!

        We hear the roar of the motorcycles and the shriek
        of the police siren - Mary smiles into Johnny's eyes.

FADE OUT.

                         THE END

4-3-37

Remember the Night

"One Man's Meat Is Another Man's Poison"

Remember the Night was an original script, and as in all of Sturges's work, we find elements taken from experiences he had and people he knew. The falling-in-love-on-a-journey motif mirrors his experience with Eleanor Hutton on a trip to Palm Beach years before, which reappeared later as a dominant narrative line in *The Palm Beach Story*. And the strong, midwestern Mrs. Sargent resembles the mother of his third wife, Louise Sargent—right down to her name.[1] Finally, the idea of a clearheaded woman like Lee who can give "matriarchal" advice to a man her own age recalls Priscilla Woolfan, who lived behind Sturges, was Sturges's age, and gave him continual no-nonsense advice.[2] Yet the script emerges as one of Sturges's most experimental works, with a life completely its own.

Frank S. Nugent reviewed *Remember the Night* for The *New York Times* following its January 1940 opening and said that it deserved to win Best Picture for 1940: "It is a memorable film in title and in quality," he wrote, "blessed with an honest script, good direction and sound performance."[3] But in a year that produced *Grapes of Wrath, The Philadelphia Story,* and the eventual winner, Hitchcock's *Rebecca,* the competition was stiff.

Sturges could not complain that year, for he did go home with the Best Original Screenplay Oscar for a later effort that year, his directorial debut film, *The Great McGinty.* We are therefore doubly rewarded by a return to the many pleasures of *Remember the Night,* a script that shows Sturges continuing to experiment, explore, and develop as a writer on his way to becoming the director he wanted to be.

We have already quoted from this delightful script in the Introduction, noting that Sturges plays with genre formulas, combining romantic comedy and courtroom drama in remarkable ways. But we should add that Sturges found this a particularly challenging project, one that almost drove him, as he put it, "to commit hara-kiri several times."[4]

The challenge was to find the right way to bring a young assistant district

A poster for *Remember the Night* with Fred MacMurray
and Barbara Stanwyck. Courtesy The Museum of
Modern Art.

attorney and a girl thief together. Sturges later remarked, "When I had Fred Mac-
Murray, as the district attorney, take Barbara Stanwyck, the girl on trial for theft,
up to the mountains to reform her, the script died of pernicious anemia. When
I had him take her up because his conscience bothered him for having had her
trial continued until after the Christmas season, it perished from lack of oxy-
gen." What we are seeing is the *process* of Sturges's thinking in working through
this problem, something he seldom allowed us to glimpse. He continues: "When
I had him take her up moved by charitable impulse and the Yuletide spirit, it ex-
pired from galloping eunuchery. So I thought of a novelty. The district attorney
takes her up to the mountains for the purpose of violating the Mann Act. This
has always been a good second act!" Translation: push the envelope, break the
rules, be a bit naughty in your writing. He concludes with the overall shape of
the project: "In *Remember the Night,* love reformed her and corrupted him, which
gave us the finely balanced moral that one man's meat is another man's poison."[5]

This script also previews many of the themes and formulas Sturges would develop elsewhere, including the motif of couples falling in love on a journey and
that of a strong trickster female redeemed by love, both of which we find in *The
Lady Eve,* where Barbara Stanwyck builds on the screen smarts we so enjoy here.

Note, too, that Sturges has blended into this script elements of yet another
genre: film noir.[6] The courtroom drama, of course, often crossed paths with film
noir, that respected "hard-boiled" American genre that emphasizes a menacing,
crime-ridden culture and strong yet often treacherous women. Billy Wilder's
Double Indemnity (1944), for instance, teamed Fred MacMurray and Barbara
Stanwyck once more for an even more memorable performance in a dark tale
of lust, greed, and intrigue. J. P. Telotte notes that film noir, as a group of films
made during the period 1941–1958, "seems fundamentally about violations: vice
corruption, unrestrained desire, and, most fundamental of all, abrogation of the
American dream's most basic promises—of hope, prosperity, and safety from
persecution." These films, he further suggests, explore the basic ambiguity of
boundaries between genres and narratives in general.[7] Although *Remember the
Night* does not pose a vision of total corruption in America, around the edges
and in several of the scenes, including the unresolved ending, the film bursts
beyond the straight-on comedy of, for example, *Easy Living.*

Sturges, as we will see, acknowledged a much darker world than he generally
portrays in *Remember the Night.* But he was unwilling to abandon comedy completely and go for the straight drama he achieved in *The Power and the Glory.* The
result is an unusual film that could be called an ironic, comic version of film noir.

Synopsis

Sequence A (26 pages)

We follow the theft of a fancy bracelet from Meyers & Co. on Fifth Avenue
in New York and the good-looking female thief's arrest in a pawn shop on Third

Avenue. Shoppers carrying wrapped gifts and a Salvation Army Santa set the scene at Christmastime.

Trial is set immediately. The young assistant district attorney, Jack Sargent, is upset that he must try this case during the holiday season, when a jury is more likely to be forgiving.

During the extended trial scene, the long-winded lawyer for the defense claims innocence for the young woman, Miss Lee Leander, saying that she was "hypnotized" by the bracelet. Sargent sharply gets the case postponed until after Christmas; such a plea, he says, needs an expert witness, and the only expert is on vacation. Bond is set at $5,000, an amount that Lee doesn't have. Jack takes pity on Lee and arranges for a certain "Fat" Mike to post bail and spring her free for the holidays.

Sequence B (21 pages)

While Jack makes his final preparations to go home to Indiana for Christmas (included here is a dialogue not in the film with his black servant, Rufus, about Christmas gifts he has or has not bought), Fat Mike shows up and deposits Lee at his apartment thinking Jack is sweet on her.

There follows the expected confusion as Lee tries to find out why Jack had her released. She thinks he is trying to have his way with her, while he only wishes her to have a happy Christmas. Since he clearly doesn't want her to stay, Lee, asking if she has the choice, declares, "Then I'll stay." The most unlikely of relationships has now officially begun. It is quickly determined that far from doing Lee a favor, Jack has created a problem, since Lee doesn't even have the money to pay her hotel bill. Once again in a Sturges script, economics rules the day. He invites her to dinner so they can solve the problem.

At a "restaurant with a dance floor," Lee and Jack are dancing. The trial judge shows up with his wife and is horrified to see Jack with Lee. There follows a rapid-fire dialogue between Jack and Lee, leading up to Jack's trying to understand why Lee is a professional thief. Lee puts him off: "I don't think you ever could understand because your mind is different. Right or wrong is the same for everybody, you see, but the *rights* and the *wrongs* aren't the same. Like in China they eat dogs." Soon after, the band plays "My Indiana Home," and Lee asks Jack to dance. Jack now discovers that Lee, too, is a Hoosier and offers to drop her at her home for Christmas and pick her up on the way back. Lee has already made it clear she hasn't been home in years, not since she ran away.

Sequence C (27 pages)

We find Jack and Lee on the road at night. They become lost and wind up in a small town, Blairs Mills. The "road," however, is bringing them together. Soon they take a "detour" and are traveling across hill and dale. In a scene not in the film, they cross a creek. At one point they crash through a fence and encounter a covered threshing machine in the fog—which they mistake at first for an ele-

Jack Sargent (Fred MacMurray) and Lee Leander (Barbara Stanwyck) stand before a small-town judge on a trespassing charge in *Remember the Night*. Courtesy The Museum of Modern Art.

phant. They drive a bit further and run into the threshing machine again—and yet again (this scene was also cut from the film). Finally they stop in a field, and Jack remembers that Rufus packed sandwiches.

At Jack's suggestion, they decide to get some rest and continue driving in the morning. They fall asleep leaning against each other and awake with a cow poking its head in Lee's window. Jack gets the bright idea to try and milk the cow into his thermos. This pure slapstick routine can't help but bring them closer together. Soon, though, an angry farmer with a rifle arrives and arrests them for trespassing and for destruction of property.

They are hauled off to the justice of the peace. Although we began the script in the legal world, here we have the law turned upside down and inside out, with the system being used against "the people," especially if they are from "out of state." Lee gives a false name, Mary Smith (which is of course the heroine's name in *Easy Living*), and she states her occupation as "bubble dancer." Jack, clearly in tune with Lee, gives his name as Henry Wadsworth Longfellow and his occupation as "steam fitter." He now shows himself to be as "playful" with facts and the law as Lee. But Lee sees that only drastic action will get them out of this fix. She drops a match in the wastebasket and chaos erupts, allowing Lee and Jack to escape. Thus at the halfway point of the script, Jack has demonstrated that he is interested enough in Lee to drop his legal persona and become a "fugitive from justice." Their final exchange has us feeling even more strongly that they are becoming a couple:

SARGENT

(Roughly)

Do you realize that house is probably in flames a mile high?

LEE

(Vehemently)

I hope it is.

SARGENT

So do I . . . but what's that got to do with the morals of the case?

LEE

(Triumphantly)

What have morals got to do with it? You've treated me like your sister.

Sturges closes the sequence with them both laughing "happily."

Sequence D (25 pages)

This is Lee's homecoming scene. At night, they arrive at "a small ramshackle house" with junk in the yard. A man "fifty-odd and disagreeable-looking" answers the door. Lee is startled when she asks for Mrs. Malone and he says, "I guess you want my wife." No real description of Lee's mother is provided; she is simply "a middle-aged woman." What follows is an extremely harsh scene that completely breaks the mood of romance and comedy established thus far. As scripted, the scene is longer, more detailed, and even harsher than in the film; it is also more explicit, for it explains that Lee "borrowed" her mother's entire savings to buy a party dress when she was fourteen. In the script, too, Lee has a sister who also ran away, and there has been newspaper coverage of Lee's arrest, thanks to a local boy, Johnny Jarvis, who "is in New York studying to be a reporter" and "sends back clippings."

Jack takes control by pointing out that they "have still fifty miles to go," and they leave. Lee "sobs once" and says, "I'd forgotten how much I hate that woman . . . and how much she hates me"—one of the bitterest comments about a mother-daughter relationship in American cinema.

The second half of this sequence focuses on Jack's homecoming. The transition is accomplished by a mention of his cross-eyed grandfather and a cut to "cross-eyed Grandpa *on the wall*." Willie, who is described in the cast sheet as "a comedy character—boy of all work—half in the family—stutters and is in hot water most of time—Sterling Holloway type or Doodles Weaver," is fixing up a room, and Jack's mother and his Aunt Emma are busy cooking and cleaning.

No contrast could be greater, of course, than between Lee's hateful home and this happy-fantasy midwestern country matriarchy. Jack arrives and there is a large welcome for him and Lee, with no chance to explain who she is. Mrs. Sargent simply says to her, "It's a joy to have you here."

They settle into the sitting room, and Jack is urged to play the piano. In the script he plays "The Road to Mandalay," but in the film he performs a version of "Swanee River" by Stephen Foster. Then it is Lee playing and Willie singing—"Rosary" in the script, but "The End of a Perfect Day" in the film. Willie sings well, with "a surprisingly beautiful tenor."

Once again we see how well matched Lee and Jack are. Dare we say they are "in tune" at this point?

Lee is to stay in the room with the cross-eyed grandfather's portrait, and Aunt Emma provides her with a striped flannelette nightgown. The sequence ends with Jack trying to explain to his mother that Lee is a crook. But Mrs. Sargent won't believe it: "That girl is as honest as all outdoors," she declares. Then she states the real theme of the film: "The poor thing. She probably didn't get enough love as a child." Just so the scene does not become too sentimental, Sturges ends this exchange with Mrs. Sargent wondering, "Do you think we ought to lock up the silver?" This is followed by one of those telegraphic descriptions that says volumes about character. "Sargent looks at his mother unbelievingly then joyously."

In her room, Lee notices the portrait of "cross-eyed Grandpa," who is "leering a little more than usual." Sturges carries this motif into other films, including *Sullivan's Travels,* when Sullivan is locked up in the widow's home and the portrait of her late husband grimaces more than usual, showing increasing disapproval.

Sequence E (9 pages)

We begin with another scene cut from the film, in church with "Holy Night" being sung and the minister preaching. The film picks up with shot E-7: Christmas morning and the opening of presents. Everyone gets gifts except Lee. Jack starts to apologize to her, but a kick from Mrs. Sargent makes it clear there are packages for Lee under the tree—including one from the perplexed Jack. It turns out to be a bottle of perfume he had given his mother the previous Christmas ("Christmas Night" in the script, but "Hour of Ecstasy" in the film).

It is then time to get ready for some community festivities. But first, in another segment dropped from the film, Lee stops by Jack's room. She mentions the upcoming trial, which he confesses he "hadn't thought of," and she kisses his hand.

LEE
(Looking into the fire)

You know, nobody would believe that we came all this way, slept

321

in adjoining rooms, neither of us old nor particularly ugly . . . and never had an evil thought.

SARGENT

(Uneasily)

No, I don't suppose they would.

With the remark "Even if it was true, they wouldn't believe it," she leaves, giving him a pat on the cheek. He remains sitting by the fire and savors the moment—then realizes his bathrobe is burning.

Sequence F (18 pages)

We begin in the kitchen with Aunt Emma giving Lee credit for having made popovers. Lee tells Jack that Aunt Emma thinks the two of them are in love. Cut to a rummage sale at the firehouse, where Lee proves her stuff by "selling" the judge an "armadillo basket."

Cut to later in the Sargent living room. There is a short exchange between Aunt Emma and Lee that was cut from the film but that in a sense points Lee in the right direction. When Lee drops a stitch knitting, Aunt Emma "firmly" states: "When you make a mistake you've got to pay for it. Otherwise you never learn."

Next we see Lee in her bedroom with Aunt Emma helping her to put on an old-fashioned corset. A box lies on the bed, wrapped in an old newspaper bearing the headline "Roosevelt Refuses Third Term." Aunt Emma pulls out a lace wedding dress, and we learn that she had considered marriage one summer a long time ago.

A barn dance follows, with "a surprisingly good orchestra" playing. Lee and Jack are dancing, and we hear Aunt Emma remark to Mrs. Sargent that the couple would have "awful cute babies." The bandleader wishes the crowd a happy New Year, and everyone embraces—including, after a pause, Lee and Jack, "smacko right on the lips."

Now they are all back home, ready to turn in. Jack, seeing Lee to her room, invites her for a goodnight cigarette, and she says she'll come soon. But as she's getting ready Mrs. Sargent arrives. She tells Lee of their poverty after her husband's death and Jack's struggle to do several jobs and to study hard to get on in his life. Then she appeals to Lee: "I'm only trying to tell you that he worked very hard to get where he is . . . *very, very* hard and . . . and nothing should be allowed to spoil it for him." Lee promises not to get in the way, and Mrs. Sargent reaches up "and kisses her." Then, with Mrs. Sargent's prodding, Lee admits her love for Jack. After Mrs. Sargent leaves, Lee cancels her rendezvous with Jack, slipping a note under his door that claims she is "too sleepy."

In a final shot cut from the film, Lee smokes and sticks out her tongue at the "stern"-looking cross-eyed Grandpa.

Sequence G (10 pages)

It's the next day and Jack and Lee are getting ready to leave. There are good-byes all around. We then cut to the Canadian border, where Jack, asked why he's going through Canada, playfully tells the official he is "a fugitive from justice."

Driving along, Jack tells Lee that if she "didn't want to go back tomorrow," he couldn't make her. She won't hear of it, though. Talk now centers on Lee's court case. For the first time, Lee understands that he sprang her because his conscience was biting him. He now explains his kid-glove "technique" for getting women convicted.

The scene dissolves to "frozen Niagara Falls at night." Jack is forceful now, pushing romantically, crossing the line of his profession. He finally confesses his love for her, and she confesses that she stole the bracelet. He shrugs off this admission by saying, "What you did yesterday and what you do today are two different things." He tries to get a declaration of love from her, but she won't cooperate.

Jack realizes that his mother has talked to her. He finally proposes in a backhanded way, stating that they will go to Niagara Falls for their honeymoon. "But we're there now, darling," she quips.

Sequence H (16 pages)

We are now back in New York inside a taxi. Jack jumps in the waiting cab and, "grin[ning] at her like a kid," shows her a marriage license. She tries to grab it, but he pockets it. This "amazing marriage" scene (the script was in fact originally titled "The Amazing Marriage") is missing from the film, which cuts to the dialogue that follows, where Lee explains that all the romantic talk by Niagara Falls was "unreal":

LEE
(Irritatedly)

That was in Niagara Falls! People aren't responsible for what they say in Niagara Falls.
(After a short pause)
This is New York . . . and this is today . . . and this is different!

Jack, though, is serious; after all, he has carried his feelings over into the "work place"—New York. Lee, trying to be practical and holding to her promise to Jack's mother, says, "Can't you see the papers? 'District attorney marries girl crook'?" The dialogue continues, wonderfully torn between pragmatic logic and Jack's heartfelt yearnings.

Finally we are in court, having come full circle. The judge and the District Attorney discuss whether Jack will "throw" the case or not. The D.A. cannot believe that the judge saw Jack and Lee together in the restaurant.

323

The case is under way and leads up to Jack's cross-examination of Lee. Jack appears to be harshly on the attack, a technique Lee knows is supposed to antagonize the jury and rebound in her favor. One juror quips, "I sat on a *murder* case and they didn't get that rough." The questioning is all about her hypnosis defense; in the script (but not the film), Lee flashes back to Jack's explanation of his technique for getting women put in jail.

The jury becomes upset with Jack's strident, aggressive behavior, and Lee has more memories of her promise to Mrs. Sargent to leave Jack alone (again, this memory "superimposition" is not used in the film). She then confesses, though Jack tries to cut her off. When the judge asks her why she wishes to plead guilty, she replies, "Because I *am* guilty," and concludes by repeating Aunt Emma's words: "and when you make a mistake you've got to pay for it . . . otherwise you never learn."

The judge closes the case, saying they will meet in a few days to fix the sentence.

We end up in the anteroom of the sheriff's office. In a final three-page dialogue Lee tells Jack, "And I love you so much." What follows is sentiment mixed with irony as they talk about waiting and love surviving a prison term. She again turns down his offer to marry her immediately before sentencing. The script ends with another confession of love from Lee as "very faintly we hear the music of 'My Indiana Home.'" Love, marriage, *and* prison seem definite for the future.

Romance and Performance: "All Juries Get Soft at Christmastime"

"Performance" comes through as a major motif for Sturges in this comedy-romance-drama. At the initial trial, for example, we learn that the verbose and melodramatic defense lawyer had indeed been on stage at one time. But Jack in his own way "acts" well in court too, stealing the show with his sudden move to postpone.

Once out of the courtroom, however, back in the "real" world, Lee appears to be the best performer. In fact, she draws attention to acting when she is dropped at Jack's apartment and the butler enters with drinks for both of them:

LEE

(Philosophically)

One of these days one of you boys is going to start one of these
scenes differently . . . and one of us girls is going to drop dead
from surprise.

The story has now been set up. Lee is the worldly woman, and Jack, the totally innocent man. We also have the one who ran away from home, Lee, and the one who has lived out the American rags-to-riches dream, Jack.

Clearly this is a narrative pattern that resonated for Sturges, for he used it again in *The Lady Eve,* which he wrote for Stanwyck, so delighted was he with her performance in *Remember the Night.*[8] In the later script, Stanwyck as Jean is even more worldly wise and an even feistier crook than Lee, and the naive male, Henry Fonda, is even more naive than Jack! The sense of performance in *The Lady Eve* is sharper as well. At one point, for example, Stanwyck, on board a luxury liner, speaks to her father while observing Fonda in her makeup mirror—sizing up their next victim. Her remarks crackle with mockery as she watches all the women trying to flirt with the clueless millionaire, Charles. (Note how Sturges the screenwriter inserts a "note" to himself as director.)

> JEAN
>
> The dropped kerchief! That hasn't been used since Lily Langtry . . . you'll have to pick it up yourself, madam . . . It's a shame, but he doesn't care for the flesh; he'll never see it.
>
> *JEAN'S HAND AND THE MIRROR—S.E. SHOT OF CHARLES IN MIRROR*
>
> *Note:* Only enough of this dialogue will be used to match the action.
>
> JEAN
>
> That's right . . . pick it up . . . It was worth trying anyway, wasn't it? . . . Look at the girl over to the left . . . look over to your left, bookworm . . . there's a girl pining for you . . . a little further . . . just a little further. THERE! Now wasn't that worth looking for? See those nice store teeth, all beaming at you.[9]

Her commentary goes on, building to a comic crescendo as she trips Charles, literally, and so begins their contact and eventual romance. The overall effect is reminiscent of the trickster-turns-romantic saved-by-love theme of *Remember the Night,* but minus the drama.

In *Remember the Night,* meanwhile, Sturges builds on the kind of structure he developed in *Easy Living,* where he set up a world—there, Wall Street and American capitalism—and then opened it up to include romance, such that both motifs, capitalism and romance, could be fused in one fairy-tale ending. We might call such an approach "triumphant romantic irony." *Remember the Night* poses as its "world" the courtroom and New York City at Christmas, then injects the all-juries-get-soft-at-Christmastime spirit to develop the comic romance between Lee and Jack.

I have quoted at length in the synopsis in an effort to convey the flavor of that developing romance in both its carefree moments and its dramatic, hard-edged moments, ones that border on film noir. In the Introduction we discussed how the film takes an unexpected dramatic turn when Lee confronts her mother, who shows not an ounce of understanding, forgiveness, or motherly love. Sturges's ambivalent feelings about his own mother undoubtedly informed that scene. Still, he may not have understood fully how much this film is about mothers, matriarchy, and the ways in which children react to the world of their upbringing. That both Lee and Jack are from small-town Indiana only reinforces Sturges's theme that "one man's meat is another man's poison."

Seen in this "motherly" light, the center of gravity (and the word is carefully chosen) of this film lies in the conflict between matriarchal "law" and the laws of the land and city, with the laws of the heart caught in the middle. Lee has been running away from home, and from herself. She is "saved" by Jack, not in any self-righteous way, but simply through his bumbling concern, which leads straight to his happy, stable home and his caring mother—elements that Sturges never had in his own life. But just when all of this hometown-at-Christmas cheer begins to feel completely staged (performance at work once more), Sturges surprises us again. This time it is the confrontation between Mrs. Sargent and Lee that throws us for a loop. The scene works so well because we realize these two strong women are equally matched and understand each other without illusions. Late on the eve of their departure back to New York, Mrs. Sargent comes to Lee's room and tells her in a long speech how hard life was for them and how hard Jack has had to work to be what he is and get where he is. Mrs. Sargent then says she knows that her son is in love with Lee, although Lee denies it. The climax of the scene is simple:

> MRS. SARGENT
> (Looking back)
>
> But you love him, don't you?
>
> *LEE—PAST MRS. SARGENT*
>
> LEE
> (After nodding "yes")
>
> I'm afraid so.

This moment, I suggest, saves the script and thus the film from falling into two completely different stories that might never find a way to connect. Sturges gambled heavily on this one, going so far as to joke that he almost committed harakiri over it. But the moment rings absolutely true and solidifies all. Mrs. Sargent is the mother Lee never had, and Jack is the man she has never found. That two Hoosiers find each other in the big city is ironic already. That they are on opposite sides of the law only increases the irony. At this point, however, Lee undergoes what few of Sturges's characters experience: a change not only of heart but of character. From this moment on she cannot be untrue to either Mrs. Sargent or Jack.

For this reason there can be no simple or even ironic comic ending to this film as there was to *Easy Living* and *The Palm Beach Story,* to mention just two. The script, as we have seen, was originally entitled "The Amazing Marriage."

But that marriage, if it takes place, must wait for Lee to serve her time. This tale begins with Lee stealing a bracelet. It ends with her on the way to her prison cell to await sentencing. Having just turned down Jack's offer to marry her on the spot, she says:

> LEE
>
> If you still wanted me afterwards . . . you'd be a sucker if you did, but if you did . . . it wouldn't be the same . . . I'd be all square . . . and you would have had plenty of time to think things over . . . a lot of things.
>
> *Sargent crushes her to him.*

And after one final speech:

> *She pats his head gently as one pats a child.*
>
> LEE
>
> I love you so.
>
> *Sargent sobs once. Very faintly we hear the music of "My Indiana Home."*

"Motherly" is the only way to describe her final gesture. She wants to marry Sargent later, if he still wants her, but in the meantime she must console him, *like a mother,* thus fulfilling an unspoken agreement with Mrs. Sargent to let no harm come to this man.

This gesture did not make it to the screen, however. In fact, Lee's final speech is cut. In the script, after Jack says he will be there and hold her hand while they sentence her, she says:

> LEE
>
> Then I won't be afraid . . .
> (She tries to laugh)
> . . . it will be kind of like a marriage at that . . .
> (Then after a pause)
> . . . and the other part won't be so bad . . . or so long . . . with your voice always in my ears, your smile always before my eyes . . . the feel of your hand always in mine.

She then pats his head and tells him she loves him. Only the first line, "Then I won't be afraid," appeared in the film, reversing the spirit of the script and making it seem as if Jack is the strong male figure instead of the child who needs a mother's reassuring hand.

I like the script's ending better. No doubt the producers saw the final cut as the more commercial and "expected" ending. As a result, though, "the amazing marriage" promised in the original title becomes a dream deferred.

NOTES

1. Diane Jacobs, *Christmas in July: The Life and Art of Preston Sturges* (Berkeley: University of California Press, 1992), 187.

2. Ibid., 141.

3. Frank S. Nugent, *"Remember the Night,"* *New York Times,* January 18, 1940, 27.

4. *Preston Sturges by Preston Sturges,* adapted and edited by Sandy Sturges (New York: Simon & Schuster, 1990), 288.

5. Ibid.

6. I am grateful to Edward Dimendberg for this observation.

7. J. P. Telotte, *Voices in the Dark: The Narrative Patterns of Film Noir* (Urbana: University of Illinois Press, 1989), 2, 4.

8. Jacobs, *Christmas in July,* 197.

9. *Five Screenplays by Preston Sturges,* edited with an introduction by Brian Henderson (Berkeley: University of California Press, 1986), 364.

CREDITS

Remember the Night

Released January 1940

Producer:	Mitchell Leisen and (uncredited) Albert Lewin
Director:	Mitchell Leisen
Screenwriter:	Preston Sturges
Cinematographer:	Ted Tetzlaff
Editor:	Doane Harrison
Art director:	Hans Dreier
Set decoration:	A. E. Freudeman
Musical score:	Frederick Hollander

CAST

Lee Leander	Barbara Stanwyck
John Sargent	Fred MacMurray
Mrs. Sargent	Beulah Bondi
Aunt Emma	Elizabeth Patterson
Frances X. O'Leary	Willard Roberston
Willie	Sterling Holloway
Judge (New York)	Charles Waldron
District attorney	Paul Guilfoyle
Tom	Charley Arnt
Hank	John Wray
Rufus	Snowflake

Produced and released by Paramount Pictures.
94 minutes. Black and white.

Remember the Night
or
THE AMAZING MARRIAGE

June 15, 1939

THE AMAZING MARRIAGE

CAST

JOHN SARGENT.................

LEE LEANDER.................

MRS. SARGENT................ John's mother - gentle, kindly, a little vague - very motherly and understanding.

AUNT EMMA................... Energetic, middle-aged spinster with heart of gold whose bark is worse than her bite.

JUDGE (Hearing Lee's
      case)............ Human and kindly - interested in his family.

FRANCIS X. O'LEARY......... The Lawyer defending Lee - spellbinder - ex-actor - unscrupulous - in it for what he can get out.

DISTRICT ATTORNEY GARVIN... A prosecuting attorney with a sense of humor, a human side - a fatherly interes in his assistants.

RUFUS...................... Sargent's man - a Stepin Fetchit - Rochester type.

TOM........................ Dumb-looking man of about 35 who very evidently got his job in the D.A.'s office through pull.

FAT MIKE................... Big, dumb, rather obliging bondsman - with mind in the gutter.

WILLIE..................... A comedy character - boy of all work - half in the family - stutters and is in hot water most of time - Sterling Holloway type or Doodles Weaver.

HANK....................... Owner of field and cow who arrests Lee and Sargent - bitter-looking man, taking out his grudge against the world and earning money on the side by running trespassers in.

MR. EMORY.................. Justice of the Peace - typical, small town grafter.

MRS. EMORY (bit)........... Frousy, disagreeable, town-gossip type.

(Continued)

CAST

LEE'S MOTHER.............. Middle-aged woman - puritanical, bitter without understanding - doing right according to her lights.

PROFESSOR KEINMETZ......... A typical, scientific-looking gent - excitable.

BITS

JEWELRY SALESMAN........... Small, with bulging eyes.

JANITOR................... Cadaverous-looking man with ringing voice.

SHERIFF................... Large, bluff gent with mean eyes.

MUG FROM SHERIFF'S OFFICE..

BRIAN..................... Uniformed court attendant with big feet that hurt.

JUDGE'S WIFE.............. Seen at restaurant - fat, comfortable-looking.

LEE'S STEPFATHER.......... Fifty-odd and disagreeable looking.

MINISTER.................. Typical.

JUDGE AT RUMMAGE SALE...... Bluff, kindly underneath.

12 jurors - 8 men - 4 women - all with lines.
Court attendants.

At restaurant - waiters, band, girl singer.

Extras at courtroom - restaurant, The Barn Dance - Rummage Sale Types

* * *

<u>SEQUENCE "A"</u>

The Main Titles are superimposed on a high-lighted
bas-relief of Justice blindfolded holding the
balance. After the last title --

DISSOLVE TO:

A-1   CLOSEUP - A MAGNIFICENT DIAMOND

We hear the babble of women shoppers' voices as the
CAMERA DRAWS BACK. We see now that the diamond is
the center stone of a beautiful bracelet around a
woman's wrist. It is being held up for inspection.
Behind a counter filled with jewelry stands a small
salesman with bulging eyes. Remember that we see
only the hand and wrist of the customer.

THE SALESMAN
Glorious, madam, isn't it?

LEE'S VOICE
Could I see that one, please?

The hand points to a bracelet in the bottom of the
showcase.

THE SALESMAN
(Cheerfully)
Yes, indeed, madam. By all means.

He opens the back of the showcase and ducks below it.
The CAMERA MOVES DOWN FOR A CLOSE SHOT of him and the
hand with the bracelet is left OUT OF THE PICTURE. The
salesman reappears close to us, like a goldfish in a
globe, reaches way into the showcase and points to a
bracelet. Now he beams, rolls his eyes upwards and
mouths:

THE SALESMAN
(Not heard)
This one?

His mouth drops as he finds that he is looking at no
one. His eyes bulge and his expression becomes panic-
stricken as he looks from right to left. Now he
scrambles out of the showcase and to his feet. The
CAMERA COMES UP WITH HIM. He bounces up above the
showcase, looks around desperately, then hurries
around the end of the counter calling:

THE SALESMAN
(Croakingly)
Mr. Meyer, Mr. Meyer, please, at once!

DISSOLVE TO:

6-15-39

334

A-2   TRUCKING SHOT AHEAD OF LEE ON <u>FIFTH AVENUE</u> - DUSK

She is a pretty girl, smartly if not richly dressed.
She looks a little nervous at the moment. She hurries past a Santa Claus tinkling his bell on the
corner and turns down a side street. The CAMERA PANS
WITH HER and watches her get small.

DISSOLVE TO:

A-3   <u>A THIRD AVENUE PAWNBROKERS</u> - NIGHT

A-4   SHOT <u>ACROSS THE STREET</u> - AT LEE

She comes slowly TOWARD US. As she goes BY THE CAMERA--

A-5   LEE - WALKING AWAY FROM US

She hesitates a moment at the door, then enters the
pawnbrokers. We wait an uncomfortably long moment.
Suddenly we hear a muffled yell, heels kicking against
a door and her voice:

> LEE'S VOICE
> (Faintly)
> Let me out of here, let me out of
> here!

DISSOLVE TO:

A-6   A GROUND GLASS DOOR PANEL ON WHICH WE READ:

> OFFICE OF THE
> DISTRICT ATTORNEY
> N.Y. COUNTY

In the lower right-hand corner it says:

> Nora H. Milqueen
> Notary Public

DISSOLVE TO:

A-7   <u>DISTRICT ATTORNEY'S OFFICE</u>

Tom is just entering with a brief which he hands to
the D.A.

6-15-39   (Continued)

A-7 (Cont'd)

                       D.A.
What's this?

                       TOM
        (Bored)
Some broad cops a bracelet outa
Meyer & Company and hocks it on
Third Avenue. Open and shut.

                       D.A.
        (Without looking up)
First offense?

                       TOM
No. She's got a record - this is
her third offense.

                       D.A.
        (Reading)
That's good....that's good... a
first offender at Christmas time
is tougher than tiger meat.
Juries get soft-hearted at Christmas,
Tommy. If you ever get a case to
prosecute and you see that "peace
on earth good will to men" look come
in their eyes, get a continuance if
you have to fall down and tell the
judge you ate green apples.

                       TOM
        (His eyes shining)
Can I handle this case, boss? I'll
get you a conviction or by......

                       D.A.
        (Interrupting him)
Quiet, Tommy, quiet. When the
right case comes along I'll give
it to you: a nice wife beater or
something like that. You have to
learn to crawl before you walk, and
besides your face isn't right to
prosecute a woman.

                       TOM
        (Looking away dis-
          gustedly)
Aw....

                       D.A.
Where's Sargent?

6-15-39   (Continued)

A-7 (Cont'd)

> TOM
> What's his face got that mine
> hasn't got?

> D.A.
> (Picking up the
> telephone)
> Get me Mr. Sargent, please.

> TOM
> He's gone home for Christmas.
> Ohio, or Oklahoma or some place
> like that. Listen, I could get
> you a conviction so quick...

> D.A.
> (Gently)
> Sh-h-h.

A-8   SARGENT'S APARTMENT

A telephone in the living room is ringing. A slow-
moving colored man comes out of the kitchenette and
reaches for the phone.

A-9   THE DOOR TO SARGENT'S BEDROOM - PAST RUFUS

Sargent hurries INTO VIEW with a razor in his hand.

> SARGENT
> If that's the office tell 'em
> I've already left.

> RUFUS
> (Into the telephone)
> Yassuh...yassuh....well, if dis
> is de office he's already lef'.

> SARGENT
> (Frothing in the
> background)
> I didn't say to say that, you
> blockheaded....

A-10   D.A. AND TOM
> D.A.
> (Into telephone)
> Oh, my no, this isn't his office!
> You just tell him a young woman

6-15-39   (Continued)

A-10 (Cont'd)

>   D.A. (Cont'd)
> wants to make an appointment with
> him.
>   (He winks at Tom)

A-11 SARGENT AND RUFUS

>   RUFUS
>   (With his hand over
>   the telephone)
> It ain't de office... a young woman
> want to make an appointment wid you.

Sargent reaches slowly for the telephone, draws his
hand back, then takes the telephone and speaks very
suspiciously.

>   SARGENT
>   (In a very bad
>   southern dialect)
> Who all wants to speak to Massuh
> Sargent?

At this feeble effort Rufus claps his hand over his
mouth.

A-12 D.A. AND TOM

D.A. has his hand over <u>his</u> mouth to stop from laughing.
Now he removes his hand talks in a voice exactly like
a girl's.

>   D.A.
> Why Jack Sargent, you couldn't fool
> a horsefly. Who do you think
> you're kidding?

A-13 SARGENT AND RUFUS

>   SARGENT
>   (In his normal voice)
> Who is this?

A-14 D.A. AND TOM

>   D.A.
>   (In his natural voice)
> This is your boss, my boy, and it's
> a good thing you didn't take up the
> stage for a living... I'll see you
> down here in fifteen minutes.

6-15-39

A-15 SARGENT AND RUFUS

       SARGENT
       (Roughly)
    Now wait a minute..... but you
    told me if I finished up the
    Mathews case........but I've seven
    hundred and thirty miles to drive
    and...........sure, and fall
    asleep at the wheel and get croaked
    ....who's defending?

Rufus exits on tip-toe.

A-16 D.A. AND TOM

       D.A.
    O'Leary. Francis X. O'Leary him-
    self.

A-17 SARGENT AT THE TELEPHONE

       SARGENT
    That windbag.....he'll give us the
    Gettysburg Address and the Declar-
    ation of Independence and....

A-18 D.A. AND TOM

       D.A.
    I'll have Tom meet you in Court and
    you'll be out of there by noon....
      (Now he scowls and
      speaks with some
      severity)
    Kindly remember who you're talking
    to and leave the pigs out of it....
    Merry Christmas yourself.

He hangs up.

DISSOLVE TO:

A-19 LOW CAMERA SHOT - UP AT A CLOCK IN THE COURTROOM

It says "4:40".

6-15-39

A-20   HIGH CAMERA SHOT - <u>DOWN ON THE COURTROOM</u>

Sargent and Tom are in the MIDDLE OF THE SHOT with
Sargent looking sourly around and UP AT US (the
clock).   Now he looks AWAY FROM US and gives his
attention to Mr. Francix X.O'Leary who is addressing
the jury.   Also giving Mr. O'Leary their attention
are the Judge, the Clerk of the Court, the Court
Stenographer, some witnesses, court attendants and a
few spectators. The Defendant has her back TO US OR
IS MASKED by a piece of furniture.

> O'LEARY
> (We have heard him, of
> course, since we CAME
> IN ON THE CLOCK)
> ...during the course of this trial
> to prove that a valuable bracelet
> was taken from the premises of Meyer
> & Company by the defendant. All of
> this has been a waste of time, ladies
> and gentlemen of the jury, of your
> time and mine, time we could spend
> to better advantage in last minute
> Christmas shopping. I know that's
> what I'd like to be doing.
> (He chuckles)

A-21   <u>THE JURY</u> - PAST O'LEARY

The eight men and four women laugh forlornly, then
give the District Attorney a dirty look.

A-22   THE ASS'T. DISTRICT ATTORNEY SARGENT, HIS ASSISTANT
TOM, AND THE JUDGE.

> SARGENT
> (Quietly)
> May it please the Court, we object,
> Your Honor. The jury's Christmas
> shopping has nothing to do with the
> case.

Sargent looks wearily toward O'Leary.

> JUDGE
> Objection sustained.
> (He turns to the
> jury)
> The jury will disregard Mr. O'Leary's
> tempting allusions to Christmas
> shopping...quite obviously we'd <u>all</u>

6-15-39   (Continued)

A-22 (Cont'd)   JUDGE (Continuing)
like to be Christmas shopping.

There is a roar of laughter and the judge pounds with
his gavel.

A-23   O'LEARY - <u>PAST THE JURY</u>

             O'LEARY
I withdraw the allusion, Your
Honor.

During the chuckle which follows he wipes his pince-
nez, then speaks forcefully.

             O'LEARY
When I say that time has been
wasted I mean that the State
has gone to great lengths to
prove that Anna-Rose Malone,
sometimes known as Lee Leander...

A-24   SARGENT AND TOM

             SARGENT
        (Quietly)
And sometimes a lot of other
things...
        (He looks sideways at
        the prisoner)

A-25   CLOSE SHOT - THE PRISONER, LEE

She glares at Sargent.

            O'LEARY'S VOICE
...did on the afternoon of
December third walk out upon
Fifth Avenue with a bracelet
which was still the property
of Meyer & Company...to prove
something she freely admits...
as if the proof of this fact
constituted a proof of guilt.
        (He removes his
        pince-nez and shakes
        it at the jury,
        warningly)
Since the dawn of civilization, ladies
and gentlemen of the jury, since the
beginnings of jurisprudence, wise
men...AND women, have refused to be

6-15-39   (Continued)

A-25 (Cont'd)   O'LEARY'S VOICE (Continuing)
                    hoodwinked by circumstantial evidence.
                    The contents of a whiskey bottle are
                    as easily cold coffee. A man who
                    staggers may be injured...and the
                    kittens born in the oven...are not
                    biscuits.

        There is a mild chuckle.

A-26   SARGENT AND TOM

                            TOM
                    I don't like the smile on that
                    jury's pan.

                            SARGENT
                    What we need here is a nice con-
                    tinuance till after Christmas.
                        (He looks at Lee)

A-27   LEE

        She looks suspiciously at Sargent, then vaguely
        at the Judge.

A-28   CLOSE SHOT - THE JUDGE

        He seems to be making copious notes.

A-29   CLOSE SHOT - THE JUDGE'S HANDS

        Already written we see:

                "For Junior:
                    1. - Super-heterosomething
                         construction kit. (Wireless)
                    1. - O-gauge electric train with
                         chime whistle and remote control."

        The hand writes:

                "1 - ..."

        The writing hand hesitates.

A-30   THE JUDGE, SARGENT AND TOM

        The Judge looks up from his writing and contemplates
        the ceiling. Sargent and Tom are whispering.

6-15-39   (Continued)

A-30   (Cont'd)   O'LEARY'S VOICE
                    (Ringingly)
                  ... temporary loss of will and
                  consciousness, now known as
                  schizophrenia, but formerly known
                  as HYPNOTISM!

The Judge jerks his eyes from the ceiling and
scowls at O'Leary. Sargent swings violently in his
chair. Tom's mouth drops open in astonishment.

A-31   CLOSE SHOT - THE JUDGE

Suddenly he writes --

A-32   JUDGE'S HANDS

He writes:

           "1 - Box magician's tricks"

A-33   SARGENT AND TOM

                     TOM
                  (Hoarsely and indignantly)
                  What do you mean, you're not
                  going to object?

                    SARGENT
                  Shut up. He's just postponed
                  the case till after Christmas.

                     TOM
                  (Blankly)
                  How do you figure that?

                     SARGENT
                  (Jabbing the index and
                  little fingers of his
                  right hand toward Tom's
                  eyes)
                 Hypnotism.

Tom's eyes cross.

A-34   O'LEARY - <u>PAST THE JURY</u>

                     O'LEARY
                  (Emphatically)
                  I said hypnotism and that is
                  exactly what I mean.
                  (He warms to his subject)

6-15-39   (Continued)

A-34   (Cont'd)

> O'LEARY
> Ladies and Gentlemen of the jury
> (He starts toward
> the prisoner)
> I want you to gaze upon this face.

A-35   CLOSE SHOT - LEE

She watches nervously as O'Leary approaches, seems
to catch his eye and remembers to cross her pretty
knees. O'Leary ENTERS THE SHOT and puts his hand
on her shoulder.

> O'LEARY
> (Challengingly)
> Is this the face of an habitual
> criminal? An outcast from society?
> A human pariah as contended by the
> learned counsel for the State?

Lee looks sadly into her lap.

A-36   SARGENT, TOM AND THE COURT

> SARGENT
> (A little wearily)
> Object, Your Honor. The learned
> counsel for the State said nothing
> of the kind.

A-37   CLOSE SHOT - O'LEARY AND LEE

> O'LEARY
> (Ferociously)
> He implied it !

Lee gives Sargent a frigid look.

A-38   SARGENT, TOM AND THE COURT

> SARGENT
> (Bored)
> Same objection.

6-15-39   (Continued)

A-38 (Cont'd)   THE COURT
Sustained. The epithets "habitual
criminal," "outcast from society,"
and "human pariah" will be stricken
out and the jury is instructed to
disregard them.

A-39   O'LEARY AND LEE - PAST THE JURY

                    O'LEARY
                (With increasing
                emotion)
This poor young girl went into this
great jewelers...why? Surely not
to buy...surely not because she
thought they would give her something
for nothing. OH, NO!
                (A titter from the
                jury)
I'll tell you why she went into
this great jewelers, ladies and
gentlemen of the jury...she went
in to look...to pretend for a
moment that she also belonged to
that ermine-wrapped and diamond-
hung elite that blooms on Fifth
Avenue at Christmas time.
                (Raising a warning
                finger)
Don't forget it is Christmas time!

A-40   SARGENT AND TOM

                    SARGENT
                (To Tom)
He's giving them a swell chance to.

A-41   O'LEARY AND LEE - PAST THE JURY

                    O'LEARY
She went in to look. Was there
anything wrong in that, ladies and
gentlemen of the jury? A cat may
look at a queen...and the starving
urchin may press his nose against
the frosted window of the bakery
shop and feast his eyes on luxuries
he's never had...and never will.
                (He pauses with a dramatic
                gesture)

6-15-39

345

A-42   TWO LADIES AND A GENT AMONGST THE JURORS

One lady wipes away a tear with a handkerchief.
The other puts a finger horizontally under her
nose and sniffles. The gent wipes the dew off
his glasses.

A-43   SARGENT AND TOM

They look at the jury in disgust.

A-44   O'LEARY - PAST THE JURY

Overcome by his own rhetoric he blows his nose
honkingly.

                    O'LEARY
          A salesman showed her the bracelet,
          URGED her to clasp it around her
          wrist, BEGGED her to examine it un-
          der a more powerful light, and then...
          excused himself. It's an old trick,
          this tempting the poor. They say,
          "Take it home and wear it for a
          few days." They say "Take it out
          and drive it all afternoon. Bring
          it back tomorrow. Buy it on your
          own terms." Consider the jewel
          scene between Mephistopheles and
          Marguerite in "Faust."

A-45   SARGENT AND TOM

                    SARGENT
                 (Quietly)
          I hope he isn't going to sing
          it.

A-46   CLOSE SHOT - THE COURT

He looks surreptitiously at his watch.

A-47   O'LEARY AND LEE - PAST THE JURY

                    O'LEARY
               (Holding up his left arm
                and looking at his wristwatch)
          The bracelet is under a powerful
6-15-39   (Continued)

A-47   (Cont'd)   O'LEARY
> light. The young girl stares at it...closer, closer. The great central stone flashes blindingly in her eyes: blue, green, purple, orange. Closer...still closer. Suddenly the colors are gone.... everything is dark. A breath of cold air brings her to her senses. But what's this? Where is the jewelry store? Where is the light she was standing under? WHAT IS SHE DOING ON FIFTH AVENUE...BLOCKS AWAY FROM MEYER AND COMPANY? With a thrill of horror she feels at her wrist...not daring to look. It's there! She steps to the light of a shop window. No doubt about it! And now...PANIC! She turns and hastens toward the great jewelers. Will they believe her? Fear turns her legs to lead...

Lee looks down at her legs, then sadly at the jury.

           O'LEARY (Continuing)
> One block. Two blocks. She goes blindly bumping into strangers who think she must be crazy. Six blocks. There at last the great windows dazzling with their gems...but no! the gems are gone! The windows are nearly bare. With a sinking heart she tries the door. It is locked. Meyer and Company has closed for the night...

A-48   SARGENT AND TOM

           TOM
> (Indignantly as he starts to his feet)

That is the ga...

           SARGENT
> (Pushing him back in his chair)

Sit down and learn something.

6-15-39

A-49   O'LEARY AND LEE

                         O'LEARY
                 What was she to do?
                         (Suddenly he points
                          a finger at a fat
                          jurywoman)
                 What would you do, madam?

A-50   CLOSE SHOT - THE FAT JURYWOMAN

She answers promptly.

                         THE JURYWOMAN
                 That's certainly a terrible spot
                 to be in... I suppose I'd....

She turns at a sharp rapping from the bench.

A-51   SARGENT, TOM AND THE COURT

Tom is goggle-eyed with indignation, Sargent is
laughing, the Court is pounding his gavel.

                         THE COURT
                         (Severely)
                 Counsel will refrain from question-
                 ing the jury and the jury will
                 refrain from answering! I've never
                 heard of such a thing!

Sargent claps his hand over his mouth to stop from
laughing.

A-52   O'LEARY AND LEE - PAST THE JURY

                         O'LEARY
                 I beg the Court's and the jury's
                 pardon....I was carried away.
                         (He pauses,
                          then con-
                          tinues)
                 What to do......suddenly an inspi-
                 ration......the phone book.....
                 S.A. Meyer & Company. S.A. Meyer
                 & Company. S.A. Meyer must

6-15-39   (Continued)

A-52 (Cont'd)

> O'LEARY (Cont'd)
> live some place, but he doesn't seem
> to... wait a minute, maybe he lives
> in the suburbs! Quick, the Westchester
> book! S.A. Meyer, S.A. Meyer, S.A.
> Meyer... maybe Long Island. S.A.
> Meyer, S.A. Meyer, S.A. MEYER!
> HERE IT IS: 324 WOODMERE ROAD,
> ROSLYN, LONG ISLAND! I'll take the
> first train. I'll be there by
> dinner time. He'll believe me.
> He's got to believe me!
> (He pauses)

A-53   SARGENT AND TOM

> TOM
> (Disgustedly)
> He should have been on the stage.

> SARGENT
> He was.

A-54   O'LEARY AND LEE

> O'LEARY
> (In a low voice)
> It costs money to go to Long Island...
> where will I get the money to go
> to Long Island?... Now a crazy idea!
> I'll hock the bracelet to get to
> Long Island to tell Mr. Meyer what
> happened. Quick, a hock shop!

A-55   SARGENT AND TOM

> SARGENT
> Quick, Watson, the needle.

A-56   O'LEARY AND LEE

> O'LEARY
> Here we are... a nice cozy pawn-
> broker's... the friend of the poor.
> Could I get some money on this,
> please? Well, well, well... I
> should say you could. Where did
> you get this piece, young lady?

6-15-39   (Continued)

A-56 (Cont'd)

> O'LEARY (Cont'd)
> Never mind where I got it. I
> need some money quick... Now don't
> get excited, everything is going
> to be all right. Just step in
> here, please... just a little further...
> BANG! You're going to get it all
> right!... Let me out of here! Look
> that door quick while I hold her
> in there... that's a boy... Hello,
> get me the police department... I
> got the thief what robbed Meyer
> & Company.

O'Leary passes his handkerchief over his forehead
then speaks very quietly.

> O'LEARY
> The defense rests.

A-57　THE JURY

They are sniffling badly and there is some honking
of noses.

A-58　SARGENT, TOM AND THE COURT

Sargent rises slowly. He seems as moved as the jury.

> SARGENT
> The hypothesis of hypnotism is a
> very interesting one... Let me be
> the first to admit it. Unfortunately
> I am no Svengali nor are you, ladies
> and gentlemen of the jury. The
> People of the State of New York will
> require the expert testimony of Dr.
> Keinmetz, the psychiatrist.

> THE COURT
> What do you want to do about it,
> then?

A-59　O'LEARY AND LEE

She looks terribly worried.

> O'LEARY
> (Furiously)
> I object!

6-15-39　　　　　　　　　　　　　　　　　　　(Continued)

A-59 (Cont'd)

>He crosses to the bench and THE CAMERA PANS WITH HIM
>BRINGING THE OTHERS INTO THE SHOT.

                    THE COURT
                  (Severely)
         How can you object to something he
         has not yet said?

                    O'LEARY
         Because I know what he's going
         to say.

                    SARGENT
                  (Politely to O'Leary)
         With your kind permission, counsel,
                  (He turns to the Judge)
         May it please the Court, the People
         request that a continuance be granted
         till after the Christmas holidays for
         the purpose of calling Dr. Keinmetz.

                    O'LEARY
                  (Loudly)
         We object, Your Honor. The defense
         has already summed up, the case was
         practically closed...

                    THE COURT
                  (Severely)
         Objection overruled. Ladies and
         gentlemen of the jury, you are
         again admonished that you are not
         to converse among yourselves or with
         anyone else connected with this trial,
         nor are you to form or express any
         opinion regarding this case until
         it is finally submitted to you. The
         defendant is remanded to the custody
         of the sheriff subject to giving a
         (new) five thousand dollar bond and
         all jurors, parties and witnesses are
         instructed to return to the Court
         Tuesday, January third. Court ad-
         journed and a very merry Christmas
         to you all.

>There is a murmur from the jury.

A-60   THE JURY - PAST COURT ATTENDANTS AND OTHERS

                    ONE JUROR
                  (Happily)
               Oh boy, oh boy!

6-15-39   (Continued)

351

A-60 (Cont'd)

>   ANOTHER JUROR
>   Hot ziggoty!

>   AN ATTENDANT
>   (Bawling)
>   Quiet, please! Quiet!

A-61   THE DOOR TO THE JUDGE'S CHAMBERS

A large uniformed attendant opens it for the approaching judge.

>   THE JUDGE
>   (Hurrying through)
>   Merry Christmas, Brian

>   BRIAN
>   The same to you, Your Honor.

A-62   THE JURORS - FILING OUT

>   A SMALL JUROR
>   (To another)
>   Well, so long.

>   THE SAME OFFICIOUS
>   ATTENDANT
>   Remember there is to be no
>   conversation between you! No
>   discussion of ....

>   THE SMALL JUROR
>   Aw, go fry a fish!

The attendant steps forward belligerently and the
SMALL JUROR ducks out of sight.

A-63   SARGENT AND TOM

>   TOM
>   (Still dazzled)
>   Boy, if that wasn't the neatest
>   fake reverse I ever saw...

>   SARGENT
>   (Laughing)
>   He fell down that one like a
>   horse down a coal hole.

6-15-39   (Continued)

A-63 (Cont'd)

> He tries to keep a straight face as O'Leary walks
> INTO THE SHOT

> > O'LEARY
> > (Indignantly)
> > That was a dirty trick you played
> > on me, Jack. It means another day
> > in Court and I don't get paid by the
> > State. I have to earn my money.
> > (He stalks out of the shot)

> > SARGENT
> > (Sadly, to Tom)
> > No more sense of humor than a grave-
> > stone. Well...
> > (He shrugs his shoulders,
> > looks back toward
> > O'Leary and calls:)
> > ... Merry Christmas anyway, Francis.

A-64   O'LEARY AND LEE

> > LEE
> > (Continuing their
> > previous conversation)
> > But how can I get a bond? I
> > haven't got any more money and
> > I don't want to spend Christmas
> > in jail... please don't let them
> > do that.

> > O'LEARY
> > (Scowling)
> > What do you mean, you haven't got
> > any more money? What have I been
> > talking for, to hear my own voice?

> Lee doesn't answer.

> > O'LEARY
> > (Considerably vexed)
> > Don't you think you should have
> > told me this at the time you gave
> > me your retainer?

> > LEE
> > I was afraid you wouldn't take
> > the case.

> > O'LEARY
> > Have you got any friends?

6-15-39

(Continued)

A-64 (Cont'd)

                    LEE
                (After a slight
                 pause)
            No.

                    O'LEARY
                (Waspishly)
            Well, it isn't any of my business.

                    LEE
                (Indignantly)
            It is _so_ your business!

A-65   SARGENT AND TOM

        Sargent and Tom turn in mild surprise and watch Lee.

A-66   O'LEARY AND LEE

                    O'LEARY
                (Furiously)
            What do you mean by that?

                    LEE
            I mean if you hadn't brought in
            that old hypnotism gag that's got
            whiskers on it down to here I'd
            be out of here right now.

                    O'LEARY
                (Cold with fury)
            Thank you. Thank you for your
            gratitude. Since I am your
            attorney of record I will see
            you here on the third. In the
            meantime I wish you a very
            pleasant holiday.
                (He turns and searches
                 for someone)

                    LEE
                (Desperately)
            Aw, please! Please don't let
            them keep me here over Christmas.

                    O'LEARY
            What could you do if you haven't
            got any money?

                    LEE
            I could walk around, couldn't I?

6-15-39   (Continued)

A-66 (Cont'd)

                O'LEARY
             (Catching the
             Sheriff's eye)
         Oh, Mr. Sheriff.

Lee cringes.

A-67   THE SHERIFF APPROACHING

He is a large bluff gent with mean eyes.

                SHERIFF
             (Cheerfully)
         Right with you, counselor.

A-68   SARGENT AND TOM

They are looking at Lee. Now Sargent turns and
speaks to Tom.

                SARGENT
         On your way out send "Fat"
         Mike in here.

                TOM
             (Surprised)
         "Fat" Mike the bondsman?

                SARGENT
         If you know any other "Fat" Mikes
         you can send them too.

                TOM
             (Beaming suddenly)
         You don't, but let it pass.

                SARGENT
         If you do, forget it.

                TOM
         Yes, sir.

He starts out. Sargent sits on the edge of the table
and takes out a pack of cigarettes.

A-69   LEE, THE SHERIFF AND O'LEARY

                SHERIFF
             (In a fatherly manner)
         ...as bad as all that. You get a
         nice little uh room and a nice

6-15-39   (Continued)

A-69 (Cont'd)

                        SHERIFF (Cont'd)
                turkey dinner on Exmas with all
                the trimmin's and....

                        LEE
                (Straightening her
                  shoulders)
                Never mind the buildup.
                    (She looks out of
                     the shot and catches
                     Sargent's eye)
                He thinks he's taking me to the
                Ritz.

A-70   SARGENT

        He smiles stupidly at this witticism, then fumbles
        for a match which he does not seem to have.

A-71   LEE, THE SHERIFF AND O'LEARY

                        LEE
                Come on, let's go.

                        SHERIFF
                    (Cheerfully)
                That's the spirit.

                        O'LEARY
                    (Perfunctorily)
                Merry Christmas.

                        LEE
                    (Violently)
                Oh, go f...
                    (She starts to say
                     "Fry an egg", then
                     thinks better of it)

        The Sheriff takes her arm and they go PAST THE CAMERA.
        O'Leary watches them go, then starts out, scowling.
        The CAMERA PANS him to Sargent.

                        SARGENT
                Have you got a match?

                        O'LEARY
                No.

        He struts past and Sargent makes a face after him, then
        looks through his clothes again for a match. Now a very
        large gent sticks his head through the door behind
        Sargent.
6-15-39

A-72   CLOSE SHOT - "FAT" MIKE

After giving Sargent the once-over he speaks greasily.

> "FAT" MIKE
> You wanta see me, Judge?

A-73   SARGENT IN THE FOREGROUND WITH MIKE IN THE BACKGROUND

> SARGENT
> (Without looking
> around)
> Yes. You got a match?

> "FAT" MIKE
> (Hurrying forward)
> Yes, sir, Judge.

He feels in his pockets, then pauses in dismay.

> "FAT" MIKE
> Well, what do you know about that?
> I coulda swore... I REMEMBER: I
> give 'em to Elmer! He comes up to
> me and he says...

> SARGENT
> (Interrupting him)
> Never mind, what do you charge
> for five thousand bail from now
> till January third?

> "FAT" MIKE
> (In a low conspirator's
> voice)
> Did they pin sumpin' on you, pal?

> SARGENT
> (Scowling)
> It isn't for me. It's for the
> young woman who was here today.

> "FAT" MIKE
> (Getting the whole
> perspective)
> Oh!

He leers at Sargent but does not wink.

> SARGENT
> How much?

6-15-39   (Continued)

A-73 (Cont'd)
                              "FAT" MIKE
                            (Beaming)
                      For a friend a yours, Judge?
                      Nuttin!
                            (He pulls out an
                             enormous roll of
                             bills)
                      ... not a red Samelka.

                              SARGENT
                            (Coldly)
                      I didn't ask you for any favors...

                              "FAT" MIKE
                            (Greasily)
                      Favors? It's a privilege.
                            (Now he seems to
                             change the subject)
                      You still livin' at the same place?

                              SARGENT
                            (Puzzled)
                      Yes.

                              "FAT" MIKE
                            (Wisely)
                      How soon you want her out?

                              SARGENT
                            (Picking up his
                             brief case)
                      Right away.

                              "FAT" MIKE
                      She's out.

                              SARGENT
                      Thanks - See you later.

Sargent starts to whistle "THE STARS AND STRIPES
FOREVER" as he exits.

A-74   A LONG HALL

        We hear Sargent's cheerful whistle before he goes
        past the CAMERA and walks happily away. Now he turns
        down some steps.

A-75   THE ROTUNDA OF THE HALL OF JUSTICE

        A cadaverous-looking gent is mopping the marble with
        slow sensuous movements. Preceded by his whistling,
        Sargent comes down the steps.

6-15-39   (Continued)

A-75 (Cont'd)

                     SARGENT
                    (Cheerfully)
         Say, have you got a match?

The janitor straightens and replies in a fine ringing
voice:

                     JANITOR
         I have not, sir! And let me
         tell you something for your own
         good: the use of nicotine is
         the scourge of civilization.

He raises a warning finger as Sargent looks at him
blankly.

                     JANITOR
                    (Continuing)
         It coerces the liver, coagulates
         the digestion and fulminates the
         mind! Consider the birds of the
         air, the quadrupeds of the field
         and the fish that ply below the
         sparkling waters supplied in liquid
         abundance by Mother Nature!

Sargent throws his cigarette on the floor and hurries
out.

                     JANITOR
                    (Continuing - warming
                      to his subject)
         Do they poison their systems
         with...

We hear a door close. The Janitor sighs and is about
to resume his mopping when he spies the cigarette
Sargent has dropped. He kills it as one would a
snake, looks at it, slugs it once more, then with a
very proud expression, resumes his rhythmic mopping.

FADE OUT.

                   <u>END OF SEQUENCE "A"</u>

6-15-39

SEQUENCE "B"

FADE IN:

B-1   THE ANTE-ROOM OF THE SHERIFF'S OFFICE - (FAIRLY DARK)

Several prisoners are waiting to be taken to the
county jail. Among them sits Lee, her hands folded
in her lap. She looks at her hands. We hear a door
open and a wedge of light widens across the floor.
All the prisoners except Lee look up hopefully.

                    A VOICE
          Hey!

Now Lee looks up slowly. After a moment she frowns a
little, points to herself and speaks almost inaudibly.

                    LEE
          Me?

B-2   THE DOORWAY TO THE SHERIFF'S OFFICE

A mug from the Sheriff's office stands in it.

                    THE MUG
          Come on, lady, willya? You're hold-
          ing up the parade.

B-3   LEE, AMONG THE OTHER PRISONERS

She swallows nervously, looks guiltily at the other
prisoners, then gets to her feet and comes forward
quickly.

B-4   THE SHERIFF'S OFFICE

Lee enters and blinks at the bright lights.

                    THE MUG
               (Closing the door
                after her)
          Okay, tootsie, that's all.

                    LEE
               (Thunderstruck)
          You mean I'm ... free? Well who ...

She looks around vaguely and suddenly recoils.

6-15-39

B-5   CLOSE SHOT - "FAT" MIKE

He tips his derby and gives her his best leer.

>   "FAT" MIKE
>   Harya, Babe?

B-6   LEE AND THE MUG

Lee backs away quickly and reaches for the door to
the prisoners' room.

>   THE MUG
>   (Stopping her)
>   Here, you can't go back in there.
>   I told you, you're free.

>   LEE
>   (With a very suspicious
>   look at "Fat" Mike)
>   Do I have to be?

B-7   CLOSE SHOT - "FAT" MIKE

He gives Lee a very indignant look and pushes his
derby on the back of his head.

DISSOLVE TO:

B-8   SARGENT'S BEDROOM

We hear him whistling "THE STARS AND STRIPES FOREVER"
but see only his hands packing quantities of gaily
wrapped Christmas presents in a large suitcase. Now
the whistling stops.

>   SARGENT'S VOICE
>   (Yelling)
>   Hey! Rufus!

B-9   RUFUS - IN THE KITCHENETTE

He is a lethargic colored man wrapping sandwiches in
oil-paper.

>   RUFUS
>   Yassuh, Mr. Sargent. I just
>   spreadin' y'all a few sanderges
>   in case y'all get hongry in de
>   middle of de ride.

He wipes his hands and starts out of the kitchenette.

6-15-39

B-10   SARGENT OVER HIS SUITCASES

> SARGENT
> Where's that Fleurs de Joy I got
> for my mother?

B-11   SARGENT - ACROSS THE <u>BED</u>

Rufus pauses in the door of the bedroom behind
Sargent.

> RUFUS
> (Very much worried)
> Perfume! You mean dat little bitty
> cheap bottle wid de bunch a pine
> needles tied onto it?

> SARGENT
> (Frowning)
> That's right.

> RUFUS
> (Extremely worried)
> Dat come in dat little green box wid
> de six-bit Christmas tree painted
> onto it?

> SARGENT
> (Roughly)
> Yes, where is it?

> RUFUS
> I ain't seen it.

> SARGENT
> (Very roughly)
> Listen: I paid thirty-seven dollars
> for that....

> RUFUS
> (Horrified)
> For dat hair oil?

> SARGENT
> (Also horrified)
> Hair oil!
> (He gives Rufus a
> paralyzing look)
> Come here!

> RUFUS
> (Coming forward
> reluctantly)
> Y-yassuh.

6-15-39   (Continued)

B-11   (Cont'd)

As he steps close Sargent grabs his head with both
hands like a basketball, takes a long whiff of it and
exhales rapidly.

> SARGENT
>
> Pew!

> RUFUS
> (Rapidly)
> I don't think your maw woulda liked
> dat stuff anyhow. Seems to me a
> nice old lady like Mrs. Sargent...

Sargent releases Rufus' head and, holding the fingers
far apart, smells of his hands.

> SARGENT
> I think you're right.

Holding his hands in front of him he starts for the
bathroom which is in sight. Now he pauses and turns.

> SARGENT
> Did you check my tires?

> RUFUS
> Yassuh. I put two new ones on de
> front wheels and de front wheels
> on de hind wheels and de hind wheels
> on de front wheels of...

> SARGENT
> (Alarmed)
> What?

> RUFUS
> (Laughing)
> On de front wheels a <u>my</u> car.

> SARGENT
> (Wearily)
> Oh.

He enters the bathroom and turns on the water.

> RUFUS
>
> Yassuh.

He looks at Sargent, passes his hand over his head,
smells of it critically, looks at Sargent again and
starts for the kitchenette.

6-15-39

B-12   THE LIVING ROOM

As Rufus crosses through it he hears a faint buzzer.
He turns at right angles and GOES BY THE CAMERA.

B-13   A SMALL FOYER

Rufus appears CLOSE TO US and opens the front door a
few inches.

>   RUFUS
> Yassuh.

B-14   "FAT" MIKE AND LEE - PAST RUFUS

Lee looks nervous, "Fat" Mike mysterious.

>   "FAT" MIKE
>   (In a stage whisper)
> The big boss in?

B-15   RUFUS - PAST "FAT" MIKE AND LEE

>   RUFUS
>   (Around the door)
> Yassuh, he's in but he ain't home.

>   "FAT" MIKE
>   (Putting a powerful
>   hand on the door)
> Save that for your radio act.

He shoves the door open with one hand, shoves Lee in
with the other and seizes Rufus' lapel between his
thumb and forefinger.

>   "FAT" MIKE
>   (Hoarsely)
> Just tell the big boss she's here,
> that's all...with the compliments
> of "Fat" Mike...you got that?

>   RUFUS
> Yassuh, Mista Mike.

>   "FAT" MIKE
>   (Hard)
> Not "Mr. Mike," "Fat" Mike.

B-15   (Cont'd)

>   RUFUS
>   Yassuh, Mr. "Fat" Mike.
>
>   "FAT" MIKE
>   (Greatly pleased with
>   himself)
>   Okay, toots, I'll seeya in Harlem.

He goes PAST THE CAMERA. Rufus gives him a last look and closes the door.

B-16   SARGENT DRYING HIS HANDS - IN THE BATHROOM

He takes another smell of them, then hangs up the towel and goes into the bedroom.

B-17   SARGENT'S BEDROOM

He enters and starts closing a suitcase. Suddenly he looks up.

>   SARGENT
>   (Impatiently)
>   What is it now?

B-18   RUFUS STANDING IN THE DOORWAY - PAST SARGENT

>   RUFUS
>   (Mysteriously)
>   She's here.
>
>   SARGENT
>   Who's here?
>
>   RUFUS
>   I dunno.

B-19   SARGENT - PAST RUFUS

>   SARGENT
>   (Wearily)
>   Then how do you know she's here?
>
>   RUFUS
>   I seen her come in.
>
>   SARGENT
>   You seen who come in?

6-15-39   (Continued)

B-19   (Cont'd)

                   RUFUS
De lady.

                   SARGENT
             (Scowling and lowering
              his voice)
You mean there's a lady in the apart-
ment?

                   RUFUS
Yessuh.

                   SARGENT
What did you let her in for? I
told you I wasn't home to anyone.

                   RUFUS
Yassuh. I told him dat but he
shoved de door open anyhow and
pushed de lady in wid his compli-
ments.

                   SARGENT
             (Indignantly)
Who did?

                   RUFUS
"Fat" Ike.

                   SARGENT
             (Scowling)
"Fat" Ike!
             (Suddenly a terrible
             expression comes
             over his face)
You mean "Fat" Mike?
             (He looks fearfully
             at Rufus)

                   RUFUS
Yassuh...he sure ain't "Thin" Mike.

Sargent rounds his eyes and scratches his head.

B-20   LEE IN SARGENT'S <u>LIVING ROOM</u>

She sits nervously on the edge of a chair, her back
to the doorway to Sargent's bedroom. Now Sargent
appears in the doorway behind her and peeks around
the jamb, trying to see her. Unable to do so he
comes a little further into the room. Suddenly she
turns and they look into each other's eyes.

6-15-39   (Continued)

B-20 (Cont'd)

                    SARGENT
                (Embarrassed)
        Oh... hello.

                    LEE
                (Warily)
        Hello.

                    SARGENT
        What are you doing here?

                    LEE
                (Suspiciously)
        I don't know yet, but I've got
        a rough idea.

                    SARGENT
                (Stalling for time)
        Well, anyway I'm glad you're
        out and --

                    LEE
        Now what do I have to do for it?

                    SARGENT
                (Indignantly)
        Well, for one thing you could say
        "Thank you," but if that doesn't
        fit in with your plans, just skip
        it.
                (He pauses, then
                begins again)
        My motives in this matter...

Now he looks around and frowns as Rufus ENTERS
THE SHOT with a tray and two clinking glasses.

                    RUFUS
        Scotch and soda?

                    LEE
                (Taking one)
        Thanks.

Silently with pantomime Sargent says to Rufus:

                    SARGENT
                (Mouthing)
        Who the hell asked you to come in
        with drinks, you flat-headed baboon.

                                    (Continued)
6/15/39

B-20 (Cont'd)

> RUFUS
> (Handing him a drink)
> Yassuh.

He exits.

> LEE
> (Philosophically)
> One of these days one of you
> boys is going to start one of
> these scenes differently...
> and one of us girls is going
> to drop dead from surprise.

> SARGENT
> (Wishing to end the
> scene)
> No doubt. Now...

> LEE
> (Interrupting)
> I suppose you do this with all
> the lady prisoners.

> SARGENT
> (Sarcastically)
> Oh, my yes! My life is just
> one long round of whoopee.

> LEE
> You're in a good spot for it.

> SARGENT
> Wonderful. I have only to wave
> a finger and I can satisfy my
> slightest vice. Now if there
> isn't...

> LEE
> (Interrupting)
> And I suppose if anybody says
> "No," you put them right back in
> the cooler.

> SARGENT
> Sure.

(Continued)

6/15/39

B-20 (Cont'd)

                    SARGENT
               (Gently)
          Look: When court reconvenes
          I'm going to try to put you in
          jail for a good long time...
          that's my business...but you
          haven't been convicted yet so
          I don't see why you shouldn't
          enjoy Christmas like the rest
          of us. That's why I told Mike
          to get you out.

                    LEE
          And bring me up <u>here</u>.

                    SARGENT
               (Belligerently)
          I did not tell him to bring
          you up here.

                    LEE
          Then why <u>did</u> that gorilla bring
          me up here?

                    SARGENT
          Because he has a mind like a
          sewer.

                    LEE
          Thanks.

                    SARGENT
          Look: I'm very glad to have been
          of service to you... and now...

                    LEE
          You mean I don't have to stay
          here if I don't want to?

                    SARGENT
               (Emphatically)
          You most certainly do not.

                    LEE
          Then I'll stay... but I won't be
          forced.

                    SARGENT
               (Wearily)
          Now wait a minute...

                                        (Continued)

6/15/39

B-20 (Cont'd)

>   LEE
> You know, there's nothing as
> dangerous as a square-shooter...
> if all men were like you there
> wouldn't be any virtuous women
> left.

>   SARGENT
>   (Boxed in again)
> Yes... well... all this is
> leading into a very interesting
> and deep-dish discussion that I
> haven't time to pursue at the
> moment. I'm going away on a
> little trip and as it's quite a
> drive and as I haven't had my
> dinner yet...
>   (He consults his
>   watch)

>   LEE
> Oh.
>   (Then in a small voice)
> You mean you want me to go.

>   SARGENT
>   (Torn between courtesy
>   and the truth)
> Well... yes.

>   LEE
> Where?

>   SARGENT
>   (Smelling more
>   complications)
> Where what?

>   LEE
> I mean I was on my way to a
> nice, comfortable jail with
> three meals a day and turkey
> for Christmas and now...
>   (She makes a helpless
>   gesture)

>   SARGENT
>   (Scowling)
> Don't you live some place?

(Continued)

6/15/39

B-20 (Cont'd)

    Lee shakes her head slowly in the negative.

                    SARGENT
          Well where have you been living...
          In a tree?

                    LEE
          I had a room in a hotel but they
          locked me out this morning.

                    SARGENT
          Oh.

    He looks at his watch again then speaks magnanimously.

                    SARGENT
          How much do you owe this hotel?

                    LEE
          Six hundred dollars.

                    SARGENT
              (Minus the magnanimity)
          Well, that doesn't solve any problems.

                    LEE
          Why don't you just put me back in
          the clink...that solves a lot of
          problems.

                    SARGENT
          For one thing I'm not sure you can
          and...well, that wasn't the idea.

    He finishes his drink and puts the glass down.

                    SARGENT
          Have you had your dinner?

                    LEE
          Not yet.

                    SARGENT
          Come on, then. We'll figure some-
          thing out.

    He helps her to her feet.

                    LEE
              (Just before leaving)
          You really didn't want me to come
          here at all then?

6/15/39   (Continued)

B-20 (Cont'd)

> SARGENT
> I'm sorry to say that I did not.

She gives him a long look - then starts out, picking
up her suitcase as she goes. Sargent scowls - then
starts to follow. Suddenly his eye is caught by
something in the kitchenette door.

B-21   RUFUS - IN THE DOOR

Rufus is beaming his approval.

> RUFUS
> Hot dawg! But don't forget you
> got to go to see your maw.

B-22   SARGENT - IN THE LIVING ROOM

He gives Rufus a dirty look, then picks up his hat
and exits.

DISSOLVE TO:

B-23   FULL SHOT - A RESTAURANT WITH A DANCE FLOOR

It has a circle of booths just outside the ringside
tables. We see an orchestra at the end of the dance
floor and couples are dancing to its music. A girl
with a throaty voice is singing. As we COME INTO THE
SHOT THE CAMERA STARTS TRUCKING ACROSS the dance
floor, through the dancers. Suddenly we come onto
Lee and Sargent dancing. WE FOLLOW THEM.

> SARGENT
> If anybody had told me this morning
> I'd be dancing with you tonight,
> well...,
>   (He breaks out laughing)

> LEE
> Who told you you were dancing?

> SARGENT
>   (Ruefully)
> Am I that bad?

                                        (Continued)

6/15/39

B-23 (Cont'd)

> LEE
> (Smiling)
> For a District Attorney you're
> marvellous.

The piece comes to an end and they stand applauding.
Suddenly another applauding gentleman turns around
and recognizes Sargent.

> THE JUDGE
> Why hello there, Jack. I want
> you to meet my wife.
> (He turns to a stout
> lady)
> Dear, this is John Sargent and uh...
> (Now he recognizes Lee
> and almost falls in a
> syncope)

> SARGENT
> (Rapidly)
> This is Miss Hrumph. Glad to
> have seen you, Judge.

> THE JUDGE
> (Dragging his wife
> away)
> Yes, yes.

Sargent leads Lee to their booth. As they sit --

B-24 CLOSE SHOT - LEE AND SARGENT

They exchange nervous smiles.

> SARGENT
> I never thought of that.

> LEE
> Gee, you're sweet. You never think
> of anything wrong, do you?

> SARGENT
> Let's try to fix up your holiday.
> (After a pause)
> Of course, I might lend you my
> apartment while I'm away.

> LEE
> (Grinning)
> That sounds like a play, doesn't it?

(Continued)

6/15/39

B-24 (Cont'd)

> SARGENT
> Yes, it sounds like a flop.

> LEE
> Don't worry about me... I can
> always chisel a hotel for a week
> or so.

> SARGENT
> That's a nice cheesy idea.

> LEE
> (Indignantly)
> Well, I'm not going to sleep in
> the subway and as far as the holi-
> day's concerned, I guess I'll get
> plenty of that when you get through
> with me.
> (Now she adds quickly)
> Not that I mean it in a disagree-
> able way, you understand.

> SARGENT
> (Almost uneasily)
> I understand.

> LEE
> Your business is your business..
> of course, some people wouldn't
> care for that kind of business...

Sargent looks but does not answer.

> LEE
> ... but SOMEBODY has to do the
> dirty work.

> SARGENT
> Thanks.

> LEE
> (Defending herself)
> I don't hold it against you, any
> more than I would if you were an
> undertaker or a ... dog-catcher or
> a ... or a HANGMAN!

Sargent's eyes bug out slightly.

> LEE
> (Concluding)
> It's just too bad it had to be
> somebody as nice as you.

6-15-39   (Continued)

B-24 (Cont'd)

                    SARGENT
          How's your salad?

                    LEE
               (Distressed)
          Now I've hurt your feelings.

                    SARGENT
          I haven't any feelings. That's
          the first thing you have to have
          removed when you get to be a
          District Attorney. Have you got
          a pin? I'll show you.

                    LEE
               (Drawing back in disgust)
          Oh, please.

                    SARGENT
               (Gently, after a pause)
          How long have you been swiping
          things?

                    LEE
               (Without looking at him)
          Always.

                    SARGENT
          Have you been caught before?

     Lee nods "yes".

                    SARGENT
          But you kept on taking things. .

     Lee shrugs.

                    SARGENT
               (Suddenly interested)
          Did you take things you didn't
          need?

                    LEE
          Sure.

                    SARGENT
          In the presence of beautiful things
          did you feel a sudden irresistible
          urge to take them in your hands and
          hurry away with them?

6-15-39   (Continued)

B-24 (Cont'd)

       LEE
     (Faintly amused)
You mean was I hypnotized?

       SARGENT
     (Hopefully)
I mean maybe you're a kleptomaniac.

       LEE
     (Placidly)
No, they tried that. You see, to
be a kleptomaniac you can't sell
any of the stuff afterwards....
or you lose your amateur standing.

       SARGENT
I don't understand it. First you
think it's environment and then..
Whitney goes to jail. Then you
think it's heredity... and you get
some bird with seven generations
of clergymen behind him.

       LEE
I don't think you ever could understand because your mind is different.
Right or wrong is the same for everybody, you see, but the _rights_ and
the _wrongs_ aren't the same. Like
in China they eat dogs.

       SARGENT
That's a lot of piffle.

       LEE
They _do_ eat dogs.

       SARGENT
I mean your theory.

       LEE
Try it like this: suppose you were
starving to death...

       SARGENT
Yes.

       LEE
... and you didn't have any food
and you didn't have any money and
you didn't have any place to get
anything.

6-15-39   (Continued)

B-24 (Cont'd)

> SARGENT
> Yes.

> LEE
> And there were some loaves of
> bread out in front of a market,
> and you were starving to death
> and the man's back was turned...
> would you swipe one?

> SARGENT
> (Vehemently)
> You bet I would!

> LEE
> (Smiling with pleasure)
> That's because you're honest.
> You see, I'd have a six-course
> dinner at the table d'hote across
> the street and then say I'd for-
> gotten my purse.

As Sargent looks at her goggle-eyed she concludes
sweetly:

> LEE
> You get the difference?

> SARGENT
> I think yours is smarter.

> LEE
> (Bitterly)
> That's it. We're smart!

Sargent takes about fifty dollars out of his pocket
and presses it into her hand.

> SARGENT
> Here's that turkey dinner I owe
> you and a room and a couple of
> breakfasts.

> LEE
> Thanks...thanks a lot.

> SARGENT
> (Motioning to the waiter)
> We'll have one night-cap...and
> then I've got to get going.
> (As the waiter approaches)
> Two Scotch and sodas, please, and
> ask the band to play "My Indiana
> Home".

6-15-39

(Continued)

377

B-24 (Cont'd)

>   THE WAITER
> Yes, sir.
>
>   LEE
> You wouldn't dance with me once
> more, would you?
>
>   SARGENT
>   (Smiling)
> Isn't that asking for trouble?
>   (Then realizing that
>   might not sound just
>   right)
> I mean, I might step on your feet.

The lights dim, the band starts playing "My Indiana
Home" and Lee rises.

>   LEE
>   (Gently)
> A couple more crunches aren't
> going to hurt them at this stage.

They start to dance.

B-25   CLOSE SHOT - LEE AND SARGENT DANCING

>   LEE
> Why did you have them play this
> piece?
>
>   SARGENT
> Because that's where I'm going.
>
>   LEE
>   (Round-eyed)
> No! Are you a Hoosier?
>
>   SARGENT
>   (Laughing)
> Wabash, Indiana. That is, a
> farm just outside of Wabash.
>
>   LEE
>   (Saying it as if
>   it were poetry)
> Wabash, Indiana! No wonder I
> liked you... I'm from Kendallville.

6-15-39   (Continued)

B-25 (Cont'd)

                      SARGENT
                    (Astonished)
No. Why, that's only about fifty
miles...

                      LEE
Yes, sir.

                      SARGENT
Well, for heaven's sake...and
we have to come here...and meet
like this.

By now they are in front of the girl singer on the
bandstand. Lee and Sargent dance OUT OF THE SHOT
and the CAMERA MOVES ONTO the singer who starts the
chorus of "My Indiana Home". After a few bars --

B-26   CLOSE SHOT - LEE AND SARGENT

Dancing.

                      SARGENT
I go home every Christmas.

                      LEE
                    (Miserably)
You do, hunh?

                      SARGENT
My Mother still runs the farm...
does all right, too. Raises
partridge Wyandottes, Poland
Chinas...

                      LEE
We never had anything that swell.

                      SARGENT
We never did either...till lately.
                    (After a pause)
How long since you've been home?

                      LEE
                    (Shaking her head)
Never.

                      SARGENT
                    (Surprised)
Why?

                      LEE
I ran away.

6-15-39

B-26 (Cont'd)

> SARGENT
> (After a pause)
> I don't know what the circumstances
> were, of course...

> LEE
> Not so hot.

> SARGENT
> Well, time takes care of those
> things. Do they write to you?

> LEE
> I got a letter from my Mother
> when my Father died.

> SARGENT
> (After a pause)
> Your mother's alive, then...

> LEE
> I hope so.

B-27   THE GIRL SINGER AT THE MICROPHONE

As she finishes the chorus, four of the musicians
step behind her and join her in close harmony for
the second chorus. After a few bars of this ——

B-28   LEE AND SARGENT — DANCING NEAR THE BOOTH

Without conversation they sit down and pick up their
drinks. Lee looks pretty blue and Sargent watches
her surreptitiously. Suddenly Lee tosses off most
of her drink, smiles an apologetic smile and looks
away. The chorus of the song is almost over by now.

> SARGENT
> (Quietly)
> How would you like to go home for
> Christmas? I could drop you on my
> way and pick you up on my way back.

> LEE
> (Frightened)
> Oh, gee.

The chorus ends on a very close chord.

FADE OUT

END OF SEQUENCE "B"

SEQUENCE "C"

FADE IN:

C-1   A DETOUR SIGN ON THE MAIN ROAD - NIGHT

It is lit by coal oil flares. An arrow points off at
ninety degrees.

C-2   LONG SHOT - DOWN A COUNTRY ROAD - NIGHT

The pin points of light appear and presently become
Sargent's car which screeches to a stop. Sargent's
head pops out one side and Lee's on the other. Now
the heads go back inside, the car turns to the right
and moves out OF THE SHOT.

C-3   LONG SHOT - DOWN A SMALL COUNTRY ROAD - NIGHT

Sargent's car hurries TOWARD US and screeches to a
stop as before. Sargent's head pops out on one side
and Lee's on the other.

C-4   AN ARROW NAILED TO A TREE AT A CROSSROAD

The arrow has worked loose on its nail and points
straight up.

C-5   THE CAR FACING US

It starts slowly to make a left turn then stops and
backs up. Now it starts to turn to the right then
backs up. Now it starts and goes straight PAST THE
CAMERA.

DISSOLVE TO:

C-6   HIGH CAMERA SHOT - A VILLAGE STREET - (NIGHT)

Across the street we see a shadowy post office on
which is painted:

"U. S. POST OFFICE
BLAIRS MILLS"

6-15-39   (Continued)

C-6 (Cont'd)

    Sargent's car COMES INTO THE SHOT and stops in front
of the post office. Lee leans out of the window.

C-7   CLOSE SHOT - <u>SARGENT'S CAR</u>

    Lee looks OVER OUR HEADS and squints up at the sign.

LEE
(Reading)
Blairs...Mills.   Blair's Mills.

    She pops her head back in the car and looks down at
her lap.

C-8   <u>INT. SARGENT'S CAR</u>

    We are SHOOTING DOWN BETWEEN Lee and Sargent. Lee
runs her finger along the map on her lap.

LEE
(Triumphantly)
Here we are: Blairs Mills. It's
in Pennsylvania.

SARGENT
(Peering down at it)
Are we supposed to go through it?

LEE
Well, it's very close to where we
were supposed to go through.

SARGENT
I was afraid of that.
(He examines the map)
Then we ought to bear north a
little bit.

LEE
About half as far as my thumbnail.

SARGENT
(Chuckling)
Well, you let me know when we've
gone that far.

C-8 (Cont'd)

>   LEE
> Where is north?

>   SARGENT
>   (Pointing on the map)
> It's up here.

>   LEE
> I mean from where we are.

>   SARGENT
>   (Pointing right across
>   her face)
> Well, it's that way.

>   LEE
> Why?

>   SARGENT
>   (Pointing to the map)
> Because we were going along here
> so naturally it's... I mean it's
> over that way...
>   (He points in a
>   different direction)

>   LEE
> Are you sure?

>   SARGENT
>   (Emphatically)
> No!

He puts the car in gear.

C-9   HIGH CAMERA SHOT - DOWN ON SARGENT'S CAR

It drives away.

DISSOLVE TO:

C-10   A WINDING BUMPY COUNTRY ROAD - (NIGHT)

Sargent's car comes around a turn preceded by the light
from its headlights. It stops very close to us and
Sargent and Lee look PAST US indignantly.

6-15-39

C-11　A RUSTIC DETOUR SIGN

A large arrow points off to a sort of cow path faintly
visible between some big bushes.

C-12　FULL ON SHOT - SARGENT'S CAR

Lee and Sargent exchange a look before the car disappears into the bushes.

C-13　A REALLY BUMPY COUNTRY ROAD - (NIGHT)

Sargent's car limps along TOWARD US. As it REACHES US
the CAMERA PANS AND WATCHES it limp away.

C-14　AN EXTREMELY STEEP HILL - FROM THE SIDE

Sargent's car creeps down it and disappears into a
clump of bushes at the bottom.

C-15　VERY CLOSE SHOT - AHEAD OF THE MOVING CAR

We watch Sargent and Lee bump up and down for a few
moments. Now Sargent stops the car quickly, sticks
his head out the side and peers ahead.

C-16　A PRETTY LITTLE STREAM GURGLING BY

C-17　INT. OF THE CAR

> LEE
> It's pretty, isn't it?

> SARGENT
> (Gritting his teeth)
> Beautiful.

He puts the car in gear.

> SARGENT
> Can you swim?

Lee laughs.

C-18　THE CAR MOVING AWAY FROM US

It creeps into the shallow water and skids its wheels
once before reaching the far side. Now it creeps up
the steep embankment and disappears.

6-15-39

C-19   <u>A VERY STEEP HILL</u>

We see the car from the side as it climbs past an opening in the bushes. Several times we hear it skid.

C-20   SHOT DOWN <u>THE HILL</u>

The car climbs up TOWARDS US and PASSES OVER THE CAMERA. With the hind wheels STILL IN SIGHT it starts again to dig itself in which makes a fine shriek in our ears. After a moment it gets its grip and goes on.

C-21   <u>THE CAR</u> CLIMBING UP TOWARD US

Suddenly it stops. Sargent and Lee stick their heads out.

C-22   <u>A FALLEN TREE WHICH BLOCKS THE ROAD</u>

A piece of cardboard has been tacked to the tree. On it a double-headed arrow is represented, pointing off in both directions.

C-23   <u>INT. OF THE CAR</u>

> SARGENT
> Which way do you want to try...
> or shall we just give the whole
> thing up?

> LEE
> (Pointing left and
> right rapidly)
> Eenie, meenie, minie, mo,
> Catch a nigger by the toe,
> If he hollers let him go,
> Eenie, meenie, minie, mo.

She ends up pointing off right.

> SARGENT
> All right.

He puts the car in gear.

> LEE
> (Pointing in the
> other direction)
> No, you'd better try that way...
> I'm not lucky.

6-15-39

                                           (Continued)

C-23 (Cont'd)

> SARGENT
> Whatever you say. One looks
> as bad as the other.

He turns the steering wheel, there is a whirring of
wheels and the car lists heavily to the left. Once
Lee gives a little scream.

> SARGENT
> Just close your eyes and
> hang on.

DISSOLVE TO:

C-24   THE EDGE OF THE RAVINE - (NIGHT)

There is a slight fog. The car grinds up over the
edge, crushes through a fence and stops NEAR US.

C-25   INT. OF THE CAR

> SARGENT
> There we are...and it wasn't
> so bad, was it?

> LEE
> (Opening her eyes)
> It was nice.

> SARGENT
> Well... we'll get out of here
> in a hurry.

> LEE
> (Pointing ahead
> suddenly)
> Look out! There's an elephant!

> SARGENT
> (Stopping the car)
> What the.....

C-26   A COVERED THRESHING MACHINE IN THE FOG

With its trunk-like pipes and things it looks not unlike an elephant.

6-15-39

C-27   INT. OF THE CAR - SHOOTING FORWARD PAST LEE AND
        SARGENT

                            LEE
                    (As if she has recogn-
                    nnized a long-lost
                    uncle)
                Why it's a threshing machine! I
                haven't seen one in years.

                            SARGENT
                Well, I'm glad you saw that one.

        He starts the car, and they drive around the machine
        and bump along a path which leads into some woods.
        They follow the sketchy road around some winding turns
        and presently come out into the open again.

                            SARGENT
                    (With relief)
                There we are!

C-28   INT. OF THE CAR - FACING SARGENT AND LEE

        He smiles at Lee.

                            SARGENT
                If at first you don't succeed,
                try, try...

                            LEE
                    (Pointing ahead
                    suddenly)
                Look out!

        Sargent jams on the brakes.

C-29   ANOTHER VIEW OF THE THRESHING MACHINE IN THE MIST

C-30   INT. OF THE CAR - SHOOTING FORWARD PAST SARGENT AND
        LEE

                            LEE
                There seem to be quite a lot
                of those around here.

                            SARGENT
                Of course it's so easy to borrow
                money from this administration.

6-15-39   (Continued)

C-30 (Cont'd)

> He drives around the thresher and into some bushes.
> The car winds back and forth, down a little hill, up
> another one, then comes out into the clear.

C-31   <u>INT. OF THE CAR</u> - FACING LEE AND SARGENT

> SARGENT
> There we are. This is a more
> traveled road than back there
> and the main road is probably...

> LEE
> (Pointing ahead weakly)
> Look out!

> Sargent stops the car and looks ahead very disgustedly.

C-32   STILL ANOTHER VIEW OF <u>THE THRESHING MACHINE IN THE
> MIST</u>

C-33   <u>INT. OF THE CAR</u> - FACING LEE AND SARGENT

> LEE
> There seems to be one on every
> farm.

> Sargent starts to laugh, then says:

> SARGENT
> We're not getting very far, are we?

> LEE
> (Philosophically)
> Well, we're holding our own.
> (She yawns)

> SARGENT
> Maybe if we took a little snooze...
> and then tried again.

> LEE
> I think that would be a lovely idea.

> She settles herself more comfortably.

> SARGENT
> I could eat the hind leg off a cow.

> LEE
> (Woefully)
> I could eat the horns.

6-15-39   (Continued)

C-33 (Cont'd)

Suddenly Sargent's scowl changes to an expression of
enthusiasm.

> SARGENT
> (Happily)
> Rufus!

He turns and fishes around behind the seat.

> LEE
> Hunh?

> SARGENT
> (Producing the lunch
> box complete with
> thermos bottle)
> There's one thing you've got to
> say about Rufus: he may be black
> but he's a yard wide.

He hands her a sandwich and fills the thermos top
with coffee.

> LEE
> Oh, boy.

> SARGENT
> Now is this better than jail or
> isn't it?

> LEE
> (After a pause)
> I'd almost forgotten I was going
> to be in jail.

> SARGENT
> (Distressed)
> I'm awfully sorry. I didn't mean
> it that way. The whole purpose of
> this trip was to forget it.

> LEE
> Thank you.

> SARGENT
> (Biting into a sandwich)
> This is made of chicken, ham, cole-
> slaw, Swiss cheese, dill pickles and...
> (He looks pensively)
> ...something else I can't identify.

6-15-39

(Continued)

C-33   (Cont'd)

>   LEE
>   (Looking over)
>   That's the paper.

>   SARGENT
>   (Examining his sand-
>   wich)
>   Oh. It isn't bad, either.

>   LEE
>   (Pausing in the mid-
>   dle of her sandwich)
>   I hope my mother will be glad to
>   see me.

>   SARGENT
>   (Indignantly)
>   Of course your mother will be glad
>   to see you.

>   LEE
>   (Doubtfully)
>   I guess she will all right.

She looks out into the night.

SLOW DISSOLVE TO:

C-34   A LEGHORN ROOSTER CROWING TO THE MORNING SUN - (DAY)

C-35   HIGH CAMERA SHOT - DOWN ON SARGENT'S CAR

It is entirely surrounded by cows which fill the
field. A cow wanders over to the car and sticks her
head into the window (we hope).

C-36   INT. OF THE CAR - SARGENT, LEE AND THE COW'S HEAD

Somehow during the night Lee's head has fallen on
Sargent's shoulder and his arm has gone around her
neck. The cow chews her cud and looks pensively at
this pretty scene. Now she snorts a little and
Sargent smiles in his sleep as the warm breath blows
on his face. THE CAMERA MOVES IN A LITTLE CLOSER
(which leaves the cow OUT OF IT) as Lee smiles also.
Now comes a powerful moo. Lee and Sargent come to
violently and the CAMERA DRAWS BACK A LITTLE as they
give the cow a surprised look.

6-15-39   (Continued)

C-36   (Cont'd)

> SARGENT
> (Patting the cow)
> Nice Bossy, nice Bossy.... we must
> have had quite a sleep....
>   (Then getting an
>   idea)
> Ever have warm milk for breakfast?

> LEE
> (Delighted)
> Would you still know how?

> SARGENT
> Would I! When I took up the law,
> Indiana lost the finest milker in
> seven counties. Just watch me.

> LEE
> What are you going to put it in?

> SARGENT
> (Looking around)
> Well....
>   (He spots the lunch
>   box thermos bottle)
> .....there doesn't seem to be much
> choice.

> LEE
> I could hold it.

> SARGENT
> Fine. Get out on that side and
> maybe I can sit on the running
> board.
>   (He turns back to
>   the cow)
> Nice Bossy, nice Bossy.

He turns to Lee who is getting out.

> SARGENT
> Try to keep her near the car.

Now he starts out himself.

> SARGENT
> (Looking back at
>   the cow)
> Don't you worry, we'll only need
> about a pint.

6-15-39

C-37   <u>THE COW SIDE OF THE CAR</u>

Lee hurries INTO THE SHOT, thermos bottle in hand, and starts scratching the cow's ears.

> LEE
> Nice Bossy, nice Bossy. Does she like to have her ears tickled?

From the inside of the car we hear a cavernous moo.

> LEE
> (Looking back over her shoulder)
> Hurry up.

Sargent hurries INTO THE SHOT.

> SARGENT
> Gimme -- where's the bottle?

> LEE
> (Holding it out)
> Here. Nice Bossy, nice Bossy. Do you want me to hold it?

> SARGENT
> (Taking the bottle)
> You'd better hold her. I can hold it between my knees. I always used to hold it that way...only I had a stool.

He sits on the running board, clamps the thermos bottle between his knees and stretches toward the cow which is a little out of reach.

> SARGENT
> Could you push her over a little bit?

> LEE
> I'll try.

She goes around to the other side of the cow and pushes. We hear another cavernous moo.

> LEE
> She doesn't seem to want to go.

C-38   THE COW <u>INSIDE THE CAR</u>

It is chewing contentedly on Lee's hat.

6-15-39

C-39   LEE, SARGENT AND THE <u>REAR OF THE COW</u> - <u>OUTSIDE</u>

> SARGENT
> Well, I'll milk her without a
> stool.

He goes to the side of the cow, squats, grips the
thermos bottle between his knees and reaches under
the cow with both hands. Nothing happens.

> SARGENT
> (Coaxingly)
> Come on, now, let's have it, let's
> have it.

> LEE
> How's it coming?

> SARGENT
> She's....

At this point the cow swats him across the face with
her tail.

> SARGENT
> Ga....

He takes his hands from under the cow and wipes his
face on the back of his sleeve.

> LEE
> What did you say?

> SARGENT
> I said she wants to be coaxed.

The cow moves away a little. Sargent spits on his
hands and reaches for the cow but cannot quite make
it. Still in the squatting position, with the thermos
between his knees, he shuffles forward.

> SARGENT
> (Grabbing her in the
> right place, coaxingly)
> Come on now, nice Bossy, nice Bossy.

A powerful squirt of milk goes into the thermos bottle.

> SARGENT
> (Delightedly)
> That's fine, that's fine.

The cow socks him in the face with her tail.

6-15-39   (Continued)

C-39   (Cont'd)

> SARGENT
> Ouch.

He shoots a squirt of milk into his lap.

C-40   LEE - PUSHING ON THE OTHER SIDE OF THE COW

> LEE
> What did you say? Are you getting
> any milk?

C-41   SARGENT ON THE FIRST SIDE OF THE COW

> SARGENT
> Yes....but don't let her....

The cow switches him in the face and moves away a
little. He shoots a squirt of milk on his shirt
front and shuffles after her.

> SARGENT
> Don't let her move! Push her back!

C-42   LEE ON THE OTHER SIDE OF THE COW

> LEE
> (Desperately)
> I'm pushing as hard as I can.

We hear a moo from the cow and she starts to move
away from Lee.

C-43   SARGENT ON THE FIRST SIDE OF THE COW

He is desperate as he feels the cow moving down on
him.

> SARGENT
> Don't push her this way, pull her
> back!

The cow slaps him in the face.

C-44   LEE PUSHES ON THE OTHER SIDE OF THE COW

> LEE
> (Breathlessly)
> Is that far enough?

6-15-39   (Continued)

C-44   (Cont'd)

> SARGENT'S VOICE
> Push her back!

> LEE
> (Leaning way down
> and looking under
> the cow)
> What did you say?

In reply she gets a squirt of milk in the face as
the cow gives way entirely and passes over the milk-
drenched Sargent. Lee wipes the milk out of her eyes,
takes one look at Sargent and becomes hysterical.

C-45   CLOSE SHOT - THE COW

It is looking around at us with the remains of Lee's
hat dangling from its mouth.

C-46   LEE, SARGENT AND THE COW

Now Sargent sees the hat and starts laughing. Lee
sees it and stops laughing. At this point the shadow
of a man with a gun ENTERS THE SHOT. Sargent sees
him out of the corner of his eye and turns. Lee sees
him also. Sargent is about to make some pleasant remark when something in the man's expression stops
him.

C-47   THE OWNER OF THE PROPERTY

He is a bitter-looking man with a gun over his arm.
At his heel stands a big nondescript dog.

> THE OWNER
> What are you doing on my property?

C-48   SARGENT AND LEE

Sargent gets to his feet and brushes himself off as
best he can.

> SARGENT
> I'm very sorry, I didn't know it
> was your property. We got onto a
> detour....

6-15-39

C-49   THE OWNER

> THE OWNER
> It's posted clear enough, ain't it?
> (He points off to
>   some trees)
> There's a sign every hundred feet.
> Can't you read?

C-50   SARGENT AND LEE - PAST THE OWNER

> SARGENT
> We happen to have got here in the
> middle of the night...

> THE OWNER
> (Interrupting)
> Yes, I saw where you busted my fence.

> SARGENT
> I'll be very glad to pay...

> THE OWNER
> (Interrupting)
> You'll pay all right. You New
> Yorkers think you can trespass on
> people's property, break their
> fences, fool around with their
> cattle, spend the night in their
> fields with I don't know what kind
> of....

> SARGENT
> (Furiously)
> Listen, you filthy-minded....

> LEE
> (Angrily)
> Listen, you fresh hick....

> THE OWNER
> You can save your language for the
> judge.

> LEE
> Who's going to arrest us?

> THE OWNER
> You're under arrest right now.

> SARGENT
> Where's your warrant...or your badge
> of office?

C-50   (Cont'd)

                     OWNER

Don't try to get cute. I'm a citizen of the United States and you're
under arrest.
         (He raises his gun
          slightly)
If you think you ain't, just try to
get away.

                     LEE
         (Looking at Sargent)
Can he do that?

                     SARGENT
Unfortunately he can.
         (Then to the owner)
What'll we do, walk?

                     THE OWNER
We'll ride. Open the rumble seat.

                     SARGENT
Open it yourself.

He helps Lee into the car.

DISSOLVE TO:

C-51   <u>A VILLAGE STREET</u>

Sargent's car is coming slowly TOWARD US.

C-52   <u>INT. OF THE CAR - LEE AND SARGENT</u>

Through the back window we see the owner and his gun.
Lee and Sargent look vastly irritated. The owner
pounds on the back window and yells:

                     OWNER
Right here!

Sargent pulls over to the curb.

                     LEE
Don't give your right name.

                     SARGENT
That's a good idea. Don't give
yours either.

                     LEE
I never do.

She opens the door and starts to get out.

6-15-39

C-53   THE CAR AT THE CURB

Lee and Sargent emerge and the owner climbs out of
the rumble seat.

                        THE OWNER
            Go on.

They start across the sidewalk and the CAMERA PANS
WITH THEM as they approach a frouzy house of the
cupola period bearing a sign on the door:

                    "CLYDE EMORY
                JUSTICE OF THE PEACE"

C-54   THE EMORY DINING ROOM

At a table sit Mr. and Mrs. Emory. Through a part
in the lace curtains we see the three coming up the
walk.

                        MRS. EMORY
            Looks like business, Clyde....
                (She cranes her neck)
            Well I declare, if that isn't a shot
            gun wedding I'll...

                        THE JUSTICE
            Hunh?
                (Now he gets a better
                 view)
            No, that's Hank. Probably got a
            couple of trespassers. With that
            new detour he gets 'em all the
            time.
                (He rises)

C-55   LEE, SARGENT AND THE OWNER - IN FRONT OF THE DOOR

The owner removes his finger from the bell and they
wait till the door is opened by Mrs. Emory.

                        THE OWNER
            Want to see the Justice of the
            Peace.

                        MRS. EMORY
                (Disagreeably)
            Kinda early, aren't you?

6-15-39   (Continued)

C-55 (Cont'd)

> THE OWNER
>
> Go in.

As they enter --

C-56   THE JUSTICE'S OFFICE

It is divided in two by a rail with an opening in it.
On one side there is a very ancient roll-top desk, a
safe, a letter press, waste basket, cardboard files,
a table and much loose paper. Also a fire extinguisher on the wall of the type that has to be turned
upside down. On the other side there are a few hard
chairs, some real estate sales notices, a calendar and
some descriptions of murderers and other fugitives
for whom rewards have been offered. The Justice is
seated at his desk as Lee and Sargent enter followed
by the owner, who stands his gun in the corner.

> SARGENT
> (Very amiably)
> Good morning, Your Honor, I'm
> afraid there's been a little mis-
> understanding here all around.
> This gentleman...
> (He indicates
> the owner)
> .....found my car parked in his
> field and naturally came to the
> conclusion.....

> THE JUSTICE
> (Interrupting)
> What's the charge, Hank?

> THE OWNER
> Trespass on posted property, wanton
> destruction of fence and petty
> larceny.

> SARGENT
> (Indignantly)
> That's a ga....

> THE JUSTICE
> (Interrupting)
> What'd they steal?

> THE OWNER
> They were milking one of my cows
> when I caught them.

6-15-39   (Continued)

C-56 (Cont'd)

> LEE
> (Indignantly)
> In a little thermos bottle that
> big.
> (She indicates)

> THE JUSTICE
> Nobody asked you anything, young
> woman. When it comes your turn
> you can talk all you like.
> (He picks up a pen)
> What's your name?

> LEE
> (Promptly)
> Mary Smith.

> THE JUSTICE
> Where do you live?

> LEE
> (Promptly)
> Ashtabula, Ohio.

> THE JUSTICE
> Occupation?

> LEE
> (Sarcastically)
> Bubble dancer.

> THE JUSTICE
> Whatever that is. All right.
> (He turns to Sargent)
> What's your name?

> SARGENT
> (Also promptly)
> Henry Wadsworth Longfellow, New
> York, New York.

> THE JUSTICE
> Occupation?

> SARGENT
> Steam fitter.

> THE JUSTICE
> All right. Do you plead "guilty"
> or "not guilty"?

6-15-39 (Continued)

C-56 (Cont'd)

                              SARGENT
                         (In his best court-
                            room manner)
                    May it please the court, I am some-
                    what familiar with legal procedure
                    having at one time contemplated the
                    law....

                              THE JUSTICE
                    Then you shouldn't have broken the
                    law.

                              SARGENT
                    It was in ignorance of the fact....

                              THE JUSTICE
                         (Interrupting)
                    Ignorance is no excuse.

                              SARGENT
                    I am aware of that, Your Honor. I
                    am also aware of what a plea of
                    "not guilty" means when made by non-
                    residents of the state.

                              THE OWNER
                         (To the Justice)
                    They're not even married.

                              SARGENT
                         (Turning on him)
                    I don't know what you mean by "even
                    married." You say "even married"
                    as if married were the least that
                    people could be, some minor unim-
                    portant arrangement instead of
                    God's greatest gift to man and
                    woman. I appeal to your sense of
                    chivalry, Your Honor, I take it
                    that you are a married man and
                    that the charming lady who opened
                    the door.....

                              THE OWNER
                         (Interrupting him)
                    And they spent the night in my
                    field.....from out of state.

                              THE JUDGE
                         (Wisely)
                    Unhunh.

        6-15-39   (Continued)

C-56 (Cont'd)

                    SARGENT
        My learned opponent, I mean this
        thug with the shotgun, is trying
        to inject into this case an ele-
        ment....

                    THE JUSTICE
        Do you plead "guilty" or "not
        guilty"?

                    SARGENT
                (Furiously)
        To what?

                    LEE
                (In a whisper
                to Sargent)
        It must feel funny to you...
                (She lights a
                cigarette)

                    THE JUSTICE
                (Consulting his
                notes)
        To trespass, destruction of pri-
        vate property and petty larceny.

                    SARGENT
                (Furiously)
        What'll you settle for?

                    THE JUSTICE
                (Also furiously)
        What'll I settle for!
                (He gets to his
                feet)
        Did you ever hear of contempt of
        court while you were studying
        the law? I think I'll just re-
        mand you to the constable and
        send you over to the county seat.

                    SARGENT
        Now wait a minute.

                    THE JUSTICE
        Wait nothing. I was trying to
        give you a fair trial, but when
        men drive girls over the state
        line....

        6-15-39   (Continued)

C-57   CLOSE SHOT - LEE

She looks around desperately, then stares at something
OUT OF THE SHOT. During this time we have heard --

>   THE JUSTICE'S VOICE
>   ....as you did, the matter is worth
>   investigating....

C-58   CLOSE SHOT - AN ENORMOUS WASTEBASKET FULL OF PAPERS

C-59   CLOSE SHOT - LEE

Making sure that she is unobserved she lights a match.

C-60   THE JUSTICE, THE PRISONERS AND THE OWNER

>   THE JUSTICE
>   ....also when they give funny names
>   like Henry Wadsworth Longfellow.
>   You may think you're dealing with
>   rubes and I'm going to give you the
>   opportunity....

A wisp of smoke drifts INTO THE SHOT.

>   LEE
>   (At the top of
>   her lungs)
>   FIRE!

She screams piercingly. The Justice looks around in
horror and the owner claws for the fire extinguisher.
He succeeds in unhooking it and pointing the hose at
the wastebasket.

>   THE JUSTICE
>   (Hysterically)
>   Turn it upside down, you gol
>   durned.....

>   SARGENT
>   I'll get some water.

He rushes into the hall and Lee follows him.

C-61   <u>THE HALLWAY OF THE JUSTICE'S HOUSE</u>

Lee and Sargent hurry in and bump into Mrs. Emory.

6-15-39   (Continued)

C-61 (Cont'd)

> MRS. EMORY
> What's the matter?

> LEE
> Get some water quick, the office
> is on fire!

Mrs. Emory tears back through the dining room.
Sargent turns to go back into the office but Lee
grabs him firmly and points to the front door.

> SARGENT
> (Stupefied)
> Hunh?

> LEE
> (Quietly but
> distinctly)
> It's only a wastebasket.

She opens the door and shoves him through it.

C-62   THE JUSTICE AND THE OWNER IN THE SMOKE-FILLED OFFICE

The extinguisher is working perfectly and the fire
is giving its last hiss.

> THE JUSTICE
> How the ding dang that ever caught
> on f.....

> THE OWNER
> (Grabbing his shoulder
> and looking around)
> Where'd they go?

> THE JUSTICE
> (Astonished)
> Hunh?

We now hear the pounding of feet and Mrs. Emory rushes
in with a bucket of water.

> MRS. EMORY
> (Hysterically)
> There!

She lets the water go and soaks both gentlemen.

DISSOLVE TO:

6-15-39

C-63   <u>PENNSYLVANIA-OHIO STATE LINE SIGN</u>

The sign has a line down the middle and the names of
the adjoining states on either side. Now the CAMERA
PANS to a LONG SHOT of the highway. Sargent's car
appears as a spot in the distance. It roars down
upon us and screeches to a stop on the other side of
the line, the CAMERA HAVING PANNED WITH IT.

C-64   <u>INT. OF THE CAR</u> - FACING LEE AND SARGENT

Sargent mops his head and relaxes a little after the
long hard drive. Lee looks at him with some appre-
hension.

                    SARGENT
          Well, that's that. Now when we
          go back I suppose we'll have to
          duck around through Canada and
          New Jersey.

                    LEE
          I guess that would be better.
                    (Now she smiles
                    faintly)
          I guess it must feel kind of
          funny to you to be a fugitive
          from justice.

                    SARGENT
                    (With a dead pan)
          Hilarious.
                    (Then after a
                    pause)
          I've been trying to figure all
          across Pennsylvania how that
          fire started. Nobody was smok-
          ing....

                    LEE
                    (In a small voice)
          I was.

                    SARGENT
                    (Looking around
                    and frowning)
          You were?

She avoids his eye.

                    SARGENT
          Did you throw anything....into
          that basket?

6-15-39   (Continued)

C-64 (Cont'd)

> LEE
> Nothing but a match.

> SARGENT
> A match!
>   (Now in horror)
> You mean...a lighted match?

> LEE
> Well, I guess there must have
> been some life in it.

> SARGENT
>   (After a pause)
> You mean you threw it in there...
> on purpose?

> LEE
> Well....I wasn't aiming for the
> spitoon.

> SARGENT
>   (Passing his hand
>   over his eyes)
> I suppose you know that's called
> "arson."

> LEE
>   (Meekly)
> I thought that was when you bit
> somebody.

> SARGENT
>   (Holding his head
>   and looking off
>   into space)
> Bit somebody.

He looks at her and she starts to defend herself.

> LEE
> Well, that's better than going
> to jail for the Mann Act, isn't
> it?

As Sargent does not reply she continues.

> LEE
> I told you my mind worked differ-
> ently.

6-15-39   (Continued)

C-64 (Cont'd)

                     SARGENT
                   (Roughly)
         Do you realize that house is
         probably in flames a mile high?

                     LEE
                   (Vehemently)
         I hope it is.

                     SARGENT
         So do I....but what's that got
         to do with the morals of the case?

                     LEE
                   (Triumphantly)
         What have morals got to do with it?
         You've treated me like your sister.

Sargent gives her an astonished look, makes a helpless gesture and puts the car in gear. Now he takes
a quick look at Lee and busts out laughing. Seeing
him restored to good humor she laughs happily.

<u>FADE OUT</u>:

           <u>END OF SEQUENCE "C"</u>

SEQUENCE "D"

FADE IN:

D-1   THE MAIN STREET OF A SMALL TOWN - (NIGHT)

If convenient, a hotel is labeled "The Kendallville
House" but it really doesn't matter. Sargent's car
appears and it is pretty dusty.

D-2   INT. MOVING CAR - FACING LEE AND SARGENT - (NIGHT)

> LEE
> (Looking around)
> It hasn't changed much...new
> drugstore.

> SARGENT
> Yes, they creep in over night.

> LEE
> (Pointing to the Elk's
> hall)
> That's where I went to my first
> dance.

> SARGENT
> First one I went to was at the
> fire house.

> LEE
> I've been to the fire house too.

> SARGENT
> Do I turn here?

> LEE
> No. Straight on...about a mile
> the other side of the tracks.
> (Now she smiles
> nervously)
> I'm getting scared.

> SARGENT
> Now, now, now.

DISSOLVE TO:

D-3   A SMALL RAMSHACKLE HOUSE - (NIGHT)

We see it quite clearly in the moonlight. No lights
are visible in the front but from the kitchen at the
side some light streams onto the junk in the yard.

(Continued)

6/15/39

D-3 (Cont'd)

    The house is back quite a way from the road and
there are some trees in front of it. We hear a
car door slam. A dog in the house starts to bark.

D-4   THE CAR BESIDE THE ROAD - (NIGHT)

    Lee stands next to the door she has just closed,
looking apprehensively at the house. Sargent goes
to the back of the car and takes out her suitcase.

>   LEE
>   (Seeing what he's
>   doing)
>   Oh, please... let's wait till...
>   she might not even live here any
>   more.

>   SARGENT
>   Oh.

    He puts the suitcase back and comes around to her.

>   SARGENT
>   Now don't be so nervous, for
>   heaven's sake.

>   LEE
>   Will you go in with me?

>   SARGENT
>   Of course I will.

    He pats her shoulder and the CAMERA PANS WITH THEM
as they start toward the house.

>   LEE
>   (After a pause)
>   You see that tree?

>   SARGENT
>   (Looking up)
>   Uhhunh.

>   LEE
>   I fell out of it when I was twelve,
>   from that branch right there... I
>   was a terrible tomboy. If I'd been
>   a man I would have run away to sea...
>   I landed on my head.

(Continued)

6/15/39

D-4 (Cont'd)

> SARGENT
> That's a better gag than
> hypnotism. Why didn't your
> lawyer use that?

> LEE
> (Wearily)
> I don't know.

> SARGENT
> You should have had me for a
> lawyer.

She chuckles nervously - then looks at the house
which is just in front of them.

> LEE
> (Stopping)
> Well, here we are.

> SARGENT
> (Gruffly)
> Come on, smile.

Lee does her best and the CAMERA PANS WITH THEM as
they climb the steps to the porch.

D-5   LEE AND SARGENT IN FRONT OF THE DOOR

Lee hesitates for a moment - then raps. The dog
in the house goes off like a fire alarm.

> LEE
> (Nervously)
> I didn't mean to knock too
> loud -- why that sounds like
> Mickie... I don't suppose it
> is, though, he'd be almost...
> here's somebody coming!

> SARGENT
> I'll pick you up on New Year's
> day -- in the afternoon.

> LEE
> Gee, you've been sweet.
> (She smiles
> nervously)

(Continued)

6/15/39

D-5 (Cont'd)

Sargent pats her shoulder and they wait. After a
moment the seldom-used front door lock squeaks and
clicks and the door is opened by a man holding a
lamp. He is fifty-odd and disagreeable-looking.
He wears slippers, pants with suspenders and woolen
underwear on the top of his body. From the kitchen
at the end of the hall we hear a radio. The dog
starts barking again.

> WOMAN'S VOICE
> Shut up!

The dog yelps.

> THE MAN
> Yes?

> LEE
> Oh, I'm terribly sorry, doesn't
> Mrs. Malone live here any more?

The man gives Lee a long look before replying.

> THE MAN
> I guess you want my wife.

> LEE
> (Startled)
> Oh.

The man turns, puts the lamp on a table and disappears into the kitchen at the end of the hall.
Lee and Sargent look at each other. Now a middle-
aged woman appears. She walks firmly toward us,
wiping her hands on an apron. She reaches the
doorway, passes her eyes over the stranger, then
looks unsmilingly at Lee.

> LEE
> (In a small voice)
> Hello, Mama.

Her mother looks at her steadily but does not answer.

> LEE
> Well, you know me, don't you?

> THE MOTHER
> Come in.

(Continued)

6/15/39

D-5 (Cont'd)

     She steps back and holds the door open. As Lee
and Sargent enter --

D-6   THE PARLOR

     We see the light in the hall through the cracks
in the door. Now the door opens and Lee's mother
comes in carrying the lamp. She is followed by
Lee and Sargent. She puts the lamp on the table
then turns with HER BACK TO US.

                  LEE
               (Nervously)
        This is Mr. uh..uh..

                SARGENT
              (Affably)
        Sargent. How do you do.

                THE MOTHER
        Sit down.

     Lee and Sargent sit on small stiff chairs but
the old woman remains standing.

                LEE
        You're looking fine, Mama.

D-7   LEE'S MOTHER - PAST LEE AND SARGENT

                THE MOTHER
        What did you come here for?
        What do you want?

D-8   LEE AND SARGENT - PAST THE MOTHER

                LEE
              (Uneasily)
        I don't want anything, Mama,
        it was just Christmas and uh
        Mr. Sargent happened to be
        driving past here...

                SARGENT
              (Brightly)
        I live in Wabash, that is, I
        used to, and I knew how glad
        you'd be --

                           (Continued)

6/15/39

D-8 (Cont'd)

                    LEE
        So he brought me with him.

D-9   THE MOTHER - PAST LEE AND SARGENT

                 THE MOTHER
        You mean they acquitted you?

D-10   LEE AND SARGENT - PAST THE MOTHER

                    LEE
            (Startled)
      What are you...talking about?
      (She looks anxiously
       at Sargent)

D-11   THE MOTHER - PAST LEE AND SARGENT

                 THE MOTHER
      You know what I'm talking about...
      and so does everybody else. The
      whole town knows about it. I'm
      talking about that bracelet you
      stole... like everything else you
      stole since you took the savings
      I put by with the sweat of my
      brow.

D-12   LEE AND SARGENT - PAST THE MOTHER

                    LEE
          (Desperately)
      I did not. I told you a thousand
      times I only borrowed it to get
      a dress you couldn't understand I
      had to have... and I'd pay you
      back out of what I'd earn during
      the summer.

During this Sargent looks at his hands in embarrassment.

D-13   THE MOTHER - PAST LEE AND SARGENT

                 THE MOTHER
         (Addressing Sargent)
      A party dress at fourteen! And
      the rest of her family out at the
      elbows!

6-15-39   (Continued)

D-13 (Cont'd)

                        THE MOTHER (Cont'd)
                     (Now she swings on Lee)
                  But you <u>didn't</u> pay me back,
                  did you? and you never paid me
                  back...and you never paid any-
                  body else back.

D-14   LEE - PAST HER MOTHER

                        LEE
                     (Almost in tears)
                  But you wouldn't give me clothes
                  to go out and work...

D-15   THE MOTHER - PAST LEE AND SARGENT

                        THE MOTHER
                  A fine lot of work you ever
                  did!
                     (She turns to Sargent)
                  The great lady! We weren't
                  good enough for her here...
                  a Christian home, a hard
                  working father and mother.

                        LEE
                  Nobody said you weren't, Mama.

                        THE MOTHER
                     (To Sargent)
                  With a crook for a daughter...
                  so the neighbors can read about
                  it in the paper...and pity me...
                  and wait for her sister to turn
                  out the same.

                        LEE
                  How is she?

                        THE MOTHER
                  She's gone too.

                        LEE
                  I'm sorry, Mama.
                     (Then after a pause)
                  How do you suppose the paper
                  knew...about me?

                                        (Continued)

6/15/39

D-15 (Cont'd)

> THE MOTHER
> The Jarvis boy is in New York
> studying to be a reporter,
> Johnny Jarvis... he sends back
> clippings.

D-16   LEE AND SARGENT - PAST THE MOTHER

> LEE
> The dumbbell.

Sargent looks at his watch, then at Lee.

> SARGENT
> And now, my dear... I don't
> want to tear you away, but as
> we have still fifty miles to
> go...

> LEE
> (Looking at him
> hopelessly)
> Oh.

> SARGENT
> (Getting to his feet)
> Are you ready?

> LEE
> (From the depths of
> her soul)
> Oh yes.

She gets to her feet.

> SARGENT
> It's been very interesting to
> meet you, Mrs. uh...

> THE MOTHER
> The name doesn't concern you.

> SARGENT
> It most certainly does not.

> LEE
> Goodbye, Mama.

(Continued)

6/15/39

D-16 (Cont'd)

She gives her mother one last look - then turns
and Sargent follows her out of the room. The
Mother turns slowly to the table, turns down the
lamp and blows it out vigorously.

D-17   TRUCKING SHOT - AHEAD AND TO ONE SIDE OF LEE AND
SARGENT

Sargent has his arm around Lee. Lee sobs once.

> SARGENT
> There, there, for heaven's
> sake.

> LEE
> I'd forgotten how much I hate
> that woman... and how much she
> hates me. It's a terrible thing
> to say, isn't it? Ever since I
> was little... she was always so
> right, and I was always so wrong.
> She was always so good and I was
> always so bad... she... thank you
> for getting me out. I'll stay
> anywhere... we can find a room.
> Only please not here... not so
> close to her.

She has been getting more and more hysterical
with the last few words. Now she bursts into
tears.

> SARGENT
> (Putting his arm
> around her)
> There, there.

> LEE
> (Pointing vaguely)
> I wish I'd ... broken my neck...
> when I fell out of that tree.

> SARGENT
> (Dryly)
> Yes. Well it's a little late to
> think about that now.

> LEE
> You won't make me stay in Kendalville?

(Continued)

6/15/39

416

D-17 (Cont'd)

                        SARGENT
I won't.

                        LEE
You'll find me a room somewhere
else?

                        SARGENT
I will.

                        LEE
Any old dump will do.

                        SARGENT
                      (Gruffly)
That's just what you're going
to get: It's only got one
window and the mattress is
stuffed with rocks and it's
got a painting of the cross-
eyedest old man you ever saw
in your life.

                        LEE
How do you know?

                        SARGENT
How do I know what...that my
grandfather was cross-eyed?

                        LEE
                    (With her face
                    working)
You mean you're taking me...
home with you?

                        SARGENT
                    (Gruffly)
Why not?

Lee bursts into tears.

                        SARGENT
                    (Throwing his arms
                    wide)
Now what?

DISSOLVE TO:

6/15/39

D-18   CLOSE SHOT - CROSS-EYED GRANDPA <u>ON THE WALL</u>

He hangs in a room which is lit from the hall outside. The CAMERA TRUCKS BACK and we see the open
door to the hall. A simple looking gent with an
armful of firewood appears in the hall and calls
to someone OUT OF THE SHOT.

>   WILLIE
>   (With somewhat of
>   a stutter)
>   Wh-where you want that f-f-fire
>   laid, Miz Sargent?

D-19   MRS. SARGENT - <u>FROM THE REAR</u>

She is deep in the linen closet. She turns with
an armful of linen.

>   MRS. SARGENT
>   Land sakes, Willie, there's
>   only one fireplace on the
>   second floor. Haven't you
>   laid that fire yet?

D-20   WILLIE - <u>IN THE HALLWAY</u>

>   WILLIE
>   (Somewhat hurt)
>   They had me p-p-peelin' puh-
>   puh-puh-puh-puh...

D-21   MRS. SARGENT - <u>COMING OUT OF THE LINEN CLOSET</u>

>   MRS. SARGENT
>   Puh-puh-potatoes.

Mrs. Sargent watches Willie go, looks once to
heaven for patience, then sniffs and looks down
over the banister.

>   MRS. SARGENT
>   (Loudly)
>   Emmy! I think those cookies
>   are burning.

6/15/39

D-22   AUNT EMMA - <u>IN THE KITCHEN</u>

She is rolling out some dough at the kitchen table.

> AUNT EMMA
> (Startled)
> Sakes alive!

She flies to the over, finds the cookies are not burning and stalks indignantly to the door and yells upstairs.

> AUNT EMMA
> Lucy Sargent, those cookies are <u>not</u> burning. I declare it's enough to drive a body crazy the way you carry on when Jack comes home. I've never burned anything yet and...

She stops in horror, sniffs, then leaps to the oven and pulls out a burning pan of cookies. She looks upstairs and almost tearfully says:

> AUNT EMMA
> There! I hope you're satisfied!

D-23   SARGENT'S ROOM

Mrs. Sargent is smoothing the bed. Willie is on his knees finishing the laying of the fire.

> MRS. SARGENT
> (Giving the bed a last pat)
> There.

> WILLIE
> You want the f-f-fire lit, Miz Sargent or wait till he g-gets here?

> MRS. SARGENT
> Does the room seem chilly Willie?

> WILLIE
> It don't seem ch-chilly Willie -- chilly to m-me but the way they ben r-runnin' me r-ragged all day I wouldn't be cha-cha-cha-cha-cha-cha...

> MRS. SARGENT
> (Closing her eyes wearily)
> Chilly.

6/15/39   (Continued)

D-23 (Cont'd)

                    WILLIE
          ...in an ice pond.

                    MRS. SARGENT
               (As severe as she
                ever gets)
          Willie Sims, if you don't stop
          complaining I declare I'll..I'll...
          well I don't know what I'll do.
          You're getting a lovely home with
          nothing but a few cows and chickens
          to...

                    WILLIE
          ...and p-pigs.

                    MRS. SARGENT
          ...What do a few pigs...

                    WILLIE
          ...and m-mules.

                    MRS. SARGENT
          They don't need any care. And
          instead of being grateful...

                    WILLIE
               (Pointing an accusing
                finger)
          And the b-b-b-b-b...b-b-b...

                    MRS. SARGENT
               (Wearily)
          All right, the bull. But even so,
          Willie...

                    WILLIE
          R-rabbits.

                    MRS. SARGENT
               (Disgustedly)
          Rabbits!

                    WILLIE
          D-ducks.

                    MRS. SARGENT
               (Folding her arms)
          Willie Sims...

          An automobile horn outside toots "Shave and a hair-
          cut, bayrum." Mrs. Sargent becomes electrified.

6-15-39   (Continued)

420

D-23 (Cont'd)

> MRS. SARGENT
> There he is!
> (At the top of her lungs)
> He's here, Emmy!

She takes a quick step toward the door - then turns
to Willie.

> MRS. SARGENT
> Go down and open the door...

Willie starts for the door.

> MRS. SARGENT
> And don't forget the fire.

Willie starts back toward the fireplace.

> MRS. SARGENT
> Bring in his bags.

> WILLIE
> B-b-but...

> MRS. SARGENT
> Give me the matches. I'll light
> it myself.

As Willie looks at her stupidly, she repeats.

> MRS. SARGENT
> The matches!

> WILLIE
> (Lost)
> The b-bags.

> MRS. SARGENT
> Here!

She snatches the matches out of his pocket and
lights the fire.

> WILLIE
> (To the world at large)
> G-g-gosh all h-h-h...

> MRS. SARGENT
> (Getting up and fin-
> ishing it for him)
> Hemlock!

She drags him out of the room.

6-15-39

421

D-24   SARGENT'S CAR - FROM THE REAR - SNOWING - (NIGHT)

He is lifting out the suitcases. Lee is still in
the car, not visible. In the background we see the
Sargent house, bright at the windows.

> SARGENT
> (Yelling toward
> the house)
> Hey!

D-25   CLOSE SHOT - THE SIDE WINDOW OF THE CAR

Lee looks longingly at the cheerful house.

D-26   MEDIUM CLOSE - THE FRONT DOOR OF THE HOUSE

It flies open and Mrs. Sargent hurries out followed
by Aunt Emma and Willie.

D-27   SARGENT - AT THE REAR OF THE CAR

He puts the last suitcase on the ground, then seeing the approaching cavalcade he steps forward,
throws his arms wide and says:

> SARGENT
> Well, well, well.

Mrs. Sargent FLASHES BY THE CAMERA and jumps into
her son's arms.

D-28   CLOSE SHOT - MRS. SARGENT IN HER SON'S ARMS

> MRS. SARGENT
> (Her eyes filled
> with tears)
> My boy, my boy.

Sargent pats her on the back, then looks at his
Aunt.

> SARGENT
> Hello, Aunt Emma.

He releases his mother gently and takes a step
forward.

6-15-39

D-29   AUNT EMMA FOLLOWED BY WILLIE

Sargent goes PAST THE CAMERA and hugs her to him.

> AUNT EMMA
> (Struggling in
> Sargent's embrace)
> John Sargent, I do declare I'm
> glad you're here.
> (She pecks him
> on the cheek)
> If only to stop your mother from
> taking leave of her senses. For
> the last week this house has been...

> WILLIE
> (Seconding the motion)
> G-gosh.

> SARGENT
> (Reaching a hand
> to Willie)
> Hello, Willie. The girls still
> chasing you?

Willie chortles idiotically.

> MRS. SARGENT
> (Coming INTO THE PICTURE)
> What made you so late? I thought
> you'd be here by six. You didn't
> have an accident?

> SARGENT
> (Wondering just how
> he's going to put it)
> I'll tell you... you see...

> WILLIE
> (Pointing to the car)
> Who's that?

Sargent, his mother and Aunt Emma turn and look at
the car. Sargent takes a side look at his mother,
then steps forward.

D-30   THE SIDE OF THE CAR

Lee looks out PAST US, wondering perhaps how she
will be received. Sargent comes INTO THE SHOT,
opens the door and helps Lee to the ground. Lee
smiles nervously.

6-15-39   (Continued)

D-30 (Cont'd)

> SARGENT
> Mother, Aunt Emma and Willie:
> this is Miss Lee Leander who's
> come to spend Christmas week
> with us.

> LEE
> (In a small voice)
> Hello...I hope I won't be too
> much trouble.

D-31   MRS. SARGENT, AUNT EMMA AND WILLIE - PAST LEE AND
> SARGENT

> MRS. SARGENT
> (Galvanized)
> Trouble? Why bless you, child,
> it's a joy to have you here...
> (Now she scowls
> at Sargent)
> ...only you might have sent a
> telegram, John Sargent! Grandpa's
> room hasn't been cleaned since your
> Aunt Clara was here for canning and ...

> AUNT EMMA
> (Indignantly)
> Lucy Sargent, that is not so!
> I had Willie in there just last
> week...

> WILLIE
> (Scowling)
> You s-s-said it!

> AUNT EMMA
> ...and it's as clean as a whistle.

> MRS. SARGENT
> (To Lee)
> I doubt it.
> (Taking Lee's arm)
> Come along, child, you must be
> freezing to death and here we are
> cackling like a couple of old --
> did you leave those cookies in the
> oven, Emmy?

6-15-39   (Continued)

D-31 (Cont'd)

>   AUNT EMMA
>   (Picking up her skirts)
>   Jeepers creepers!
>   (She gallops into the
>   house)

>   WILLIE
>   (Delighted)
>   Hot z-z-ziggoty!

Lee and Sargent burst out laughing which causes
Mrs. Sargent to join them.

>   MRS. SARGENT
>   (Dragging Lee toward
>   the house)
>   Come along, now.

Sargent picks up a suitcase and Willie picks up
the other two.

>   WILLIE
>   Oh, b-b-b-boy!

>   SARGENT
>   What?

>   WILLIE
>   Ain't she a pup-pup-pup-pup-
>   pup-pupppeacherino?

>   SARGENT
>   What? Who? Oh!

>   WILLIE
>   Hot d-d-d-dog!
>   (He gives Sargent
>   a big wink)

D-32   THE SARGENT KITCHEN

Aunt Emma is washing dishes. Lee and Sargent are
drying, each with a big apron around them.

>   SARGENT
>   If I do say so myself --- eek
>   (This means a
>   hiccup)
>   my Aunt Emma is probably -- eek
>   the second best cook in the world.

6-15-39   (Continued)

D-32 (Cont'd)

                              AUNT EMMA
                          (Embarrassed)
               How you talk, Jack...
                          (Now she frowns)
               Who's the first best?

Sargent and Lee laugh happily. Mrs. Sargent comes
into the kitchen followed by Willie who is covered
with cleaning apparatus and carries two pails.
Mrs. Sargent has a duster around her head which
she now removes.

                              MRS. SARGENT
               There. The room is still far
               from clean, Lee, but it's passable.

                              AUNT EMMA
                          (Frowning)
               It was pretty passable before, too.

                              WILLIE
                          (Dismally)
               Well, it's p-p-perfeck now.
                          (He clanks his pails
                           on the floor)

                              MRS. SARGENT
                          (To Lee)
               Won't you come in the sitting room,
               dear?
                          (She nods toward
                           the dishes)
               I don't know why she made you do
               that, Willie could have done them
               easily.

                              WILLIE
                          (Looking around
                           indignantly)
               Sh-sure.

                              LEE
               I liked doing them. I've lived
               in hotels and... and places so
               long I haven't been as much around
               a house as I'd like to be.

                              WILLIE
               Your f-folks dead?

                              MRS. SARGENT
                          (Shocked)
               Willie!

6-15-39   (Continued)

D-32 (Cont'd)

       WILLIE
      (Surprised)
 Hunh?

       LEE
 My father's dead. My mother's...
 remarried.

      MRS. SARGENT
     (Sympathetically)
 I always say that's so hard on the
 children. It doesn't matter how
 nice the new parent is, it just
 isn't the same. Now everybody
 come into the parlor while Jack
 plays the piano.

      SARGENT
 I had fourteen dollars worth of
 piano lessons and they've never
 forgotten it.

They start out.

D-33 THE SITTING ROOM

  It contains a square piano and some nice old furniture, also a decorated Christmas tree. Mrs. Sargent
  enters, followed by Lee, Sargent and Aunt Emma.

      MRS. SARGENT
     (Beginning with Lee)
 Now you sit here, dear, and you
 sit there, Emmy and I'll sit here.

      SARGENT
     (To Lee)
 Until you have heard this, you
 have heard nothing.

      MRS. SARGENT
     (To Lee)
 He plays very nicely when you
 consider the size of his hands.
 Play "The Road to Mandalay."

      AUNT EMMA
 And sing it.

  He sits at the piano and strikes a fearful discord —
  then cracks his knuckles like a great pianist.

6-15-39

            (Continued)

D-33 (Cont'd)

      SARGENT
   Are we all set?
     (He turns back to
      the piano)
   Let 'er go, Gallagher.

With which he gives a stupefying rendition
(condensed) of the "The Road to Mandalay". Concluding, he slams the piano shut and rises.

      SARGENT
   And that is that.

     MRS. SARGENT
   Oh, play one more piece.

      SARGENT
   Not till next year.

     MRS. SARGENT
   Oh, please.

      WILLIE
   C-c-come on, now.

      SARGENT
   You forget, Mother, we have a guest.

      LEE
   I'll play you a piece. I used to
   play in the ten cent store.

      WILLIE
   I can sing the "R-r-rosary."

      AUNT EMMA
   Now Willie.

      WILLIE
   Well I - I can.

     MRS. SARGENT
    (Gently)
   So can everybody else, Willie.

      SARGENT
   Then let's all sing it.

Lee seats herself at the piano, loosens her fingers
with some very swell chords, then turns to Willie.

6-15-39   (Continued)

D-33 (Cont'd)

> LEE
> All right, Willie.

In a surprisingly beautiful tenor and with only an
occasional stutter, Willie begins the "Rosary".
Lee joins him in harmony, then Sargent comes in
with a fairly accurate bass. With the others already in, Mrs. Sargent and Aunt Emma add their
quavering sopranos to the melody. As the song
ends --

DISSOLVE TO:

D-34   <u>EXT. HOUSE - (NIGHT)</u>

Lights are going on on the second floor while lights
are being turned off on the ground floor.

D-35   <u>THE CROSS-EYED GRANDFATHER'S ROOM</u>

Aunt Emma's turning down the bed. Lee opens a suitcase and takes out her nightgown.

> AUNT EMMA
> (Feeling of the nightgown)
> Land sakes, child, you want to catch
> pneumonia?

She pulls open a drawer of a bureau and takes out a
superb nightgown of striped flannelette with long
sleeves and a high neck.

> AUNT EMMA
> There. And I think you'd better
> have a hot water bottle too. You
> look a little peaked.

> LEE
> I'm as strong as a horse.

> AUNT EMMA
> (Exiting)
> Well, many a horse has frizz in
> this weather.

She exits. Lee looks after her, touched. Now she
takes off the top of her dress, slips her shoulder
straps down.

6-15-39

D-36   SARGENT AND HIS MOTHER - IN THE SITTING ROOM

He is knocking out his pipe in the fireplace while his mother puts out the lights. As she starts for the last light he stops her with a word.

> SARGENT
>
> Mother.

> MRS. SARGENT
> (Gently)
> Yes, dear?

> SARGENT
>
> I don't know whether to tell you this or not, but I don't like to bring somebody under your roof without your knowing exactly who she is.

> MRS. SARGENT
> (Romantically)
> I think I can guess.

> SARGENT
>
> What?
> (Then getting her
> meaning)
> Oh, no. Not at all. This young woman isn't even a friend of mine.

> MRS. SARGENT
>
> Why I think she's charming. She reminds me of your father's cousin Winifred who died when her second was born, the lovely, sweet thing. I was just saying to Emmy --

> SARGENT
>
> This girl is a crook, Mother. I'm going to put her in jail. In the meanwhile she had no place to go for Christmas.

> MRS. SARGENT
> (Distressed)
> Why the poor lamb!
> (Now she scowls
> at her son)
> You'll do no such a thing, John Sargent. That girl is as honest as all outdoors, I can tell by

                         (Continued)

D-36 (Cont'd)

      MRS. SARGENT (Cont'd)
looking at her face. If she did
take anything, I am sure it was
entirely by mistake. She's probably a ... hypochondriac.

Sargent puts his arm around his mother and laughs.

      SARGENT
She might be at that.

      MRS. SARGENT
    (Hopefully)
She hasn't really taken things...
you're just making a bad joke,
aren't you?

      SARGENT
    (Soberly)
No. I'm afraid this isn't even
her first offense..but that doesn't
mean that she wasn't unhappy, and
lonely, and a human being like the
rest of us.

      MRS. SARGENT
    (Distressed)
The poor thing. She probably
didn't get enough love as a child.
Do you remember how bad you were...
not really but -- d'you remember
the time you took my egg-money I
was going to get a new dress with?
... and then how hard you worked
to pay it back when you understood?

      SARGENT
    (Gently)
You made me understand.

      MRS. SARGENT
It was love that made you understand...I do hope she'll enjoy her
stay here! We must do everything
to make her happy and comfortable
and feel like a member of the
family.
    (Now she has another thought)
Do you think we ought to lock up the
silver?

Sargent looks at his mother unbelievingly then
joyously.

6-15-39

D-37   LEE – **IN HER ROOM**

She stands bare-footed adjusting the voluminous
nightgown. Now she examines herself in a mirror.
Suddenly she turns and gives a startled look OUT
OF THE PICTURE.

D-38   CROSS-EYED GRANDPA <u>ON THE WALL</u>

He seems to be leering a little more than usual.

D-39   LEE – LOOKING UP AT GRANDPA

She pulls the nightgown a little tighter closed at
the throat, then laughs at herself, bounds into bed,
pulls the cover up to her nose and blows out the
candle. After a moment of adjustment the window
PAST THE BED becomes visible. Lee's head comes
BEFORE IT IN SILHOUETTE as she watches the snow
falling softly. Suddenly we hear a sob and Lee's
head goes back on the pillow.

<u>FADE OUT</u>

<u>END OF SEQUENCE "D"</u>

<u>SEQUENCE "E"</u>

FADE IN:

E-1   <u>A STAINED GLASS WINDOW OF CHRIST</u>

The morning sun slants through it. We hear the
congregation and the choir singing "Holy Night"
to organ accompaniment, as the CAMERA MOVES DOWN
SLOWLY OVER massed flowers onto a gentle looking
minister who leads the music while singing.

E-2   MRS. SARGENT, SARGENT, LEE AND AUNT EMMA

They stand in a front pew singing enthusiastically.
The song ends and they sit down.

E-3   CLOSE SHOT - THE MINISTER

                  THE MINISTER
          The Lord is my shepherd; I shall
          not want. He maketh me to lie
          down in green pastures; He leadeth
          me beside the still waters.

E-4   LEE AND SARGENT

               THE MINISTER'S VOICE
          He restoreth my soul; He leadeth me
          in the paths of righteousness for
          his name's sake. Yea, though I
          walk through the valley of the shadow
          of death, I will fear no evil; for
          Thou art with me; Thy rod and Thy
          staff they comfort me.

Lee looks slowly up at the minister.

E-5   CLOSE SHOT - THE MINISTER

                  THE MINISTER
          Thou preparest a table before me
          in the presence of my enemies;
          Thou anoitest my head with oil; my
          cup runneth over.

E-6   CLOSE SHOT - LEE

Her eyes are dim with tears.

6-15-39   (Continued)

E-6 (Cont'd)

                     THE MINISTER'S VOICE
         Surely goodness and mercy shall
         follow me all the days of my life:
         and I will dwell in the house of
         the Lord forever.

The organ peals out as we --

DISSOLVE TO:

E-7   THE FAMILY AT THE CHRISTMAS TREE

Sargent is busy handing out presents.

                     MRS. SARGENT
                (Looking at a bottle
                of perfume)
         Why Jack, I haven't even started
         that bottle of "Christmas Night"
         you gave me last year.

Aunt Emma gives her a warning look and Mrs. Sargent
looks distressed.

                     SARGENT
         This is the latest.
                (He points to Aunt
                Emma's present)
         So is that.

                     AUNT EMMA
                (Holding up a com-
                pletely transparent
                nightgown)
         What's this supposed to be?

Now she sees it's a nightgown and slaps it back in
the box.

                     AUNT EMMA
         Why Jack Sargent, you ought to be
         ashamed of yourself.

                     WILLIE
         Haw-haw!

                     AUNT EMMA
                (Severely)
         Willie!

6-15-39   (Continued)

E-7 (Cont'd)

> WILLIE
> Yes, m'am.

> SARGENT
> (Handing him a
> package)
> Here, Willie.

Willie tears open his present and pulls out a round
Tyrolian hat complete with badger and badges. As
Willie looks at it round-eyed, Sargent speaks with
authority.

> SARGENT
> The latest.

> WILLIE
> (Putting it on the
> top of his head)
> Is that a f-fact.

> SARGENT
> (Solemnly)
> Only you have to yodel with it.

> WILLIE
> Oh.

He does a magnificent yodel, beams and announces:

> WILLIE
> Pretty sna-sna-sna-sna-sna-
> sna-snazzy I'll say. Got to
> f-f-find me a mirror.

He hurries out.

> SARGENT
> (Picking up a couple
> of boxes)
> Well, for heaven's sake.

He pulls out a magnificent sweater.

> SARGENT
> Thank you, Mother.
> (He kisses her)
> It's a beauty.

He opens the other package and pulls out three pairs
of socks.

6-15-39   (Continued)

E-7 (Cont'd)

> SARGENT
> And thank you, Aunt Emma.

> AUNT EMMA
> Not so fancy but they'll keep your
> feet warm.

He holds both the old women to him and smiles at
Lee.

> SARGENT
> Pretty lucky, hunh?

> LEE
> You bet.

Suddenly Sargent's face falls.

> SARGENT
> I'm sorry about the present
> situation...if we'd only known
> sooner....

His mother kicks him from one side and his Aunt from
the other. Mrs. Sargent indicates the sofa near
the door. Sargent looks over and sees three packages
there. He crosses and picks up the boxes.

> SARGENT
> (Reading the inscrip-
> tions)
> Well, well. You can always trust...
> Santa Claus.

Suddenly he puts the three packages in Lee's arms.

> SARGENT
> Merry Christmas.

> LEE
> (Distressed)
> Oh, no. You shouldn't have...gone
> to all that trouble.

> AUNT EMMA
> Open them up, now.

From the first one Lee removes a beautiful handmade
pin cushion. She looks at the card then takes Mrs.
Sargent's hand.

6-15-39   (Continued)

E-7 (Cont'd)

> LEE
> Oh thank you. It's so pretty.

> MRS. SARGENT
> Why, it's nothing at all. Just
> scraps and things that I collected
> over a period of years.

> LEE
> It's lovely.

Now she opens the next package and pulls out a pair
of bedsocks. She looks up and smiles at Aunt Emma.

> AUNT EMMA
> Not so fancy but wonderful on a
> cold night...for a spinster lady.

> LEE
> (Embarrassed)
> That's awfully sweet of you.

Now she opens the third and smallest package.

> SARGENT
> (Perplexed)
> Who's that from, Willie?

> MRS. SARGENT
> (Giving him the wink)
> You, you big dunce. Can't you re-
> member anything?

Completely perplexed Sargent points to himself and
mouths the word "Me?" His mother nods assent.
Sargent turns to Lee and watches with great curiosity
until she takes out a bottle of perfume.

> LEE
> Oh, thank you....and "Christmas
> Night."

> SARGENT
> The latest.

He rolls his eyes toward his mother.

> LEE
> You're all much too kind. I don't
> think I've ever met anyone so thought-
> ful and so...

6-15-39   (Continued)

E-7 (Cont'd)

                    MRS. SARGENT
                 (Interrupting her)
Oh, nonsense, child. We're so
happy to have you and so anxious
for you to enjoy your stay. There
isn't much to do so you'll just
have to make the best of it. Some
friends are coming and we'll bob
for apples tonight, then tomorrow
the young people are having a
treasure hunt in the snow, then
the day after we have the taffy
pull.....

                    AUNT EMMA
And will _that_ gum the house up.

                    MRS. SARGENT
Oh, pshaw. It don't amount to a
row of pins. Then we have the
rummage sale and charity buffet
down at the fire house. A pretty
girl like you will be a big help.
They're so tight you almost have
to pick their pockets.

                    LEE
I'll do my best.

                    AUNT EMMA
My specialty is short-changing 'em.

                    MRS. SARGENT
Then we rest up for a day and the
next day is New Year's Eve. This
year we're having an old-fashioned
barn dance like the hicks we're
supposed to be.

                    SARGENT
                 (Sarcastically)
And that's all there is...farmers'
wives don't die of boredom any
more....they die of heart failure.

DISSOLVE TO:

E-8   CLOSE SHOT - LEE AND SARGENT ON EITHER SIDE OF A
       WASHTUB FULL OF WATER ON WHICH FLOATS A BIG APPLE

       They are playing apple polo: the object of each being
       to remove the apple with the teeth and prevent the.

       6-15-39   (Continued)

                           438

E-8 (Cont'd)

opponent from doing it. This makes a very wet game
greatly enjoyed by the spectators. The climax comes
when both lose their balance and duck their heads in
the tub.

> MRS. SARGENT
> (Handing Lee a bath
> towel)
> You go right upstairs and change
> your dress. Of all the silly
> games I've ever heard.
> (She turns to Sargent)
> And you too, you big smarty. Your
> shirt is wringing.

> SARGENT
> (Taking Lee's arm)
> Come on, the last one up is a
> cross-eyed skunk.

They race out of the room and up the stairs. The
guests look after them and an old gentleman beams
at Mrs. Sargent.

> THE JUDGE
> They certainly make a handsome
> couple, don't they?

> MRS. SARGENT
> (Amiably)
> Yes, don't they, Judge.
> (Now she looks a
> little worried)
> They certainly do.

DISSOLVE TO:

E-9   <u>SARGENT'S ROOM</u>

Sargent is peeled to the waist drying himself.
There is a knock at the door. He puts on a wrapper.

> SARGENT
> Come in.

E-10   <u>THE DOORWAY</u> - PAST SARGENT

Lee sticks her head in. She has a bath towel around
it. For the rest she also wears a wrapper and
carries a spare towel.

6-15-39   (Continued)

E-10 (Cont'd)

>   LEE
> Could I dry my hair in front of
> your fireplace? I really got it
> soaked.

>   SARGENT
> Why certainly. Come on in.

Lee enters and closes the door after her. Now Lee
sees that the fire isn't lit.

>   LEE
> Oh, don't bother if it isn't
> lit.
>   (She sneezes)

>   SARGENT
>   (Crossing to the
>   fireplace)
> It's no bother.
>   (He also sneezes)
> It's a darn good idea.

He strikes a match and lights the fire which blazes
up at once.

>   LEE
> Thanks.

She sits on the hearth, takes the bath towel off her
head and shakes her hair out.

>   SARGENT
>   (After a moment)
> Enjoying yourself?

>   LEE
> You bet I am.....I hate to think
> of the third.

>   SARGENT
> The third?
>   (Now he remembers)
> Oh, you mean the third.
>   (Then after a pause)
> I hadn't thought of it.

She takes his hand, examines it slowly, then kisses
it.

6-15-39   (Continued)

E-10 (Cont'd)

                          SARGENT
                      (Embarrassed)
              What's the idea?

                          LEE
                      (Shrugging)
              I felt like doing it....

Sargent looks vaguely uneasy.

                          LEE
                      (Looking into the
                       fire)
              You know, nobody would believe
              that we came all this way, slept
              in adjoining rooms, neither of
              us old nor particularly ugly...
              and never had an evil thought.

                          SARGENT
                      (Uneasily)
              No, I don't suppose they would.

Lee feels that her hair is dry, then rises and
stretches like a cat. After this she looks at
Sargent quizzically.

                          LEE
              Even if it was true, they wouldn't
              believe it.

She pats him on the cheek, crosses to the door and
exits slowly. Sargent turns on the hearth and
stares after her with his mouth a little open. This
brings him pretty close to the fire. Suddenly he
leaps to his feet with the rear of his bathrobe
smoking.

FADE OUT:

                    END OF SEQUENCE "E"

SEQUENCE "F"

FADE IN:

F-1   AUNT EMMA AND LEE <u>IN THE SARGENT KITCHEN</u> - (DAY)

They stand near the stove.

> LEE
> (Nervously)
> Do you suppose they've popped?

> AUNT EMMA
> (Proudly)
> I'm positive they've popped.

> LEE
> I wish I could be that sure.

> AUNT EMMA
> You will be when I've told you the
> secret...but you must never let it
> out of the family.

> LEE
> (Taken aback)
> Oh, but I'm not...

> AUNT EMMA
> (Ignoring her)
> Now listen carefully...

She looks to right and left, then pulls Lee's head
down and whispers in her ear, waving her finger em-
phatically the while.

> LEE
> (Astonished)
> No!

> AUNT EMMA
> Yes!

> LEE
> Are you sure?

> AUNT EMMA
> (Crossly)
> Look for yourself.

Lee opens the oven and pulls out a pan of the world's
finest popovers.

> SARGENT
> (Entering)
> How about some breakfa...

6-15-39   (Continued)

> SARGENT   (Cont'd)
> (Now he sees the
>   popovers)
> Holy smoke!

> AUNT EMMA
> (Valiantly)
> And she made them entirely by her-
> self.

> SARGENT
> Oh, boy! Bring 'em in!

He hurries into the dining room.

> LEE
> (Aghast to Aunt Emma)
> What did you tell him that for?

> AUNT EMMA
> (Scowling)
> Don't you know the shortcut to a
> man's heart is through his gizzard?
> Take 'em in while they're hot.

She shoves Lee into the dining room.

F-2   THE DINING ROOM

Sargent is at the table. As Lee enters he finishes
tying a big napkin around his neck, then holds his
knife and fork at attention.

> SARGENT
> I didn't know you could cook.

> LEE
> (In a whisper)
> I didn't make these...she just said
> I did...

> SARGENT
> (Breaking a popover in
>   two and buttering it)
> Why?

> LEE
> Because she's taught me how but I
> guess she thought if you thought
> I already knew how, why that would
> make everything go faster.

> SARGENT
> Make what go faster?

6-15-39   (Continued)

F-2   (Cont'd)

>   LEE
>   (After a pause)
>   You see, she thinks you brought
>   me out here because...you're in
>   love with me.

>   SARGENT
>   Oh.

He guffaws with his mouth full of popover.

>   LEE
>   (With an edge to
>   her voice)
>   Funny, isn't it?

>   SARGENT
>   (A little uneasy now)
>   Yeah.

>   LEE
>   (With a trace of
>   toughness)
>   Well, if you think I couldn't make
>   a popover as good as that you're
>   nuts!

She hurries into the kitchen and Sargent looks after
her in surprise.

DISSOLVE TO:

F-3   <u>THE RUMMAGE SALE IN THE FIREHOUSE</u> - (DAY)

On all sides women are stalking the unfortunate
fathers of families brought there by their females.

F-4   MRS. SARGENT AND THE JUDGE WE SAW AT HER HOUSE

She has him by the arm and is holding an armadillo
basket under his nose.

>   MRS. SARGENT
>   (Holding onto him)
>   Lee!

F-5   LEE AND AUNT EMMA

They are counting a boxful of money. Lee turns,
sizes up the situation at a glance and starts for
the scene of action.

6-15-39   (Continued)

F-5   (Cont'd)

>   LEE
>   (To Aunt Emma)
>   Come on.

Aunt Emma trots after her with a determined look.

F-6   MRS. SARGENT - HOLDING ONTO THE JUDGE

Lee ENTERS THE SHOT instantly followed by Aunt Emma.

>   LEE
>   (To Aunt Emma)
>   Mark down one armadillo basket,
>   Aunt Emma. The seven dollar size.

>   THE JUDGE
>   Now just a minute.

>   LEE
>   That's all right, you can have it
>   for six and kiss Aunt Emma into
>   the bargain.

>   THE JUDGE
>   My dear Miss...

She forces the armadillo basket into his arms,
reaches into his breast pocket, takes out his wallet,
removes all the money from it and throws it into
Aunt Emma's box.

>   LEE
>   (Holding up one
>   finger)
>   Three dollars change, please.

>   AUNT EMMA
>   (Repeating)
>   Three dollars change.

She hands Lee a dollar which the latter pops back
into the wallet, then sticks the wallet back in the
Judge's breast pocket.

>   LEE
>   Thank you, call again.

>   THE JUDGE
>   (Furiously)
>   Now really, Mrs. Sargent, I think
>   that this joke...

Sargent steps INTO THE SCENE and puts his arm around
the Judge.

6-15-39   (Continued)

F-6   (Cont'd)

> THE JUDGE
> (Indignantly)
> John Sargent...

> SARGENT
> No one is forcing you to buy, but
> we must keep the aisles clear.
> Right this way, please.

He strong-arms the Judge OUT OF THE PICTURE.

DISSOLVE TO:

F-7   <u>THE SARGENT LIVING ROOM</u> - (NIGHT)

Mrs. Sargent and her son are playing dominoes. Aunt
Emma is knitting and Lee sits next to her, learning
to knit. Willie is asleep in an easy chair with a
copy of Screen Classics in his lap. There is some
faint radio music. There is silence for a few moments broken by an exclamation from Mrs. Sargent.

> MRS. SARGENT
> Why Jack Sargent, you're cheating!!...
> you can't put a five on a six.

> SARGENT
> I thought you had your other glasses
> on.

> MRS. SARGENT
> If you use tactics like that in New
> York I'm surprised they haven't put
> you in ja--oh!

She looks hastily toward Lee.

> SARGENT
> You're not as surprised as I am.

He smiles reassuringly at his mother.

F-8   CLOSER SHOT - LEE AND AUNT EMMA

> AUNT EMMA
> (Looking over at
> Lee's work)
> You dropped one.

> LEE
> (Dismayed)
> Oh, darn it!

6-15-39   (Continued)

F-8   (Cont'd)

> AUNT EMMA
> (Firmly)
> No. When you make a mistake you've
> got to pay for it. Otherwise you
> never learn.

Lee picks up the end of the yarn dismally.

> AUNT EMMA
> (Firmly)
> Go on, now.

Lee pulls out almost a whole row.

> AUNT EMMA
> Now start again and start right.

Lee starts to knit a little clumsily. Willie snores
and Aunt Emma gives him quite a look.

> AUNT EMMA
> (After a moment)
> What are you going to wear at the
> barn dance?

> LEE
> Well, Willie said he'd lend me a
> pair of his overalls...

> AUNT EMMA
> Pew!

> LEE
> (Quickly)
> Clean ones, of course, and then I
> thought I'd...

> AUNT EMMA
> (Interrupting her)
> Nonsense! Women belong in skirts.
> It's the mystery that gets 'em.

Willie snores again.

> LEE
> Well, I just thought that would
> be easy.

> AUNT EMMA
> How big are you around the waist?

> LEE
> Oh, I don't know, about twenty-five,
> twenty-six I guess.

6-15-39   (Continued)

F-8 (Cont'd)

> AUNT EMMA
> (Sneeringly)
> Hunh!
> (Then after a pause)
> When I was a girl we thought nine-
> teen was big.

> LEE
> (Astonished)
> Nineteen! How could anybody be
> nineteen?

> AUNT EMMA
> It takes a little pulling but it
> can be done.

F-9 CLOSE SHOT - WILLIE

He gives out an horrendous snore.

F-10 FULL SHOT - THE LIVING ROOM

> SARGENT
> (Scowling around at
> Willie)
> You know, there's a cure for that.

> MRS. SARGENT
> (Anxiously)
> What, dear?

> SARGENT
> An ax.

DISSOLVE TO:

F-11 VERY CLOSE SHOT - LEE

Her hair has been prettily arranged in the style of
1906 but she seems very miserable at the moment.

> LEE
> (Gasping)
> A-a-ah!

> AUNT EMMA'S VOICE
> Let your breath out.

Lee puffs out her cheeks.

> AUNT EMMA
> Go on now.

6-15-39   (Continued)

F-11 (Cont'd)

Lee blows some more.

      AUNT EMMA'S VOICE
  Now: one...two...

F-12 LEE AND AUNT EMMA - IN THE LATTER'S BEDROOM

Lee is in her underclothes and an old-fashioned corset. Aunt Emma holds the laces like a charioteer
and has one foot in the small of Lee's back.

      AUNT EMMA
  THREE!

She pulls Lee down to size nineteen and takes a quic'
hitch on the laces.

      AUNT EMMA
   (With great satis-
    faction)
  There! How does that feel?

Lee points to her stomach and seems to say that it
feels like hell but no sound issues from her moving
lips.

      AUNT EMMA
   (Phi.osophically)
  You'll get used to it...the rest
  of us did.

Lee points to her stomach and speaks desperately but
soundlessly.

      AUNT EMMA
  Oh, fiddlesticks.

She crosses to her bed and takes a layer of brown
paper off a dress box. Lee follows her. The dress
box is now seen to be wrapped in newspaper. A headline says:

  "ROOSEVELT REFUSES THIRD TERM"

Beneath this we see "Teddy" smiling with all his
teeth. Aunt Emma opens the box and lifts out a
beautiful lace wedding dress.

      LEE
   (Startled)
  Oh, but it's beautiful!

6-15-39   (Continued)

F-12   (Cont'd)

> AUNT EMMA
> I thought your voice would come
> back.

> LEE
> But it's too nice to wear to a
> barn dance.

> AUNT EMMA
> You let the others look like
> scarecrows. It never hurts to
> wear the best.

> LEE
> (Looking away
> in embarrassment)
> Was that...was that your wedding
> dress?

> AUNT EMMA
> (Dryly)
> I twiddled around with the idea
> one summer.

> LEE
> (Sympathetically)
> Oh.

> AUNT EMMA
> But I was all right again by fall.

DISSOLVE TO:

F-13   <u>THE BARN DANCE</u>

A surprisingly good orchestra is playing a waltz,
and the floor is crowded with dancers in overalls,
and jack boots and peanut hats and chin-whiskers.

F-14   LEE AND SARGENT DANCING BY

Lee is gorgeous in Aunt Emma's white dress. Sargent
wears a conventional hick outfit.

F-15   MRS. SARGENT AND AUNT EMMA

They wear farm dresses and sunbonnets.

6-15-39   (Continued)

F-15 (Cont'd)

                    AUNT EMMA
                 (Watching Lee)
        Beautiful, isn't she?

                    MRS. SARGENT
                 (Faintly worried)
        Yes.

                    AUNT EMMA
        They'd have awful cute babies.

                    MRS. SARGENT
                 (Almost crossly)
        Jack isn't in love, Emmy. Wherever
        did you get such an idea?

                    AUNT EMMA
        Fiddlesticks !

                    MRS. SARGENT
                 (More and more
                    nervously)
        Well, I tell you they're not.
        I'm not going to tell you why
        or anything, but they..they just
        can't be, that's all. You don't
        know about these things, Emmy,
        and...

                    AUNT EMMA
                 (Coldly)
        If you're referring to the fact
        that I never married, I would
        like to point out that you don't
        have to be a horse to judge a
        horse show. If ever I saw two
        people...

                    MRS. SARGENT
                 (Looking up at
                    the dancers)
        Sh !

F-16   CLOSE SHOT - LEE AND SARGENT DANCING

                    LEE
                 (Wistfully)
        Almost over....

                    SARGENT
        Gone quickly, hasn't it?

6-15-39   (Continued)

F-16   (Cont'd)

               LEE
        So quickly...

F-17   MRS. SARGENT AND AUNT EMMA

              AUNT EMMA
        If that isn't as plain as
        Pike's Peak I'm a...

             MRS. SARGENT
          (Crossly)
        Oh, Fiddlesticks!

F-18   CLOSE SHOT - LEE AND SARGENT DANCING

              LEE
        You've all been so sweet...
        no matter what happens after
        we get back...it won't matter
        so much - I'll have some wonder-
        ful memories.

Sargent looks at her in embarrassment.

F-19   THE LEADER OF THE ORCHESTRA

He has his watch in his hand and seems poised for
flight.   Now he motions the musicians to be quiet.

              THE LEADER
        Ladies and gentlemen, I have
        the honor to wish you all...a
        very........HAPPY NEW YEAR!

He waves frantically to his musicians and they play
deafeningly.

F-20   AN OLD MAN AND HIS WIFE

They embrace fondly.

F-21   A LITTLE BOY AND A LITTLE GIRL ABOUT TWELVE YEARS
        OLD

They kiss shyly.

6-15-39

F-22   WILLIE AND A VERY TALL PARTNER

        She bends slightly for him to kiss her. As this is
        still too high he leaps into her arms.

F-23   MRS. SARGENT AND AUNT EMMA

        With tears in their eyes they peck each other on
        the cheek, then look out across the floor.

F-24   LEE AND SARGENT

        They stand about a foot apart holding each other's
        hands. The din is terrific. Sargent smiles at her
        and forms the words: "Happy New Year." Lee smiles
        and says: "Happy New Year." Now they both stop
        smiling and look at each other anxiously. Sargent
        bends down a little. Lee reaches up a little. Sudde-
        ly he crushes her in his arms and kisses her smacko
        right on the lips. After three seconds we LEAVE
        THEM kissing and CUT AWAY TO:

F-25   MRS. SARGENT AND AUNT EMMA

        They watch goggle-eyed for another three seconds.
        Now Aunt Emma looks at her sister, sees her worried
        expression, slaps her sister on the knee and bursts
        into hilarious laughter.

F-26   LEE AND SARGENT

        They come out of the kiss and look at each other
        strangely.

        DISSOLVE TO:

F-27   THE UPPER HALL OF THE SARGENT HOUSE

                              SARGENT'S, LEE'S
                              AUNT EMMA'S AND
                              MRS. SARGENT'S
                              VOICES TOGETHER:
                    Goodnight, Willie...sleep tight...
                    you can sleep till six-thirty
                    tomorrow...and not a minute
                    longer.

6-15-39   (Continued)

453

F-27   (Cont'd)

> WILLIE'S VOICE
> G-g-goodnight, all. S-s-some fun,
> hunh?

Mrs. Sargent, Aunt Emma, then Lee and Sargent
APPEAR up the stairs.

> AUNT EMMA
> (Beaming)
> Goodnight, children. Sweet dreams.
> I'll have your breakfast by seven-
> fifteen.

She kisses Lee, then Sargent.

> AUNT EMMA
> (To Lee)
> You want flannel cakes or fried
> mush?

> LEE
> I think we'll ride better on
> the mush.

> AUNT EMMA
> All right, and happy New Year.

She pinches Lee's cheek and trots off to her room.

> MRS. SARGENT
> (To Lee)
> Goodnight, dear. Get a good rest.

> LEE
> Thank you. Thank you for everything.
> (She turns to
> Sargent)
> Goodnight, Jack.

> SARGENT
> Goodnight.

Lee goes into her room and closes the door.

> MRS. SARGENT
> (Taking her son in
> her arms)
> Goodnight, dear, and the best
> of all things to you for the
> New Year.

6-15-39   (Continued)

F-27   (Cont'd)

    They kiss fondly and she departs for her room
leaving Sargent in front of Lee's door. As we
hear Mrs. Sargent's door close, Sargent taps lightly
on Lee's door. After a second Lee appears.

                    SARGENT
      You sleepy?

                    LEE
      Not very.

                    SARGENT
          (Huskily)
      You want to come in and have a
      goodnight cigarette?

                    LEE
      Well...
          (Now she makes up
          her mind)
      I'll be in in a minute.

    She closes the door slowly. Sargent starts cheer-
fully for his room.

F-28   MRS. SARGENT'S ROOM

    She stands by her desk drumming her fingers nervous-
ly. After a moment she turns and goes out into the
hall.

F-29   LEE - IN HER ROOM

    Actually we see her reflection in the mirror as
she touches up her makeup. She wears an attractive
wrapper. There is a light knock at the door.
Lipstick in hand Lee looks at the door nervously.

                    LEE
      Come in.

F-30   THE DOORWAY

    Mrs. Sargent comes in and smiles apologetically.

                  MRS. SARGENT
      I'm sorry to disturb you, dear,
      but you'll be in such a rush
      tomorrow morning.

6-15-39

F-31   LEE - PAST MRS. SARGENT

She looks quite puzzled.

                         LEE
              Of course you're not disturbing me.

F-32   MRS. SARGENT - AT THE DOOR

                         MRS. SARGENT
                           (Sweetly)
              Thank you.

She closes the door after her and comes forward.
The CAMERA TRUCKS AHEAD OF HER AND STOPS WHEN
LEE IS IN THE SHOT.

                         MRS. SARGENT
              First of all I want you to know
              how glad we are to have had you
              here...and how much I hope you've
              enjoyed your stay.

                         LEE
              You'll never know how much.

                         MRS. SARGENT
                           (Nervously)
              And then...I want you to know how
              sorry I am that you're in trouble
              ...and how much I hope it will come
              out all right.

                         LEE
                           (Looking away)
              I didn't know you knew about that.

                         MRS. SARGENT
                           (Taking her hand)
              You poor child...you can be sure
              I never would have mentioned it
              now ... only ... only ... has
              Jack ever told you anything about
              his childhood?

                         LEE
              No...why?

Absentmindedly she lights a cigarette.

6-15-39   (Continued)

F-32   (Cont'd)

                    MRS. SARGENT
We were very poor after my
husband died...in fact we had
nothing. Jack had to do the
chores before school and after
school, then when he went to
high school, he drove a delivery
truck in the afternoon to earn
a little money, and then after
the chores, he studied in the
evenings to try to get into
college, and then he had to work
his way through college and through
law school -- I don't mean there's
anything unusual about it..
thousands of boys in the United
States are doing the same thing
right this minute, I'M only trying
to tell you that he worked very
hard to get where he is...very,
very hard and...and nothing should
be allowed to spoil it for him.

                    LEE
I see - I don't see why anything
should spoil it for him, do you?

                    MRS. SARGENT
He's in love with you.

                    LEE
Oh, but he isn't in love with me!
He's never had any more interest
in me than...than some panhandler
you buy a meal for.

                    MRS. SARGENT
Are you sure?

                    LEE
Of course I'm sure.

                    MRS. SARGENT
He kissed you tonight.

                    LEE
     (Shrugging)
Well, I'm not ugly.
     (Then after giving .
     it some thought)
Oh, he might have a little lech
for me, you wouldn't know what

F-32 (Cont'd)

> LEE (Continued)
> that means, but it isn't going
> any further....and it hasn't been
> any place, either.
> (After a pause)
> He's no fool, and even if he was
> I wouldn't hurt him...or you...
> or Aunt Emmy...or even Willie.

Mrs. Sargent reaches up and kisses her. Lee pats
her on the back. Now Mrs. Sargent crosses to the
door and opens it.

> MRS. SARGENT
> (Looking back)
> But you love him, don't you?

F-33   LEE - PAST MRS. SARGENT

> LEE
> (After nodding "yes")
> I'm afraid so.

Mrs. Sargent looks at her for a moment, then closes
the door and starts for her room.

DISSOLVE TO:

F-34   SARGENT - IN HIS ROOM

He paces up and down, smoking. Suddenly he stops
and looks down at the floor in front of his door.
He starts for it

F-35   CLOSE SHOT - A FOLDED PAPER STUCK UNDER THE DOOR

Sargent's hand comes INTO THE SHOT and picks it up.

F-36   SARGENT

He completes the movement of straightening up,
then reads the paper.

F-37   THE PAPER IN SARGENT'S HANDS

In a large erratic handwriting we read:

6-15-39   (Continued)

F-37 (Cont'd)

            "Too sleepy

             Goodnight

               -- Lee."

F-38   SARGENT - LOOKING AT THE NOTE

          He crumples it and throws it in the fir.

F-39   LEE - IN HER BEDROOM

          She is lounging disgustedly on the top of her
          bed, smoking. As she happens to look up her
          eyes fix on cross-eyed Grandpa.

F-40   CROSS-EYED GRANDPA ON THE WALL

          He looks down at us sternly.

F-41   LEE - ON THE BED

          She gives the cross-eyed grandpa a long disapproving
          look, then sticks her tongue out at him.

          FADE OUT:

                  END OF SEQUENCE "F"

6-15-39

G-1   SARGENT'S CAR IN FRONT OF THE HOUSE - MORNING

        It is pointing in the direction from which it arrived
        last week. Willie appears in his Tyrolian hat, carry-
        ing suitcases. Behind him come the others.

G-2   CLOSE TRUCKING SHOT - AHEAD OF THE FOUR

                            MRS. SARGENT
                        (To Lee)
                    Goodbye, dear, goodbye, and
                    remember there's always a room
                    upstairs for you...and my sister
                    and I... and Willie... will be only
                    too happy to have you... that is
                    if everything turns out all right...
                    I mean, of course it will.

                            LEE
                        (Gently)
                    I know it will.

                            AUNT EMMA
                        (As Lee and Sargent get
                         into the car)
                    And don't drive too fast. If you
                    get tired just pull into a field
                    some place and go to sleep.

                            SARGENT
                    No thanks - that's why we're going
                    back through Canada.

                            AUNT EMMA
                    Whatever are you talking about?

                            SARGENT
                    Well... I held up a cow... she burned
                    down a Pennsylvania courthouse -- all
                    in fun, of course, so... we're going
                    back through Canada.

                            MRS. SARGENT
                        (Laughing)
                    You big dunce.
                        (She kisses her son)
                    Goodbye, dear. Goodbye, Lee.

                            SARGENT
                    Goodbye, Aunt Emma.

6-15-39   (Continued)

G-2 (Cont'd)

                               LEE
                  Goodbye, Aunt Emma.

                          SARGENT
                  Goodbye, Willie.

                              LEE
                  Goodbye, Willie... and thank you
                  all for everything... I'll never
                  forget it.

The car starts out.

                          MRS. SARGENT
                    (Calling)
                  Are you going through Scranton
                  or Pittsburgh?

                          SARGENT
                    (Calling back)
                  Canada.

The car pulls OUT OF THE SHOT, leaving Mrs. Sargent,
Aunt Emma and Willie by the roadside.

                          WILLIE
                    (Calling after the car)
                  D-don't forget to write.

                        AUNT EMMA
                    (Sharply)
                  And don't you forget to chop
                  some wood. Christmas is over.

                          WILLIE
                    (Sadly)
                  Ain't it the truth.

He sighs and follows Aunt Emma toward the house.
Mrs. Sargent sniffs into a handkerchief.

DISSOLVE TO:

G-3   THE OFFICIAL BORDER AT WINDSOR, CANADA - DAY

        There is a queue of United States cars passing
        through slowly.

G-4   SARGENT'S CAR AT THE HEAD OF THE LINE

        A very pleasant official stands at the window. We
        see the car from the rear.

6-15-39   (Continued)

G-4 (Cont'd)

                           SARGENT
              Just passing through.

                           THE OFFICIAL
              Any cigarettes, cigars, uncut gems
              or spiritous liquors to declare?

                           SARGENT
              I've got four Chinamen and a bale
              of opium in the rumble seat but
              that's all.

                           THE OFFICIAL
                    (Trying not to laugh)
              And what is your reason for going
              through Canada, sir?

                           SARGENT
              I'm a fugitive from justice.

                           LEE
              You sound like a fugitive from
              a nut house.

                           THE OFFICIAL
                    (Laughing)
              Go ahead, sir, go ahead.

The car draws away and the official looks after it,
chuckling.

G-5   INT. OF THE CAR - FACING LEE AND SARGENT

         Sargent thinks for a moment then looks at her
         quizzically.

                           SARGENT
              You know something?

                           LEE
              What?

                           SARGENT
              You're in Canada now.

                           LEE
              What about it?

                           SARGENT
                    (Looking around at her)
              If you didn't want to go back
              tomorrow I couldn't make you.

6-15-39   (Continued)

G-5 (Cont'd)

>   LEE
>   (Pointing ahead)
>   Watch where you're driving.

>   SARGENT
>   (After a moment)
>   Did you hear what I said?

>   LEE
>   I heard you.

Sargent shrugs. Then after a pause --

>   SARGENT
>   Why didn't you come in last
>   night for that cigarette?

>   LEE
>   I didn't feel like smoking.

Sargent gives her a quick look, then watches the road
ahead.

>   LEE
>   (After a pause)
>   I hope you don't bust out laugh-
>   ing when you look at me in court.

>   SARGENT
>   I won't feel much like laughing.

>   LEE
>   (After looking at him
>   quickly)
>   It's funny that of all the people
>   in that courtroom you were the only
>   one who had a heart...you'd think
>   you'd be the last one.

>   SARGENT
>   Don't give me any credit. I played
>   you a fairly dirty trick and I guess
>   I felt bad about it. That's all.

>   LEE
>   (Puzzled and interested)
>   How did you play me a dirty trick?

>   SARGENT
>   (Almost harshly)
>   In having your case put over till
>   after the holidays...when I saw the
>   jury was going to acquit you for
>   Christmas.

6-15-39   (Continued)

G-5 (Cont'd)
                              LEE
                         (Mildly)
                    Why you dirty so-and-so!
                         (Then with admiration)
                    That was pretty smart of you all
                    right.

                              SARGENT
                    It's part of the business.

                              LEE
                         (Beginning to
                          understand)
                    Then when that fat slob got me
                    out if was because your conscience
                    was biting you.

                              SARGENT
                    A little.

                              LEE
                         (Ruefully)
                    And all the time I thought it
                    was my legs.
                         (She chuckles, then
                          speaks seriously again)
                    I didn't even know you were
                    against me...oh, I knew you were
                    supposed to be trying to put me
                    in jail, but you were so gentle...

                              SARGENT
                         (Dryly)
                    That's part of the technique. If
                    you don't treat a woman with kid
                    gloves every man on the jury wants
                    to punch you in the nose, you have
                    to handle them with kid gloves too
                    or you get it right in the verdict.
                    It's very hard to put a woman in
                    jail...no matter what she's done.
                         (Then after a pause)
                    I'm a kind of a specialist at it.

                              LEE
                         (Quickly)
                    Oh, no you're not.

                              SARGENT
                         (Harshly)
                    Sure I am.

6-15-39   (Continued)

464

G-5 (Cont'd)

> LEE
> (Almost pleadingly)
> You're just trying to make me hate
> you so you won't feel so bad...when
> you give me the business. Aren't
> you?

Sargent doesn't answer.

> LEE
> (Pleadingly)
> You are, aren't you?

Sargent looks ahead.

DISSOLVE TO:

G-6   FROZEN NIAGARA FALLS AT NIGHT

It is brilliantly lit and very spectacular.

G-7   LEE AND SARGENT - ON THE EDGE OF THE GORGE

They walk slowly looking at the wonders below. Lee
shivers and Sargent puts his arm around her.

> SARGENT
> (Continuing a conversation)
> I mean it.

> LEE
> I wish you'd stop talking nonsense.

> SARGENT
> It isn't nonsense. I'm not a police-
> man. It isn't any of my business
> whether you go back or not.

> LEE
> (After a pause)
> Anyway, I haven't got any money.

> SARGENT
> You wouldn't have to worry about
> that.

> LEE
> And I can just see the phizz on
> your fat friend if he had to shell
> out that five grand.

6-15-39   (Continued)

G-7 (Cont'd)

                         SARGENT
           You don't have to worry about
           that either.

                         LEE
           I can worry about it if I want to.

Sargent continues to look down at the spectacle below.

                         LEE
           A fine District Attorney you are!

                         SARGENT
                       (Looking at her)
           You know I love you, don't you?

                         LEE
                       (Quietly)
           Don't say that.

                         SARGENT
                       (Almost roughly)
           Why shouldn't I say it? Because
           some chiseling jeweler claims you
           swiped one of his bracelets?

                         LEE
           I did swipe it.

                         SARGENT
           The jury will tell you whether
           you took it or not...and he's
           got it back, hasn't he? Anyway,
           what you did yesterday and what
           you do today are two different
           things. All the State wants you
           to do is to lay off other people's
           property...it doesn't care how
           that condition is arrived at.
           Once you were with me you
           wouldn't pull any of that stuff.

                         LEE
           I might.

                         SARGENT
           And get your ears slapped down.

He pulls her close to him.

                         LEE
           Please...

G-7 (Cont'd)

                    SARGENT
You love me, don't you?

                    LEE
No.

                    SARGENT
                 (Passionately)
I suppose that's why you've
looked at me the way you have,
and danced with me the way you
did and kissed me the way you
did, and your hand has always
found mine and mine has always
found yours when they were any-
where near each other.

                    LEE
                 (Pleadingly)
Don't be a sucker. Naturally,
you're a good-looking man...
and I'm human. But everything
you said about the State not
caring, or staying here, or how
I'd be when we were together is
the bunk, Jack. You've got to
remember how hard you worked to
get where you are...how you drove
a truck after school, and did
the chores, and...

                    SARGENT
My mother's been talking to you.

                    LEE
Why shouldn't she? She's got
something to be proud of! And
you've got to be proud and think
about it too instead of telling
people to jump bail and...and
falling for the first pretty pair
of eyes that...

Sargent cuts this off with a kiss.

                    LEE
              (A little breathlessly)
You know perfectly well that
what I'm saying...

Sargent kisses her again.

6-15-39   (Continued)

G-7 (Cont'd)

> LEE
> Don't be unfair.

> SARGENT
> I love you.

This time she reaches up and kisses him, then speaks
against his cheek.

> LEE
> It'll be awful hard to lose you.

> SARGENT
> You know what I wish?

> LEE
> What?

> SARGENT
> I wish the case was over...and
> you'd been acquitted...

> LEE
> Then you shouldn't have had it
> postponed.

> SARGENT
> That's true, but if I hadn't I
> wouldn't have met you.

> LEE
> That's true.

> SARGENT
> So the case is over and you've
> been acquitted....

> LEE
> Knock wood.

> SARGENT
> ...and I pull out a marriage
> license...

> LEE
> (Dreamily)
> Oh, gee.

> SARGENT
> ...and we march right into the
> judge's chambers and have him
> marry us.

6-15-39   (Continued)

G-7 (Cont'd)

                    LEE
        I can see his mug from here.

                    SARGENT
        Wouldn't that be something?

                    LEE
        It would be a novelty.

                    SARGENT
        And then we go down and hop
        into our car...

                    LEE
        You know you're talking like a
        four-year-old, don't you?

                    SARGENT
        ...and fill 'er up with gas...

                    LEE
        Opium would be better.

                    SARGENT
        ...and you know where we're
        going for our honeymoon?

                    LEE
            (As to a child)
        Where, stoopid?

                    SARGENT
            (Triumphantly)
        Niagara Falls!

Lee looks at him adoringly before speaking.

                    LEE
        But we're there now, darling...

He takes her in his arms.

FADE OUT:

                END OF SEQUENCE "G"

6-15-39

SEQUENCE "H"

FADE IN:

H-1 LEE <u>IN A WAITING TAXICAB</u> - DAY

The motor is running and we see a BACKGROUND of downtown New York. Now she looks up quickly as Sargent jumps into the car and calls to the driver.

    SARGENT
Criminal courts building.

The taxi pulls away.

    LEE
What did you stop for?

Sargent grins at her like a kid, then pulls a document out of his pocket and shows it to her. Lee looks distressed.

H-2 CLOSE SHOT - A MARRIAGE LICENSE

For the sum of two dollars John Wesley Sargent is permitted to espouse Anna Rose Malone.

H-3 SARGENT AND LEE <u>IN THE TAXICAB</u>

    LEE
   (Dismayed)
But you're crazy! Give me that!

She makes a grab for it but Sargent snatches it away and puts it back in his pocket.

    LEE
   (Desperately)
I tell you you're crazy, Jack...

    SARGENT
   (Interrupting)
I thought that was all settled.

    LEE
   (Irritatedly)
That was in Niagara Falls!
People aren't responsible for
what they say in Niagara Falls.
   (After a short pause)
This is New York...and this is
today...and this is different!

H-3 (Cont'd)

       SARGENT
      (Gaily)
   As my Mother would say: fiddlesticks.

       LEE
      (Almost angrily)
   Well it isn't fiddlesticks! In
   the first place there's no reason
   why they should acquit me, but even
   if they did I wouldn't marry you...
   so you might as well tear that
   thing up.

       SARGENT
      (In mock anguish)
   Don't you love me any more, dear?

Lee looks away and speaks with trembling lips.

       LEE
   I never loved you.

       SARGENT
      (Mockingly)
   Were you just toying with me?

       LEE
      (Violently)
   Oh, shut up!

       SARGENT
      (Gaily)
   You will have to develop more
   courtesy and respect for your
   husband or I shall fall back on
   strong measures. A woman, a dog
   and a hickory tree, the better
   ye beat them, the better they be.

       LEE
      (Miserably)
   Aw quit it, will you?

       SARGENT
      (Gently)
   Suppose you begin.

       LEE
   I can't argue with you...imagine
   being married to a man who argues
   for a living. You know it isn't
   right. Can't you see the papers?
   "District attorney marries girl
   crook"? I'd only hurt you, Jack.

6-15-39   (Continued)

H-3 (Cont'd)

> LEE (Cont'd)
> Don't you remember how the judge
> acted when he saw us in that place?

> SARGENT
> But you won't be a crook! You'll
> be acquitted!

> LEE
> (Quickly)
> How do you know?

> SARGENT
> (With an uneasy eye)
> I don't know... but I think
> you've got a good chance.

> LEE
> (Looking at him
> suspiciously)
> You wouldn't do anything to make
> them acquit me, would you?

> SARGENT
> (Uneasily)
> What could I do?

> LEE
> (Almost indignantly)
> That would be a fine thing!

After a moment Sargent leans forward and speaks to
the driver.

> SARGENT
> Stop at the next corner a moment.
> (Then to Lee)
> We'd better not go in together...
> there's no use pushing things too
> far.

Now he puts his arm around her.

> SARGENT
> Good luck.

> LEE
> (Worried)
> Thanks.

> SARGENT
> Don't be unhappy.

6-15-39   (Continued)

H-3 (Cont'd)

>   LEE
> I'm not unhappy...I'm all balled up.

>   SARGENT
>   (Holding her gently)
> Everything's going to come out
> all right.

>   LEE
> It's got to come out all right.

The taxi stops. Sargent tries to kiss her. Lee turns
her head away, takes the kiss on the cheek and hurries
out of the cab. Sargent smiles after her, then speaks
to the driver.

>   SARGENT
> Stop in the middle of the block.

H-4   THE JUDGE IN HIS CHAMBERS

He is adjusting his gown while talking to someone
OUTSIDE THE SHOT.

>   THE JUDGE
>   (Angrily)
> I tell you I did see them...
> dancing in a cafe..., two hours
> after he was prosecuting her in
> this very courtroom.

H-5   THE DISTRICT ATTORNEY - PAST THE JUDGE

>   DISTRICT ATTORNEY
>   (Angrily)
> And I tell you you're mistaken.
> That boy is dead on the level and
> if he weren't quite as honest as
> he is I'd say he had a big future
> in politics.

>   THE JUDGE
>   (Quiveringly)
> I tell you I stood as close to him...

>   DISTRICT ATTORNEY
>   (Interrupting him)
> You forget that you're an old man!
> Your eyes aren't...

6-15-39   (Continued)

H-5 (Cont'd)

> THE JUDGE
> (Triumphantly)
> I happened to speak to him and
> he answered me!

> DISTRICT ATTORNEY
> (Gratingly)
> Anybody would answer you, that's
> only common politeness.

> THE JUDGE
> I called him Jack.

> DISTRICT ATTORNEY
> There are millions of people
> called Jack. You haven't got a
> leg to stand on. You're trying
> to make a case out against this
> boy...

There is a perfunctory rap on the door and a court
attendant comes in.

> BRIAN
> All ready, Your Honor.

> THE JUDGE
> Be right in.

> BRIAN
> Yes, sir.

He goes out, leaving the door open.

> DISTRICT ATTORNEY
> So now I suppose you think he's
> going to throw the case.

> THE JUDGE
> (Piously)
> Those are your words, Henry, not
> mine.

> DISTRICT ATTORNEY
> Well I tell you he wouldn't throw
> a case if he were trying his own
> brother.

> THE JUDGE
> (Gently)
> Not if he knew you were in the
> room he wouldn't.

H-5 (Cont'd)

                    DISTRICT ATTORNEY
          Then I'll listen from here.

                    THE JUDGE
               (Gently)
          That's all I wanted, Henry.
          That, and your apology later.

                    DISTRICT ATTORNEY
          You'll get that in a pig's eye.

The Judge smiles sweetly and steps through the doorway.
Immediately we hear:

                    A VOICE
          Hear ye, hear ye, hear ye!
          All ye who have business draw
          near, give attention and ye
          shall be heard.

The District Attorney scowls toward the door and takes
out a cigar.

                    THE JUDGE'S VOICE
          The People versus Malone.
          Stipulate the jurors are all
          present and the defendant is
          in court?

                    O'LEARY'S VOICE
          So stipulated.

                    SARGENT'S VOICE
          So stipulated.

                    JUDGE'S VOICE
          The record may so show. You may
          resume.

The District Attorney bites off the end of his cigar,
spits it onto the floor, lights the cigar and flops
into a chair.

DISSOLVE TO:

H-6   LEE ON THE WITNESS STAND - PAST O'LEARY

                    O'LEARY
          You heard Dr. Keinmetz define
          the condition known as "hypno-
          leptic catalepsis?"

6-15-39   (Continued)

475

H-6 (Cont'd)

> LEE
> Yes, sir.

> O'LEARY
> Would you say that was the condition
> you were in?

> LEE
> I guess so. Yes, sir.

> O'LEARY
> That is all.

Lee looks around vaguely, then starts getting off
the witness stand.

H-7   SARGENT RISING

He seems in a faintly bad humor.

> SARGENT
> Just a moment, Miss Leander.

H-8   LEE - PAST SARGENT

She gets back into the witness chair slowly.

H-9   SARGENT - PAST LEE

> SARGENT
> Now, young lady...

Suddenly he turns and frowns toward the jury.

H-10   CLOSE SHOT - A FAT LADY IN THE JURY LEANING TOWARD
A THIN LADY NEXT TO HER

> FAT LADY
> (Acidly)
> They think because they're
> young and cross their legs
> they can get away with anything.

> THIN LADY
> She was about as hypnotized as
> I am.

6-15-39

H-11   SARGENT - PAST LEE

He looks from the talking jurors back to the judge.

> SARGENT
> If your Honor would instruct the
> jurors to listen to the testimony
> rather than mumble amongst them-
> selves...

H-12   THE JUDGE

He looks at Sargent stonily, then raps once with
his gavel.

> THE JUDGE
> The jurors will cease whispering
> and give their entire attention
> to the case at hand. Proceed,

H-13   THE FAT WOMAN AND THE THIN WOMAN

The fat lady is talking indignantly to a male juror.

> FAT LADY
> Why I never missed a word that
> was said! What's the matter
> with that fresh gink?

H-14   SARGENT - PAST LEE

He looks back at the talking fat lady then up
at the Judge.

> SARGENT
> Your Honor...

We hear a smack of the gavel.

> JUDGE'S VOICE
> Proceed with the case.

> SARGENT
> (To the Judge)
> You can't hear yourself think.
> (Now he turns and
> scowls at Lee)
> You said that you were hypnotized
> at the time you left the jewelry
> store and walked up Fifth Avenue?

6-15-39   (Continued)

H-14   (Cont'd)

>   As there is no answer, he raises his voice slightly.

>   SARGENT
>   Didn't you?

H-15   LEE - ON THE WITNESS STAND - PAST SARGENT

>   LEE
>   Well...

>   She looks at him miserably.

>   SARGENT
>   (Roughly)
>   Did you or didn't you?

>   LEE
>   Well, my lawyer said so.

H-16   SARGENT AND O'LEARY - PAST LEE

>   SARGENT
>   (Triumphantly)
>   Oh!

>   He gives the jury a knowing look then speaks quickly.

>   SARGENT
>   Are we to understand then that
>   you and your lawyer do not agree
>   exactly as to what happened?

>   O'LEARY
>   (Leaping to his feet)
>   Don't answer that question!
>   Object, Your Honor. The question
>   is entirely improper, irrelevant
>   and immaterial and I ask that it
>   be stricken from the record.

H-17   CLOSE SHOT - THE JUDGE

>   THE JUDGE
>   Sustained. The jury will dis-
>   regard the question.

H-18   TWO MALE JURORS

>   FIRST JUROR
>   That's easier to say than to do.

6-15-39   (Continued)

H-18   (Cont'd)   SECOND JUROR
                              Why did he ask it if it was
                              irrevelant?

H-19   LEE AND SARGENT - PAST THE JUDGE

                                   SARGENT
                              (Pointing to the
                               talking jurors)
                         Your Honor, those jurors are...

                                  THE JUDGE
                              (Pounding his gavel)
                         Proceed with the case.

H-20   TWO SHOT - SARGENT AND LEE

                                   SARGENT
                              (Roughly)
                         Were you hypnotized or weren't you?

                                    LEE
                         Well, I suppose...

                                   SARGENT
                              (Still rougher)
                         We don't want your suppositions,
                         we want to know whether you were
                         hypnotized or not.

H-21   THE DISTRICT ATTORNEY - IN THE JUDGE'S CHAMBERS

         Through the half-open door he is listening to the
         case with astonishment and dawning suspicion.

                                  LEE'S VOICE
                         Yes.
                                 SARGENT'S VOICE
                         Yes what?

                                  LEE'S VOICE
                         I guess I was hypnotized.

                                SARGENT'S VOICE
                              (Sarcastically)
                         You"guess" you were hypnotized!
                         First you "suppose" you were
                         hypnotized, now you "guess" you
                         were. Kindly remember you're
                         under oath! Do you know the
                         penalty for perjury?
6-15-39   (Continued)

H-21   (Cont'd)

                    O'LEARY'S VOICE
Object, Your Honor.

                    JUDGE'S VOICE
Sustained.

                    DISTRICT ATTORNEY
              (In a low voice)
Not so rough, Jack! How many times
have I told you when you're working
with a woman...

Now he scowls and clamps his mouth shut.

                    SARGENT'S VOICE
              (Roughly)
Well, which is it? A guess or a
supposition?

H-22   TWO MORE MEMBERS OF THE JURY

                    THIRD JUROR
              (Scowling)
What's he getting so tough about?

                    FOURTH JUROR
He's just naturally mean.

                    THIRD JUROR
I sat on a murder case and they
didn't get that rough.

H-23   SARGENT, LEE, O'LEARY AND THE JUDGE

                    SARGENT
Your Honor, those jurors are gab-
bing again.

As the Judge looks at the jury --

H-24   THE THIRD JUROR

Between clenched teeth he mutters soundlessly: "How
sorry you'll be."

H-25   LEE - PAST SARGENT

                    SARGENT
Miss Leander, will you kindly tell
us how it feels to be hypnotized?

6-15-39   (Continued)

H-25   (Cont'd)

>   O'LEARY'S VOICE
>   Object, Your Honor.
>
>   JUDGE'S VOICE
>   Sustained.
>
>   SARGENT
>   How old were you when you began
>   to steal things?
>
>   O'LEARY'S VOICE
>   Object.
>
>   JUDGE'S VOICE
>   Sustained.

During the above scene Lee has started looking at
Sargent in puzzlement.

H-26   THE THIRD, FOURTH AND FIFTH JURORS

>   FOURTH JUROR
>   What's that got to do with this?
>
>   FIFTH JUROR
>   He's just trying to get her in
>   wrong.

H-27   SARGENT AND LEE - PAST THE JUDGE

>   SARGENT
>   (Indicating them)
>   Your Honor, those jurors are at
>   it again.

H-28   THE JUDGE - PAST LEE AND SARGENT

>   THE JUDGE
>   (After pounding his
>   gavel)
>   Mr. Sargent, I'm perfectly capable
>   of running this courtroom without
>   promptings from counsel.
>   (He bangs his gavel)
>   If there's any more whispering
>   amongst the jurors I'll hold the
>   offenders in contempt.
>   (He bangs his gavel
>   again)
>   Now proceed with this case.

6-15-39   (Continued)

H-28   (Cont'd)

> SARGENT
> How many times have you been hypno-
> tized by beautiful jewelry?

The CAMERA STARTS TO MOVE SLOWLY IN ON LEE whose
expression is very peculiar.

> O'LEARY'S VOICE
> Object.

> LEE
> (In a strange voice)
> I guess quite a lot of times.

> O'LEARY'S VOICE
> Please don't answer questions after
> I've objected to them.

Lee frowns faintly as she searches her memory. THE
SHOT IS NOW FAIRLY CLOSE OF HER.

> JUDGE'S VOICE
> Objection sustained. The jury will
> disregard the question and the an-
> swer.

> SARGENT'S VOICE
> Did you hear Dr. Keinmetz' opinion
> about hypnotism?

Lee seems lost in thought.

> SARGENT'S VOICE
> (Very roughly)
> Will you answer my questions and
> not keep us here all day?

Suddenly Lee remembers. Her expression changes and
OVER THE CLOSEUP APPEARS A SUPERIMPOSED SHOT OF LEE
AND SARGENT DRIVING IN CANADA.

> SARGENT (SUPERIMPOSED)
> If you don't treat a woman with kid
> gloves every man on the jury wants
> to punch you in the nose...

> SARGENT'S VOICE
> (Roughly)
> Will you answer my question?

> SARGENT (SUPERIMPOSED)
> ...you get it right in the verdict.
> It's very hard to put a woman in
> jail.

6-15-39   (Continued)

H-28   (Cont'd)

Lee, that is the Lee IN THE CLOSEUP, shakes her head
and mutters:

> LEE
> Oh, no.

H-29   SARGENT AND LEE - PAST THE JUDGE

He turns helplessly to the Judge.

> SARGENT
> Your honor, if the witness refuses
> to answer my questions there's noth-
> ing more I can do.

H-30   TWO MORE JURORS

In the background we hear the judge speaking severely
to Lee.

> SIXTH JUROR
> Now he's getting her in wrong with
> the Judge.

> SEVENTH JUROR
> I'd like to punch that guy right on
> the schnozzola.

H-31   THE FAT LADY AND THE THIN LADY

> FAT LADY
> Look, she's crying.

Her chins tremble.

> THIN LADY
> The poor thing.

She reaches for her handkerchief.

H-32   LEE - PAST SARGENT

Her eyes are full of tears and she watches Sargent
almost ecstatically.

> SARGENT
> Did Mr. Keinmetz sound as if he
> knew what he was talking about?

> LEE
> (Quickly)
> Yes, sir.

6-15-39   (Continued)

H-32 (Cont'd)

                    O'LEARY
               (Hurrying INTO THE
               SHOT)
          Please don't answer so quickly!
          Give me time to object!

He turns to the Judge.

H-33 THE JUDGE

                    THE JUDGE
          The question has already been
          answered. Proceed.

H-34 CLOSE SHOT OF LEE - PAST SARGENT

                    SARGENT
               (Sarcastically)
          When you said "yes" just now you
          meant "no," didn't you?

                    LEE
               (Smiling faintly
                through her tears)
          No. I meant "yes."

OVER THIS SHOT DISSOLVES IN A SUPERIMPOSED SHOT OF
LEE AND MRS. SARGENT IN THE BEDROOM

                    SARGENT
               (Mimicking her)
          No you meant yes or yes you meant
          no! Which was it?

                    LEE
          Well, I think...

Her lips tremble.

                    LEE (SUPERIMPOSED)
          He's no fool, and even if he was
          I wouldn't hurt him...or you...or
          Aunt Emmy...or even Willie.

                    SARGENT
               (Loudly)
          Don't tell us what you think...tell
          us which it was.

                    MRS. SARGENT (SUPERIMPOSED)
          But you do love him, don't you?

                    LEE (SUPERIMPOSED)
          I'm afraid so.

6-15-39   (Continued)

H-34 (Cont'd)

The SUPERIMPOSED SHOT FADES.

>   SARGENT
>   (Roughly)
>   Come on, which was it?

Lee tries to talk but can't.

>   SARGENT
>   (Sneering as he
>   offers her his
>   handkerchief)
>   Can I lend you my handkerchief?

Lee tries to smile at him and turns slowly toward
the judge.

>   LEE
>   (In a small voice)
>   Your Honor...

H-35   SARGENT AND THE JUDGE - PAST LEE

>   SARGENT
>   (Faintly worried)
>   Kindly address your answers to
>   me...over here.

H-36   CLOSE SHOT - LEE - LOOKING UP AT THE JUDGE

>   LEE
>   Your Honor, I want to plead
>   guilt....

H-37   SARGENT, O'LEARY AND THE JUDGE - PAST LEE

>   SARGENT
>   (Interrupting loudly)
>   Your Honor, I don't believe
>   this young woman is well. I
>   believe a five-minute recess...

H-38   CLOSE SHOT - LEE - LOOKING UP AT THE JUDGE

As she speaks Sargent tries to drown her out in
the background which forces Lee to raise her voice
a little.

>   (Continued)

6/15/39

H-38 (Cont'd)

>   LEE
> I want to plead guilty.
>
>   SARGENT'S VOICE
>   (Simultaneously)
> ...would be sufficient for her
> to recover. I am undoubtedly
> responsible for having made her...
>
>   LEE
>   (Doggedly)
> I want to plead guilty.

H-39   SARGENT, O'LEARY AND THE JUDGE - PAST LEE

>   O'LEARY
> Your Honor, it is perfectly
> apparent that this young woman
> has been made hysterical by...
>
>   SARGENT
>   (Simultaneously)
> Just a few minutes' recess. She's
> quite obviously in the throes of
> an emotion during which she is not
> responsible for what she says.

H-40   LEE AND THE JUDGE - PAST SARGENT AND O'LEARY

Lee reaches out and puts her hand on Sargent's
shoulder.

>   LEE
>   (Gently)
> I'm all right... I just want to
> plead guilty.
>
>   SARGENT
>   (Furiously)
> IF YOUR HONOR WOULD KINDLY GRANT
> A FIVE MINUTE RECESS!

Lee looks back at the Judge. He pounds his gavel
for silence.

>   THE JUDGE
>   (Almost gently)
> Why do you wish to plead guilty,
> my dear?

                                        (Continued)

6/15/39

H-40 (Cont'd)

> LEE
> (Very simply)
> Because I am guilty...
> (She looks away as
> if remembering
> something)
> ...and when you make a mistake
> you've got to pay for it...
> otherwise you never learn.

The Judge looks from Lee to Sargent and O'Leary.

H-41   LEE, SARGENT AND O'LEARY - PAST THE JUDGE

> O'LEARY
> (Desperately)
> It must be perfectly clear to
> Your Honor that this is not
> normal behavior.

> SARGENT
> (To O'Leary)
> Perfectly clear.
> (He turns to the
> Judge)
> And the State has no wish to
> take advantage of a temporary
> aberration...
> (He looks furiously
> at Lee)
> ...a..a stupid...

Lee puts a hand on his shoulder.

> LEE
> (Serenely)
> There isn't anything temporary
> about this.
> (She looks back up
> at the Judge)
> You can see that I'm in my right
> mind, can't you?

H-42   THE JUDGE - PAST SARGENT AND LEE

> THE JUDGE
> (After a pause)
> In that case there is nothing
> more to be said.

(Continued)

6/15/39

H-42 (Cont'd)

> He clears his throat, then continues in a more
> business-like tone.

> > THE JUDGE
> > The Court at this time will
> > fix next Friday, January sixth,
> > at ten a.m. as time for passing
> > sentence. The prisoner is
> > remanded to the custody of the
> > sheriff.
> > > (He bangs the gavel)
> > The jury is dismissed!

H-43   LEE AND SARGENT - PAST THE JUDGE

> > LEE
> > (Gently)
> > Thank you, Your Honor.

> She looks into Sargent's eyes for a second, then
> turns away from him toward the Sheriff who is
> approaching.

H-44   THE DISTRICT ATTORNEY - <u>IN THE JUDGE'S CHAMBERS</u>

> He looks completely mystified. The Judge comes
> in slowly. Now the District Attorney scowls and
> looks at him accusingly.

> > THE DISTRICT ATTORNEY
> > (Raspingly)
> > Well?

> In answer the Judge throws his arms wide, then
> lets them fall to his side, then scratches his head.

DISSOLVE TO:

H-45   <u>THE ANTE-ROOM OF THE SHERIFF'S OFFICE</u>

> Lee is looking out the window, away from us. We
> hear a door open.. Lee turns guiltily and looks
> PAST THE CAMERA. Now she lowers her eyes and looks
> away again as Sargent GOES PAST THE CAMERA and
> stops near her.

> > SARGENT
> > (Hoarsely)
> > Are you crazy?

> > > > (Continued)

6/15/39

H-45 (Cont'd)

Lee shrugs.

> SARGENT
> Do you know what you've done?

Lee neither replies nor nods.

> SARGENT
> Do you know it can't be undone?

Lee does not move.

> SARGENT
> (Roughly)
> You understand there's no appeal..
> no retrial...no mistrial...nothing
> but jail.

> LEE
> How long will I get?

> SARGENT
> How do I know? Maybe not very
> long, but if you'd kept your
> trap shut you wouldn't have had
> to go at all.

> LEE
> There wasn't anything else to do..
> you're so strong and you argue so
> well....and I love you so much.

> SARGENT
> You certainly proved that!

> LEE
> (Ignoring him)
> I'd always do what you wanted....
> even if it wasn't good for you.
> I'd never have a chance against you..
> and you'd never have a chance...with
> me...like just now when you were
> trying to lose the case. Aren't you
> ashamed.

> SARGENT
> (Roughly)
> Hog wash! High-flown hog wash and
> sentimental sheep dip! Oh, I know
> what you were trying to do: save

6-15-39   (Continued)

489

H-45 (Cont'd)

> SARGENT (Cont'd)
> little Willie's career from the bad,
> bad woman! You poor sap! Don't
> you think I'm the best judge of
> what's good for me or what I want
> in this world?

> LEE
> No.

> SARGENT
> And while you were making your
> big gesture did you stop to think
> how much you'd be hurting me?
> Do you think I'll stop loving you
> just because they lock you up with
> hopheads and street walkers for the
> next few years?

> LEE
> I'm not much better.

> SARGENT
> (Savagely)
> Well, you were good enough for me.

His own chin trembles.

> LEE
> (Compassionately)
> Oh.

She puts her arms around him and pats him.

> LEE
> Will you come and see me some
> time?

> SARGENT
> (Indignantly)
> Come and see you! I'm going to
> take you into the Judge and marry
> you right this minute!

> LEE
> (Almost amused)
> Oh no....but thank you just the
> same.

She kisses him on the cheek, then looks away. After
a moment she speaks hesitantly.

6-15-39   (Continued)

H-45 (Cont'd)

> LEE
>
> If you still wanted me afterwards...
> you'd be a sucker if you did, but
> if you did....it wouldn't be the
> same...I'd be all square.....and
> you would have had plenty of time
> to think things over....a lot of
> things.

Sargent crushes her to him.

> LEE
> (Looking over
> his shoulder)
> Will you stand beside me and hold
> my hand when they sentence me?

> SARGENT
> (Huskily)
> Of course I will.

> LEE
> Then I won't be afraid...
> (She tries to laugh)
> .....it will be kind of like a
> marriage at that....
> (Then after a pause)
> ....and the other part won't be
> so bad...or so long...with your
> voice always in my ears, your
> smile always before my eyes...
> the feel of your hand always in
> mine.

She pats his head gently as one pats a child.

> LEE
> I love you so.

Sargent sobs once. Very faintly we hear the music
of "My Indiana Home."

FADE OUT:

THE END

Compositor: Integrated Composition Systems, Inc.
Text: 10/12 Times Roman
Display: American Typewriter Medium
Printer and binder: Edwards Brothers, Inc.